The United States, Germany, and Japan – the world's three most powerful and successful free market societies – differ strikingly in how their governments relate to their economies. *Comparing Policy Networks* reports the results of collaborative research by three teams investigating the social organization and policy-making processes of national labor policy domains in the United States, Germany, and Japan during the 1980s.

Through data collected from interviews with more than 350 key labor policy organizations, including labor unions, business associations, professional societies, public interest groups, advisory boards, governmental agencies and ministries, political parties, and legislative committees, the researchers uncovered fundamental business-labor cleavages underlying the labor policy domains in all three societies. These patterns were revealed in both the contemporary policy debates and the historical development of each national domain.

Labor legislation fights were structured by action sets, or coalitions of organizations, that shared preferences on specific policy events and worked together to affect their outcomes. An irreconcilable labor-business antagonism seemed most evident in the U.S., whereas a more accommodating stance was apparent in Germany and in Japan. Each domain's power structure reflected a distinctive national variation on the organizational theme: Japan had a single corporatist center comprised of the government and Liberal Democratic Party that dominated all players; Germany's pluralistic twin centers coalesced around the party partners of the conservative government; and the U.S. was polarized between party and class organizations, reflecting its divided federal government in the Reagan era.

COMPARING POLICY NETWORKS

CAMBRIDGE STUDIES IN COMPARATIVE POLITICS

General Editor

PETER LANGE Duke University

Associate Editors

ELLEN COMISSO University of California, San Diego
PETER HALL Harvard University
JOEL MIGDAL University of Washington
HELEN MILNER Columbia University
RONALD ROGOWSKI University of California, Los Angeles
SIDNEY TARROW Cornell University

OTHER BOOKS IN THE SERIES

Catherine Boone, *Merchant Capital and the Roots of State Power in Senegal, 1930–1985*
Donatella della Porta, *Social Movements, Political Violence, and the State*
Roberto Franzosi, *The Puzzle of Strikes: Class and State Strategies in Postwar Italy*
Ellen Immergut, *Health Politics: Interests and Institutions in Western Europe*
Thomas Janoski and Alexander M. Hicks, eds., *The Comparative Political Economy of the Welfare State*
Allan Kornberg and Harold D. Clarke, *Citizens and Community: Political Support in a Representative Democracy*
David D. Laitin, *Language Repertories and State Construction in Africa*
Doug McAdam, John McCarthy, and Mayer Zald, *Comparative Perspectives on Social Movements*
Joel S. Migdal, Atul Kohli, and Vivienne Shue, *State Power and Social Forces: Domination and Transformation in the Third World*
Paul Pierson, *Dismantling the Welfare State: Reagan, Thatcher and the Politics of Retrenchment*
Yossi Shain and Juan Linz, *Inerim Governments and Democratic Transitions*
Theda Skocpol, *Social Revolutions in the Modern World*
Sven Steinmo, Kathleen Thelan, and Frank Longstreth, eds., *Structuring Politics: Historical Institutionalism in Comparative Analysis*
Sidney Tarrow, *Power in Movement: Social Protest, Reform, and Revolution*
Ashutosh Varshney, *Democracy, Development, and the Countryside*

COMPARING POLICY NETWORKS

Labor politics in the U.S., Germany, and Japan

DAVID KNOKE
University of Minnesota

FRANZ URBAN PAPPI
Universität Mannheim

JEFFREY BROADBENT
University of Minnesota

YUTAKA TSUJINAKA
University of Tsukuba

Published by the Press Syndicate of the University of Cambridge
The Pitt Building, Trumpington Street, Cambridge CB2 1RP
40 West 20th Street, New York, NY 10011–4211, USA
10 Stamford Road, Oakleigh, Melbourne 3166, Australia

First published 1996

Printed in the United States of America

Library of Congress Cataloging-in-Publication Data

Comparing policy network: labor politics in the U.S., Germany, and Japan /David Knoke . . . [et al.].

p. cm. — (Cambridge studies in comparative politics)

Includes bibliographical references (p.).

ISBN 0–521–49588–1 (hardcover). – ISBN 0–521–49927–5 (pbk.)

1. Labor policy – United States. 2. Labor policy – Germany. 3. Labor policy – Japan. 4. Industrial policy – United States. 5. Industrial policy – Germany. 6. Industrial policy – Japan.

I. Knoke, David. II. Series.

HD8072.5.C66 1996
331.12 – dc20

95-12513
CIP

ISBN 0–521–49588–1 Hardcover
0–521–49927–5 Paperback

Contents

Tables and figures

TABLES

FIGURES

Preface

The United States, Germany, and Japan – the world's three most powerful and successful free market societies – differ strikingly in how their governments relate to their economies, running the gamut from low to high market intervention. Each nation varies in the basic institutions that shape its social, political, and economic structures and processes, in the balance of power among contending groups, and in the rules of its political games. In a fractious world whose leading nations fret about who buys cars from whom, such seemingly minor distinctions assume vast significance. A nation's economic health and that of its citizens turns on such mundane matters. And all national governments, especially that of Japan, take increasingly enlarged stances toward directing growth and trade strategies.

In this struggle, a key public arena is labor policy, which modulates the condition of the working populace. Numerous government policies – ranging from restructuring the entire economy, to imposing taxes, to regulating wages and working conditions, to designing welfare "safety nets" to catch workers when they lose their jobs – comprise the labor policy domain. Following Otto Bismarck's late-19th-century creation of worker protection and welfare laws for Imperial Germany, national governments have embraced, with greater or lesser enthusiasm, an expanding responsibility for mediating the relationships between employers and employees. These policies greatly affect the productivity and health of the entire economy, including the growth and export rates so evident among international competitors.

Dual crises of fiscal austerity and retrenchment, originating in the rapid oil price rises of the 1970s, struck all three nations hard in the 1980s. Each country elected conservative politicians preaching the gospel of reduced government expenditures to achieve fiscal restraint. These politicians embarked on unique programs, implementing labor policies that revealed the distinctive tenor of each nation's approach. In the U.S., the Reagan Administration on the one hand launched a program of tax-rate reductions, union bashing, and welfare slashing. On the other hand, it paradoxically fostered vastly increased spending on high-tech military industries that caused public spending and debt to mushroom. During this decade, U.S. labor policy stagnated under a national government deadlocked between a Republican executive and a Democratic legislature. By contrast, Japan's Liberal

Democratic Party (LDP) government successfully reduced public expenditures by privatizing some major government-owned industries, thereby changing the legal status of those industries' massive labor unions, as well as altering their political positions within the party arrangement and the labor movement. Japan created programs for assisting depressed regions and industries and for retraining workers for new jobs by business-labor cooperation. In addition, Japan made considerable efforts to remodel the labor legal framework and to create new laws for adjusting labor to the transformed environment, despite having a "conservative" LDP cabinet. Germany's Christian Democratic Union (CDU) government, faced with similar fiscal austerity problems, also successfully retrenched its public budget. Like Japan, it did not eliminate programs vital to its national economy. Germany continued to invest heavily in worker education and retraining and to maintain essential welfare safety nets despite continuing high unemployment. These contrasting policy choices reflected not so much the different problems confronting each government as they did the distinct reactions of American, German, and Japanese decision-making institutions to comparable problems. The key question is, then, what aspects of those institutions led to these large differences in policy response, when the objective problems were very similar?

These evident divergences in economic performances and in policy responses raise the question "why?" and invite deeper investigation. In this book, we contend that the different labor policies of the U.S., Germany, and Japan result from institutional differences deeply embedded in the very fabric of state and civil society. We reached this conclusion after rigorous empirical research on the political influence relationships among the most powerful organizations occupying the central positions in the three national labor policy-making networks. Many previous investigators dug into the institutional particularities of one or the other country and often unearthed interesting findings. Some sought to compare several nations in these respects. But few possessed the detailed data, methodology, and explanatory framework necessary for nuanced examination and comparison of those policy networks in operation. Our advantage lay in applying an organizational state perspective to explain German, Japanese, and U.S. labor policy domains in the 1980s.

Chapter 1 presents the organizational state perspective, which designates the core political organizations and their relationships, indicates the relevant network and event concepts, and specifies analytic methods for explaining social organization and policy processes. The labor histories and policy-making institutions of the three nations are recapitulated in Chapter 2, which concludes with a discussion of the purposes and advantages of comparative analysis. The data collection procedures are briefly discussed in Chapter 3.

Chapter 4 begins the empirical analyses by comparing the policy issue interests of the core organizations as a necessary precursor to their policy influence actions. In Chapter 5, we investigate the network structures for exchanging valuable policy information and political support and how organizations' locations in these networks contribute to their reputations and their participation in policy events.

Chapter 6 shows how political collaboration arises from organizations' shared issue interests, network connections, and policy event preferences, creating opposing circles of policy advocates and coalitions that struggle for leverage over the outcomes of national labor legislation decisions. Chapter 7 carries this process further by examining political exchanges among public authorities and interest groups, testing a series of models to determine which ones best account for the organizational power and legislative outcomes in the three nations' labor domains. The power structure analyses of Chapter 8 reveal how intimately the informal policy network relations are intertwined with the formal institutions of each nation to produce characteristic power configurations between government and opposition parties and interest groups. Finally, Chapter 9 assesses what the organizational state perspective teaches us about national policy-making, what alternative theoretical interpretations we might make from our investigation, and what might be some future directions from comparative research on national policy systems.

This book describes labor policy-making in the three countries, paying special attention to the structure of policy domain networks. These descriptions are grounded in network data that were collected by rigorous measurement techniques that were duplicated in each nation. From time to time, our results deviate from the rich pictures painted by field researchers using exclusively qualitative data. We do not aim to reconcile all our results with the abundance of descriptive models of policy-making in Japan, Germany, or the U.S. Rather, we claim that good primary data, especially of the network type, constitute a solid basis for depicting power structures and for explaining policy outcomes. Now let the games begin.

Acknowledgements

Support for research in the United States was provided to the first author by a grant from the National Science Foundation (SES-8615909), by grants-in-aid from the University of Minnesota, by a Fulbright Senior Research Fellowship, and by a fellowship at the Center for Advanced Study in the Behavioral Sciences (supported by NSF grant SES-9022192). The German data collection was supported by a grant to the second author from the Volkswagen Stiftung. The Japanese data collection was supported by grants to the third author from the Japan – U.S. Educational Commission (JUSEC) Fellowship, U.S. Department of Education Fulbright-Hayes Fellowship (Prog. 84.019, App. P019A80047), and the National Science Foundation (NSF/INT-8821714). Earlier versions of various analyses were presented at several meetings, conferences, and colloquia, including those organized by the International Institute of Sociology (1993); the European Conference on Social Network Analysis (1989, 1991, and 1993); the Association for Asian Studies (1992); the American Sociological Association (1989 and 1990); the International Sunbelt Social Network Conference (1989 and 1991); the American Political Science Association (1986); the International Sociological Association (1994); the Max-Planck-Institut für Gesellschaftsforschung in Cologne's Workshops on Policy Networks (1989) and on Games in Hierarchies and Networks (1991); the Theory Boundaries and Units Conference in Enfield, New Hampshire (1991); the Cornell University Organizations Research Group (1991); the Stanford Center for Organizational Research (1993); the Reischauer Institute of Harvard University (1993); Mercator University (1994); University of Bremen (1994); the Harvard – MIT Center for European Studies (1993); the Center for Advanced Study in the Behavioral Sciences (1993); and the Citizenship and Social Policy Thematic Group at Duke University (1994). Comments from the audiences at these sessions were greatly appreciated, and we particularly acknowledge suggestions by Philip Anderson, Richard Braungart, Paul Burstein, John Freeman, Joseph Galaskiewicz, Mauro Guillen, Thomas Janoski, Peter Kappelhoff, Gerald Marwell, Gwen Moore, Robert Nelson, Charles Manski, Bernd Marin, Renate Mayntz, W. Richard Scott, Fritz Scharpf, Frans Stokman, Jan Van den Bos, J. Allen Whitt, William Julius Wilson, and several anonymous reviewers. We especially thank our research assistants for their diligent work during the many years of this project:

Suzanne Bisson, Frank Burleigh, Denise Floe, Yoshito Ishio, Naomi Kaufman, Thomas König, Willi Schnorpfeil, and Nancy Wisely. The third author wishes especially to thank Ezra Vogel, Shinyasu Hoshino, Yoshiaki Kobayashi, and Toru Shinoda for their help and cooperation with the data collection in Japan.

1

Policy-making in the organizational state

With the end of the Cold War, the titanic struggle between capitalism and communism no longer preoccupied politicians, the public, and social scientists. Instead, the world entered an era of "competing capitalisms" where the United States, Germany, and Japan played the leading roles. Important international frictions in this new era hinged heavily on economic relationships within and between these nations. During the 1980s, the rapid growth and economic successes of Germany and Japan provoked great consternation in the U.S., which suffered from ballooning trade deficits with both of these competitors. The spectacular economic resurrections of Germany and Japan from the ashes of World War II seemed to originate, at least in part, from relationships among state, industry, labor, and market that differed qualitatively from those in the U.S. Although neither nation developed the bureaucratically centralized command economy of the failed Soviet Union, both Germany and Japan exhibited stronger governmental roles and greater coordination of the business and labor sectors than occurred in the U.S. The ultimate resolution of this increasing international economic friction will depend, importantly, on how Germany, Japan, and the U.S. manage their economies and on how their respective national governments intervene in business-labor relations.

Numerous scholarly studies have uncovered substantial divergences among these three countries' politics, civil societies, and state-society interactions that strongly affect their productivity and growth trajectories. The U.S. long prided itself on being a noninterventionist state, contending that "leaving things to the market" would produce optimal economic outcomes. However, America's declining international competitiveness casts this laissez-faire ideology into doubt. In comparison, Germany and Japan each developed markedly more intimate forms of state-society coordination in economic policy-making, although they evolved along divergent paths. For instance, Germany emphasized the "codetermination" of industry governance through union participation on company boards of directors. Japan, on the other hand, emphasized a national-level coordination of policy-making involving the government and a highly integrated business community, while a variety of informal and semi-formal consultation mechanisms developed among business, labor, and government. Despite the apparent importance of national institutional differences for understanding the fates of these nations in the emerging era of competitive capitalisms, and their potency as paradigms for developing nations, they have not been subjected to systematic comparisons.

Our research provides the first comparative analyses of these nations to examine empirical evidence about their state–civil society relationships. The multidisciplinary field of political economy abounds with competing theoretical explanations of the social organization and exercise of political and economic power in capitalist democracies. Over the past century, numerous analysts have contributed to alternative theoretical accounts of how power is created, concentrated, dispersed, or destroyed. The four major explanatory models are the class, elite, pluralist, and corporatist models. Each explanation postulates a different locus of power in society, degree and purpose of state economic intervention, and relative political advantage for the business and labor sectors in the political process. Each theory tends to lump all industrialized capitalist democracies together, treating their differences as minor variations on the favored theme. But because every theorist argues for the universal superiority of his or her preferred paradigm, the result is a babel of theoretical voices.

When we began our search for a useful framework to describe and explain policy-making in the U.S., Germany, and Japan, the available theoretical models offered helpful starting points. The class, elite, pluralist, and corporatist accounts posed provocative questions even though they provided no fully satisfying answers regarding the uniformity or the differentiation of power processes across these three powerful nations. As a group, these alternative explanations performed limited service by identifying each nation's important political and economic features. They oriented us to significant questions about how public policies, especially those in the economic arena, are made and implemented. However, these theoretical perspectives were premised on untenable assumptions about, and employed inadequate methods to disclose, the core social-structure differences among the three societies. Therefore, the available models finally proved unproductive in guiding our three-nation comparative investigation.

As an alternative, we adapted an organizational state perspective that was inductively synthesized from an earlier analysis of U.S. energy and health policy-making (Laumann and Knoke, 1986, 1987, 1989; see Knoke and Burleigh, 1989, and Knoke, 1986, 1990b, 1992a, 1992b, for elaborations). The application of this approach in the U.S. produced several insightful results about that political system. We regard the organizational state as an analytic framework that is useful for making comparisons among nations. We seek to assess how well this generic approach enables us to gain new insight into the social structures and collective actions of national policy-making systems. Because the organizational state has previously been applied only to the U.S., we are most confident in its ability to explain the policy processes of that country. However, we surmise that this perspective is demonstrably applicable to most advanced industrial capitalist democracies. For this project, we have chosen two other nations, Germany and Japan, whose radically divergent histories and institutional systems maximize the potential contrasts with the U.S. In applying the organizational state perspective to these three countries, we wish to see how far the substantive results from the earlier U.S. study could be generalized to these potentially divergent cases. Nothing in our empirical methods precludes the possibility that we might find substantive outcomes quite different from those observed in the earlier project. As will be seen in the chapters that follow, the organizational state approach reveals new aspects of policy-making in each nation.

The remainder of this chapter develops the core conceptual features of the general organizational state perspective. Because its distinctive vocabularies may be unfamiliar to analysts working within other theoretical traditions, we ask the reader's forbearance as we elaborate its elements in great detail. This effort will pay off in the succeeding chapters as we examine labor policy-making in the three nations. The organizational state approach is an orienting analytic framework. Its conceptual components argue that modern state-society relationships have increasingly become blurred, merging into a mélange of interorganizational influence and power relations. In this aspect, the organizational state stands on a plane with other political economy theories whose explanations are subject to rigorous empirical examination. Moreover, in its methodological and sensitizing aspects, the organizational state perspective provides a distinctive conceptual bridge linking the abstract macro-structures of institutional power, which previous theories sought to characterize, to the concrete micro-structural relations of informal power and influence occurring among organizations in specific societies. Its central methodology involves quantitatively measuring networks of information exchange and political support that connect a nation's politically active organizations. By explicitly connecting macro-levels and micro-levels, the organizational state perspective leads to investigations of these dual structures that are more rigorously empirical than analyses previously generated by alternative theoretical paradigms.

Interorganizational networks enable us to describe and analyze interactions among all the significant policy actors, from legislative parties and government ministries to business associations, labor unions, professional societies, and public interest groups. The organizational state framework provides the conceptual basis to describe macro-structures of decision making, so that operational explanations about collective decisions can be tested. It is satisfactory for describing decision-making systems that contain both public and private actors whose boundaries have not been arbitrarily restricted by institutional rules imposed by researchers (as is the case when political scientists study decision-making institutions). As an empirical system, the organizational state lacks full support of legal regulations. Its effective appearance reflects both the formal and informal decision-making power flowing through state and society. Therefore, its analysis relies heavily on the understandings that the system's participants acquire about their own situations. This procedure enables us to uncover meso-structural aspects of power built by the participants' social relationships, especially the detailed communication and support interactions between individual organizations. Previous macro-theoretical models only alluded to such elusive but important aspects of the political economy. By applying the organizational state approach, we can discern and measure differences in the interorganizational policy-making networks among the three nations. In other words, we can accurately capture the policy-relevant practices, processes, and performances of the major competing capitalisms.

Of course, the web of relevant relationships among all the politically active organizations in any advanced industrial society is extremely large, dense, varied, and complex. This immensity is impossible to measure in its totality. Accordingly, we limit our empirical inquiry to one economic policy domain with critical impact on the productivity and economic competitiveness of the U.S., Germany, and Japan – labor policy. And we concentrate on basic political relationships among organizations, such as policy communication, coalitions, political support, and mutual nominations for power and influence. We argue that the possession and exchange of information and of resources like public support substantially shape effective power distribution in the policy-making process.

We investigated government policies that directly or indirectly affected the condition of the labor forces in each nation. Among the varieties of public policy, labor policy most directly affects the fate of the labor force, as well as being central to the concerns of management and capital ownership. We examined major labor policy proposals ranging from shop-floor practices concerning health and safety, worker retraining programs, unemployment compensation standards, and fair employment laws to large-scale corporate restructuring and broad economic regulations affecting labor conditions. Choosing this policy domain gave us a direct window on essential mechanisms of economic policy-making within the three major industrial capitalist democracies.

As a context for and prelude to outlining the organizational state framework, the next section considers how various theorists have conceptualized the uneasy relationships between national states and their civil societies. A major implication is that rigid boundaries between these two forms of social organization are increasingly impossible to draw. Hence, any investigation of national policy-making must encompass all relevant political actors.

THE STATE AND CIVIL SOCIETY

Since the Enlightenment, social theorists have posited the state as distinct from its civil society – the private spheres of economic, cultural, and social organization. They have stridently disagreed about appropriate state–civil society relations. In Europe, the fragmented, hierarchical, and autonomous systems of feudal patrimonialism gave way to centralized political institutions that tried to subordinate many private spheres to a larger "public interest" (Poggi, 1978: 117–22). Indeed, state-formation can be viewed as a progressive surrender of private autonomy in exchange for public citizenship rights defined and enforced by the centralizing state (King, 1986: 51). But the historical origins and legal bases of sovereignty – kings or people, in Reinhard Bendix's (1978) telling phrase – remains the subject of considerable dispute. In Georg Hegel's intricate idealism, the state could refer either to the whole social existence of a people or to just the highest political unity of *das Volk* (Dyson 1980: 21). Standing Hegel on his head, Karl Marx asserted that the state is a mere superstructure resting on the real foundation of economic structures (Marx, 1978: 4). Thus, the state ultimately reflects the underlying condition of social relations within the civil society, in particular its class-ridden conflicts (Giddens, 1985: 20). Similarly, in Emile Durkheim's functionalism the state was entirely a product of its society, an "organ of social thought" ultimately responsible for translating social activities into moral purposes and protecting individual rights (Horowitz, 1982). Liberal philosophers, such as John Locke and John Stuart Mill, advocated a greatly restrained state to safeguard individual liberty within private spheres that were to remain inaccessible to capricious governments. As a remedy to predatory mercantilism, Adam Smith's (1776) model of a market economy likewise proscribed state intervention in the invisible-hand economy. Alexis de Tocqueville's (1945 [reprint]) cogent analyses of American civic and political associations inquired into democratic mechanisms sufficient for a populace to govern itself. The modern debate about state–civil society relations continues this theme, turning on state managers' autonomy and discretion and on how far they should penetrate into and subordinate other social formations (Lindblom, 1977; Hollingsworth, Schmitter, and Streeck, 1994). Is the state merely an arena within which societal forces struggle, or does it reserve the power to shape and channel that struggle?

In Japan and many other non-Western countries, the relationship between the state and civil society was less distinct (Johnson, 1982) then it was in Europe or the U.S. First, the modern Japanese state developed not within the context of a capitalist civil society but in order to defend the society and polity against Western imperialistic encroachment. Second, Japanese state institutions were imported from the West. The oligarchic elite that guided the Meiji Restoration of 1868 imported numerous institutions to Japan, such as the constitutional monarchy; legislative democracy; and the nation's military, police, administrative, and educational systems. As a result, these "public" institutions were, at the behest of the state, more-or-less exact transplants of their Western counterparts. As in many developing and late-industrializing countries, the Japanese public sector consisted of imported, quasi-Western institutions that did not develop indigenously and had an uneasy relationship with civil society. Third, in addition to this modernization or political development path, traditional Japanese concepts of public and private spheres made less of a distinction between the two spheres than did Western concepts. In Japan there was a "shared feeling that all the people are performing some of the public functions" (p. 15). Despite the imported administrative institutions, the traditional fusion of the public and private spheres still justified informal negotiations in politics. This tendency grew strong in the Japan of the 1980s as the power of the state declined vis-à-vis that of the civil society.

All three national examples, then, give us warrant to look for "a blurring of public and private spheres" (Wilensky and Turner, 1987; 10; Cawson, 1986: 35; Lehman, 1988: 818). One formulation of this trend sees a growing similarity of contemporary organizational forms in state and society due to a pervasive rationalizing of ends–means relations and imperatives of efficiency that pervade all spheres of social life:

> . . . [I]nstitutionalism suggests that the interpenetration of environments with organizing (and its actors and technical functions) is especially great with those features of the social environments that are themselves highly rationalized, that is, with elements of what was traditionally called "civil society." Formal organization is not only interdependent with, but interpenetrated with, the various elements of rationalized society: modern actors with their "interests," legitimated functions and their functionaries, and agents of the modern collectivity such as state elites, and legal and professional theorists and practitioners. (Jepperson and Meyer, 1991: 205)

A precise boundary between state and civil society is rendered indistinct due to highly complex patterns of mutual penetration (Block, 1987: 21; Streeck, 1983: 265–6). Continuously evolving interactions redefine the meaning of public and private spheres. As groups and organizations compete for access to and influence over public policy officials, the state managers in turn try to institutionalize interest group "responsibility" for disciplining their members' political behavior. The degree and form of state–civil society permeation varies greatly across nations. An extreme example occurs in consociational societies, such as Belgium or Canada, where subcultures are so antagonistic that civil strife is avoided only because "the group actors are often in fact a *part* of the state" (Scholten, 1987: 27). Even in less socially polarized nations, a steady devolution of nominally public authority into quasi-governmental organizations (Barker, 1982) blurs the boundaries:

> The boundaries between "state" and "civil society" are never fixed, but constantly changing. Public and private are not natural divisions, but socially and historically constructed ones. One of the ways in which the state expands its reach is to re-draw the public/private boundaries, and reconstitute the definition of the private, so as to make it legitimate for the state to intervene in areas which had hitherto been considered inviolable. (Hall, 1984: 21)

As organized interests become increasingly integrated into the policy-making process and acquire greater sophistication in obtaining and using political resources, new governing structures arise. These formations are neither state nor society in an earlier sense, but hybrid structures that carry out their functions. Thus, the state's legally constituted governing bodies are permeated by diffuse sets of policy networks – advisory and quasi-official relations that connect state managers to organized interest associations (Mann, 1986: 1; Dunleavy, 1982: 205).

Policy networks link heterogeneous communities of policy actors into intricate webs of common benefit-seeking actions (Heclo, 1978; Katzenstein, 1978; Wilks and Wright, 1987). The implications of these networks for public policy outcomes are as ambiguous as the state-society boundaries themselves. Earlier images of business lobbyists conspiring with government officials in closed "iron triangles" have been replaced by images of open networks whose diffuse participants may be less predictable, more intransigent, and biased toward consensual collective agreements (Jordan, 1981). On the other hand, "it is conceivable that where decision-making networks are more complex, whose external interests more intrusively invade government, and where agreements have to be forged to carry out policy decisions, the results may have broader support and will ultimately prove to be less contentious" (Rockman, 1989: 185). An important objective in our project is to determine how networks among nominally public and private actors shape the national state's policy-making processes in the U.S., Germany, and Japan.

COMPONENTS OF THE ORGANIZATIONAL STATE

Given the necessity to include both state and civil society social formations in any investigation of public policy-making, we now present the major components of the organizational state perspective. Although these conceptual components originated in the U.S. energy and health research project mentioned earlier (see Laumann and Knoke, 1987: 380–7), they were subsequently elaborated as a general paradigm of contemporary policy-making. As already noted, we use this perspective to guide our empirical analyses of the American, German, and Japanese labor policy domains, assessing how well it accounts for similarities and differences among the three nations. The summary statements in this section encapsulate the core analytic assumptions, principles, and relationships of the framework. Following this overview, we turn to a detailed exposition of the key concepts whose empirical investigation engages our efforts in the remainder of this book.

In every modern polity the distinction between state and civil society has become blurred. By definition, government actors possess various kinds of formal authority to make legally binding decisions. But so-called private-sector organizations also possess various kinds of formal and informal rights and powers to participate in decision making. Because policy-making results from complex interactions among governmental and nongovernmental actors, the organizational state concept encompasses both kinds of actors within its boundaries.

The central actors in the organizational state are formal organizations, not individual persons. Elite individuals participate only as agents of collectivities. Both governmental and nongovernmental organizations are rationally motivated to participate. They pursue the interests of the organization and its main constituents, seeking in those terms to gain advantages or to minimize losses. Corporations pursue broader markets and greater profits, unions fight for higher wages and better working conditions, politicians promote ideologies and covet votes for reelection, bureaucrats seek to enforce their agencies' mandates or enhance their budgets, social movements hope to improve the conditions of the oppressed. No organization acts solely and entirely on behalf of a generalized "public interest," although some may do so more than others.

The primary function of the organizational state is to produce collectively binding decisions in specific policy events. These decisions may take the form of legislative acts, regulatory decrees, court rulings, or strong bureaucratic leadership. In common, such decisions reinforce or alter the rules of the game that all participants must follow, at least until new decisions change the rules.

Governmental organizations are generally not neutral arbiters in policy fights. Although bureaucratic agencies are charged with following mandates given by political decision makers, the political parties in the legislature and commanding the bureaus are responsive to the constituencies that funded them and elected them to office. The extent to which governments actively participate as partisans supporting one side or another varies with the particular events. Hence, governmental actors resemble other participants whose involvements depend on the degree to which their interests are at stake in the outcome of a policy decision.

The organizational state does not have a unified ideology. Clashing beliefs about the role of the state, free enterprise, the public good, and technical expertise are advocated by organizations claiming legitimacy to participate and influence policy outcomes. Many policy decisions carry heavy ideological freight as symbolic expressions of their proponents' values. Which political vision dominates a system at a given moment is the result of opposing forces marshalled on behalf of each policy position.

The scope of policy-making is narrow. Most policy events occur within specialized spheres, or domains, having restricted access. These policy domains develop fairly stable power structures dominated by a core of peak associations and governmental actors. Access to central positions requires information (both technical expertise and political knowledge) and resources (both material and symbolic). The social organization of a policy domain is structured by its networks of information and resource exchanges that confer advantages on some actors and disadvantages on other. These structures can be represented by spatial or other relational configurations that locate some actors toward the center or at the top of the social space and others toward the peripheral regions.

The main sources of political change in policy domains are social-demographic shifts and, increasingly, the international economic system. Most challengers have difficulty entering the highly restricted domains unless they acquire sufficient political clout, especially connections to powerful organizations in the information and resource exchange networks.

An actor's influence over policy decisions varies over time with the intensity of its own efforts and of those of other participants attempting to shape event outcomes. Actors realize their policy interests primarily through interorganizational alliances. Policy cohesion is always problematic, as the cost of sustaining alliances is high. Coalitions must be continually reconstituted with new members, because attention and resources are limited and organizations must ration their use. Alliances shift from event to event, because the substantive contents of interest to potential participants vary.

Both governmental and private-sector organizations pool their resources, coordinate their influence efforts, and negotiate with the authorities to gain advantages on events of interest. These actions lead to the formation of coalitions with other actors having the same policy preferences concerning single events. Strategic behavior across sequences of policy events may require participants to logroll, trading off their support on events of lesser interest in return for help on events of higher concern. A logic of political exchange leads in our version to an exchange of access to political deciders, where actors realize their interests better than they can without exchange. The consequences of making collective decisions feed back into the structure of a policy domain, socially reconstructing the interorganizational field on which succeeding policy battles must be fought.

The following subsections elaborate these basic elements of the organizational state, developing the technical vocabulary and research expectations necessary for designing a testable project on the three national labor policy domains.

Policy domains

The basic unit of analysis in the organizational state is the *policy domain,* a complex social organization in which collectively binding decisions are made, implemented, and evaluated with regard to specific topics. It is "identified by a substantively defined criterion of mutual relevance or common orientation among a set of consequential actors concerned with formulating, advocating, and selecting courses of action (i.e., policy options) that are intended to resolve the delimited substantive problems in question" (Knoke and Laumann, 1982: 256). In short, a policy domain is an input-throughout-output-feedback process by which the governance of delimited societal structures takes place. A policy domain consists only of actors having common interests in certain types of public policies (but not identical preferences) who must take one another into account in their efforts to influence those policy decisions. Every domain encompasses a diversity of controversial policy matters and numerous claimant groups and public authorities, each seeking in varying degrees to influence the ultimate decisions about matters of importance to them and to their constituencies. Burstein (1991) argued that each policy domain also develops a logically coherent substantive or functional basis for framing its policies and that its participants usually construct a common culture about how society does and should work.

Complex industrial societies with highly differentiated social, political, and economic structures give rise to numerous relatively autonomous policy domains. Every distinctive domain is organized around some central substantive concerns, or set of societal problems and their proposed solutions, with which the domain's participants must deal on a continuing basis. Thus, by the late 20th century, liberal democratic polities had created such narrow policy domains as natural resource development, environmental protection, energy production, surface transportation, and space exploration. Commonly, new domains are formally recognized by creating cabinet ministries, departments, and special administrative units to deal with their conditions. Such institutions publicly acknowledge domain participants, legitimize their concerns, and establish formal procedures through which policy solutions can be attempted. Each newly emerged ministry stakes out a policy turf from which it tries to exclude all intruders who might thwart its aims. The historical formation of U.S. cabinet-level departments indicates that they resulted largely from political entrepreneurs' initiatives, stimulated by the appearance of new problems, to carve out distinct niches within which they hoped to gain special advantages unavailable in existing domains. A recent example was the creation of the U.S. Department of Education as a separate cabinet post from the previous Department of Health, Education, and Welfare. It was clearly a reward to organized teachers' unions for their support of Jimmy Carter's successful 1976 presidential campaign (Bell, 1988). A similar political deal elevated Veterans Affairs to cabinet rank, but interagency rivalries denied President Bush's "drug czar" an equivalent status. We can find similar occurrences in Japan and in Germany. For example, the Japanese Environmental Agency (*Kankyocho*) was established as an administrative response to pollution in 1971, when the level of pollution and the antipollution movement reached a peak. This formative action, which legitimized public opinion against pollution, obviously formalized the environmental policy domain in Japan. Although the question of how executive-branch agencies are created is fascinating, our analytic framework is not concerned with this particular dynamic. It concentrates instead on processes occurring after a policy domain has clearly emerged.

Moreover, we argue that a policy domain's boundaries are not synonymous with formal state ministries. Historical patterns of institutionalization and sheer, obstinate reality conspire to produce societal problems not conveniently confined within even the most rationally crafted governance plans. Typically, many formal government organizations overlap across several domains, whereas other domains' problems are parceled out among diverse and competing institutions. For example, occupational safety and health is simultaneously a medical, labor, and social welfare concern, and vocational training is both an educational and a labor matter. Multipurpose nongovernmental actors also divide their attention among several domains and view their interconnections from unique standpoints. Determining where the boundaries of a particular policy domain fall – which components lie inside which domain – is often problematic. Policy domains are not legally recognized entities whose membership criteria are clear-cut and enforced by a central authority (Laumann, Marsden and Prensky, 1983; Pappi, 1984). Rather, all domain boundaries are more or less fuzzy and porous, allowing various participants, problems, and policy proposals to enter and leave in disorderly fashion. Indeed, identifying a policy domain is primarily a social construction whose meanings result from its participants' collective symbolization and negotiations (Laumann and Knoke, 1987: 93). Hence, we should expect to find a gradient from greater to lesser intensity of involvement, where participation shades off rather rapidly with the actors' social distances from a domain's core concerns.

At its most abstract conceptual level, the internal structure of a policy domain is constructed from four basic components: policy actors, policy interests, power relations, and collective actions (Knoke, 1992a). Table 1.1 gives several examples of these elements. The configurations of these components at any time provide policy analysts with comprehensive maps, or multidimensional snapshots, of the domain's social structures and activities. A given combination of the four elements locates specific sets of policy actors holding diverse substantive policy interests

Table 1.1. *Components of the policy domain framework*

ANALYTIC ELEMENTS	EXAMPLES
ORGANIZATIONAL ACTORS	
Interest Groups	Unions; trade groups; PIGS; corporations; bureaucracies
Peak Associations	Federations; chambers; quasi-official advisory bodies
Government Institutions	Legislatures; courts; ministries; regulators; official advisory councils
POLICY INTERESTS	
Subfields	Broad areas of focal concern: collective bargaining; markets
Issues	General substantive matters: wages, hours, conditions
Events	Legislative bills; court suits; regulatory proclamations
POWER RELATIONS	
Information exchange	Ideas, data, strategies, advice
Resource exchange	Funds, facilities, votes, coercion
COLLECTIVE ACTIONS	
Mobilization	Coalition building; social movements
Publicity	Mass media blitzes; targeted mailings
Lobbying	Contacts with government officials; legal suits
JOINTLY OCCUPIED POSITIONS	
Issue publics	Shared profiles of interests in all domain issues
Event publics	Interests in a specific event, regardless of outcome preferences
Advocacy circles	Shared preferences for a specific event outcome
Action sets	Active collaboration to produce favorable event outcome

into network positions possessing differential power, whose collective actions are targeted on the ultimate policy makers. By investigating how the four components interrelate across a series of policy decisions, a researcher can accurately describe and analyze a domain's policy-making processes. To appreciate fully how our policy domain framework guides the empirical investigation of labor politics in the U.S., Germany, and Japan, we next consider details of the four basic components.

Policy actors

The generic term *actor* indicates any social entity able to pursue its goals in a unitary manner. From the organizational state perspective, the policy actors in national policy domains are formal organizations, not individual persons. A formal organization enables many individuals to coordinate their actions in attempting to affect the outcome of a policy decision, thereby magnifying their strength many fold. In pooling their resources for coordinated action, actors give up exclusive control over the uses to which their contributions are put (Coleman, 1973b). Individuals participate mostly as agents of formal organizations, such as professional societies, corporations, government agencies, law firms, labor unions, voluntary associations, business councils, and the like. Only organizations can mobilize sufficient resources to monitor continuously the policy activities within a national domain and to intervene effectively to affect collective decisions. The enormous costs of bringing power to bear within any national decision system – to maintain an on-going physical presence at the geographic sites where domain decisions are made; to communicate interests and intentions to decision makers, allies, and opponents; to offer sanctions sufficient to have an impact on the other players – are generally beyond the capacity of most individuals to pay. In the U.S., even such dedicated policy altruists as Ralph Nader have found advantages to channeling their efforts through organizations such as Public Citizen and Congress Watch. Increasingly, these resource requirements may also be beyond the ability of all but the very richest organizations to sustain on a broad scale (Salisbury, 1984; March and Olsen, 1984).

Policy domain actors include organizations from both the "public" and "private" sectors. As already pointed out, the nominal distinctions between these sectors tend to blur under closer scrutiny. The vastly increased scale and scope of capital and labor in the late-19th-century industrial societies produced "an interpenetration of state and market, a blurring of the boundaries separating the activities of the state, unions, and employers' associations" (Marks, 1989: 79). Although governmental organizations possess the ultimate legal authority to make laws, regulations, and court rulings, in many polities nongovernmental actors increasingly are deeply enmeshed in policy-making processes. An important conceptual distinction must be maintained between policy actors as corporate advocacy organizations and in those roles in which they must abide by collective resolutions of conflicts that may go against their preferences. These contrasting roles emerge in the legislative arena. The labor committees of the U.S. Congress, and the labor and social policy committees of the German *Bundestag* and Japanese Diet – each consisting of elected members from several political parties – have authority to block or to mark up bills for consideration by the full legislature. As committee members, the political parties thus participate in a "collective decider" whose outcomes become binding on all the participants. A legislative chamber is another collective decider, which follows explicit procedures to enact legal statutes binding on the entire body. Because committees and legislative chambers as deliberative bodies lack the unity necessary for acting collectively in pursuit of common interests, we do not consider them to be meaningful participants in the organizational state. In contrast, a given political party's legislative delegation *can* act as a unified corporate entity (except where party discipline has collapsed), and thus these entities must be included among the key domain actors. For example, the German Social Democrats (SPD) routinely ally themselves with the German Labor Federation (DGB) to promote labor bills in the *Bundestag* Committee for Labor and Social Politics that typically are opposed by the Christian Democratic Union (CDU) in coalition with the Federal Association of German Employers (BDA). However, this partisan activity by the SPD and CDU clashes with their legal obligations as committee members to cast votes toward a majority decision that is then binding on the entire committee. We will avoid much confusion by recognizing that party organizations play distinct dual roles, as members of collective deciders and as corporate advocacy actors.

Perhaps thousands of organizations express some interest in a given domain's policy concerns, but far fewer make discernable impacts. Policy researchers need not take account of marginal actors and can concentrate on consequential participants whose actions are most likely to shape collective decisions. An iron-clad definition of consequentiality is impossible to state, but, fortunately, domain actors' expressed orientations are useful in identifying core participants. If two actors are compelled to take one another's actions into consideration, then both must be deemed consequential domain participants. But if an organization's preferences and actions can be safely ignored by the other actors, then that organization undoubtedly lacks standing within the domain (although it could well be a core member of some other domain). This mutual-relevance criterion (Laumann and Knoke, 1987: 11) seems sufficient to identify the relatively small number of domain movers-and-shakers, although a precise boundary between core and peripheral actors can never be rigidly drawn. Obviously, an actor's consequentiality may fluctuate as a result of its successes and failures. So, policy analysts are well advised to apply a generous boundary criterion when delimiting a domain population of mutually relevant, consequential actors.

Policy interests

Organizations bring a variety of *policy interests* into their involvement in a policy domain. Interests orient social actors toward specific preferred ends and away from others. To say that an actor has an interest in a policy means that the outcome of a decision has consequences for that organization and its constituents. Hence, organizations with policy interests are likely to attend to and become involved in any activities where those interests are at stake. How an organization acquires its interests and how it collectively decides to act on those interests are not relevant for our purposes. Some organizations may follow an ideology-driven agenda that dictates when and how they must participate. Others may engage in rational cost-benefit calculations to determine whether an effort to affect policy decisions would be worthwhile. Still others may act to repay favors done for them by allies at an earlier time. Presumably, most policy objectives emerge from the political dynamics within organizations' internal polities. Our organizational state perspective has nothing to say about how organizational interests and goals develop. Rather, just as economists do not try to explain consumers' taste for Coke or for Pepsi, we simply take as given the particular configuration of policy interests expressed by each organization participating in a policy domain.

The organizational state approach analyzes organizational interests at three levels of decreasing breadth: subfield, issue, and event. We view them as nested concepts.

(1) Subfield interests. Every policy domain contains several specialized *subfields*, which categorize topics of interest to particular participants, such as "disadvantaged populations in the labor market." For example, in the energy policy domain, different fuel types (nuclear, oil, gas, coal, solar) might comprise distinct subfields. In practice, identifying subfields depends critically on an analyst's understanding of how the players themselves make sense of their socially constructed world views. And, just as policy domain boundaries are fuzzy, so subfields are porous and overlapping with regard to the issues and events they contain. Generic principles for identifying basic subfields are difficult to specify, although cleavages between producer and consumer interests do seem to span many economic domains, such as energy, health, agriculture, manufacturing, services, and other basic sectors. Other common cleavages can involve technological, geographical, population, and status axes along which domain participant differentiation occurs.

(2) Issue interests. An *issue* is a broadly characterized set of substantive matters that attract the attention of some domain actors. For example, "affirmative action policies for minorities" is an issue within the disadvantaged population subfield of the labor domain. Although any issue may ultimately lead to one or more concrete policy proposals, issues are not framed in terms of specific plans of action. Rather, an issue is primarily framed by policy domain actors at fairly abstract levels that identify the salient problem(s) believed to require policy decision, but do not stipulate what course(s) of action should be taken. A short descriptive label often suffices to identify an issue to interested actors: minimum wage rates; collective bargaining; job discrimination; sweatshops; and so on. Because issues can be expressed in fairly general terms, they are susceptible to modification in at least two main directions. Through refinement, an issue can be broken into more detailed components, each of which can take on a life of its own. Thus, occupational safety and health issues can be subdivided into toxic substances, repetitive motion injuries, smoking in the workplace, video terminal radiation, and so forth. Or, through aggregation, two seemingly independent issues can be linked and made to appear as just one element in a more complex bundle. For example, automobile import quotas and immigration could be conjoined as elements of a labor market protection issue.

Some domain policy actors become issue entrepreneurs who develop and promote issues favorable to themselves, whereas other actors are either reactive or passive in their responses. This variation in level of involvement implies that intensity of interest is the basic relationship linking actors to issues. When an organization's agents express "strong interest" in an issue, they assert that policies proposed to deal with the issue may have important consequences for the organization. Similarly, weak or no interest in an issue implies that an organization is unconcerned about the impact a policy proposal might have on the organization's fate. The scope of policy actors' interests varies markedly across the set of domain issues. Some organizations are specialists; others are generalists (Hannan and Freeman, 1977). Generalists maintain a broad portfolio of issue interests, with high levels of concern spanning numerous substantive matters. Specialists concentrate their interests and efforts on a handful of narrowly defined issues (e.g., job training for the handicapped). Thus, both the distribution of interests in single issues and the profile of organizational interests across all current issues are important dimensions characterizing domain interest structures.

(*3*) *Event interests.* An *event* is a "critical, temporally located decision point in a collective decision-making sequence that must occur in order for a policy option to be finally selected" (Laumann and Knoke, 1987: 251). Every event occurs at a specific time and place. Its outcome, whether a success or a failure in the view of its advocates, marks a definitive collective judgment either to change or to continue existing practices. Events can be classified according to their institutional jurisdictions: judicial, executive, or legislative. Other classification schemes slice the policy pie differently, as does, for example, the famous distributive-redistributive-regulatory trinity of Lowi (1964), where the substantive intent of a proposal is the chief criterion. Kingdon (1984: 99–105) distinguished an event's prominence, with "focusing" events, such as crises and disasters, attracting heavier actor attention and participation than "routine" events. Laumann and Knoke (1987: 252) classified U.S. energy and health domain events as program-initiation, program-termination, regulative, and funding types. However, because our analyses focus only on legislative events, such elaborate distinctions among events are not necessary.

The organizational state paradigm examines the entire policy-making process from initial conceptualization to final evaluation and reassessment, depicting interests as embedded in an event-policy cycle (see Downs, 1972; Pappi, 1988) and in an actor-involvement cycle (Broadbent, 1989a, 1989b). The policy process begins with actors' efforts to attach generic issues to specific incidents or conditions in the larger society. Thus, a major oil tanker spill in an Alaskan sound raises cries for the reform of hazardous materials transport policies. Or, a slaughter of school children by an Uzi-wielding maniac pumps new life into a campaign to outlaw the import of automatic weapons. At this policy-formulation stage, many diagnoses may surface and many vague, tentative proposals may be put forward. The media are an especially likely arena for "trial balloons," with many launched by anonymous sources wanting to see whether an idea will float or burst in the public spotlight. Policy events at this stage most closely resemble a garbage can: many suggestions trying to latch onto sponsoring actors, and many actors hoping to ride a winning issue (March and Olsen, 1976). Which particular policy proposals slip through the narrow windows of opportunity to the next stage may be more a matter of luck and timing than of intrinsic merit (Kingdon, 1984).

At any given moment, participants in an already complex and overburdened policy domain have only limited time and energy to consider new policy proposals. Out of the many contenders for serious attention, only a handful of potential events will emerge to fill slots on policy actors' agendas (Cobb and Elder, 1983). Although media attention can still help raise a proposal's salience, in order for matters to move forward, proposals at the agenda-setting stage require precise statement in the language and format of the particular institutional arena where they are being pushed (e.g., in the form of a legislative bill, executive regulation, or court suit). Sponsorship by inside players is indispensable, because only legislators can toss a bill into the hopper, only agency bureaucrats can promulgate a new set of regulations, only judges can accept an appeal. Unless a proposal tickles the fancy or kicks the inertia of authoritative gatekeepers, its prospects for becoming an agenda item are vanishingly small. Even then, serious discussion is unlikely to follow if key sponsors in the arena's power structure do not adopt the proposal. At this stage, organized interest groups seek to insert their specifications into the agenda item: at legislative hearings, during office visits, in friend-of-the-court briefs, by regulatory testimony. Deals for sponsorship often are cut behind the scenes, not only with the claimant organizations, but also among the public authorities who seek to roll logs for their own pet proposals.

Once a proposal begins to move forward on an arena's agenda, events follow one of a limited number of well-worn tracks. For example, in the U.S. Congress, hearings on a bill are followed by committee mark-up, a committee vote, House and Senate debates and votes, a reconciliation conference, final votes, and the president's signature on the act (Oleszek, 1989). At each point, substantive modification of the proposal's contents is still possible, in the form of substitutions, amendments, and, ultimately, a presidential veto. Hence, lobbying by claimant organizations and among public authorities can still reshape the proposal's contents or at least limit its damage. The few proposals that pass into public policy in the form of law, regulation, or legal precedent are binding on all societal actors covered under its provisions. If a proposal fails to pass, as most do, the policy cycle is interrupted at this stage. If the issue is not completely dead, it must begin the cycle again with a reformulated proposal.

In the Japanese polity, a new policy usually originates in the drafts of middle-ranking government bureaucrats. They locate in the hub of various information flows stemming mainly from the proposal's supporting interest groups and relevant local government departments. Through these networks, bureaucrats deliberately collect, examine, and evaluate the need for policy innovations. After giving a policy proposal its initial form, they feed it into an informal discussion and deliberation process, first inside the bureau and ministry, then between the ministry and the ruling political party (from 1955 to 1993 the Liberal Democratic Party). Once the party and related ministries internally approve the proposal, a new formal policy draft is prepared for submission to deliberation and consultation involving formal advisory councils and the Japanese cabinet. A large proportion of cabinet bills drafted by the bureaucracy pass the Diet with little change. Hence, in our investigations, we assume that ministerial-level policy preferences and actions reasonably reflect the interests of their middle-level bureaucrats.

For routine legislation, the German process is similar to the Japanese case. But important bills receive much public attention, with the political parties seen as the major policy advocates. Coalition contracts that are negotiated at the beginning of a legislative period contain a legislative program that the coalition partners agree to initiate and guide over the parliamentary hurdles.

In general, once a policy proposal is enacted, its provisions must be implemented via some type of performance agency. Some agencies involve simply changing a few name plates and shuffling office personnel around; others require creating an entirely new organization from scratch, with new buildings, computers, employees, paperwork, and tasks to perform. Because no legislation, regulation, or court ruling anticipates and mandates every iota of activity for a performance agency, many holes for discretionary implementation remain (Pressman and Wildavsky, 1984), and they may be big enough to drive the proverbial truck through. Thus, even at this allegedly pure administrative stage of the policy cycle, interested actors seek to affect agency performance. Recurring procurement scandals at the Pentagon are costly reminders that implementation events are a vital part of every policy cycle.

After initial implementation experiences, some type of program assessment typically follows. Oversight commissions responsible for program evaluation may conduct research or collect testimony from staff members, clientele, and the general public about the performance agency's performance. Funds for such evaluations may be built into the original program, with continued agency funding contingent on passing periodic reviews. If the policy is not operating as originally mandated, or inadequately deals with changed circumstances, the oversight commission may propose modifications. Because the performing agency's bureaucrats now have a stake in the continuation and expansion of the program, they become significant players in the evaluation phase. By selectively controlling information about agency operations, and by cultivating protective political relations with arena authorities and claimant organizations, the bureaucracy tries to become entrenched in the policy domain's institutional muscle. "Iron triangles," "cozy triangles," and the "Ruling Triad" reflect popular perceptions of such incestuous relations (Ripley and Franklin, 1978; Smith, 1988: 173–9; Kabashima and Broadbent, 1986). Only disastrous performance breakdowns, such as NASA's Challenger explosion or the payoff scandals that brought down Japan's Liberal Democratic government, may shake policy actors out of their complaisance and launch a new round in the policy event cycle.

Power relations

Uncovering power relations among the core domain organizations is a critical objective in the organizational state approach. In relational terms, *power* has two aspects. The first is "the capacity of some persons to produce intended or foreseen effects on others" (Wrong, 1979: 2). That is, power occurs in an instance of one social actor obtaining another actor's obedience to a command, whether the latter resists or consents. In many situations, compliance with commands occurs as willing consent without any overtly coercive compulsion. Whether force is needed or voluntary assent is present, the exercise of power requires interaction among social actors, thus permitting its analysis as networks of exchange relations. At the same time, actors' ultimate objectives in attempting to exercise power are to affect policy outcomes, not just to exert some control over other actors.

The second aspect of power is an organization's control over policy outcomes, irrespective of its specific exercise of interorganizational control (Alford and Friedland, 1975). Power accrues to those policy actors who control scarce material and intangible resources that are highly valued by others. By exchanging these resources in return for obedience to their commands, or by mutual exchange leading to a negotiated consensus, resourceful actors can coordinate collective actions toward the achievement of their preferred policy objectives. The emergence of stable exchange networks in a policy domain reflects the differing capacities of actors to gain access to resources essential for participating in and shaping policy decisions. But these networks also take on a degree of institutionalized stability as network structures, further reinforcing inequalities. The networks do not reflect only opportunistic exchanges of convenience; they are habitual structures "embedded" in the polity (Granovetter 1985). Access to resources and their exchange confer unequal positional advantages, which can be represented as the actors' locations either near the centers or on the peripheries of resource networks' social spaces. Actors who are well-connected to important other actors thereby gain important advantages through their access to flows of political resources. Actors at the network margins, whose ties connect them mainly to other peripheral actors, cannot tap sufficient quantities of quality political resources to participate effectively in collective actions. Thus, policy actors who control scarce resources, which are unavailable from alternative suppliers, can more readily affect system actions. These major players occupy positions that are targets of importuning by needy actors seeking essential material and symbolic rewards. The resource controllers can reward others' cooperation in (and punish their resistance to) helping to produce the collective ends sought by the core actors.

The two policy networks especially relevant to our analysis are information exchange and resource networks. Information is an intangible asset – such as scientific, legal, or political knowledge – whose transmission from one actor to another does not result in its loss to the first possessor. Resources are physical commodities – such as money, labor power, or facilities – whose control can be transmitted from one actor to another. This differentiation between intangible and physical resources is a recurrent theme in analytic power typologies. For example, French and Raven (1959) distinguished among coercive, inducement, expert, legitimacy, and referent bases of power (Broadbent [1986] added persuasion as a sixth basis). Etzioni (1975: 12) trichotomized participants' compliance within organizations into coercive, normative, and utilitarian bases. Clark (1968: 57–67) inventoried 13 power resources (including money and credit, social status, knowledge and specialized skills, and followers' commitment), and Laumann and Pappi (1976: 185–215) proposed eight categories fitting a Parsonsian scheme (e.g., economic resources, expert knowledge, connections to influential persons). Our focus on two exchange networks most closely parallels Knoke's (1990b: 11–16; 1992a) analytic distinction between two basic network power relations: persuasive communications intended to change others' beliefs and perceptions regarding political actions (which Knoke labeled "influence") and transactions of physical benefits (or harms) in return for compliance with commands (labeled "domination").

The information and resource exchange networks constitute two fundamental political structures in modern societies. Although governmental agencies typically possess enormous resource stocks (particularly their formal legal authority over collective decisions), the core positions in both types of power networks are not exclusively occupied by state institutions. Rather, as resource exchanges become increasingly diffuse, their global structures lead to an interpenetration of state and civil society that can be captured with network imagery.

A central task for policy domain analysts is to uncover the structural relations in the political networks among the core organizations. Although structural relationships are easily observed in small networks, policy domain analyses typically involve dozens or hundreds of actors. Fortunately, computer programs for analyzing matrix representations of large networks have become widely available in recent years (Burt, 1980; Knoke and Kuklinski, 1982; Pappi, 1987; Freeman, 1988). Many techniques reduce network complexity by clustering, or grouping together, subsets of actors that exhibit identical or very similar patterns of relations with others in the system. Summary measures can then be computed for these jointly occupied network positions. In the empirical chapters of this book, we further specify the relevant network methodologies in greater detail as they are needed.

Collective actions

Analyses of network structures are ultimately valuable only if they improve our understanding of how core policy domain organizations interact in making policy decisions. The basic proposition is that the networks represent organizations' attempts to bring sufficient political power to bear on other policy domain actors, most saliently on the public authorities responsible for deciding a policy event, to sway the collective decision in their favor. Organizations on each side of an event try to increase the probability that these authorities will choose the outcome they prefer. To a great extent, actors use preexisting information and resource exchange networks in their influence efforts on specific events. In a word, these networks are institutionalized. An organization's current position within an institutionalized power network, which is the result of its earlier political activities, partly determines its credibility and hence its power. Therefore, organizations' positions in the already-existing information and resource exchange networks are important factors both in generating participation and in determining the outcomes of policy events. During the course of political struggles, various coalitions or alliances among organizations may arise to undertake coordinated political actions aimed at furthering their common interests. A *collective action* involves three or more organizations working together in an effort to obtain their preferred policy event outcome. The necessary preconditions for collective action involve mutual recognition by organizations that they share common goals, followed by formation of linkages that enable them to undertake cooperative activity. As shown in Table 1.1, the major types of collective actions in which such coalitions may engage are

(1) *Mobilization*: freeing up and applying some of the resources held by the collaborating organizations, with the aim of achieving the collective goal.
(2) *Publicity*: expressing preferences via the media to audiences that include both governmental officials and nongovernmental organizations, as well as to the general public.
(3) *Lobbying*: attempting to persuade governmental authorities to make favorable decisions.

Some of these collective actions are aimed at supporters or potential supporters, whereas others are targeted toward neutral observers (e.g., the media and the general public) and against active opponents (more often to dissuade them from action than to convert them to one's side). But the most important targets in any policy domain are the governmental officials who possess the legal or customary authority to make a decision about an event that is binding on the domain as a whole.

Organizations that form coalitions to pool their political resources are generally more successful in realizing their goals than are actors attempting by themselves to affect policies. Because considerable resource expenditures are involved, only organizations holding high interests in a particular policy event typically pursue their preferences collaboratively with others. The configurations of allied and opposing actors may be quite fluid and complex when examined over time (Broadbent, 1989b). Further, because events reflect numerous decision points within a continuing policy stream, the interweaving of actors, relations, and actions is best considered across multiple, sequential policy events. A large sample of events can reveal both stability and change in policy network structures as well as the impact of event outcomes on subsequent policy struggles.

Events can span more than one institutional arena, and they may refer to the numerous types of decisions just described. Given the enormous complexity and often ponderous decision making of liberal democratic states, a potentially inexhaustible number of decision points might be examined. Unfortunately, conceptualizing the total number of decision points, both in space and time, that make up the complete event process lags far behind the parallel problem of identifying and selecting elite organizations. Most researchers resort to purposively selecting only highly visible and controversial events, where core actor participation is exceptionally great. However, overemphasizing exciting rather than routine events risks distorting how policy participation occurs. Nor do social scientists yet understand the full implications of singular events embedded within much larger temporal sequences (Abbott, 1984; Abbott and Hrycak, 1990). Although we lack definitive solutions to event definition and sampling, by studying relatively large numbers of salient policy events in three countries we hope to uncover factors associated with organizational participation as well as event outcomes.

In the organizational state approach, the most important social structural formations are *jointly occupied positions* within networks (Lorrain and White, 1971; Burt, 1976). These locations are defined both by organizational interests in specific events and by exchange ties among organizations. In the order of increasingly stringent criteria and, hence, of smaller size, the following nested positions occur:

(1) An *issue public* consists of all organizations expressing similar interests in all policy domain issues. Because issues are not framed in terms of particular policy proposals, an issue public is very likely to encompass many organizations that take opposing sides on specific policy proposals relevant to the issues in which they are interested. Hence, an issue public resembles a "social circle" (Kadushin, 1968; Alba and Kadushin, 1976) whose members also share a common orientation toward some substantive matter without necessarily agreeing about what is to be done. But a social circle presumes relatively dense communication linkages among its members, whereas we require only that an issue public's members share common orientations toward the issues (see Laumann and Knoke, 1987: 127–8). Such publics form a broad category rather than an interacting network.

(2) An *event public* is a subset of domain actors that expresses interest in a specific event, no matter how slight. Like issue publics, event publics are heterogeneous audiences with regard to which policy outcomes they prefer. Both proponents and opponents as well as neutral observers who merely monitor the scene may all be involved in a specific event public. Thus, an event public consists of the broadest possible subset of domain organizations from which the more intensely committed participants may be recruited. The criterion of membership does not include maintaining direct or even indirect communication ties to one another. Indeed, the primary mode of attention to an event for some organizations may be via mass media channels. Each event attracts a distinct public, which may overlap to greater or lesser degree with the members of other event publics.

(3) An *advocacy circle* consists of three or more formal organizations within an event public who communicate directly or indirectly among themselves about policy matters and who prefer the same outcome on that event. (This concept is identical with the "collective actor" of Laumann and Marsden [1979] and Knoke and Pappi [1991], but it is a more descriptively accurate term and is similar to Sabatier's [1988] concept of "advocacy coalition.") Inclusion in an advocacy circle does not necessarily indicate that all members engage in efforts to influence a policy decision, but requires only that participants share the same preference. Requiring at least three members avoids cluttering the analysis with trivial subsets. Members of one advocacy circle all support the "pro" outcome on an event, whereas members of a second advocacy circle all prefer the "con" outcome for that decision. For other events, differing subsets constitute distinct advocacy circles. Typically, advocacy circle members for different events overlap only partially. Indeed, the degree of coincidence among advocacy circles across numerous events is important evidence about the cleavage structure prevailing in a policy domain. The advocacy circle concept does not distinguish between organizations that work closely together to influence a concrete policy decision and those that are passive policy proponents.

(4) The *action set* concept further restricts its scope to members of an advocacy circle who consciously coordinate their policy influence activities (Knoke and Pappi, 1991).

> Group cohesion is the essential feature: all members of an action set prefer the same policy outcome for the event; are directly or indirectly linked together in communication or other networks; and jointly engage in lobbying and other policy influence activities (Knoke and Burleigh, 1989). If communication channels are weak and disjointed, more than one action set favoring the same policy event outcome many emerge from a given advocacy circle. More typically, single action sets emerge on two opposing sides of a contested event (a "pro" and a "con" action set).

Because issue publics do not form around specific policy events, their members are not nested in the other three formations, although we would expect them to be disproportionally attracted to events where these issues are at stake. Indeed, an important proposition in the organizational state approach asserts that organizations' issue interests are a major determinant of their participation in policy-making activities.

Because event publics, advocacy circles, and action sets are social formations unique to a specific event, they cannot by themselves reveal global structures in a policy domain. During any political era, many policy fights take place and each event stimulates the formation of distinct organizational clusters. An important question for a policy domain analyst is whether an overarching opposition structure emerges across these multiple events. For example, organizations *A* and *B* may collaborate in the same pro-action set for event *W*; belong to different con-action sets on event *X*; work in opposing action sets on event *Y*; and sit out event *Z* entirely. Similar diverse patterns apply to advocacy circles formed around each event. Because dozens of other organizations are involved in many events, measuring their advocacy circle and action set activity becomes critical to understanding a domain's global social structure. To uncover these relationships, analysts can take advantage of the duality of organization-to-event connections: Some organizations participate in the same events, and some events attract the same organizations. Mapping these organization-event co-occurrences reveals the entire structure, tying together advocacy circles and action sets across multiple policy events.

More formally, an *opposition network* is the pattern of overlapping memberships among all advocacy circles or action sets that form around the entire set of policy events during some period. A domain opposition network's structure is a function of overlapping memberships among its advocacy circles or action sets. These relations can be spatially represented in two or more dimensions by treating the degree of overlap between advocacy circles or action sets as a measure of social proximity. Figure 1.1 illustrates four fundamental cleavage patterns of opposition networks in a two-dimensional space. Each small circle represents a specific event's advocacy circle or action set; thus, three or more organizations may be included inside each circle. In diagram A, the circles are located close together because the organizations comprising the advocacy circle or action sets for each event are virtually identical. In contrast, the polarized pattern in diagram B arises because each event produces two differentiated groupings, one taking the pro position and a second taking the con position. For each event, the pro and con clus-

Figure 1.1 *Hypothetical domain cleavage structures*

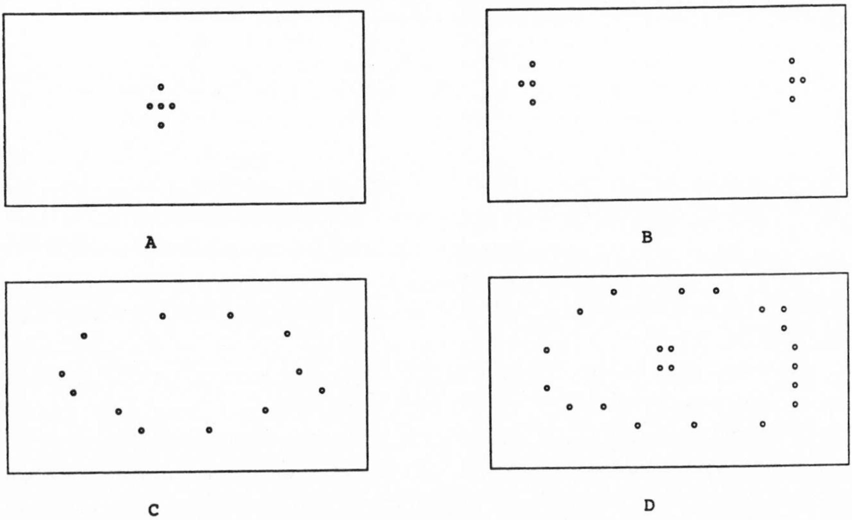

ters consist of almost the same organizations. However, if each event's advocacy circles or action sets tend to recruit different combinations of members, their infrequent overlaps will result in pro and con groups that are scattered and interspersed throughout the domain's topographical space. Diagram C represents a circular or rim structure with a hollow core, while diagram D contains a few advocacy circles or action sets at the center but locates most in specialized sectors at the periphery.

A policy domain's opposition network structure has important implications for the resolution of domain policy conflicts. Polarized structures indicate bitter divisions whose great gulfs cannot be easily bridged, because few or no members exist in common that could serve as mediators of disputes. More diffuse configurations indicate a system's greater capacity to bargain and negotiate a compromise solution to an event conflict. Because some actors appear as members of the pro and con groupings on different events, they have the potential to serve as brokers. The few empirical analyses of such opposition networks have generally found patterns that imply linkages between proponents and opponents across events, rather than extremely polarized structures. Based on analyses of a German community elite system, Laumann and Pappi (1976: 142) proposed two generic structuring principles: sectoral differentiation and integrative centrality. A policy domain's social space is divided into relatively homogeneous sectors occupied by actors who are likely to share common values, attitudes, and interests. Located at a network's center are policy actors who play the key coordinating roles in the domain, whereas the periphery is occupied by actors with less integrative importance. Similar patterns have been uncovered in the U.S. for information and resource exchange networks among urban organizations (Galaskiewicz, 1979: 61–90), national energy and health policy domain organizations (Laumann and Knoke, 1987: 242–8), and national labor policy domain organizations (Knoke, 1990b: 163–71). Laumann and Knoke (1987: 245) succinctly summarized the spatial structure: "The core is dominated by governmental actors with the most broad-reaching policy mandates; the first circle is dominated by the major special interests of particular sectors; and the peripheries are occupied by the minor claimants. In effect, the aggregative interest groups serve as intermediate communication filters that link the peripheries with the core."

A notable exception is a study of Washington lawyers' helping ties with the 72 most prominent and influential persons in four national policy domains (agriculture, energy, health, and labor), which revealed a "roughly spherical structure with a hollow core" (Heinz, Laumann, Nelson, and Salisbury, 1993: 300). No autonomous brokers capable of bridging the empty center of the four policy areas were uncovered. Rather, client type, economic ideology, and political party affiliation produced sharply polarized sectors in which "communication among influentials takes place mostly with the elites of adjacent, politically compatible interest groups. They deal with their allies not with their adversaries" (p. 301). The labor domain exhibited a particularly wide gulf between union and business representatives. The authors speculated that government officials, who were not included in their list of notables, might serve as mediators or arbiters of domain disputes on at least some issues, thus binding the policy system together. Because our project includes *all* the key labor policy domain organizations, the organizational state anticipates that the spatial core in each nation is filled by both the most consequential governmental organizations and the peak private-sector organizations, whereas distinct peripheral sectors are occupied by specialized organizations. A contrasting state-centric hypothesis argues that governmental actors dominate the core to the exclusion of civil society interest groups.

Event outcomes

The policy-making process progressively winnows both the organizations occupying key network positions and the proposed policy alternatives as an event moves over time toward a definitive collective resolution. The metaphor of a funnel is apt: Successively fewer mobilized positions remain to carry on the policy fight as the outflow nears. Figure 1.2 depicts this mobilization funnel in terms of the relative proportions of organizations participating in issue publics, event publics, advocacy circles, and action sets according to organizational types. At the broad inflow end of the funnel are numerous individual persons in their social statuses (such as employees, consumers, professionals) and informal collectivities (such as classes, groups, communities). Although many actors have latent structural interests or even consciously held concerns about particular policy events (e.g., automobile assembly workers' worries about import policies), most lack the resources, including time, for effective participation. Perhaps only a small minor-

Figure 1.2 *Funnel of mobilization by organizational types*

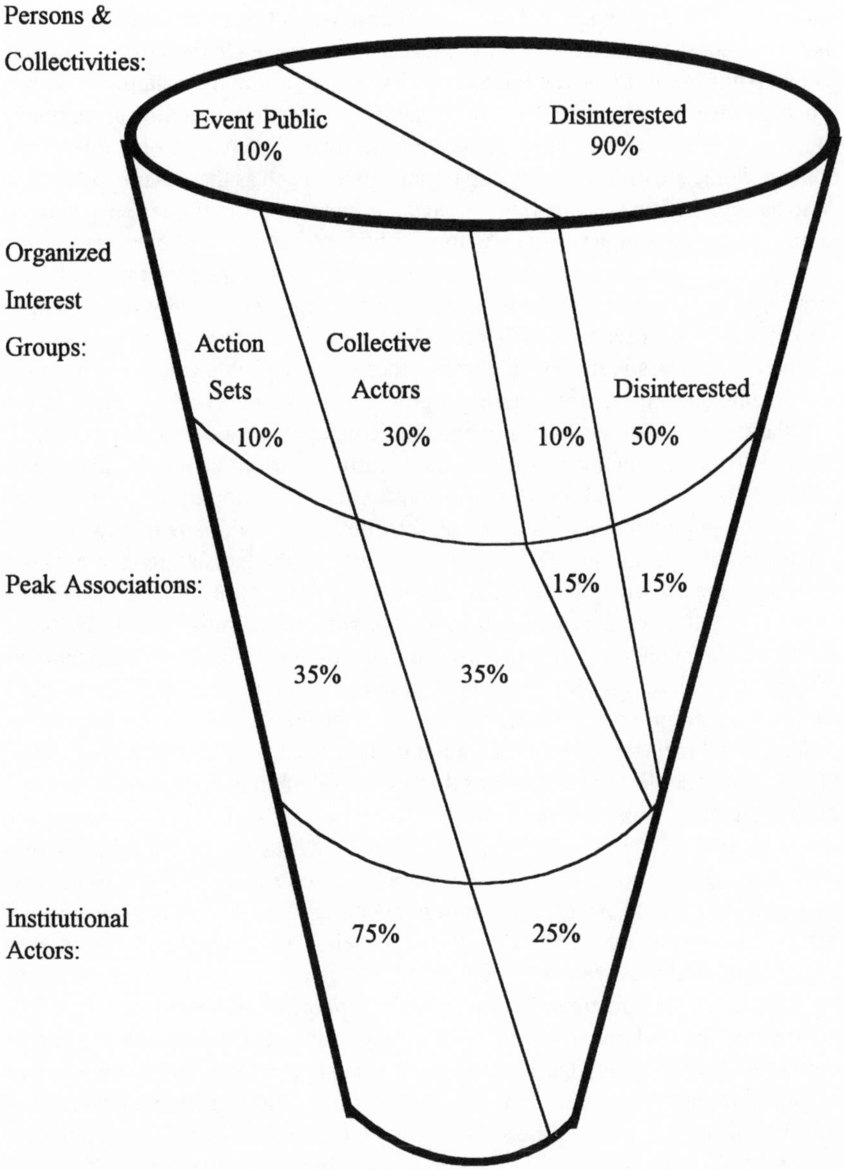

ity comprise a meaningful issue public for any particular event; the vast majority are simply disinterested and hence uninvolved.

Still near the funnel's wide end, organized interest groups are much more likely to perceive that their interests are at stake in a policy event. However, many will have either narrow policy mandates, charters that proscribe partisan activity, or insufficient power resources to become involved in every campaign. Perhaps half or more of them remain passive, but most of those with clear policy preferences are likely to choose sides as the events' alternatives become clearly defined. Hence, membership in an advocacy circle is fairly common among organized interest groups. However, relatively few will collaborate with others as action set partners. The next segment of the funnel consists of the "peak" interest associations of the domain. Some are mass membership organizations, such as the American Medical Association, the Buraku Liberation League in Japan, and the single German labor unions. Others are organizations with institutional members, like the AFL-CIO, the Japanese Federation of Economic Organizations, and the Federation of German Industry. Peak organizations typically have large and wealthy memberships who give their professional staffs broad latitude to select from the domain's policy menu. Comparatively few in number, these highly visible actors often cannot avoid being sucked into many policy fights. Their members and constituents expect them to pursue their commitments to a core agenda, and their partners from previous collective actions expect them to fulfill their obligations to participate reciprocally when called on. Hence, a substantial proportion of a domain's peak association population belong to action sets. Finally, the ultimate policy decision makers in the relevant institutional arenas – such as the legislature or regulatory agencies – are shown at the funnel's narrow end. Virtually all these actors participate, as a collective decision is not possible without definitive action by them. Hence, the large majority of these institutional participants are mobilized into one of the pro or con action sets where they collaborate with the key peak associations and interest groups preferring the same policy outcome.

The funnel metaphor implies a temporal procession from earlier activities that involve broad publics to later actions that are settled among a small number of key decision makers. Most real policy events, however, are unlikely to conform to so tidy a sequential scenario. Institutional actors, such as the prime minister or a regulatory agency, are as likely to initiate policy proposals as they are to be reactors to events raised by pressure groups. Peak associations may activate their grass roots members to lobby directly with their legislators. Passionate interest groups may bolt their peak associations to pursue an idiosyncratic agenda (e.g., the Chemical Manufacturers' Association's support of a workplace safety bill opposed by the Chamber of Commerce). Despite such chaotic thrusts and parries during the heat of policy battles, the conceptual simplicity of the funnel remains helpful in highlighting a persistent pattern: As a policy proposal moves ever closer toward concrete resolution, the subset of domain actors with sufficient power to affect the final decision generally becomes smaller rather than larger. Ordinary voters and association members may express general preferences toward one side or another of a proposal, but they rarely sit down with legislative committee staff to design sections of a bill. Organized interest groups may prowl the corridors of a regulatory agency, but when the rate structures are being marked up, only the lobbyists for peak associations are likely to get their phone calls returned. The mobilization funnel captures the tendency of policy-making to be an exclusionary process – locking out both actors and alternatives – rather than an inclusionary one. Rare instances where mass participation has an impact, such as the successful revolt of the U.S. elderly against catastrophic medical insurance premiums, prove the rule.

The distinction made about political parties in their corporate advocacy and their collective decider roles is also relevant to the funnel's dynamics. As partisan supporters of one side or another in a public policy dispute, politicians typically join the fray early in the process, forming coalitions with interest groups and peak associations to enact their preferred outcomes. But their roles as members of a collective decider – a committee or a legislative chamber – are enacted only toward the very end of the conflict, when they must cast the ballots that yield a final settlement binding winners and losers alike to that collective decision. By distinguishing between their adversarial and conflict-resolution roles, we can see that public actors participate in distinct ways at various policy process stages.

The eventual success or failure of a policy event fight depends on which side of the controversy can activate enough power resources to overcome the advantages on the other side. Such resources are gathered from every stage of the funnel. Public opinion and election votes come from persons and collectivities; publicity and grass roots lobbying are contributed by interest groups; peak associations pour professional fundraisers and lobbyists into the offices of bureaucrats and politicians; and within the institutional arena itself, lawmakers and regulators twist arms and trade support for their pet projects.

The outcomes of public policy controversies are also related to network connections among elites interested in collective decisions. Winning or losing a policy fight depends on which of the opposing sides best deploys its network connections to mobilize and coordinate greater quantities of political resources. Galaskiewicz (1979: 140–1) proposed simple but elegant concepts of interorganizational resource inflows and outflows. First, each organization could tap resources from its support system. An organization with many contacts offering money, information, and moral support has potentially greater access to the resources of those partners than does an organization with fewer such connections. Second, an organization's resource dependents – the organizations to which it sends money, information, and support – are also potential sources of resources that could be obtained by calling in political debts. These inflow and outflow linkages significantly affect both an organization's influence reputation and its success in affecting domain events, independent of the organization's own funds, personnel, and purposes.

Parallel efforts to explain collective decision making as a network of exchanges, have generated a collective action model (Coleman, 1973, 1977, 1990; Marsden, 1981, 1982, 1983). In essence, Coleman's approach considers how policy actors with interests in different events exchange resources that influence the event outcomes. Following from resource dependence principles, actors are more powerful, and hence more likely to achieve their preferred outcomes, if they possess resources that control events in which other actors have strong interests. Event outcomes depend on the intensity of the actors' interests in the various events and on the resources the actors control. In a pure market situation, every pair of actors can directly exchange with one another. But, in political elite systems, where mutual trust is essential before such transactions take place, resource exchanges most likely occur only through well-established communication networks comprised of direct and indirect connections (Marsden, 1983). Brokerage relations may also be critical in bringing potential exchange partners together (Gould and Fernandez, 1989; Fernandez and Gould, 1994). The absence of a communication channel between actors signals a lack of information or access needed for making an exchange on one event that could be reciprocated on a later event. Political exchange models have been applied to only a few real collective action situations, with varying degrees of success (Marsden and Laumann, 1977; Pappi and Kappelhoff, 1984; Pappi and Melbeck, 1984; Kappelhoff, 1989; Pappi and Knoke, 1992). Laumann and Knoke with Kim (1987: 343–73) applied a modified version of Coleman's exchange model to 16 American energy and health policy domain event outcomes. The model quite accurately predicted the collective outcome of every event, failing in only one of the eight health events to designate the actual result correctly. Stokman and Van den Bos (1992) proposed a two-stage model of policy-making that integrated a preliminary stage of mutual interactor influence and a final stage of decision made only by the actors entitled to vote on the binding decision (i.e., governmental authorities). Applied to the U.S. energy domain data, they found that the positional power of various types of organizations is especially dependent on both their resources and their voting power, indicating that the distinction between governmental and nongovernmental actors is important to preserve. Another intriguing advancement was Kappelhoff's (1989) extension of exchange network power beyond Marsden's reformulation, taking into account clientelistic dependency (using Bonacich's [1987] measure of centrality) and barter exchange relations among actors. Our empirical investigation of the three national labor policy domains examines a new version of the resource exchange model to explain the outcomes of more than six dozen labor legislation events.

COMPARISONS AMONG THREE NATIONS

We now explore the policy-making realities of the U.S., Germany, and Japan using the organizational state approach. The fundamental questions we seek to answer are the same in each case, the perennial questions asked by all political researchers: Who rules and what difference does it make? Specifically, we want to know more about the central policy actors, the power relations between the state and civil society, the state's main governance functions, the sociopolitical organization of civil society, the patterns of alliances and conflicts, the totality of the national power structures, and the relationships of information- and resource-exchange patterns to the power structure. We feel that an organizational state approach can yield new insights on these questions. Our analyses focus on such topics as the distribution and intensity of interests in different labor issues among the organizations; the relative centrality of different actors in communication and political support networks, and how well this centrality predicts their reputations for influence; the composition of different interorganizational coalitions, and how successful they are; and the overall patterns of each national power structure. Unlike most earlier studies, the organizational state approach necessitates the collection of data from all key labor domain actors, thus enabling us to look at politics in new, more comprehensive ways. These lines of investigation provide us with new angles of vision on the perennial questions about political power that we have raised.

To some degree, in power structure studies as in any other type of research, the methods and approaches one uses will affect the findings one reaches (Ricci, 1971). For the analysis of advanced, capitalist, industrial democracies, the predominant research methods have been secondary institutional studies and individual-level survey data. These studies have produced manifold images of the power structure. Those images include the well-known pluralist, elite, class, state-autonomy, and corporatist-ideal typifications (for details, see Knoke, 1981; Alford, 1975; Alford and Friedland, 1985). Each power structure perspective has its ardent advocates, and each has contributed in varying degrees to an improved understanding of policy-making. We do not claim that our use of the organizational state approach and its empirical findings will adjudicate among these alternative images' validities nor definitively settle their disputes. However, our results can provide some new insights into their relevance for the three nations under study, so we comment on these alternative images in passing throughout the book.

When the U.S., Germany, and Japan are viewed from the organizational state perspective, new dimensions of similarity and difference should emerge. These dimensions should offer fresh insight into the institutional forces that contribute to national differences in policy responses. Present-day Japan and Germany evolved from historical and institutional backgrounds that are very different from each other's and from those of the U.S. Similarities might indicate that the three nations have converged over the years since World War II. The possibility of observing strong variation among these three cases is important. Because the organizational state was originally induced from research on U.S. policy domains, to some extent it may still assume or reflect peculiar characteristics of the U.S. To the extent that our applying the organizational state approach produces useful and convincing insights into the politics of the three nations, it will have demonstrated a much wider relevance.

Japan, Germany, and the U.S. were each governed by conservative regimes during the research period. Presumably, this commonality should have enhanced their power-structural similarities. Yet despite this apparent similarity their responses to common problems of fiscal austerity in the 1980s were quite different. Their respective labor policies reflected this difference. This diversity of response indicates the profound institutional differences that modified and channeled their actual policy outputs. Our approach clarifies the dynamics and structures of these institutions.

In the U.S., in its policy responses to austerity in the 1980s, the Reagan Administration cut taxes and increased military spending while reducing social programs and labor benefits. These actions induced a temporary economic expansion but did not respond effectively to real fiscal limits. To the contrary, they led to a massive debt buildup that made the long-term fiscal problems of the U.S. much worse. In Germany, the Kohl government started the early 1980s with a fiscal austerity program and minor deregulation of the labor market, immediately raising major controversies with opposition parties and the unions. But in contrast to what occurred in the U.S. and Japan at this time, in Germany social benefits and labor's position vis-à-vis capital were weakened less and the gulf separating the conservative coalition and its opponents could at times be bridged by particular policies (such as worker retraining to ease economic readjustment). In Japan, the Nakasone and successor regimes took the most radically conservative path of all. They not only cut numerous social benefits to save money but also raised taxes. Furthermore, the Japanese government embarked on a vigorous program of structural reform to weaken the organizational and political forces pushing for high state expenditures. This program involved privatizing government-held railroad and communications corporations, which made these corporations more efficient. It also weakened the huge leftist labor unions, which were bastions of the opposition labor movement and its affiliated Socialist Party, and strengthened the alternative, more compliant labor federation.

Contemporary scholarship on these three countries proposes a variety of reasons for their divergent policy responses. In their current political images, the U.S. is seen as a pluralistic political system in which most groups can readily participate. Germany is typically regarded as a corporatistic system in which peak business and labor federations negotiate with the government to set labor policy and coopt resistance. And Japan is often viewed as a political system whose society is controlled by its strong state, which guides it to the government's preferred goals. Each of these conventional images is a subject of controversy. Each contender touches upon central theoretical questions about the basic nature of politics and power in advanced, capitalist, industrialized democracies. However, rather than further sketch these controversies and images, we will turn, in the following chapters, to a detailed presentation of the results of our comparative organizational state analyses.

CONCLUSION

The organizational state approach combines elements of exchange theory, network analysis, and interorganizational relations into a distinctive framework for analyzing the behavior of national policy domains in the modern state. The concepts of core policy actors, policy interests, political exchange relations, and collective actions suffice to construct an account of domain social structures and processes.

Our empirical analyses of U.S., German, and Japanese labor policy domains are premised on these basic organizational state principles. At the broadest level, a common pattern of social organization should occur because the three nations share many social, economic, and political properties. But differences can be anticipated to occur. They can arise from these societies' different institutional histories, in terms of, for example, executive-legislative unity, business-labor antagonism, or collectivist-individualist ethos. In particular, we expect to find a more corporatist and state-centered polity in Japan than in the federalist U.S., with Germany intermediate. The next chapter reviews the labor policy histories of these three nations, setting the stage for our subsequent assessment of the organizational state's relevance to their contemporary experiences.

2

Three labor policy domains

This chapter introduces the three nations whose labor policy domains we investigate using the organizational state model – the United States, Germany, and Japan. We begin with an overview of recent changes in their economies and labor forces and then turn to short historical explications of their labor politics in the early 20th century. We conclude with a discussion of analytic strategies for drawing inferences about sociopolitical behavior through cross-national comparisons.

ECONOMIES AND LABOR FORCES

Following their recoveries from the devastation of World War II, both Germany and Japan rapidly joined the U.S. in dominating the world economy during the quarter-century from the early 1960s to the late 1980s. These three nations were clearly the world's upper-class societies: Despite having less than 10 percent of the global population, their combined gross domestic products comprised 51.6% of the $1.756 trillion world GDP in 1965, and by 1988 they accounted for 52.3% of the $17.018 trillion world GDP (calculated from the World Bank, 1990: 183). During this era, Japan's economy grew the fastest of the three, so that its share of world GDP leaped from 5.2% to 16.7%. Germany's share remained roughly constant (6.5% and 7.1%), but the U.S. portion tumbled from 39.9% to 28.5%. By 1988 their citizens' per capita annual incomes were roughly identical (Germany = $18,480; U.S. = $19,840; Japan = $21,020), a plateau matched only by the four Scandinavian countries and exceeded only by tiny financial powerhouse Switzerland (p. 179).

The three national labor forces continued some major transformations that began earlier in the century. Although the majority of their populations had long ago left agricultural pursuits, the transition from industrial-based to service-based economies proceeded apace. As shown in Figure 2.1, service-sector employment reached a majority of workers in each country, with the U.S. considerably in the lead. Employment in industry followed a converse pattern in Germany and the U.S., falling to 39% and 27% of employment, respectively. The Japanese industrial labor force actually rose early in the period before settling around 34%,

Figure 2.1. *Percent of labor force in services*

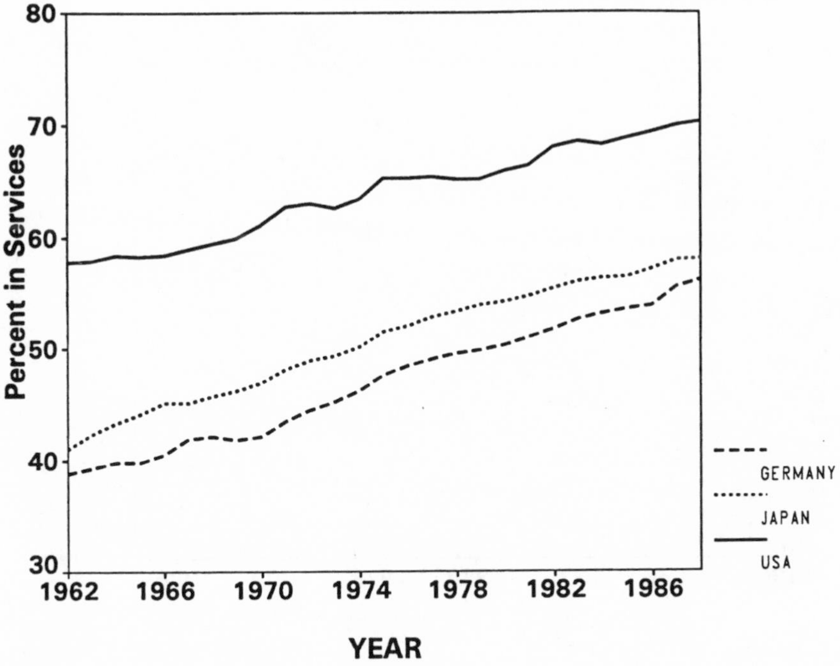

mainly because Japan was still reducing its agricultural workforce from more than a quarter to less than a tenth of its populace.

Another remarkable transformation during this quarter-century was the incorporation of women into the paid labor force. Figure 2.2 plots the annual percentages of working women in the female population age 15–64 years. The U.S. trend was a steady upward expansion of about one percent each year, topping two-thirds in 1987. The German line was virtually flat until the mid-1980s, when a majority of women finally entered the paid labor force. Japan initially reduced its very high female labor force participation level until the mid-1970s, when women again began to enter at a rate somewhat below that of the U.S. The result was a U-shape curve that left the percentage of women in the labor force in Japan intermediate to the percentages in the U.S. and Germany. The recent surges in numbers of women working outside the home reflected major changes in both marital ages and family sizes, as well as changes in families' needs for additional wage earners to sustain their living standards. With women comprising growing proportions in many national labor forces, their concerns about comparable pay, child care, career advancement, and pension equity have become increasingly salient political issues.

Finally, still another noteworthy set of trends is in the union representation of workers. Unionization levels peaked during the immediate postwar period in each

Figure 2.2. *Percent of women in labor force*

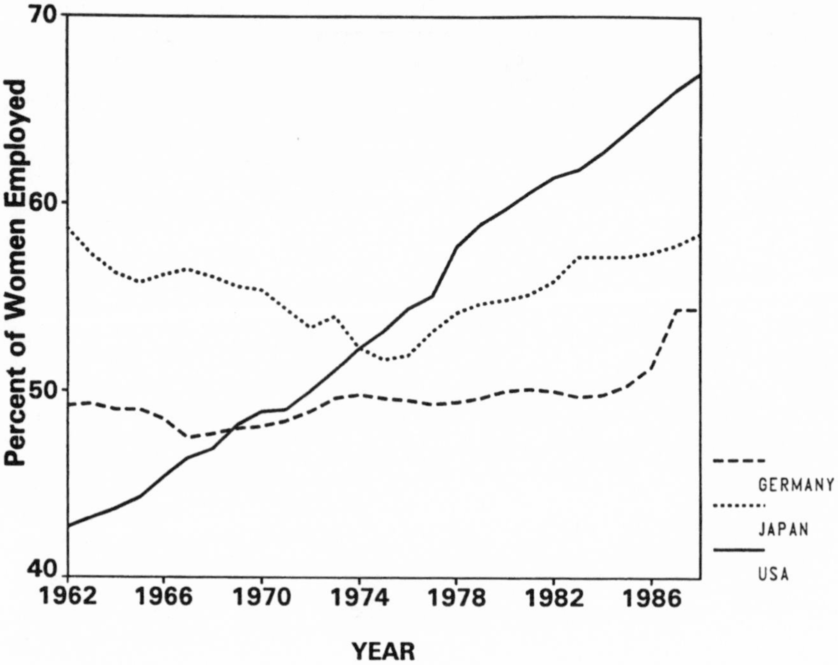

nation (Japan at 55.8% in 1949; Germany at 39.3% in 1951; and the U.S. at 34.7% in 1954; reported respectively in Nihon Seisansei Honbu, 1988: 160; Armingeon, 1988; and Goldfield, 1987: 10). As shown in Figure 2.3, the subsequent trends diverged markedly from 1962–87. The U.S.'s unionization levels deteriorated markedly until barely one nonagricultural employee in five was represented by a union. Japanese unions maintained a roughly constant rate until the late 1970s, when enrollments began falling in parallel to the U.S., eventually accounting for slightly more than one in four workers. Only the German union movement managed to increase its representation, reaching almost one-third of the labor force, the highest unionization level, in 1987. These shifting fortunes underlay the differential political clout exercised by organized labor in each nation.

Labor productivity and unemployment problems began to plague the three nations as the 20th century drew to a close. Japan's robust productivity gains were concentrated in the 1960s and 1970s. By the mid-1970s, all three national trends had settled into the range below two percent annually, with the U.S. experiencing frequent periods of null-to-negative productivity that accompanied two major domestic recessions. Except for a brief interlude induced by the Vietnam War, U.S. unemployment never fell below five percent. In contrast, Japan's unemployment rate was always under three percent. Germany's *Wirtschaftswunder* (economic miracle) persisted into the 1960s, with spectacularly low unemployment figures

Figure 2.3. *Percent of labor force unionized*

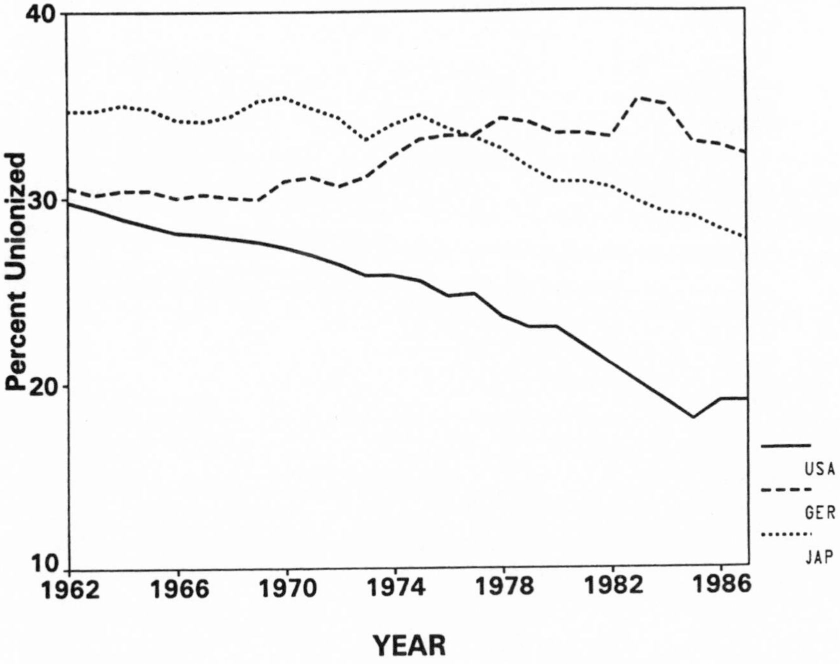

that even Japan could envy. But the twin "oil shocks" of the 1970s caused by the Organization of Petroleum Exporting Countries (OPEC) cartel's sudden price hikes rapidly transformed the German economy into a high-unemployment regime almost indistinguishable from the U.S. Japan, however, coped with both oil shocks much better, holding down its unemployment and making industrial adjustments. In sum, the expansionary, high-prosperity economies enjoyed by Japan, Germany, and the U.S. during the early post–World War II era began to show considerable signs of erosion by the 1980s. The three nations' changing labor forces and increasingly complex trade and productivity problems raised a host of new issues with which their labor policy domains grappled.

LABOR POLITICS IN THREE NATIONS

This section recapitulates the major political events that shaped the national labor policies of the U.S., Germany, and Japan in the 20th century up to the beginning of our empirical study. Space limitations permit only brief summaries of each domain's history. In order to concentrate on the critical labor, management, and government developments at the highest strategic and policy-making levels, we forego inquiry into such specialized topics as industry collective bargaining, corporate personnel policy, and workplace relations (Kochan, Katz, and McKersie,

1986: 17). We also do not provide information here about national governmental institutions, but descriptive summaries of U.S., German, and Japanese legislative processes may be found in Appendix 1.

Each nation's labor policy domains became historically differentiated to varying degrees from their social-welfare practices. Thus, those with the necessary qualifications receive old age, poverty, disability, maternity, sickness, and work-accident benefits, with the amounts provided to recipients tied to their families' labor market participation and performances in quite different ways. Beginning with Bismarck's conservative policies in the late 19th century, the German state actively promoted a wide variety of compulsory social insurance benefits whose levels were tied to socioeconomic status and market inequalities (Schmidt, 1989: 66–7). The U.S. welfare system remained mired in 19th-century laissez-faire notions of limited government intervention and produced stigmatized, temporary benefits rather than permanent, collective welfare rights (Amenta and Skocpol, 1989; Skocpol, 1992). Japan's social-welfare policies exhibited characteristics typical of many late-industrializing countries. Although some of Japan's welfare and social security policies grew out of the war-mobilization experience, their relatively low costs are explained by two factors (Tominaga, 1988: 123). First, the Japanese population was predominantly concentrated in the younger age strata, although aging will become a more critical problem for Japan than for Germany and the U.S. in the next century. Second, because Japan's welfare system began later, it matured much later. All social welfare and social security programs require more than a few decades to mature. Prior to maturity, they cost less because relatively few people qualify as beneficiaries. These historically diverse legacies of each nation persist today in distinctive national images of their labor policy domains.

The United States

The key events shaping the 20th-century labor policy domain in the United States were legislative acts passed by the Congress and federal court decisions that defined the rights and limitations of organized labor. The rise of a limited welfare state, the civil rights movements of racial minorities, and the struggles of women for labor force equity each contributed to making the federal government the central institutional arena where labor policies were hammered out.

Until the latter 19th century, the U.S. labor force was predominantly rural and agricultural. As large-scale urban industries begin to develop after the Civil War, national unions pressed workers' grievances over low wages, long hours, workplace disputes, child labor, and female labor (Ware, 1935). The American Federation of Labor (AFL), formed in 1886, represented skilled crafts unions that refrained from an overtly political approach. Instead, Samuel Gompers, the AFL president for four decades, initially advocated an ideology of voluntarism and economism, or "business unionism," more compatible with the individualism of ordinary workers (Taft, 1957). This conservative orientation proved successful in attracting new members: Between 1898 and 1904, the AFL unions increased six-fold to more than a million, reaching a peak of four million by 1920. Total union strength as a percentage of the nonfarm labor force grew from 6.5% in 1900 to 17.6% in 1920 (Troy and Sheflin, 1985; all U.S. union enrollments cited in this section come from that source).

Propelled by the rise of large industrial corporations, the U.S. was transformed from a set of regional economies into an integrated national economy. This change accompanied increasingly ruthless competition among economic groups in the national political arena. Rudimentary institutions and policies for regulating an increasingly complex labor market were lacking. The U.S. labor policy domain remained decentralized and dominated by employers through the judicial system. The federal Department of Labor, created in the cabinet in 1913, lacked authority to decide which unions were certified, what bargaining units were recognized, and what labor relations practices and standards were legitimate.

In self-preservation, the AFL was forced in a more politically active direction. It created a lobbying committee in 1896 and endorsed its first presidential candidate (the Democrat, William Jennings Bryan) in 1908 (Karson, 1958). Spurred by its own socialist and progressive minorities and by competition from radical unions such as the Industrial Workers of the World (Wobblies), the AFL championed moderate reforms for child labor, women's hours, government workers, and retirees (Greenstone, 1969: 27–8). Several states passed innovative regulatory legislation, and union officials participated in administering factory inspections, accident insurance, and unemployment insurance plans. During World War I, the War Labor Board coordinated collective negotiation of labor-management disputes, while the AFL appointed its leaders to numerous other government panels. But these modest corporatist interventions into the economy were quickly dismantled after the war ended.

Court rulings once again freed employers to ignore union bargaining demands and to retaliate against workers who joined unions. Anti-labor decisions by the courts and militant employer opposition undermined working-class organization (Griffin, Wallace, and Rubin, 1986). Resurgent employer associations such as the National Association of Manufacturers (NAM) and the National Civic Foundation aggressively used federal court injunctions against strikes and boycotts. Effective application of the Sherman Anti-Trust Act prevented closed-shop unions (Marks, 1989: 70–1). Throughout the 1920s, union strength steadily declined, reaching its all-time low of 12% of the nonfarm labor force on the eve of the stock market crash of 1929. But the business community's inability to ameliorate the havoc wrought by the Great Depression soon resuscitated the union movement and brought it a powerful ally, the national Democratic Party.

President Franklin Roosevelt's New Deal restructured the U.S. national labor policy domain. It created a complex of legislative, executive, and regulatory institutions to counterbalance labor's interests with capital's. The alliance between the AFL and congressional liberals led by Senator Robert Wagner "made collective bargaining a matter of public concern, conducted by institutions with statutorily-defined rights within a framework shaped by state agencies" (Tomlins, 1985:

101). By recognizing workers' rights to organize and bargain with employers, the New Deal empowered unions to expand their memberships vastly. Six major acts established an industry-based collective bargaining system that prevailed in the U.S. for the rest of the century:

(1) The Davis-Bacon Act (1931) required locally prevailing rates of pay on federally financed construction projects, primarily employing construction workers from craft unions.
(2) The Anti-Injunction (Norris-LaGuardia) Act (1932) greatly restricted employers' use of court injunctions against union organizing and made yellow-dog contracts unenforceable.
(3) The National Industrial Recovery Act (1933) organized employee rights to organize, bargain collectively, and choose their own union representations without interference from employers. Business associations were required to design their own codes of fair competition concerning hours and wages. The Supreme Court declared the NIRA unconstitutional in 1935.
(4) The National Labor Relations (Wagner) Act (1935) replaced the NIRA. It set regulations to create bargaining representation through majority vote of workers in a unit, and it defined unfair labor practices by employers. Most importantly, it provided an enforcement mechanism. The National Labor Relations Board was empowered to issue cessation orders to company anti-union activities, to supervise collective bargaining unit elections, and to hear and adjudicate labor-management grievances in a courtlike manner.
(5) The Walsh-Healey Act (1936) specified minimum labor standards for government contractors.
(6) The Fair Labor Standards Act (1938) extended coverage to more workers. It set a minimum wage, a 40-hour work week for 1940, and a time-and-a-half for overtime work, and it restricted child labor under age 16.

A potent alliance between the labor movement and the national Democratic Party was clearly crucial to passage and enforcement of key labor relations laws (Fine, 1966; Greenstone, 1969: 40–52). The militant Congress of Industrial Organizations (CIO), whose unions broke from the AFL in the mid-1930s, waged aggressive organizing campaigns in major industries (steel, autos, clothing, textiles, rubber), broadening labor's base among semiskilled factory workers and blacks. Union membership in the nonfarm labor force more than doubled, from 14.7% in 1930 to 30.4% in 1945. The CIO's creation of Labor's Nonpartisan League (1936) and its reincarnation as the Political Action Committee (PAC) (1943) solidified unionized labor as a core constituency in the Democratic Party (Foster, 1975). New constraints were imposed during World War II, as the War Labor Board encouraged management to accept collective bargaining agreements in return for union no-strike pledges and narrow grievance procedures binding on their members (Kochan, Katz, and McKersie, 1986: 32). With many white males off to combat, blacks and women entered the urban labor force in enormous numbers, posing persistent problems for a union movement built on white male skilled labor, despite retrenchments occurring after the war ended.

Business was on the political defensive during much of the New Deal, fighting unsuccessfully to prevent or limit the federal government's guarantee of rights to labor and the elderly. Though they lost this fight, they did establish a political presence in Washington that would serve them well in coming decades, most notably by forming the Business Council (McQuaid, 1982: 30–7) and the Committee for Economic Development (Collins, 1981). With the lifting of wartime controls, business associations learned how to combat the unions politically. In 1947, employer associations lobbied successfully for major revisions of the NLRA. A Republican-controlled Congress allied with conservative Southern Democrats to enact the sprawling Labor Management Relations (Taft-Hartley) Act over President Harry Truman's veto (Millis and Brown, 1950). Although it maintained the general liberal framework of administrative regulation, the Taft-Hartley Act shifted power to employers by recognizing the right of individual workers to abandon collective goals (Rainsberger, 1990: 98). Jurisdictional strikes and secondary boycotts were banned, supervisory personnel were prevented from bargaining collectively, and a mandatory 80-day cooling-off period could be imposed by federal mediators on striking unions. Taft-Hartley allowed state legislatures to adopt "right-to-work" laws banning closed union shops. Eventually, 20 states, mostly in the south and west, enacted legislation that kept unions out of service sectors and peripheral industries and small and medium firms (Fillipelli, 1990: 158). Organized labor's postwar strength was confined to large mass-production industries at the economy's core. Its impact was restricted to bargaining over job-related issues of wages, fringe benefits, and working conditions. In 1959, the Republican-sponsored Labor-Management Reporting and Disclosure (Landrum-Griffin) Act sought to combat union corruption by regulating internal union governance. Despite these constraints, union enrollments continued to swell, reaching the all-time peak of 34.7% of the nonfarm labor force in 1954. Union organizing in the public sector was boosted by President Kennedy's Executive Order 10988, which authorized federal employees to bargain collectively. Many states followed suit for their own employees.

Faced with business efforts to strangle unions through legislative containment, the AFL and CIO finally agreed to merge in 1955 under George Meany's presidency. The militant CIO unions and laissez-faire AFL unions converged on a pragmatic centrism with strengthened ties to the Democratic Party through its Committee on Political Education (COPE), successor to the PAC (Greenstone, 1969: 52–8). COPE conducted registration and voter education drives and provided substantial financial and campaign worker support to numerous Democratic candidates (Rehmus, 1966; Wilson, 1979: 16–35). Union endorsements and resources appear to have affected both the election outcomes and congressional decisions (Freeman and Medoff, 1984: 191–206). But comparable electoral effects of opposing business expenditures also can be identified (Esty and Caves, 1983).

During the early 1950s, the union-Democratic alliance could be read as a successful effort to prevent the New Deal's partial welfare-state programs from being dismantled by a reinvigorated Republican-business coalition. President Eisenhower's acceptance of the New Deal institutions signaled that conflicts over the scope of the federal state would thenceforth be fought at the margins. The business community would always push for less government intervention in the marketplace and fewer restrictions on management's prerogatives to run their factories unimpeded by organized labor. The landslide Democratic congressional victories in 1964 temporarily upset this balance, enabling passage of President Lyndon Johnson's Great Society legislation, which vastly expanded public welfare and government authority over business (Vogel, 1989: 36). An array of new regulatory agencies – Environmental Protection (EPA), Occupational Safety and Health (OSHA), and Consumer Product Safety (CPSC) – drove up the costs of compliance and provoked a militant business counterattack, with far-reaching consequences for the labor policy domain.

Richard Nixon's election as president in 1968 heralded a revitalized conservative political era. Although the Congress remained largely under Democratic control, Republican candidates won five of the six presidential races spanning the next quarter century. This politically divided national government spelled prolonged failure for the labor movement to pass legislation "most important to them as institutions and to their monopoly power" (Freeman and Medoff, 1984: 192). Management grew increasingly sophisticated at mobilizing opposition to union-power bills that would be most costly to business. Employer groups could win simply by not losing on the key labor-law reforms proposed by the labor-Democrat alliance. Meanwhile, they could pursue further restrictions on union power through the courts and the NLRB. As a result of tightened limits on workplace organizing, collective bargaining, strikes, pensions, and unemployment insurance, U.S. labor unions faced an increasingly hostile regulatory environment (Rainsberger, 1990: 100).

Organized labor's political woes were exacerbated by intense international competition that eroded the U.S.'s world economic position, as noted at the beginning of this chapter. Declining market shares in key manufacturing industries (steel, autos, appliances, apparel, consumer electronics), a worsening international trade balance, and a shift toward a white-collar service economy eliminated hundreds of thousands of unionized jobs (Bluestone and Harrison, 1982). Apart from the public sector, the overall trend in union membership was steadily downward, falling from 29.6% of the nonfarm labor force in 1970 to 19.5% in 1984. Union busting by management consultants and wage-and-benefit concessions by unions to save jobs became tactics for desperate times (Cappelli and McKersie, 1985). The nadir of labor's plight was President Reagan's firing of striking air traffic controllers during his first months in office.

The U.S. labor policy domain was altered by fragmentation of power in Congress and the executive branch, by changes in campaign finance laws, and by a rapid influx of interest groups bringing innovative pressure tactics to Washington. Congressional procedural reforms in the early 1970s reduced the power of committee chairmen and enhanced that of subcommittees (Oleszek, 1978: 65). Numerous points of policy access were created for interest groups to press their claims. New regulatory bodies, such as OSHA and EPA, generated thousands of pages of federal regulations that provoked their business targets to seek political redress. And post-Watergate election law reforms, although limiting contributor donations, also stimulated formation of numerous political action committees. Ironically, although originally pioneered by labor unions, PACs rapidly became business's preferred tool for electing candidates disposed to support their policy agendas (Eismeier and Pollock, 1988; Clawson, Neustadtl, and Scott, 1992).

Most dramatic of all were the thousands of organizations establishing continuing presences in the capital. Many either kept a Washington office or headquarters or retained legal counsel to monitor legislative and administrative decisions of interest to them (Heinz, Laumann, Nelson, and Salisbury, 1993). This population deployed large resource holdings through effective political tactics to influence government policy makers. In their repertoires were electronic mass media, computerized direct mailing, constituency-legislator linkages, political action committees, congressional and regulatory testimony, personal contacts with officials, and coalitions with other interest groups (Berry, 1984; Kingdon, 1984; Schlozman and Tierney, 1986; Knoke, 1990a). The density and intensity of lobbying actions raised the temperature of many public policy battles. Following a quiescent period during which severe regulatory restrictions were enacted, resurgent business reentered the political fray with a vengeance (Levitan and Cooper, 1984; Vogel, 1989: 193–239). Led by the Chamber of Commerce, National Association of Manufacturers (NAM), Business Roundtable, and a host of specialized employer associations, corporations pursued their agendas in an increasingly receptive political environment (Salisbury, 1984).

The business offensive worsened the position of an already weakened labor movement. Management's most spectacular political victories over labor came during the mid-1970s. In its 1976 legislative drive to overturn the Taft-Hartley Act's ban on secondary boycotts, organized labor had the support of President Gerald Ford's labor secretary, John Dunlop. Although Congress passed a common-site picketing bill, an intense lobbying effort by construction contractors and business associations persuaded Ford to reverse his announced support. Under pressure from Ronald Reagan, his rival for the 1976 Republican Party nomination, Ford vetoed the bill and Dunlop resigned (Levitan and Cooper, 1984: 120–2; Ornstein and Elder, 1978: 123–53). This legislative battle was a classic example of interest group lobbying: "The strategies and tactics of the pro- and anti-common-site groups were similar in many respects: the use of computers to generate grass-roots pressure in crucial districts; provision of 'hard facts' to members of Congress; analyses of vote breakdowns and trends; face-to-face contact between members of Congress and group lobbyists; and last-minute lobbying 'blitzes' and 'fly-ins' of group representatives from the member's home district" (Ornstein and Elder, 1978: 152–3). The following year, despite Democratic control of both the White House and Congress, organized labor was unable to secure House passage of a weaker bill that would have exempted much of the construction industry from coverage. And it failed to reform labor laws to expedite the NLRB's administrative and adjudicative functions. Labor mobilized a broad-based coalition of religious, minority, and civil rights groups, whereas business coordinated massive grass roots opposition through the "Big Three": the Chamber of Commerce, NAM, and

Business Roundtable. Skillful coalition building, member mobilization, and favorable media publicity won both legislative fights for business "against considerable odds" (Levitan and Cooper, 1984: 136).

Because labor policy-making in the two Reagan Administrations (1981–9) is the focus of the remainder of this book, we delay its detailed examination until Chapter 6. In retrospect, Reagan's broader policy agenda tried to reduce federal intervention in the market economy, to strengthen the military, and to champion public morality issues (antiabortion, school prayer) favored by conservative-fundamentalist religious groups (Glazer, 1986; Heclo, 1986). Under a "supply-side economics" rubric, deep tax cuts and increased defense spending generated enormous federal deficits that paralyzed any new liberal policy initiatives. Labor and social welfare interest groups fought rearguard actions to salvage programs threatened by the looming budgetary cuts imposed by Gramm-Rudman deficit-reduction targets (Wolman and Teitelbaum, 1984). In this austere political and fiscal climate, business interests held a strategic advantage over their labor union and minority-group opponents: Simply by blocking changes within every institutional arena, they could prevent major changes in the status quo, which thus allowed management to continue dominating their employees' work lives.

Germany

The early years of the Weimar Republic, immediately after World War I, were the decisive era for the institutionalization of German labor policy as a domain in its own right. Weimar laid the foundations of labor law as a separate legal field whose principles function today as a common frame of reference for the actors of this policy domain. The early Weimar compromise among unions, employers, and the state must be seen as an outcome of preceding developments in a political climate favorable to unions and the Social Democratic Party (SPD). Although the political situation changed drastically after the Weimar Republic collapsed, the general thrust of German labor policy remained heavily influenced by this take-off phase. This persistence was true for all democratic German governments and is verified by the fact that all labor ministers were affiliated with the unions.

Industrialization began much later in Germany than it did in England and France, but, from the middle of the 19th century on, it proceeded in Germany more vigorously, especially in the Ruhr valley. Such liberal concepts as freedom of contract and of trade were not implemented at the same time in the many German states, but as national unification proceeded, economic liberalism became the dominant political ideology. The 1869 Business Code, abandoning the older doctrine that all combinations of workers or employers are illegal cartels against freedom of trade, guaranteed freedom of association to industrial workers (Hentschel, 1983). Following the British example, many industrializing European states allowed unions and strikes, even when they did not protect collective bargaining and even if strikes could be costly for workers due to civil law consequences. The freedom of contract between employer and employee was supposed to be a more valuable good than the protection of groups with less-favorable market positions. But liberalism did not hinder the protection of certain groups in the labor force unable to speak for themselves (such as children), or whose protection could be legitimized by middle-class norms of family life (such as protecting working women's hours or maternity leaves).

During the Bismarck government's liberal phase before 1878, craft unions grew steadily and were able to organize large strikes, especially during the economic boom until 1873. Ideologically, the union movement was divided into socialist and liberal wings. The Hirsch-Duncker liberal unions took a more moderate attitude toward strikes, as did the Christian unions that gained importance by the 1890s. After the big strike wave of 1873, the imperial government began a repressive policy against unions (Tessendorf Era) (Schönhoven, 1987: 42). In 1878 Bismarck ended his collaboration with the National Liberals. Besides introducing protective import duties, the Anti-Socialist Law (enacted in 1878 and prolonged until 1890) marked the conservative turning point of government policy. But those 12 years of repressive policy were simultaneously the start of the German welfare state. Repression of the socialist movement and introduction of a mandatory social insurance system were two sides of a policy seeking to pacify the socialist workers and integrate these politically pacified workers into German society. In 1883, the law on a compulsory sickness insurance was enacted. One year later, accident insurance was added, and in 1889, a system of old age and disability pensions was started. These laws were consolidated in the Reich Social Insurance Act of 1911, supplemented by an insurance system for white-collar workers.

The German welfare state regime is sometimes characterized as the prototype of a corporatist system, in contrast to a liberal regime "in which means-tested assistance, modest universal transfers, or modest social insurance plans predominate" (Esping-Andersen, 1990: 26). Liberal systems uphold traditional work-ethic norms, with the consequence that labor market mechanisms remain the most important device for allocating income. The U.S. exemplifies this type of welfare system. The German version of the corporatist welfare state purportedly preserves status differences. Hence, it is much more closely linked than are liberal welfare regimes to welfare recipients' current or former employment statuses, and thus, to labor policy in general.

One important consequence of Bismarck's social legislation was the creation of mandatory corporate actors that participate in labor policy-making. The sickness and pension funds were designed as self-governing corporations with both workers and their employers represented on the supervisory boards according to their share of the financial contribution. For example, the workers originally paid two-thirds of the sickness funds and had a two-thirds majority. This representation made the state and local insurance associations (*Ortskrankenkassen*) a stronghold of the Social Democrats, who were employed as full-time bureaucrats in these newly created institutions. Employers were liable for work accidents and had to pay the full cost of the insurance. This system is administered today by industrial mutual associations wholly controlled by the employers. Old-age pensions for workers are paid by regional insurance corporations, and the Reichs Insurance Institution, founded in 1911, collects contributions and pays pensions for disabled and retired white-collar workers. The more common practice is for regional institutions to form a federal association for the purpose of lobbying at the federal level. In a way, the regulation of safety and physical conditions of work remains a separate subfield within the more general labor policy domain.

Bismarck's Anti-Socialist Law delayed, but failed to suppress, the growth of a politically autonomous socialist working-class movement. After 1890, the socialist unions gained even more momentum, accompanied by growing numbers of Social Democratic voters and party members. Three models of union development are distinguished in the labor movement literature (Slomp, 1990: 33–8): the British, the French, and the German models. The British system, which developed gradually in the 19th century, remained basically a craft union system only loosely coupled to the Trade Union Congress. The French syndicalist movement stressed direct action, such as striking for political goals, but did not build strong organizations. In Germany, where both the Social Democratic Party and the free (i.e., socialist) unions were heavily influenced by Marxism, "the ideal was industrial unionism rather than craft unionism" (Slomp, 1990: 33). Party and union were twin components of a strong working-class movement led by the Social Democratic Party. As unions gained more strength, due to both their mass basis and their effective internal coordination by a general commission, they reached a compromise with the party at the 1906 Mannheim Congress that enabled them gradually to implement collective bargaining with employers. More orthodox Marxists in the SPD were at first opposed to this policy of gradualism instead of a more direct route toward the collapse of capitalism. The unions made progress with their policy only in the less-important industries. In 1913, the employers' associations finally founded a peak organization for their own sociopolitical aims, the Confederation of German Employers Associations (*Vereinigung der Deutschen Arbeitgeberverbände*). But full implementation of a collective bargaining system had to wait until after World War I, when the last stronghold of capitalist dominance, heavy industry in the Ruhr region, finally accepted the new system.

During the war, the government and especially the army leadership recognized their dependence on the unions in their endeavor to maximize the war economy's output. The unions decided to cooperate under the terms of the Auxiliary War Service Law of 1916 (Schönhoven, 1987: 104–9). The unions' acceptance as equal partners in this corporatist arrangement could not be withdrawn later. They became even more valuable bargaining partners during the last months of the war and the revolutionary events of November 1918. The big industrialists realized that their only choice lay between a pro-labor institutionalization of industrial relations within a parliamentary system and a radical works council system within a soviet-type government that would have some backing from union members. The socialist union leader Carl Legien, and Hugo Stinnes, the most influential industrialist of the Ruhr region, reached their famous Stinnes-Legien Agreement of November 15, 1918, which promulgated a new era of labor legislation: negotiated collective wage agreements, which were binding for individual labor contracts; parity councils for the regulation of conflicts; works councils at the plant level; and, last but not least, an eight-hour working day in all industries (Feldmann, 1981: 170). The state merely ratified this agreement, partially in the Weimar Constitution and partially by new laws, such as the Works Council Act of 1920, or, in urgent cases, by decree.

The actual practice of collective bargaining was considered less successful than its original institutionalization (Hentschel, 1983: 71–8). After the immediate postwar period, many employers were no longer convinced that German industry could be run effectively under the burden of the 1918 concessions. They began to undermine cooperation with the unions, with the consequence that compulsory arbitration by the state became increasingly common, especially from 1929 onward due to the economic recession. Some employers even began to support the growing Nazi movement. The Weimar period has been called a period of transition "providing institutional precedents for a mode of labor-management cooperation which survived the Nazi era . . . and reappeared after 1945" (Bunn, 1984: 1971). During Weimar, the socialist unions developed a concept of economic democracy that had a decisive impact after World War II on union support for the codetermination idea.

The institutional innovations of Weimar were not restricted to the collective bargaining system. Labor courts were created in 1926 as a special branch of the court system, thereby giving prominence to a self-contained labor law. Representatives of labor and of employers served as honorary lay judges in addition to a professional judge. This system was taken over by the Federal Republic with only slight changes. In 1927, an unemployment compensation program was introduced as the final pillar of the German social security system. In the midst of this labor policy activity, the national government also created the most powerful state agency to deal with labor policy, a separate ministry of labor. During World War I the imperial government had created a bureau responsible for both economic and labor policies. But the revolutionary government decided very early in 1919 in favor of a special ministry with jurisdiction over both labor law and the social insurance system (Reindt and Saffert, 1968). This combination is indicated even in its present name – the Federal Ministry for Labor and Social Policy (*Bundesministerium für Arbeit und Sozialordnung*).

Nazi government policy from 1933–45 can best be described as state corporatist. The Nazis created compulsory organizations for both labor and business, dissolved the independent unions in 1933, outlawed strikes, and abolished collective bargaining (Weitbrecht and Berger, 1985: 496–8). Employers were more successful than workers in keeping at least some independence. Former employees of employers' organizations became responsible for wage regulations by the Labor Ministry. Apart from their general policy of forced unity and their imposition of the leadership principle (*Führerprinzip*) in place of domestic self-governance, the Nazis did not pursue a special labor policy. Although Nazi organizations propagated populistic ideas of the folk community, labor policy-making remained the prerogative of the Labor Ministry. The German social insurance system was not changed (Hentschel, 1983: 136–44). A few bills drafted by the civil servants of this ministry were re-enacted with minor changes after World War II. Despite these institutional continuities, the factual power relations in industry were heavily biased in favor of employers. The Nazis brutally canceled the class compromise of the Weimar period.

Immediately after World War II, the West German unions again enjoyed a stronger position than the employers, as they had after World War I. The Allies allowed them to rebuild their organizations before the employers were permitted to do so. For the first time, German labor surmounted its ideological splits and formed a united labor movement in which both Socialists and Christian Democrats worked together. One further obstacle faced by the industrialists must be mentioned: The larger enterprises were decartelized by the Allied military governments and were supervised in the interim by agents of the occupational powers, not by their owners or original managers (Hirsch-Weber, 1959). This situation changed in the late 1940s with the founding of the Federal Republic of Germany. As a result of the first federal election, a bourgeois coalition led by Chancellor Konrad Adenauer favored a market economy with a heavy emphasis on welfare politics. West Germany became increasingly skeptical of socialist solutions, even though some Christian Democrats had such leanings immediately after the war. Many leftist German writers label the 1950s a period of restoration. They are correct with respect to the weakening of the unions' political influence under the conservative federal government.

For labor policy, 1951 divides the immediate postwar period in which many political groups nurtured socialist ideas, from the long period of economically successful governments led by the Christian Democrat and Christian Social unions (CDU/CSU). The Codetermination Act of the Mining, Iron, and Steel Industries was passed in 1951 with votes from both the CDU/CSU and the opposition Social Democratic Party, but was opposed by the liberal Free Democratic Party (FDP), which participated in Adenauer's coalition government (Hirsch-Weber, 1959). This bill was the last major political success of the unions for a long time to come. It provided for equal numbers of seats for labor and capital on the supervisory boards of mining, iron, and steel enterprises. It created the position of "labor director," usually a former union leader, who serves on the management board of the German dual-board system. This director could not be elected against the labor votes of the supervisory board (Helm, 1986).

In 1952, the Works Constitution Law (*Betriebsverfassungsgesetz*) was passed. Similar to its Weimar forerunner, it guaranteed codetermination in the plant-level works councils. It also provided codetermination at the enterprise level, but required only one-third instead of half of the supervisory board to be labor representatives. However, the unions had fought for the same solution as enacted in the mining, iron, and steel industries. Thus they lost an important battle, whereas the employers welcomed the new law. Another important labor bill, the Wage Agreement Law (*Tarifvertragsgesetz*), had already been passed by the Economic Council of the American and British occupation zones before the founding of the Federal Republic. It regulated the collective bargaining process along lines equivalent to the Weimar Republic law, but with different consequences in the Federal Republic. Compulsory arbitration was almost never practiced in West Germany, because both employers and unions prized their autonomy in collective bargaining as an end in itself.

A new era of labor policy began in 1966 when the Social Democrats entered the federal government, first as a junior partner of the CDU/CSU during the Grand Coalition and, from 1969–82, as the senior partner with the FDP. Some major laws were revised, with solutions generally more favorable to the unions (e.g., the Works Constitution Law of 1972), and some bills were passed that partially responded to union demands. The most controversial law was the Codetermination Law of 1976. The solution finally enacted was opposed by both employers and unions. The employers felt restricted in their ownership rights. The unions opposed it because full parity in the supervisory board was not achieved. Although half the board members were supposed to be labor representatives, the law provided that one member on the labor side must be elected, not by all employees, but only by management. The unions' failure, despite the SPD's role as the leading government party, can be explained by the FDP's influence. This small liberal party, which has always advocated a market economy, favored the business community's political demands and opposed corporatist arrangements that would create a more privileged position for organized labor.

Postwar social legislation has provoked less controversy than bills in labor policy proper. This proposition held at least during the early period, when unemployment rates were low and the economy boomed during the first years of the SPD-FDP government. After the CDU/CSU-FDP coalition was formed in 1982, some welfare payments were cut back (see Chapter 6 for details). But despite a public debate over retrenchment of social services and the danger of new poverty, until national reunification in 1990 the German welfare system adjusted to new exigencies very much along the same lines as it had in the socialist-liberal coalition.

Within the German labor policy domain, the unions have traditionally been the proactive side, a position weakened in times of high unemployment. In the early 1980s the public debate was influenced more than usual by Liberal arguments in favor of deregulation. But labor regained its old strength. In Germany, labor interests are represented by a powerful united union movement based on the industrial unions of the German Trade Union Federation (*Deutscher Gewerkschaftsbund*: DGB). The major adversary of the unions is also a powerful business peak organization. Outside the public sector, 80 percent of German enterprises are organized by the Confederation of German Employers Associations (*Bundesvereinigung der Deutschen Arbeitgeberverbände*: BDA). This organization specializes in labor and social policy and coordinates the collective bargaining strategy of the diverse sectoral employers' organizations. Business interests in other policy domains, especially in economic policy, are represented by other organizations, for example the Federation of German Industry (*Bundesverband der Deutschen Industrie*: BDI). The third important corporate actor in labor policy is the Federal Ministry for Labor and Social Policy, supported by several federal agencies, most notably the Federal Labor Institute (*Bundesanstalt für Arbeit*). The strength with which labor law is institutionalized in Germany can be seen from events during the German reunification begun in 1990. There was almost no public debate about which parts of the labor law and the social security system should be carried over from East Germany. All consequential actors in the labor policy domain were convinced that the only possible solution was a complete replacement of the East German by the West German system. As the history of German labor policy shows, this decision could be justified because labor law was not just a Federal Republic (West German) invention but went back in its essential parts to the Weimar Republic, the first democratic system in Germany.

Japan

Although Japanese labor-management relations and national labor politics and policies are often considered unique, in fact they have gone through developmental stages similar to the stages of other advanced industrial nations with some time lag (Mori, 1981; Tominaga, 1981; Campbell, 1992: 21). The basic structure of labor policy as well as the Japanese constitution was created under guidance from Occupation Headquarters by U.S. leadership. The key policy events that restructured the Japanese labor policy domain in the postwar era were legislative acts passed by the Japanese Diet, judicial decisions of the Supreme Court, and quasi-judicial decisions by the National Labor Committee. In turn, these events reflected the changing positions of major political actors and included a series of big domestic strikes as well as international events such as the 1973 and 1979 OPEC "oil shocks." Over the postwar decades, Japanese labor policy evolved as part of an emerging welfare "capitalism" (stress on capitalism by Shinkawa, 1993) that took shape in the 1960s and 1970s as part of a "creative conservatism" (Pempel, 1982) reflecting "crisis compensation" (Calder, 1988) under the one-party dominant system.

Despite the common image that Japan has an inadequate welfare system, Japan's relatively low percentage of welfare expenditures can be explained by the simple fact of its late start in creating a welfare system. Social pensions especially had to await the system's maturity, and the real increase in aging population did not start until the 1950s. However, the political situation of labor policy-making in prewar Japan was considerably different from that in the postwar era, as it was in other countries. This break can be understood by corresponding changes in the responsible state agencies that were in charge of labor policies. Originally, the main agencies in Japan were the Ministry of Agriculture and Commerce (the Industrial Bureau) and the Home Ministry (the Police and Safety Bureau). In the next stage, starting from 1922, the Social Bureau of the Home Ministry seemed to take over the actual role of formulating labor policy. In the third stage, from 1938, the

Ministry of Health and Welfare emerged as the solid driving force for mobilizing and controlling labor for war purposes. By 1947 the Ministry of Labor was established as a descendant of the previous ministry, and this ministry continues to formulate conventional labor policy today (Takemae, 1982: 397–8).

Japan was a late developer relative to Western industrializing countries, lagging behind by almost a century but catching up very quickly by the 1930s as one of the world's major industrialized countries, at a level similar to France and Italy. This delay conferred several characterizations on Japan, such as being a "late modernizer"; experiencing a "late starter effect" for importing advanced technologies and learning foreign industrial relations; and maintaining a "double structure" of economic, social, and cultural life that reflects both modern and traditional aspects. In 1896, the vice minister of Agriculture and Commerce noted, regarding the labor movement, that "the advantage of being one of those who follows is that it gives one the opportunity to take note of the history of those who have gone before, and to avoid taking the same path" (Pempel and Tsunekawa, 1979: 254). This remark reveals the imperial government's generally paternalistic attitude toward the labor movement, initially regulative and oppressive, later partially cooptative. It also expresses the business elites' aversion to autonomous organized labor.

Following the Sino-Japan War of 1894, the first buds of unionization appeared in Japan, but the Public Peace Police Law (1900) nipped them almost immediately. Until the 1922 establishment of the Social Bureau of the Home Ministry, labor policy in Japan was subsumed under the Ministry of Agriculture and Commerce, through the Mining Industry Law (1905) and the Factory Law (1911) and under the domestic security mandate of the Police and Safety Bureau. Under strong state industrial policies and martial-like direction from the administration, Japanese capitalism developed smoothly. Wars in 1904 and 1914 accelerated industrialization, and the labor movement gradually developed along with it. By the start of the 20th century, several labor unions re-emerged. Several strike waves in the 1920s and 1930s brought unionization to its prewar peak, but only at the level of less than 8 percent of the labor force (Ministry of Labor, 1978; all figures on Japanese unions come from this source). The first national federation of labor, formed in 1912, took the name Japanese Federation of Labor (*Nihon Rodo Sodomei*) in 1921. However, it suffered several secessions and weakened after 1925.

This initial wave of unionization was led by moderate unionists, such as Sen Katayama and Fusataro Takano, a former activist in the American AFL and an advocate of Samuel Gompers's policies. Adversarial and suppressive reactions from business and government pushed the labor movement into a radical antiestablishment stance. Simultaneously, unions suffered internal ideological splits and secessions influenced by anarcho-syndicalism and Leninist bolshevism. During the pre–World War II era, union legal status was in limbo, neither recognized nor denied. There was no legal ban against forming labor unions. Before World War II, unions were primarily organized along occupational and industrial lines (Komatsu, 1989: 27). Excluded by business and government, they conducted their activities outside the enterprise. Although enterprise unionism, which became very common in postwar Japan, was not supported by labor leaders, some of its basic elements first appeared in this era. Supported by the Home Ministry and reformist capitalists, enterprise unions – later transformed into company unions – were established in big industries after 1921 (Komatsu, 1989: 30).

In the 1920s Japan entered a stage of limited party democracy under the constitutional emperor system similar to monarchies in the West. A kind of accommodating-inclusive labor policy was promoted by progressive bureaucrats in the Social Bureau of the Home Ministry (for a compact description and analysis of state-labor policy and relations, see Garon, 1987). Although the bureaucrats wanted to give unions some formal recognition and status primarily in order to correspond to Japan's International Labor Organization (ILO) affiliation, the imperial government failed five times in the 1920s to pass the Labor Union Law (Ministry of Labor, 1961, vol. 1). However, social health insurance began in this period, with the Health Insurance Law targeting factory workers in 1922. The government seemed to recognize the status of labor unions in the process of electing Japan's labor representatives to the ILO in 1923. And, in order to end accusations of labor offenses, it abolished the more repressive aspects of the Public Peace Police Law in 1925 (Ministry of Labor, 1961, vol. 1). Despite passage of the Industrial Relations Mediation Law in 1926, the law's procedures were actually used only six times. Instead, the Special Higher Police gained substantial mediation power in labor disputes (Inagami, 1989: 100). A few labor protection laws, such as the Minimum Age for Factory Workers Law and revisions of the Factory Law, were enacted in the 1910s and 1920s, but their impact was limited and reflected militarist intentions. The imperial government clearly treated labor as a national security problem during this era (Inagami, 1989: 97; Takemae, 1982: 395).

Japanese capitalists demonstrated strong class solidarity against the labor movement, especially in opposing union bills in the late 1920s (Hazama, 1981: 120). Despite the limited scale of the labor movement, the business community, led by the Japan Manufacturers' Club, took all possible measures to suppress it. In 1931, business interests, encouraged by the failure to pass legislation for a labor union law, established the National Federation of Industrial Associations (*Zenkoku Sangyo Dantai Rengokai*), a national peak association to deal with labor problems, and many business associations were created to control each business sector.

The establishment of the Health and Welfare Ministry (HWM) in 1938 and its takeover of all labor policies from the Home Ministry should be understood primarily in the context of national mobilization and human resource control for the war. The HWM prepared the first draft of the National Mobilization Law (1938), which provided the legal basis for a variety of wartime labor control orders, such as the Wage Control Order in 1939. The president of the National Patriotic Industrial Association was the minister of the HWM. In addition, a number of social security policies have their prototypes in this period, prior to the occupational reforms. The HWM created the National Health Insurance (1939) and Labor Pension Insurance (1941) in attempting to create a nationwide comprehensive social insurance system. Although all suffered from the devastation of the war that followed, the endeavor itself was very advanced in the world (Ito and Momose, 1990: 212).

Meanwhile, the Home Ministry and some business activists tried to nurture more cooperative industrial relations. The home minister promoted a system of factory committees (labor-management cooperative consultive bodies) and, with the help of businessmen in 1919, formed the Cooperative Association, which soon functioned as a mediator for business interests (Hazama, 1981: 174; Garon, 1987: 74). These cooperatives became the nucleus of the Patriotic Industrial Association Movement during wartime (Hazama, 1981: 211; Inagami, 1989: 103), which soon accounted for more than three-quarters of the labor force (Sakurabayashi, 1985: 1). In a sense, this movement laid the foundation for the thorough organization of labor across all enterprises after World War II (Takemae, 1982: 897).

In sum, the prewar heritage of the labor and social policy domain in Japan left a skeleton of state corporatist structures and some seeds for postwar development. Whether to consider this prewar heritage as substantial and critical in the labor domain is one of the most controversial agendas in Japanese social science (Wolferen, 1989). Garon (1987: 232) concluded, "Any discussion of the Japanese government's policies toward the labor movement after World War II must consider the complex legacy of these earlier programs and relationships," such as the "persistence of the social bureaucrats" and the "corporatist" relations among state, business, and labor. The influence of history on the contemporary labor policy domain in Japan is not to be found in the tangible structures, however, but in more subtle ways.

After Japan's defeat in 1945, accompanied by terrible damage to industrial production, the General Headquarters of the Allied Occupation (GHQ) under General Douglas MacArthur spearheaded a revolutionary restructuring and redefinition of the Japanese national labor policy domain. The GHQ considered labor reform to be a critical prerequisite for fulfilling its goals of demilitarization and democratization (Richardson and Flanagan, 1984: 30). It enacted the Labor Union Law and electoral laws, abolished prewar security laws, and purged war-related persons before allowing deliberation on the new constitution in 1946. The Labor Union Law defined labor unions and labor agreements and established labor committees to guarantee the equal status of labor with employers. The Labor Relations Adjustment Law of 1946 created a system of mediation and arbitration by labor committees for the purpose of settling labor disputes. Under the Katayama "Socialist"-led coalition cabinet (a type of cabinet that did not appear again until the Murayama cabinet of 1994), the Ministry of Labor was established in 1947, and three rights of labor – to organize, to bargain, and to act collectively – were first guaranteed by the government. The term "labor" was very new to the government. In order to enact labor laws, some of the Communist Party leaders were mobilized in the advisory councils (Takemae, 1982: 398). Finally, the Labor Standards Law of 1947 prescribed the minimum standards in labor contracts for wages, working hours and holidays, safety and sanitary conditions, and so forth. The revolutionary impact of these reforms reactivated the labor movement. From basically zero in 1945, union membership exploded to 55.8 percent of the Japanese labor force by 1949, a dramatic contrast to the prewar rate.

The new unions differed greatly from the prewar ones. They were enterprise unions, organized within workplaces and including both white- and blue-collar employees in the same unions. These two principles received support from new labor leaders as well as from business. Radical labor activists affiliated with communist-led unions used enterprise unions to organize and mobilize members, whereas business leaders believed the enterprise unions would moderate movement militancy. The Congress of Industrial Unions of Japan (CIU), a communist-controlled peak labor association created in 1946, led the labor movement during the upheaval of democratization and labor offensives. The CIU promoted the general strike as a tactic for founding a communist government. In the workplace, "union control of production" was pushed in several major industries. During the late 1940s, labor even dominated the joint labor-management works councils.

Business interests established the Japan Federation of Employers' Associations (*Nikkeiren,* or FEA) in 1948 to protect management from labor assaults. The FEA struggled with labor to consolidate management rights. In 1950, the Federation of Economic Organizations (*Keidanren,* or FEO) reorganized as a big business peak association, divesting itself of the Chamber of Commerce and Industry and the Japan Smaller Enterprise League.

Facing both domestic political unrest and the emerging Cold War, the GHQ shifted its labor policy from pro-labor to conservative readjustment, mainly by limiting the rights of civil servants and employees of public enterprises, which comprised 40 percent of organized labor at that time. General MacArthur ordered a halt to the general strike scheduled for February 1, 1947, forced revisions of the National Public Servant Law and Public Corporation and National Enterprise Labor Relations Law in 1948 that deprived public servants of the right to strike, and introduced American principles of industrial relations into the Labor Union Law revision in 1948. In 1950, the GHQ carried out a Red Purge inside government and private companies in which it fired workers suspected of affiliation with the Communist Party. The GHQ supported the establishment in 1950 of the General Council of Trade Unions of Japan (*Sohyo,* or GCTU) to counter the influence of communists in the CIU. The GCTU promptly attracted a majority of labor union members, taking over the initiative from the CIU.

Contrary to GHQ expectations, however, the GCTU soon transformed itself from a timid federation into an unruly one, insisting on the four peace principles against war and Japanese rearmament. The GCTU's drastic shift of policy illustrates the Japanese adage "the transformation from a hen into a duck." Formed from the major public-sector unions, consisting of postal, educational, municipal, and railway workers, it exerted its power in electoral campaigns for the Japan Socialist Party, especially its left wing.

During the 1950s, the conservative Liberal Democratic government pursued a "reverse course" policy, trying to nullify the reforms of the Occupation. It attempted unsuccessfully to revise the constitution but did successfully revise other fundamental postwar laws. Labor unions within the GCTU allied themselves with the Japan Socialist Party (GCTU-JSP bloc) to block this reverse course effort. The period was marked by conflict in industrial and labor relations, including many big strikes and disputes in such industries as electricity, steel, metals, mining, national railways, and education. The era ended when the conservative government, management, and labor unions realized the high social costs of these conflicts.

Beginning in 1960, the Liberal Democratic Party (LDP) government moved gradually to the pluralistic position with a moderate welfare policy that Pempel (1982) termed "creative conservatism." Regarding labor policy, the government arrived at a set of basic characteristics: guaranteeing a certain degree of "protection" to labor unions, promoting "liberal collective bargaining" and "the principle of autonomy by management and labor unions," and regulating workers in the public sector to some degree (Inagami, 1989; Gordon, 1988: 386–411). The era is called the Ishida labor policy period, after the famous labor minister Hirohide Ishida who developed the approach starting in the late 1950s through the 1960s. Ishida established the custom of implementing the completely arbitrary awards made by the National Enterprise Labor Committee, ratified the ILO 87 Treaty on the protection of the right to labor organization, and drafted the Labor Charter of the LDP (*Rosei Kenkyukai* 1978). The government practiced a cautious labor policy, passing several minor supplementary labor laws and focusing on the situation of white-collar and women workers, as is shown by enactment of the Law for the Promotion of Workers' Property Accumulation and the Industrial Homework Law in 1971 and the First Year Declaration of the Completed Welfare System in 1973. The judicial branch generally supported moderate government policies and recognized labor rights in line with the constitution in the 1960s and early 1970s.

In this relatively favorable milieu, fostered by governmental appeasement of labor and a high-growth economic policy like the Income Doubling Plan of the Ikeda Cabinet in 1960, collective bargaining and labor management consultative systems became a stable means of settling industrial problems at the enterprise level. The Spring Wage Bargaining Round (*Shunto*), started in 1955 as an amalgamation of increasing economic demands with political radicalism, occurred frequently throughout Japan in the 1960s. Millions of workers increasingly participated in these annual sessions. The symbolic event of the 1964 *Shunto* was a "summit meeting" between Prime Minister Hayato Ikeda and the GCTU leader, Kaoru Ota. Their meeting symbolized the LDP government's formal recognition of *Shunto* tactics (Takagi, 1976: 67–71, 79–81). It also confirmed the role of the Public Enterprise Labor Committee: the demonstration effect of private companies' wage increases for other sectors, including public enterprise. In spite of surface radicalization, the Spring Wage Bargaining Round increasingly became a moderating mechanism for wage determination through the ritualized mobilization of workers. This change is shown by the fact that, although the number of labor disputes doubled in the 1960s compared to the 1950s, the number of lost work days in the 1960s fell to half the 1950s' rate.

Once the unions established regular connections to a variety of industrial networks, such as *keiretsu* (the vertical networks of parental companies and subcontractors and the horizontal networks, or "families," of corporations) and interindustrial and intersectorial networks (between private and public sectors), the Spring Wage Bargaining Round increasingly gave priority to economic over political issues. Along with this change, initiative slowly shifted from the GCTU, led by the big public-enterprise unions, to private-sector industry unions (Shimizu, 1981: 340–5). Private-sector unions established the International Metal Workers' Federation–Japan Council (IMFJC) and the Japan Confederation of Labor (*Domei,* or JCL) in 1964. Thereafter, the GCTU gradually lost its position as the leading peak labor association.

By the mid-1960s, when Japanese industry had to overcome the threat of liberalized international trade and a decrease in protectionism, both labor and management recognized the mutual benefits in keeping industrial peace within companies. This recognition spurred the consolidation of the enterprise union system. By 1964, enterprise unions comprised 94 percent of the total number of unions and 85 percent of the total number of members, a dominance that continues today. As a result of the cooperation between enterprise unions and managers, enterprise-level labor leaders very commonly were promoted to positions as company executives in big industries. More than half of all companies had executives who were former labor leaders by 1976 (Shakai, 1977).

Several other informal means of cooperation developed in big industries: quality control circles, enterprise-level labor-management joint consultation bodies, industry-level joint consultation councils, and the Productivity Promotion Movement. The latter movement proposed industrial-level consultative councils in 1959; thus far 20 councils have been established in major industries, with councils at the enterprise level. By 1986, 70 percent of all unions and 90 percent of big unions were participating in them (Fujita, 1988: 89). In Japan, the distinction between collective bargaining and joint consultation of labor and management is not clear, because the representatives of the employers and those of the union members often belong to the same enterprise union.

During the one-party dominant era, the LDP government refrained from intervening in industrial relations, relying on informal, cooperative, liberal industrial relations independent from the government, especially at the micro-level. Under the era's successful economic growth, the weight of labor policy became lighter and lighter at the national level, as can be seen from the labor ministry's declining proportion in the national budget (Tsujinaka, 1987: 67).

As the LDP began to adjust in the 1960s to the emerging industrialized and urban society, the Japan Socialist Party experienced setbacks in attracting private union members' votes, as well as the votes of nonunion workers, because of its heavy reliance on public-sector worker unions and on radical socialist ideology. The JSP lost urban voters, a fundamental cause of the opposition parties' fragmentation vis-à-vis the expanding domination of the LDP, despite the favorable environment of an increasing worker population in the industrialized society.

A series of international events in the early 1970s deeply "shocked" Japan. The Nixon Shock terminated the fixed-rate currency exchange system in 1971, and the first Oil Shock, in 1973, radically raised oil import prices. These shocks created critical problems for the LDP, including a rapidly appreciating yen, greater inflation, more unemployment, and a need to respond to these industrial and political crises due to shrinking electoral support for the LDP in the mid-1970s (Calder, 1988). These problems made national labor policy significant once again. The government had to cooperate with private labor unions as well as with business. Informal consultation mechanisms were used and a Round Table Meeting of Industry and Labor was established in the 1970s (Tsujinaka, 1986: 256–9; Mori, 1981: 237–310).

Two events were critical turning points in labor policy as well as in the labor movement in Japan (Oomi, 1994): the 1975 Spring Wage Bargaining Round and the Eight-day Strike for the Right to Strike. After an enormous wage increase (33 percent) in the 1974 bargaining round, government and management sought to confine subsequent wage raises within a 15 percent range. The International Metal-Workers Union-Japan Council (IMF-JC) and the Japan Confederation of Labor supported the government's policy in exchange for employment security and a stronger policy-making role for private-sector unions (Tsujinaka, 1986; Shinoda, 1989: 102). Wages were to be keyed to actual economic growth. Although government and business decided not to impose a formal income policy, favorable wage-raise guidelines were obtained by the late 1970s. In this issue, a variety of informal labor-management (and government) consultation networks worked well to achieve consensus through information sharing (Shimada, 1983).

In 1975, affiliates of the Public Employees' Union and the Public Enterprise Union Council embarked on their longest strike to recover the formal strike rights they had lost in 1948. On the surface, radicalism in the mass movement appeared to be still alive, and the increasing number of progressive (socialist and communist-affiliated) municipal governments seemed to demonstrate the opposition's strength. Led by the public unions, however, the GCTU was isolated from the private-sector unions. In fact, the weight of the public sector was in relative decline in the national economy. Therefore, in spite of the public unions' enthusiasm, the ultimate defeat of this strike heralded their weakening (Shimizu, 1981: 516). In the end, the unions gained only harsh criticism from the public and a government fine of over 20 billion yen to compensate for damages.

The number of labor disputes fell drastically, down to close to zero. In 1976, the Labor Union Council for Policy Promotion (LUCPP) was founded by private union leaders who overlapped with those of the IMF-JC. This group eventually became the nucleus for a new peak labor union in 1989: the Japanese Labor Union Confederation (*Rengo,* or JLUC). The initiative started to shift from the GCTU to the LUCPP. On the other hand, the Liberal Democratic Party became informally allied with other political parties (the Democratic Socialist Party [DSP] and the Clean Government Party [CGP]) and with private labor unions. These alliances continued at least until the late 1980s.

After the Oil Shock of 1973, these alliances spurred three developments in the labor policy domain. First, under the impact of a worldwide recession, the LDP government enforced a series of adjustment policies, including a positive employment policy and an industrial policy for economic restructuring. Private-sector union leaders began to participate in some of the most important economic advisory councils (Shinoda, 1989: 94–7). This corporatist inclusion of labor at the industrial and national level was a clear extension of corporatism at the enterprise level (welfare corporatism [Dore, 1973]). In exchange for labor cooperation, companies enriched their employee welfare plans beginning in the late 1970s (Fujita, 1983).

Second, to tackle the budget deficits of the 1980s, the government embarked on administrative reforms for the sake of retrenchment and established several large-scale advisory councils for this purpose. Private union leaders participated in these councils and were allied with business leaders in their position against GCTU and public-union leaders. Throughout this process, the private union leaders cultivated access to networks of the major ministries and the peak economic and social organizations, such as the Federation of Economic Organizations (Shinoda, 1989; Tsujinaka, 1986). As a result of the government's administrative reform efforts, such important public enterprises as the Telephone and Telecommunication Corporation and the National Railway were largely privatized. This transformation destroyed their large public-employee unions and weakened the GCTU support base. Hence, the GCTU was left with no choice but to be absorbed into the JLUC in 1989.

Third, since the mid-1980s, the Japanese labor policy domain seemed to be surrounded by a new environment characterized by increasing emphasis on service and information industries; increasing flexibility in the labor market, especially in emerging high-technology industries; increasing numbers of women and elderly workers; rapid internationalization and multinationalization of Japanese companies; increasing numbers of foreign workers from developing countries; increasing friction with foreign countries over trade issues; and international pressures to equalize labor conditions in Japan with those in other advanced countries (Nakamura, 1988). The Japanese labor policies of the 1980s that deal with these issues are examined in greater detail elsewhere in this book (see Chapter 6).

In conclusion, this section has provided evidence for three structural eras in the history of the Japanese labor policy domain: the prewar state corporatist era with the contemporary legacy of the state social bureaucrats, the postwar Occupation-imposed labor structure as a basic legal line, and informal networklike relations as the substance of policy-making developed from the 1960s through the 1980s.

THE COMPARATIVE METHOD

The preceding brief labor histories of the U.S., Germany, and Japan provide the background for our comparative analysis of the effects of their institutional structures on their national labor policy domains in the 1980s. Comparative research involves decisions about many serious issues, ranging from which cases to select, to the details of questionnaire construction, to the interpretation of findings and their theoretical implications. We address issues of conceptual equivalence across the three survey instruments in Chapter 3. This section discusses alternative methods for making analytic comparisons across nations and our expectations about the three labor policy domains.

Because the three nations are all advanced, capitalist, industrialized democracies (ACID), many potentially broad sources of social variation are controlled. Many theories of the modern state advance undifferentiated global characterizations as if they applied uniformly to every ACID society. For example, some institutional theorists assert that a universal expansion of state jurisdictions fosters strikingly similar social activities and identities among modern national polities, particularly, intense rationalization of ends–means relations and formal organizing in rules of efficiency and effectiveness (Jepperson and Meyer, 1991; Meyer, Boli, and Thomas, 1987; Kamens and Lunde, 1987). Competitive monitoring and diffusion of institutional forms across national boundaries sustains an underlying homogeneity at many levels of analysis: "There is a common, highly legitimated, boundaryless (now worldwide) polity that confers authority on and guides the action of subordinate entities (states, individuals, and other subunits), often resulting in sacralized entities and structures" (Boli, 1987: 75).

The more integrated a nation-state is into the world system, these theorists argue, the greater its conformity to these extranational cultural values. Consequently, institutional theory predicts that the most advanced of the ACID polities – in particular, the three under investigation here – should exhibit marked commonalities in state structures, processes, and policy outcomes. On the other hand, significant differences do exist among ACID nations' political and social institutional structures. These divergences may produce distinctive state responses to similar policy problems. At the broadest comparative level, our research explores how these structural differences shape the three nations' policy decisions. Our empirical data permit us to explore fine-grained distinctions among them that universalizing theories cannot easily explain. The unique German, Japanese, and American historical experiences and institutional components already described led us to anticipate finding differences among their labor domains' political networks and power structures that may ultimately affect policy outputs and economic performance.

COMPARATIVE STRATEGIES

Given equivalent data on labor domains in three nations, our project addresses several types and levels of questions. We treat nations both as units of analysis and as contexts of analysis. We investigate within-nation relationships between structures and outcomes, such as the effect of network positions on organizational reputations. We also view these relations as characteristics of the national political systems that affect those systems' behaviors. On that basis, we compare relationships across the three nations. Tilly called this approach "variation-finding," in the sense of comparing the relationships between the same variables in different national settings (Tilly, 1984: 80–6). This approach stands distinct from treatments in which the nation is either the object of analysis (explaining its unique historical or institutional properties), a unit of observation (representing values on cross-national variables, such as percent literate), or one element within a larger system (for instance, its position in the world trade system) (see Kohn, 1987, 1989). Rather, our main strategy is to treat each nation as a context that holds a set of social, economic, and political institutions relating to policy-making.

Within each nation, we focus on relationships among organizations, the so-called meso-level of analysis, and how these interactions construct political power structures and affect policy outcomes. Through the lens of network analysis, we identify patterns of interorganizational interests, network centrality, and collective decision making in each nation. A basic comparative question concerns the relative importance of information versus political support networks in shaping organizations' political behavior. Other important comparative questions concern the breadth of organizational interests in policy issues, the distributions of organizational reputations and participation in policy events, the locations of organizations occupying the most central network positions, and the dynamics of legislative influence efforts. All these structures and processes potentially affect a nation's responsiveness to problems of labor policy, including which issues gain salience and the specific solutions produced (e.g., the level of minimum wage rates, or the enforcement of female wage equality).

Most power structure analysts, whether comparativists or otherwise, have usually built their models by examining organizational behavior in one or a small number of important, yet illustrative, policy events (such as the passage of social security legislation). Due to the small number of within-nation events studied, this approach has not yielded great confidence that the findings represent generic properties of a nation's entire political structure. Because our project examines more than two dozen policy-making events in each nation, the research design produces greater reliability in this regard. The larger number of events greatly increases the chances that the resultant pattern truly represents the institutional structures of the labor domain, at least for that country during the historical period under investigation.

The organizational state perspective expects strong similarities of meso-patterns and relationships across the three nations. Some other theories also predict similarities, although each expects a different structure of power distribution among actors. Too often, theories of the state or of power relations use global, undifferentiated characterizations as if they applied equally to each society. The methodology of political network analysis permits a much finer distinction between varieties and modalities of state-society interaction than previously possible. In addition, our detailed survey data more precisely measure the variables we consider, such as organizational reputations. Taken together, these techniques permit us to make finer distinctions among structures and outcomes across the three nations that more illustrative methods and global theories cannot easily handle. For instance, we can discern the participation by ministries, business associations, and labor unions in specific policy events. This precision allows a more detailed comparative examination of the policy-making processes than has been performed by previous comparative analysts using other theoretical and methodological approaches.

CASE SELECTION

The numbers of cases examined in cross-national comparative research runs the gamut from few to many. Some critics of macro-societal comparative analysis, like Stanley Lieberson (1991), disparage research relying on a small number of cases because the logic rests on very strong assumptions that normally cannot be met: "a deterministic set of forces, the existence of only one cause, the absence of interaction effects, confidence that all possible causes are measured, the absence of measurement error, and the assumption that the same clean pattern would occur if data were obtained on all relevant cases" (p. 315). If such conditions hold, systematic comparisons seek to identify the sources of variation among cases, by applying the logic of John Stuart Mill's methods of difference and agreement (Mill, 1974). Applying the former method when outcomes are not the same for all cases, researchers search for an explanatory variable that is perfectly correlated with the outcome. In the situation where all case outcomes are identical, the method of agreement seeks to isolate the causal factor that is constant across all observations. Given the heavy data demands imposed by these methods, small-*N* comparative research allegedly cannot reach meaningful conclusions about macro-societal problems.

Other comparative researchers, like Melvin Kohn, advocate using only a few cases as contexts for intensive analyses of middle-range phenomena: ". . . the deliberate choice of a small number of countries for systematic, intensive study offers the maximum leverage for testing general propositions about social process" (Kohn, 1987: 726). Our study takes that approach. As the world's most highly industrialized nations serving as models for others, Germany, Japan, and the U.S. have an intrinsic importance for studying labor politics. Cross-national research is most useful, Kohn continues, when it can resolve a theoretical dispute. For example, one key theoretical dispute concerns the argument that pluralistic political institutions (where "all legitimate interest groups have an appreciable share of influence" [Huber and Form, 1973: 132]) should produce more populist, welfare-oriented social and labor policies than those generated by corporatist political systems.

As contexts for comparative research, the three nations exhibit major variations in historical and current institutional conditions that may affect their policy outputs. Japan, Germany, and the U.S. span a range on important attributes: East to West in terms of culture and social relations (groupist to individualist), divergent political institutions (state-centric versus pluralistic), and distinctive state–civil society relationships (corporatist to atomistic). Japan's Eastern cultural origins differ radically from the cultural origins of the U.S. and Germany. Reputedly, Japan also has a more centralized and state-dominated polity. Both Germany and Japan represent "late developers," whose initial economic growth was orchestrated by the state and was manifested during the World War II era as a state-dominated fascistic corporatism (Dore, 1973: 12). In contrast, the U.S. industrialization history was more purely business-led with a continuous democratic polity (albeit a polity dominated by the privileged classes). The three cases arguably span the full scope of historical and institutional variation within the population of about 25 ACID nations, giving us more confidence in the limits to generality of our conclusions.

MESO-QUESTIONS

Our meso-level of analysis looks at the networks that organizations construct in their pursuit of political influence. At the same time, these networks, to some degree, comprise the on-going institutions that help to determine the policy impact of the organizations embedded in them. The field of political network studies has developed its own set of hypotheses on these issues (Knoke, 1990b). These expectations concern the nature of the exchanges among organizations and how these interactions affect both the relative power of organizations and the macro-structure itself. A key question concerns how networks contribute to policy-making outcomes. To investigate these dynamics, we collected data about organizations' communication and political support networks.

The context of network relations differs across the three nations. Their formal political institutions differ (see Appendix 1), as do their state–civil society relations and internal state structures. Examining the exchanges of the same types of resources across these varied institutional contexts, essentially treating the nation as context to assess whether relational patterns vary among them, is our strategy for detecting whatever regularities may exist (Kohn, 1987: 714; Scheuch, 1967).

Japan is often characterized as a vertically organized, "consensus-building" society (Okimoto and Rohlen, 1988: 173; Nakane, 1970). Indeed, Kumon (1992: 124) asserted that Japanese society "is more like a network organization, or even a societal network, than a modern state." This blending of the state into the larger society is consistent with the organizational state expectation of blurred boundaries between government and civil interests. Because reaching consensual agreements depends on long discussion, a reasonable hypothesis is that the volume of information flowing between organizations would be greater in Japan than in the other two countries. This difference may be so because Japan did not break with its authoritarian past as thoroughly as Germany did. Many members of the wartime bureaucratic elite retained and even augmented their positions under the Allied Occupation. Soon after MacArthur departed, others who had been purged returned to positions of power (Baerwald, 1973: 41). Consequently, Japan's dominant elites might reflect the wartime values of a centralized, patriarchal, paternalistic, homogeneous, and popularly deferential political culture. (On the traditional vertical hierarchy, see Ishida, 1984; on contemporary elite attitudes, see Verba and Kelman, 1987: 185–6; Richardson and Flanagan, 1984: 72). At the same time, the forces set in motion by the Occupation and by Japan's own rapid growth have partly broken down the elite's ability to impose that paternalistic institutional style.

Building on this historical legacy, Japan is still regarded as a "state-centric" polity (Johnson, 1982). Accordingly, government ministries can be expected to occupy the central positions in the communication network. But both business and labor sectors follow a horizontal as well as vertical corporatistic organization of the various sectoral organizations under a few peak organizations, which represent their collective opinions to the state. Those peak organizations are likely to be located at or near the center of the highly integrated (decentralized but well-knitted) polity, under a bureaucratic-elitist state and a dominant single political party that receives their opinions (Broadbent, 1989b). Among these three sectors, the state should exercise the most autonomous control over policy decisions, independent of pressures from business, labor, and other groups, and should transmit its decisions through corporatistic relations. Within that structure, by some accounts, the voice of organized labor should play a much weaker political role in Japan than it does in Germany (Pempel and Tsunekawa, 1979). On the other hand, some scholars contend that the voice of labor seeps into the policy arena (Tsujinaka, 1993). Interest groups are bound into continuous dialogue with the government over policy matters through their participation in a multitude of advisory councils established by government ministries for every policy topic. A group-loyalty-oriented culture and strong affective bonding in social relations further cement the political institutions (Nakane, 1970).

Germany made a more decisive institutional break with wartime authoritarian corporatism and the elites that dominated it. It has a collaborative federalist state (Katzenstein, 1987: 43; Kuster, 1980: 38) that governs a moderately corporatist political economy (Lehmbruch, 1979; Schmitter, 1981: 294; Hancock, 1989: 75–8). By most accounts, the German state gives a greater voice to organized labor than does the Japanese polity. German corporatism implies a great volume of policy information flowing between peak associations. This pattern might place Germany between Japan and the U.S. in the density and centralization of its communication network. Because of the strong German socialist party, labor participates more effectively in corporatist policy-making. Therefore, we expect to find a highly communicative partnership among ministries, business, and labor peak organizations at the core of the German system.

In some ways, Germany retained a more rigid social structure than Japan, but it is more pluralistic in other ways. Like Japan, it retained its "prewar structure of capital and wealth" (Kuster, 1980: 38) and approval of state centralism, upon which democracy was imposed by the Allied Occupation. Corporatist theorists often give an impression of a German managerial state that develops policy in conjunction with highly structured interest group sectors. Both business and labor operate under strong peak organizations, with each sector having considerable voice in the labor policy-making process. The national state grants considerable autonomy to the state governments (*Länder*), which also participate extensively in national policy-making institutions. German culture and social relations, less individualistic than these relations in the U.S., support this corporatist form, which shows strong commitment to the whole community (Isaak, 1980: 34 and passim). But German social relations also exhibit considerable instrumental flexibility. German organizations outside the core government and peak associations have many points of entry into the political process. Such multiple access alone should create a more pluralistic power structure than in Japan.

In contrast to the other two cases, the U.S. is usually characterized as a highly pluralistic and atomized polity, with relatively little overt government coordination or corporatist inclusion of policy actors (Salisbury, 1979; Wilson, 1983). The federal government generally takes a noninterventionist approach, resulting in a flexible, spontaneous pattern of influence relations among the private-sector actors (Laumann, Knoke, and Kim, 1985). Hence, information exchanges should be relatively diffuse and only poorly predict organizations' influence reputations or policy control. Rather, because "money talks" in the American polity (Clawson, Neustadl, and Scott, 1992), the control and exchange of political support should have a greater impact on American organizations' reputations and policy activities than in the other two societies. Such transactions should occur mainly between organizations in the civil society, with the state agencies playing a more peripheral role. The spontaneous quality of the American polity is reinforced by a highly individualistic culture and instrumental, issue-specific forms of social relations (Bellah et al., 1985; Chapter 6). This pervasive individualism makes for a highly participatory polity, but one that cannot get much done – except during times of national crisis. In this fragmented situation, U.S. organizations should reveal relatively little consensus compared to organizations in Japan and Germany. Thus, American exchange networks should be relatively more diffuse, and their relevance for policy outcomes should be the weakest among the three societies.

MACRO-QUESTIONS

At the macro-level, we seek to learn which theoretical power structure is most consistent with our network observations on each nation. Proponents of some theoretical models might argue that our interorganizational networks are cast at levels of social organization so distant from their global models that we cannot properly test their explanatory value. Although we understand this objection, our research design affords an unparalleled opportunity for comparatively assessing these heatedly debated explanations (debates that too often "talk past" one another). In this respect, the organizational state thesis developed in the U.S. leads to an expectation that all ACID nations will exhibit substantial structural similarities: a diffuse state, high political pluralism, and organizational autonomy. But, in contrast, developmental theories emphasize unique historical and institutional configurations, using these differences to explain divergent processes and outcomes (Eisenstadt, 1973: 28; Cardoso and Faletto, 1979: 27). Because we employed an equivalent data collection method in each labor policy domain (see Chapter 3), we can examine fundamental questions about the macro-structural level.

To understand national labor policy domains, we must look closely at the state agencies most responsible for labor. As a theoretical object, the national labor ministry (or labor department, in the U.S.) sits at the crux of several important institutional theories, providing a crucial vantage point for research on the state. These issues include the extent of state policy-making autonomy from organized business interests and the amount of internal state cohesion.

To the degree that business interests dominate the state, the labor ministry should be more concerned with controlling labor than with advocating its interests. Correlatively, labor unions should experience little success in influencing public policy, which instead would mostly be constructed to benefit business interests. Alternately, the more autonomy that the state exhibits from business interests, the less the labor ministry and its policies should automatically reflect business demands and desires (Evans, Rueschemeyer, and Skocpol, 1985: 6 and passim). Under conditions of greater state autonomy, the state either will set policy according to its own agenda (a state-centric expectation) or a more balanced representation of the policy demands by labor and other interest groups will occur (a pluralist hypothesis). The theoretical perspective of corporatism, which concerns the degree to which peak associations representing business and labor participate directly in state policy formation (instead of indirectly through representative legislatures), obviously fits within this larger theoretical context (Schmitter and Lehmbruch, 1979).

The question of internal state cohesion also concerns the labor ministry's role in policy-making. Many theorists reify the state, speaking of its "purposes" (Alford and Friedland, 1985: 220). In contrast to this Weberian image of centralized bureaucracy, much recent research emphasizes that state agencies enjoy considerable freedom from central control in policy-making and policy implementation, whether because of inherent autonomy (Allison, 1971: 139), coordination difficulties (Pressman and Wildavsky, 1973: 110–20), or cooptation by outside constituencies (Selznick, 1949: 145). To the extent that the state is a congeries of autonomous agencies under minimal central control, it cannot be treated as a unified actor having a single purpose. The question then arises, to what extent *is* the state unified under a central authority? Alternately, is it merely an arena of disparate agencies each going its own way for one reason or another (Campbell, 1984)? Our project does not assume that the state is necessarily a unitary actor in all policy matters. Rather, we examine data from the relevant ministries, departments, and government agencies and, in some cases, from specific bureaus housed inside them. This disaggregation of the state apparatus allows us to investigate their individual political interests and actions and thus allows us to answer questions about the state's unity and autonomy.

THEORETICAL IMPLICATIONS OF RESULTS

Were we to find substantial cross-similarity in meso-level relationships despite the many national differences noted, our results would support a conclusion that strong homogenizing tendencies have been at work in all three nations. In such instances, Melvin Kohn urged that the explanation need not "be focused on the particular . . . circumstances of each country, but instead should focus on social-structural regularities common to them all" (Kohn, 1987: 719). Finding similar patterns would dictate a search for structurally similar antecedent causal conditions, rather than an interpretation focusing on different origins (Kohn, 1987: 716). Observing regularities across distinct national and institutional contexts provides evidence of universal sociological processes at work (Kohn, 1987: 714). For instance, Kohn and his colleagues found that "for Poland as for the United States, higher social-stratification position is associated with valuing self-direction." Also, "in the main, the findings for Japan are markedly consistent with those for the United States and Poland" (Kohn, 1989: 81–2). Such consistencies arise because universal principles operate in all industrialized societies (Kohn, 1987: 719). To the extent that we find similar political processes and outcomes in the U.S., Germany, and Japan, Kohn's principles would urge us to consider whether similar causes operate. The institutional and functional requirements for highly efficient ACID societies, plus the reforms of the Allied Occupations of Germany and Japan, may have compelled these nations to discard the unique influences of their disparate pasts and, by the late 20th century, to establish very similar political networks and power structures.

In contrast to Kohn's point of view, a conclusion of common causality on that basis could be erroneous. Ragin argued that causality is complex, multiple, and conjunctural (1987: 23–6, 83). In the complex realm of social causation, differing combinations of social forces can generate similar outcomes. Hence, finding cross-national similarities does not allow us to identify a single set of unique causes. This problem exceeds the limits of our data, the situation noted earlier by Lieberson (1991). As is typical of most cross-national studies, we have more candidates for the causal variables than we have cases, and so we cannot systematically examine all the possible combinations of causes for the patterns we empirically observe.

The complex and conjunctural nature of causality becomes all the more apparent when processes and outcomes differ between nations. "But when the relationships . . . differ," Kohn went on, "then we must look to what is idiosyncratic about the particular countries" (Kohn, 1989: 79). Different network patterns and power structures may arise from the divergent historical and institutional dynamics of each nation. This situation requires a somewhat different comparative strategy. It could take either an individualizing or a variation-finding approach. Treating each case as a separate object of analysis (Tilly's "individualizing" strategy) would produce a separate and unique explanation for each national pattern. In the absence of systematic comparative background data, the explanation could go only that far.

Bendix (1978), for example, used this strategy in his historical study of kingship and citizenship. The point of an individualizing comparison is to contrast cases in order to illuminate their peculiar qualities. The strength of this strategy rests on illuminating the intricacies of different complex, conjunctural, and ideographic causal processes. It does not attempt to prove what universal sociological process causes one case to differ from another. The best one can hope for with this approach is a clarification of specific events that produced the observations and a plausible interpretation of those outcomes in light of prior theoretical expectations. On the other hand, the variation-finding approach would try to attribute the case variation to differences in common institutions, such as capital and land-holding patterns (e.g., Paige, 1975).

The comparative analysis strategies just outlined need not be taken as rigid alternatives, but may be combined within a single project. Were we to observe similar political network patterns in all three nations, we would have to evaluate the claim that the similarity arose from identical causal sources. Those sources might be the imprint of similar ACID institutions: capitalism, industrialization, and democracy. Such a conclusion would resemble the contentions of the older "modernization" and "convergence" arguments. But these interpretations would ultimately remain tentative, because we cannot eliminate all the rival explanations. The observed similarities might have arisen from yet other unobserved causes, common to all three cases, which we failed to consider. Even similarities consistent with one theoretical explanation would not allow us to generalize that process to other ACID nations. The conditions generating our observations might occur only in our three cases, but have nothing to do with capitalism, industrialization, or democracy. Or, each case could have its own causal origins. The nature of these origins remains for further empirical exploration.

3

Finding domain actors

Identifying the important organizations, relations, issues, and events in a policy domain requires researchers to make both conceptual and empirical decisions. We sought to map the essential features of the U.S., German, and Japanese national labor policy domains during the 1980s, but without capturing so much detail that our pictures became too cluttered for comprehension. Our task involved painstaking choices among empirical indicators of the conceptual elements described in Chapter 1. This chapter outlines the data collection and measurement procedures that we followed and the results that we obtained.

SPECIFYING DOMAIN BOUNDARIES

Which analytic components fall inside a national policy domain, and which ones fall outside? Every domain is a continually changing bundle of organizations, events, and activities. Because convenient membership lists do not exist, researchers must develop methods for identifying the members that are unique to each domain. In their cogent discussion of the boundary specification problem in network analysis, Laumann, Marsden, and Prensky (1983) offered two "metaphysical perspectives," the realist and the nominalist. The *realist approach* relies on participants to be knowledgeable informants. It assumes that all or most actors share a subjective awareness of who belongs to a social system. Thus, a representative cross-section of the social system's participants can inform a researcher about who are its members and which activities are significant. We find the realist perspective less compelling for large, complex national policy domains. Some participants are aware of only small portions of the entire structure. Other informants may confound the separate domains in which they simultaneously operate.

By contrast, the *nominalist approach* imposes a conceptual framework designed according to the researcher's theoretical agenda. Network boundaries are delineated by a priori criteria, without regard to members' subjective perceptions (although the overlap between the two approaches may itself be an interesting research question). The nominalist perspective allows us to generate data more closely attuned to the organizational state perspective. Of course, as outside observers, we may perceive more rigid structures than actually exist in the welter of daily occurrences. The trade-off between subjective representation of social life and analytic rigor is a continuing struggle for all researchers; we resolve the dilemma for our project by combining aspects of both strategies.

Conceptual differences among the three countries constrained the potential comparisons. The term "labor politics" has somewhat the same meaning for Americans and Japanese, but for Germans *Arbeitspolitik* is quite different. Recent German political science understands labor policy to mean the "technical, economic, social and political problems of labor- and production-processes within firms" and their "direct and indirect regulation" (Jürgens and Naschold, 1982: 328). Indeed, in Jürgens's view, apart from the connection between "labor- and social-policy, . . . an institutionally defined labor policy field does not exist" (1987: 208). Thus, German policy researchers tend to restrict the term "labor politics" to mean "politics in the workplace," which is not what we have in mind. These local struggles over pay, conditions, and status take place below the national level, between the workers and managers within individual enterprises and are consistent with a Marxist notion of the "politics of production" (Burawoy, 1979). Labor politics in this sense should not stand directly "under the domination of policy-oriented investigations" (Jürgens, 1987: 210). Under similar background, Japanese social scientists had deemphasized the labor politics realm, concentrating their energies instead on the politics of the workplace (Shimizu, 1982). Foreign observers have also been interested in politics-and-productivity issues (Johnson, Tyson, and Zysman, 1989) and in micro-level company practices such as welfare corporatism (Dore, 1973). To ensure consistent treatment, we apply the terms "labor politics" and "labor policy" only to collective decisions at the national level and not to power relations at lower levels of analysis.

To delineate the boundaries of the three national labor policy domains, we first imposed a nominalist definition:

> Labor relations occur within market economies where workers exchange their labor power for monetary compensation from employers, in either the so-called public or private sectors. All governmental policies that shape the conditions under which these labor-capital relations occur are encompassed by the labor policy domain. The regulatory policies of the domain are identical to those codified in labor law statues, including collective bargaining rights, union election procedures, and workplace regulations. The domain also includes those aspects of social welfare contributions that are directly tied to workers' wages and employers' contributions, and not only indirectly to general taxes. And it embraces some aspects of macro-economic policies that attempt to regulate the labor market.

Second, we also considered whether the domain organizations took their interests into account in acting with respect to one another. A strictly realist procedure would only have asked the participants whom they viewed as important and what substantive contents they subjectively considered to be relevant to domain policymaking. Such procedures would have rendered cross-national comparisons quite problematic. Our approach insured that the three national policy domains would be analytically equivalent. The empirical task was to determine whether each domain actually structures the mutual orientations among the participating organizations.

For each nation, we classified the various dimensions implied by our formal definition as labor policy domain subfields. As shown in Table 3.1, identical subfields were created for the U.S. and Japan. However, three major differences exist in Germany. For Germany, labor law courts (*Arbeitsgerichtsbarkeit*) are a distinct entity, and two other subfields are each further subdivided. Labor-management participation consists of formal representation of workers at the enterprise level (*Unternehmensmitbestimmung*) and codetermination at the plant level (*Betriebsverfassung*). Similarly, the employment conditions subfield is separated into labor contracts law (*Arbeitsvertragsrecht*) and labor hours standards (*Arbeitszeitschutz*). For stricter comparisons, we dropped the German labor court subdomain and combined the responses to the two subdivided pairs.

As Chapter 2 notes, each nation's labor history spans more than a century, but we could effectively collect original network data on domain activities for only the most recent decade. To make comparisons appropriate and manageable, we confined our investigation to the years 1981–7 in U.S., 1983–8 in Germany (prior to reunification), and 1982–8 in Japan. These dates effectively span the U.S. Reagan, German Kohl, and Japanese Nakasone governments (specifically, the Suzuki Cabinet, July 1982–November 1982; Nakasone Cabinet, November 1982–November 1987; Takeshita Cabinet, November 1987–June 1989. All were Liberal Democratic Party governments), which were notably conservative regimes with regard to labor policy. The core organizations in the U.S., German, and Japanese national labor policy domains include labor unions, trade associations, professional societies, business corporations, governmental bureaucracies, advisory councils, political parties, and legislative committees that are primarily concerned about relations between labor and capital. But the domain also involves various groups, such as civil rights, women's, health, education, and elder organizations having specialized interests in the employment relations of their constituencies. Because many informants who participated in the labor policy-making activities of their organizations still held office during our field research, we were able to reconstruct detailed histories of the three domains with high reliability. The following sections discuss how we identified the actors, relations, interests, and events necessary for our empirical analyses.

POLICY ACTORS

For the U.S., a list of potential national labor policy domain organizations was compiled from four sources:

(1) Organizations testifying before the Senate and House of Representatives labor committees and subcommittees. Abstracts were scanned for all hearings dealing with labor or vocational education before the House Committee on Education and Labor and the Senate Committee on Labor and Human Resources for the 98th, 99th, 100th, and 101st Congresses (*Congressional Information Service* volumes). At these 297 hearings, representatives of approximately one thousand organizations appeared, although most testified only once or twice during the seven years.

Table 3.1. *Subfields of the labor policy domains*

1. Collective Bargaining Regulations

2. Participation of Labor in Management and Control of Enterprises, Employee Stock Ownership Plans (In Germany, formal worker representation at the enterprise level [Unternehmensmitbestimmung] and codetermination at the plant level [Betriebsverfassung])

3. Internal Organization and Governance of Labor Unions and Employer Associations

4. Working Conditions: Safety and Physical Conditions

5. Employment Conditions: Hiring, Promotion, Firing, Layoff, Retirement, Time and Wages (In Germany, labor contracts law [Arbeitsvertragsrecht] and labor hours standards [Arbeitszeitschutz])

6. Social Policies: Pensions, Insurance, Maternity Leave, Job Rights

7. Disadvantaged Populations in the Labor Market: Women, Minorities, Handicapped Youth, Elderly, Veterans, Welfare, Vocational Education and Retraining

8. Discrimination in Employment

9. Labor Market Policies: Job Creation, Immigration, Underground Economy, Plant Closings

10. Labor Law Court (In Germany only [Arbeitsgerichtsbarkeit])

(2) Organizations mentioned in *New York Times* labor articles. Annual abstracts from 1981 through mid-1987 were read, and all references to actions and statements by national organizations and their agents were tabulated. As with congressional testimony, news coverage is highly skewed, with most actors appearing only once, although a handful are mentioned numerous times.
(3) Registration as a congressional lobbyist for labor policies. The 1981–8 volumes of the *Congressional Quarterly* list all organizations registering as lobbyists with the House and Senate.
(4) Supreme Court *amicus curiae* briefs filed. A computer search of the *LEXIS* data base was made for friend-of-the-court briefs filed in 16 major labor cases that were appealed to and decided by the Supreme Court. A total of 81 briefs were filed by 99 organizations, again with few filing in more than one brief.

Selection of the U.S. organizations to be interviewed was based primarily on the number of appearances in these four types of public document during the seven years. Registering as a lobbyist in one or more years was counted as only a single appearance, but the instances of congressional testimonies, *New York Times* abstract mentions, and Supreme Court briefs were each counted as separate appearances. From more than one thousand organizations, 112 were identified with five or more mentions. An additional 23 governmental organizations were added, including five major units within the Department of Labor and the Republican and Democratic "members and staff" of the House and Senate full committees and specific subcommittees. A total of 135 organization names were recorded on the various lists used when interviewing the organizational informants. However, during the field period, interviews with congressional subcommittees were determined to be redundant to the four full committees. Hence, the final target number for interviews in the U.S. labor policy domain was reduced to 117 organizations.

Convenient compendia of legislative and judicial participants were not available for Germany. Instead we selected all organizations that: (1) had formal jurisdiction over labor policy in the German federal government agencies, *Bundestag* (the parliamentary chamber of popularly elected representatives), and *Bundesrat* (the second parliamentary chamber of the then-eleven German states [*Länder*]); or (2) were interest groups invited to participate in hearings by the relevant *Bundestag* committees and federal ministries at the preparation of legislative bills. The latter criterion was crucial for identifying the interest groups: we required them to participate at least twice in hearings of the Committee for Labor and Social Policy between 1983 and 1988. In this manner, a total of 85 interest groups were uncovered. Also identified were the work councils of four major enterprises and the managements of three enterprises that testified at two or more hearings. By inspecting attendance lists for all the committee's sittings, we also ascertained which departments of various federal ministries and which representatives from the German states were frequently present at committee consultations. As a result, we included all 11 state representatives, the departments of the Federal Ministry of Labor, and five other federal ministries: Interior; Justice; Finance; Economy; and Youth, Family, Women and Health.

For the German political parties, we decided on theoretical grounds to treat the four *Bundestag* parties (Christian Democrat Union, Free Democrats, Social Democrats, and Greens) as unitary actors. Thus, for each party we included its Bundestag faction and, in addition, its members in the Committee for Labor and Social Policy as two separate corporate actors. The interviewed informant for the *Bundestag* faction was the faction's governing board member responsible for labor politics, and the informant for the labor committee members was the official speaker for that party in the committee. The regional Christian Social Union Party was represented by its Bavarian headquarters, whereas the headquarters of the other parties were all located in Bonn and were also treated as separate corporate actors. Also added for the SPD and CDU were important party caucuses like the Labor Association for Employee Questions of the SPD and the Social Committee, the Economic Advisors, and the Small Business Association of the CDU/CSU. These procedures produced a total of 126 German labor policy domain organizations. During the field interviews, agents of each organization were asked to suggest other influential actors not on the list. Only the German Farmers Association received sufficient mentions to be added, for a total of 127 target organizations.

For Japan, a master list of about 580 organizations was assembled from mentions in articles appearing in the *Asahi* newspaper, in the *Weekly Labor News* (*Shukan Rodo Nyusu,* published by the Japan Institute of Labor, which was founded by the Ministry of Labor), and in the Labor Year Book of Japan (*Nihon Rodo Nenkan,* compiled by the Ohara Institute of Social Research), and from membership lists of the major business and labor federations and government ministries and their departments. We decided to take business associations rather than companies to represent business interests, because the population of companies is too large and because all major companies are core members of some type of business association. This master list was submitted to a panel of five Japanese experts in labor politics from different backgrounds and political orientations, who then selected the most active and powerful organizations, also adding others they felt were important. In this process, mass media like NHK (Japan Broadcasting) and major newspapers were omitted. Those organizations that were checked by three or more panel members, a total of 128, were included in our final list of organizations in the Japanese labor policy domain. During the course of interviewing, six organizations that proved to be either redundant, no longer in existence, or inactive in labor politics were dropped. Three other organizations, including the powerful Ministry of Finance, were active and therefore interviewed, yielding a total of 125 target organizations.

All interviews took place in Tokyo. Among the organizations are the two peak labor and five peak business federations, plus 34 labor union–sector associations and 33 business-sector associations (of which three were defunct or inoperative in the labor domain). We also included public interest groups and cross-sector (business-labor-party) discussion forums. Government ministries appeared as unitary actors represented by their labor bureaus, except for the Labor and Welfare ministries, where five bureaus and three bureaus were interviewed, respectively. Advisory councils were represented by their chairs. We interviewed the policy affairs experts for six major political parties.

For all three nations, we classified each organization's objective interests according to their primary mandates, based on constituencies or clienteles served by the organization. First, we distinguished between two sectors: organizations possessing governmental authority over policies and those lacking such authority. Within this basic dichotomy we further distinguished among: (1) legislative committees and political parties; (2) federal agencies (executive or bureaucratic); (3) in Germany, the 11 state governments (*Länderregierungen*) that participate directly in national policy-making through the *Bundesrat*; (4) labor unions and work councils (representing employees in firm governance); (5) business associations and corporations (representing employers); (6) professional societies (primarily health and education); (7) "public interest groups" (PIGs); and (8) in Germany, the mandatory social insurance associations, and in Japan, the advisory boards *(Shingikai)* comprised of representatives of business, labor, and citizen groups that make policy recommendations to the national government. These boards seemed to be uniquely significant organizations in Japan. Appendix 2 is a complete list of all the core labor policy domain organizations in each nation, classified according to this typology.

The "public interest group" label has sparked much controversy in the U.S. Berry (1977: 7) identified more than 80 U.S. national associations fitting his definition: "A public interest group is one that seeks a collective good, the achievement of which will not selectively and materially benefit the membership or activists of the organization" (see also Berry [1984: 22] and Schlozman and Tierney [1986: 29], who labeled them "citizens' groups"). Because the ability to appear as a disinterested actor is highly prized in policy rhetoric, many groups claim the label while still pursuing policy agendas that mainly benefit narrow segments of the society. Given the difficulty of determining when an organization is clearly acting on behalf of the general public's interests, we apply the PIG label to *all* nongovernmental organizations that do not represent overt economic interests (i.e., employers, workers, or professionals).

Table 3.2 compares the distributions of types of organizations for the three nations. The Japanese domain contains the larger percentages of both labor unions and business associations, more than half its total. The largest proportions of public interest groups appear in the U.S. and Germany, whereas both Japan and the U.S. have about the same proportions of federal agencies. The German domain has the most professional society, legislative committee, and political party actors. And, of course, the German state representatives (*Länder*) in the *Bundesrat* and the Japanese advisory groups (*Shingikai*) have no counterparts in the other labor domains. These national differences reflect only some of the research design choices among the three projects, such as the decision not to interview the U.S. Congress subcommittees. They also reveal substantively meaningful contrasts in the social organization of each domain, for example, the greater German prominence of official and political organizations, the greater American involvement of interest groups, and the greater Japanese emphasis on cross-sectoral consultative bodies and industry- and firm-specific organization of business and labor.

DOMAIN ISSUES

No sound theoretical basis exists for specifying a priori what policy matters are likely to be salient to domain participants. Identifying and selecting a comprehensive set of important labor policy issues requires careful empirical work. Only a portion of all potential concerns are sufficiently salient to attract serious consideration by the core actors. Issues that are temporarily disposed or that fail to gain sponsorship do not warrant inclusion. But the full range of conspicuous problems must be represented in order to characterize a policy domain's global-issue structure.

In the U.S., the same four sets of public media used to identify actors were further ransacked to find the substantive contents of the diverse debates, proposals, hearings, bills, and court cases. The important issues in German labor policy were obtained by coding the contents of pending laws, the annual index of the newspaper *Das Parlament* from 1983–8, and the publications of interest groups (especially the peak union and employer associations). For the Japanese case, the issues used for the U.S. were slightly modified to fit the Japanese situation; for instance, the types of minorities involved in targeted opportunity policies. These procedures

Table 3.2. *Types of labor policy domain actors*

TYPE OF ORGANIZATION	PERCENT OF ACTORS U.S.	Germany	Japan
Labor Unions and Work Councils	17.1	14.2	27.7
Business Associations and Corporations	25.6	18.9	30.0
Professional Societies	8.6	10.2	0.8
Public Interest Groups & Mandatory Social Insurance Associations	29.9	24.4	11.5
Federal Agencies	15.4	10.2	14.6
Legislative Committees & Political Parties	3.4	13.4	6.9
Länder/Advisory Council	--	8.7	8.5
TOTAL	100.0	100.0	100.0
(N)	(117)	(127)	(130)

produced a total of 53 U.S., 45 German, and 51 Japanese issues that were included in the interview schedule. During the interview, informants were shown the list and asked to indicate how much interest their organization had in each, using a six-point scale. Appendix 3 presents these issues, based on the hierarchical cluster analyses of the organizations' interests discussed in Chapter 4.

POLICY EVENTS

Organizational participation in the labor policy events of the Reagan, Kohl, and Nakasone eras is the central focus in our research. Because events are decision points in the process of selecting a collectively binding decision, potentially innumerable activities could be identified. In practice, we selected only the major decision points at which large numbers of actors were likely to seek influence and about which especially reliable recall data might be obtained from informants. In most chapters, we considered the relative influence of all actors. We also collected some data on all types of important policy decisions, including legislative, administrative, judicial, and regulatory events. But in order to maximize cross-national comparability, we restrict our analysis in Chapters 6 and 7 to events in which the legislatures made the decisions. Other chapters take the full spectrum of interest groups and decision-making authorities into account.

U.S. senators and representatives each year toss thousands of proposed bills into the hopper. Relatively few of these bills emerge for serious consideration by an appropriate committee, and only about three percent eventually become law. All hearings by House and Senate labor committees and subcommittees were scrutinized using the *Congressional Information Service* abstracts. Hearings concerned with agency or program oversight, investigations, nominations, or other general information exchanges were eliminated. We kept only hearings at which one or more legislative bills, or "acts" (identified by an "H.R." or "S." number), were under consideration. Four bills originating in other committees, but which had substantial labor policy implications, were also included. This population of 137 hearings about new acts or about amendments to old acts was then grouped into 79 "scenarios" (Laumann and Knoke, 1987: 17–18), that is, chains of related events (e.g., a bill that had hearings in several Congresses). Most scenarios (52) consisted of only a single hearing, whereas 11 received two hearings and 16 went to three or more hearings. To ensure inclusion of major bills, 20 scenarios were designated for certain inclusion (primarily, but not exclusively, scenarios that had multiple hearings). Another five minor scenarios were selected randomly from the remainder, yielding a total of 25 legislative policy events for the interview schedule.

In German policy-making, the primary federal legislative institution is the *Bundestag* (see Appendix 1). The event population consists of all bills concerning labor policy introduced by the government or by legislators and discharged bills concerning labor policy. We examined the German *Federal Registry* for the 10th and 11th legislative periods, under the categories "Labor and Social," "Interior," "Justice," "Education and Science," and "Youth, Family and Health." International agreements and the main budgetary authorizations were excluded, but not occasional budgetary amendments concerning entitlement programs. Guidelines of the Federal Ministry for Labor and Social Policy served as the orienting point for our classification of legislative bills (Halbach et al., 1987). A total of 112 policy events were identified for the period 1983 to June 1988. In the final selection, we took 32 *Bundestag* bills. All 22 proposals with hearings before the labor-social policy committee were included, along with 10 randomly chosen bills.

For Japan, 31 labor policy events were identified from mentions in *Asahi,* the *Weekly Labor News,* and the Labor Year Book of Japan, to which our expert panel added three more, making a total of 34 candidate events. For selection, an event had to be checked as important by at least one panelist. The events included 22 bills reported out to a vote in the Diet. Two tax bills, which would have fallen outside the labor policy domain as defined for the U.S. and Germany, were included, because new taxes increased the tax burdens on employees and other groups. These bills provoked intense mobilization of many social groups.

During the interviews, informants were shown the list of legislative events and asked about their organizations' involvement with each one. These actions included taking a position for or against the bill, formulating proposal contents, mobilizing their members, contacting public officials, and working with other organizations. Brief descriptions of each legislative event appear in Appendix 4.

DATA COLLECTION

Most organizational informants were interviewed in person from 45 minutes to an hour or more (particularly in the Japanese case). In the overwhelming majority of interviews, the key organizational informant was the head of the office that handled governmental policy affairs, lobbying, or legislative liaison. These persons typically had participated directly in the policy influence activities about which they were questioned, and they responded in a manner indicating great depth of familiarity with those events. In the occasional instance of uncertainty due to an informant's newness on the job or poor memory of distant events, we recorded the information as missing and later attempted to fill in details from public documents. After the interview, those German informants who needed to consult with other organization members (especially in larger organizations) mailed back a questionnaire about the policy events.

An interview schedule, or questionnaire, was jointly constructed by the U.S. and German investigators in the fall of 1987, cross-translating all items into identical English and German meanings. The major sections of the questionnaire covered organizational interests in labor policy subfields, informant perceptions of the most influential organizations in the domain and subfields, communication of subfield policy information with other domain organizations, organizational interests in labor policy domain issues, organizational participation in labor domain events, and various background information about the organization and its relations with other domain actors. The Japanese version was created in early 1989 by translating the U.S. instrument, paying careful attention to accuracy of meanings. Exact wordings for many questionnaire items are presented in later chapters when those variables are analyzed.

The U.S. interviews were conducted from April to June 1988, primarily in Washington, D.C., where most organizations had headquarters or branch offices. Of the 117 targeted organizations, only the E. I. du Pont Corporation and the American Council on Life Insurance refused to grant interviews. Thus, the completion rate was 98.3%, exceeding the high levels achieved by a 1981 study of the U.S. national energy (94.3%) and health (89.4%) policy domains (Laumann and Knoke, 1987: 98). German data collection took place between October 1988 and March 1989. Only one enterprise failed to participate in the study, because the director responsible for labor policy had retired and was unavailable for an interview during the fieldwork period. Therefore, the German completion rate among the 127 organizations was 99.2%. The Japanese field period spanned almost two years, from September 1988 to August 1990. This long time was required because of the difficulties of doing research in a foreign country (Broadbent conducted 75% of the Japanese interviews) and because of the painstaking negotiations required to obtain introductions and consent to interviews. Ironically, more than half the organizations (labor unions excepted) probably would have refused to be interviewed by a Japanese academic but relented or were even quite solicitous of a foreign investigator. Although only one of the 125 target organizations ultimately refused to be interviewed, two others could not be interviewed because they no longer existed or had their labor affairs handled by another organization in the study. Thus, the Japanese response rate was 97.6%.

In conclusion, the data collection phase of our three-nation project was highly successful. Nearly identical data sets provide very detailed information about the interests and actions of almost all major labor policy domain organizations spanning much of the 1980s. This trove of data, precisely tailored to requirements of the organizational state perspective, is analyzed in the following chapters.

4

Organizational policy interests

with Naomi J. Kaufman[1]

As the High Risk Occupational Disease Notification Prevention Act, designed to allow workers exposed to hazardous chemicals to receive medical attention before health problems arose, moved through the U.S. Congress in 1987, business lobbyists attempted to block its passage. Testifying at a Senate Labor Subcommittee hearing, the Chemical Manufacturers Association (CMA) echoed sentiments typical of the business community: A new law was unnecessary because existing statutes were adequate, an avalanche of ruinous lawsuits would ensue, and the high costs of monitoring employees would burden firm resources, especially for small businesses. Yet, within six months, the CMA along with the American Electronics Association and several companies switched sides, joining organized labor, insurance companies, and health associations to support a significantly modified high-risk bill. "When the language was changed so that it literally represented what a lot of our industry is currently doing voluntarily, it made sense to support it," a CMA spokesperson said (Moretz, 1987: 114). Although ultimately defeated by a coalition of Republican politicians and business organizations, the bill made strange bedfellows of some traditionally opposed interest groups, illustrating the inherent malleability of political issues. As powerful social actors come to identify their interests at stake in national political controversies, so are they motivated to struggle collectively on one side or the other of these conflicts.

This chapter examines the patterns of interests in broad subfields and specific labor policy issues of the 1980s that were expressed by the core organizations in the U.S., German, and Japanese national labor policy domains. Organizations' mutual interests in subfields and issues generate distinctive "issue publics" – in graphic terms, jointly occupied positions in a multidimensional space (issue space) representing their general policy preferences. Organizations located in a common issue public give policy information to each other at high rates. The relevance of issue publics for national policy-making lies in the greater susceptibility of their members "to activation whenever policy events strike at the heart of their interests" (Laumann and Knoke, 1987: 125). Organizations sharing similar issue in-

1. An earlier version of this chapter was published as David Knoke, Franz Urban Pappi, Jeffrey Broadbent, Naomi J. Kaufman, and Yutaka Tsujinaka, 1992, "Issue Publics in the U.S., German, and Japanese Labor-Policy Domains," *Research in Politics and Society* 4:255–294.

terest profiles are more likely to pay attention to opportunities and threats that arise in policy-making institutions than are the members of issue publics whose attention is concentrated elsewhere. By their continual monitoring of issues in anticipation of intervening in the policy process, issue public members are more likely to communicate with one another than they are with organizations not sharing their concerns. Both potential allies and prospective antagonists within an issue public are prone to exchange information about their concerns and intentions. Therefore, careful attention to the details of labor domain organizations' interests in policy issues is an essential prerequisite to understanding their subsequent patterns of mobilization on policy events.

OBJECTIVE AND SUBJECTIVE INTERESTS

We agree with Max Weber that "Not ideas, but material and ideal interests, govern men's conduct" (Weber, 1946: 280). Social researchers require a vocabulary to order the relationships among the various elements that motivate social actors to express and to act on their interests. Brian Barry (1965: 184) offered a generic definition of an actor's interest that relates means to ends: "'x is in A's interest' means 'x increases A's opportunities to get what he wants.'" In other words, "x" is an instrumental means to attain the goal to which A's interests point. Social actors also have negative interests in avoiding any "x" that would reduce the probability of achieving goals. An interest is not identical to a "want"; wants are diffuse, whereas interests are more concrete. Interests orient social actors toward specific preferred ends. Wants may generate interests, which then motivate actors to seek the means to their attainment. An actor will perform some type of social action in order to enjoy some benefit (or to avoid some harm). A causal connection exists between wants, interests, and means, even if not in the actor's conscious perceptions. For example, a worker has an interest in a union-representation election, regardless of whether she favors or opposes unionization. The election outcome affects the worker's opportunities to achieve various wants – wages, retirement benefits, working conditions, grievance negotiations, and so forth. She takes a means – voting for or against unionization – to achieve them. Some social scientists also refer to actor "preferences" for a specific alternative among several possible choices, for example, preferring a candidate most likely to implement desired public policies (Riker and Ordeshook, 1973: 1–3; Enelow and Hinich, 1984). Rational actors make decisions that they believe lead to a higher probability of achieving the desired goal. In our terms, an actor's preference is essentially equivalent to an interest in achieving a particular end among the alternatives available. To avoid confusion, we use *preference* in the sense of being in favor of or against a particular policy solution, whereas *interest* designates the intensity of utility differences that these possible policy problem solutions have for an actor. The higher the utility differences of alternative solutions for a certain problem, the higher the actor's interest in this policy problem or in this subfield of the policy domain.

How best to define the interests of actors driven by particular wants continues to stir controversy among political and social theorists (see Balbus, 1971; Connolly, 1972; Wall, 1975). In simplified form, the debates revolve around two controversies: (1) the rationality or irrationality of interests and means; and (2) the materialism or idealism of wants and goals, and hence their degree of "objectivity." Although these features are most germane to individual actors, they require some attention before we turn to a central question for our project: What is the structure of organizational policy interests?

Interests initially encompassed the totality of human aspirations. Only in recent times have they come to connote predominantly material welfare. In his highly influential treatise *On the Wealth of Nations,* Adam Smith (1776) reduced all noneconomic (ideal) interests to the drive for economic advantage (Hirschman, 1977: 109). Consequently, contemporary economists and many other social scientists now conceptualize interests as solely oriented toward material goals, using mainly utilitarian means. The monetary metric conveniently allows actors rationally to calculate their costs and benefits in pursuing their chosen goals. This short-sighted view overlooks how noneconomic interests (altruism and emotion) can constrain and even supersede material interests. To be sure, in Weber's well-known discussion of human habits and motivations, *Zweckrationalität* (goal rationality), the dominant social force of the modern era, emphasizes the instrumentality of action driven by calculable interests (Weber, 1968: 26). However, Weber was careful not to restrict interests exclusively to material self-maximization. He stressed that idealized wants may also channel, structure, and define people's interests. His classic *Protestant Ethic and the Spirit of Capitalism* (1930) reconstructed a historical era during which mortal passions for otherworldly salvation shaped the Calvinist businessmen's interests in accumulating wealth as a sign of election. The same want – salvation in the afterlife – could become linked to radically different means of goal attainment – ascetic Protestantism, Buddhist renunciation – through the mechanism of socially shared ideologies, and hence to different interests and goals – capital accumulation or mental quiescence. More recently, collective norms and emotional affective ties among social actors have been shown to be very important motivators of member contributions, such as the provision of material benefits, to collective action organizations (Fireman and Gamson, 1979; Broadbent, 1986; Knoke, 1990a: 27–45). Material goals can certainly be the object of powerful interests, but they are not the only significant ones. Ideal and social goals, such as promoting civic virtue and fostering personal friendships, can also motivate action.

The second debate disputes the degree of subjectivity or objectivity of wants. As Schlozman and Tierney (1986: 17–23) characterized them, the alternatives are either to accept wants as subjective preferences stated by an actor himself or for a disinterested observer to impute them to the actor. In the latter case, an "informed, dispassionate observer" may either (1) agree with an actor's conscious wants but reject his means and interests as unlikely to accomplish that goal, or (2) reject the actor's stated wants as injurious and impute other ones as the "real interests"

(Reeve and Ware, 1983). Typically, objective interests are inferred by conceiving them as generated from an actor's potential for economic maximization from a position in a social system, regardless of whether the actor is aware of them (March and Olsen, 1989: 147). In both cases, the analyst arrogates the right to judge whether an actor really knows what is best for herself and how best to achieve it. "False consciousness" about true wants, interests, and means is thus possible (Connolly, 1972: 463). Commonly, neutral observers point to severe long-term negative consequences of an interest that offset the short-term benefits that are all that the actor sees. For example, both automobile companies and workers may support restrictive quotas on foreign cars and trucks in hopes of saving profits and jobs, but, in the long run, such restrictions can decimate the domestic auto industry through overpricing, poor quality, customer exits, and inefficient productivity.

The major difficulty with the objective interests approach, as Schlozman and Tierney (1986: 22) recognized, is its failure to take account of differences in "tastes" between actors and observers. If an actor's subjective preferences fail to agree with the interests imputed by an external observer, the discrepancy probably lies with the observer's inability to assess accurately the ideal interests (interest in ideal goals): the complex values, preferences, and sociocultural forces shaping an actor's interests, goals, and probable means of reaching them. If an observer's purpose is to understand how people make practical choices in the real situations they face, then an analysis of how they consciously but subjectively view their conditions and prospects should yield more accurate explanations of their observed behaviors. Weber's advocacy of a sociological approach that comprehends actors' subjective understandings (*Verstehen*) was proposed as an alternative to the imputation of interests from objective positional analyses.

In view of these considerations, we feel that policy domain organizations' wants and interests cannot be accurately imputed from the organizations' objective social positions. Rather, we rely on their subjective expressions to indicate their policy aims. As will be explained, we believe this conceptualization is appropriate for measuring and interpreting national policy domain structures and for explaining the sources of labor policy participation. However, we must first consider how organizational interests differ from those of individuals.

ORGANIZATIONAL INTERESTS

Organizations cannot be viewed simply as individuals writ large. The most important difference is that an individual is a unitary actor in making decisions (although subject to shifting internal forces), whereas organizations are formally structured plural actors whose decisions are made through social processes involving many individual participants with different capacities to affect binding decisions. Though "it is neither reasonable nor possible to specify the psychic state of a corporate actor, it is possible to determine its actions" through analysis of its agents' interests (Coleman, 1990: 527; also 941–6). Organizational interests are the outcome of internal decision processes that take into account the interests of the corporate actor's principals and agents, under the constraint of an organizational charter that expresses the original rationale for pooling those principals' resources. The dominant coalition, a subset of organizational members in authority positions, typically seeks to impose its preferences on the entire collectivity despite the resistance or indifference of other members (Cyert and Marsh, 1963; Pennings and Goodman, 1977: 152).

If internal disunity is not paralyzing, the interests expressed by an organization's dominant coalition may be shaped by various social forces. Among the most important sources of collective interest formation are mandates, ideologies, pragmatism, and obligations that orient an organization to the achievement of preferred ends. A *mandate* is an official statement of purposes and goals, such as a charter or constitution, stipulating in general terms what product or service should be provided to which constituencies. Organizational *ideologies* are shared belief systems that reflect participants' common understandings of the enterprise's ultimate values. In contrast to mandates, which may reflect outmoded formal myths (Meyer and Rowan, 1977), an ideology expresses the living corporate culture, its members' institutional thought structure (Warren, Rose, and Bergunder, 1974). *Pragmatic interests* are mundane aims vital to maintaining the organizational political economy and ranging from balancing the budget to adopting technological innovations. Finally, organizations incur *obligations* to support the preferences of other domain actors on matters of little intrinsic interest, thus paying off favors granted in the past (Prensky, 1985). The relative impact of these four processes in shaping collective organizational interests are difficult to disentangle, and our research design does not allow a rigorous assessment. Regardless of their exact origins, organizations' expressed interests in labor policies serve as basic means by which they orient themselves to achieving significant objectives.

NESTED SETS OF INTERESTS

We conceptualize organizations' interests as nested across three levels of increasing specificity: policy domains, subfields, and policy issues. As defined in Chapter 1, every *policy domain* encompasses a diversity of controversial policy matters and numerous claimant groups and public authorities, each seeking in varying degrees to influence the ultimate decisions about matters of importance to them and their constituencies. Labor policy domains involve national decision making that regulates relations between capital and labor and affects the resource distributions between these factors of production.

A *subfield* is a major category within a national policy domain. Each subfield typically spans may decades of development and experiences differential cycles of activity and neglect. For example, collective bargaining was the critical labor domain problem in the late 19th and early 20th centuries as large-scale industrial economies expanded. Although workplace safety and health emerged as a distinct labor subfield in Germany in the 19th century, it developed in the U.S. only during the late 20th century. Disadvantaged populations and discrimination problems became more salient labor policy subfields only recently, long after the institutionalization of other subfields dealing with problems of the core industrial labor force. An important research question is how new subfields become institutionalized. Unfortunately, we lack the appropriate data to track these longitudinal processes. Instead, we have the contemporary residues of these historical developments, revealing the contemporary differentiation and specialization of labor domains into subfields.

Policy issues, in contrast, often seem to have a time horizon of years rather than of decades. Media attention and public opinion raise the salience of issues and bring them into short-term prominence in the policy domain (Downs, 1972; Kingdon, 1984: 61–4, 68–71). Typically, a policy issue is presented not as something requiring immediate action, but as a persistent "problem" whose solution is not evident, thus inviting a variety of advocates to propose their preferred treatments. For example, within the working conditions subfield, "use of polygraphs and drug testing of employees" emerged in the 1980s as a prominent U.S. issue. Substance abuse in the workplace had reached pandemic proportions, adversely affecting worker productivity, shop safety, and medical insurance costs. Many firms pondered alternative methods to screen job applicants and to identify current workers with problems. The issue raised troubling questions about employee privacy, test accuracy, and company control of the workplace. All the labor policy domain organizations that expressed high interest in the workplace substance abuse issue did not necessarily agree with one another about a single policy solution to this problem. By phrasing the substance abuse issue in such broad terms, the subset of policy domain organizations commonly oriented toward this specific matter could be identified – labor unions, employer associations, civil libertarians, medical professions, and governmental agencies – despite the diversity of the policy outcomes they preferred to enact.

Organizations' interests in policy domains, subfields, and policy issues form a nested set. That is, every policy issue is subsumed under a primary subfield within a national domain. Thus, if an organization has a high level of interest in a particular issue, theoretically it should also express high interest in the corresponding subfield and devote part of its political effort to the domain. The empirical reality may not consistently and precisely correspond to this predicted set inclusion. Social actors' perceptions of the policy environment are formed through social processes to which we, as outside observers, are not directly privy. Hence, our measures inevitably fail to capture the subtle, idiosyncratic filters that organizations use to interpret their realities. For example, although the underground economy appears to us primarily as an issue in the labor market subfield, a Hispanic organization might see it as part of the disadvantaged population subfield, a medical society could classify it under the working conditions subfield, and a vocational education association might consider it to be a matter falling in the education policy domain rather than in the labor domain. Because our standardized questionnaire cannot reveal the nuances of every informant's subjective motives, we must examine the degree of nesting in the domain-subfield-issue interest trinity.

The results that follow suggest that this structure approximates informants' collective perceptions.

RESEARCH EXPECTATIONS

Our network approach depicts the structures and processes within national policy domains as social-spatial relations among organizations expressing interest in policy matters. Here we specifically analyze U.S., German, and Japanese organizations' attention to the labor policy domain, its subfields, and its issues. Consistent with the substantive findings from Laumann and Knoke's earlier study of the U.S. national energy and health policy domains (1987: 109–51), we expected that organizations in these three labor policy domains would collectively perceive the subfield and issue spaces in sharply differentiated and highly specialized ways. Constrained by narrow mandates and limited resources, most organizations cannot afford to devote extensive attention to many concerns at one time. Consequently, the spatial arrangement of labor policy subfields and issues should resemble donuts – rim or circle structures with hollow centers – indicating that most domain affairs attract the interest of specialized audiences. Each segment along the circumference consists of topics closely resembling one another in the kinds of organizations that express passion or indifference about them. Segments widely separated in social space contain substantive matters whose audiences are largely disjoint. The expected absence of any central core to the space reflects the scarcity of overarching issues or subfields capable of attracting the interests of the entire policy domain population.

Turning the interest structures inside out, we also investigate how patterns of expressed policy interests bring organizations together in specialized social formations. Our central analytic concept is the *issue public,* a subset among the core domain actors exhibiting similar profiles of interest in the entire range of domain policy issues. Organizations belonging to a particular issue public express very similar profiles of concern about, and disregard of, *all* issues currently under scrutiny within the domain. That is, the spatial graph represents a pair of organizations as close to the degree that they hold a common orientation toward the entire agenda of policy matters. However, this similarity depends only on the intensity of their concerns about each issue, *not* on the specific policy solutions to problems that they advocate. Two organizations may share a common orientation to every domain issue without agreeing at all about their preferred policy solutions. For example, an employer association and a labor union may both express intense interest in collective bargaining and workplace safety issues but be unconcerned with vocational education and immigration. Hence, both organizations belong to the same issue public, even though they may propose different solutions to the bargaining and safety questions. Indeed, issue public members may as often be antagonists as allies in political conflicts over appropriate policies to resolve the issues. Organizations belonging to different issue publics, and issue publics that sharply diverge from one another, exhibit quite dissimilar interest profiles across the full set of domain issues. Hence, they are located at great distances apart within a domain's issue public space. Again, following the U.S. energy and health domain results, we expect to observe within each national labor policy domain a circular or rim structure whose specialized segments are occupied by the members of similar issue publics but whose centers are empty (Laumann and Knoke, 1987: 142–3).

ORGANIZATIONAL EFFORTS

Our initial inquiry is whether most of the organizations we identified as core labor policy domain actors actually devote a substantial portion of their efforts to monitoring and participating in labor affairs. Some organizations are specialists that concentrate exclusively on labor policy; others are generalists for whom labor policy is just one among several domains competing for attention. For example, employer associations typically also attend to international trade, technology development, and tax policies. We asked informants, "Taking into account [organization name]'s efforts to influence national policy in *all* areas – such as domestic policy, foreign affairs, etc. – what percentage of this total effort is direct toward national labor policy?"[2]

Table 4.1 shows the mean percentages of effort spent on labor matters across the basic organizational types. On average, the U.S. and German labor domain organizations devoted about half their effort to labor affairs, but Japanese organizations spent the majority of their time in other domains. No statistically significant differences in effort occurred between organization types in Germany, whereas mean effort levels varied among the U.S. and Japanese types. The patterns in both nations were similar: Federal agencies and labor unions exerted the most effort, while business associations and professional societies gave the least attention to the labor domain. The eta-squares (correlation ratios), produced by one-way analyses of variance within each nation, reveal that the half-dozen organizational types explain about one-fifth of the variance in U.S. and Japanese organizations' labor policy domain efforts.

SUBFIELD INTERESTS

Based on our understanding of the basic labor policy domain dimensions, our questionnaires presented nine broadly defined labor domain subfields common to all three nations, plus one subfield that is unique to Germany (see Table 3.1 in Chapter 3 for the list). Informants circled one of six numbers to report how much interest their organization had in each subfield, from "almost none" (0) through "moderate" (3) to "very strong" (5). For each nation, Table 4.2 displays the mean

2. We later discovered that the German questionnaire was worded in such a way that some informants may have interpreted this question to apply to their personal, rather than organizational, allocation of time to the labor policy domain. Thus, some of the differences across nations may arise from measurement rather than from substantive effects.

Table 4.1. *Organizational effort in the labor policy domain*

ORGANIZATION TYPE	MEAN PERCENT OF EFFORT U.S.	Germany	Japan
Labor Unions	71.5	62.8	64.6
Business Associations	38.0	41.0	24.6
Professional Societies	37.7	41.5	5.0
Public Interest Groups	43.9	51.1	26.7
Federal Agencies	72.9	50.9	55.8
Political Parties	42.5	58.5	35.7
State Governments (Länder)	--	57.3	--
Advisory Boards (Shingikai)	--	--	47.1
All Organizations	50.7	51.8	43.3
Eta^2	.208***	.055	.243***

***$p < .001$

organizational interests in each subfield and the percentages expressing "strong" or "very strong" interests (4 or 5 on the six-point interest scale). Comparing subfield means across nations, we observe significant differences in all but one subfield (labor market policies), although the size of the eta-squares discloses that "nation" explains only 1 percent to 11 percent of the variance in organizational interest levels. The social policies subfield attracted the most interest in the U.S. and Germany, with disadvantaged populations second in both countries. Employment conditions ranked first in Japan, while social policies attracted the next highest interest. The largest disparities among the nations arose in the discrimination and disadvantaged populations subfields, with the German and especially the Japanese domains clearly less concerned about these matters than the American organizations. These large differences presumably originate in the more diverse U.S. population and its seasoned racial, gender, and age movements that politicized these topics much more extensively than in the homogeneous and culturally conservative German and Japanese societies. Substantial cross-national contrasts also occurred in working conditions, where Germany lagged behind Japan and the U.S., and in collective bargaining and management participation, which was far more important to the German organizations than to the U.S. and Japanese. Although internal governance did not evoke strong interest from a majority of any domain, it was clearly of greater concern to German organizations. Neither social

Table 4.2. *Organizational interests in labor policy subfields*

SUBFIELDS	MEAN INTEREST U.S.	Germany	Japan	PERCENT STRONG U.S.	Germany	Japan	Eta²
1. Social Policies	4.07	4.30	4.05	76.6	82.8	74.6	.010*
2. Disadvantaged Populations	3.98	3.87	3.51	74.8	71.1	55.7	.022*
3. Discrimination	3.95	3.40	3.07	71.1	50.4	41.3	.059***
4. Employment Conditions	3.94	3.54[a]	4.25	72.1	63.3	80.2	.048**
5. Working Conditions	3.48	2.88	3.63	56.7	39.2	62.0	.041***
6. Labor Market Policies	3.75	3.89	3.68	67.5	68.1	61.5	.004
7. Collective Bargaining	2.51	3.46	2.74	34.2	57.8	34.7	.055***
8. Internal Governance	1.96	2.91	2.62	20.7	41.1	27.3	.055***
9. Management Participation	1.90	3.25[b]	2.79	19.8	46.6	37.2	.108***
10. Labor Courts	–	2.68	–	–	31.9	–	–
(N)	(111)	(124)	(121)	(111)	(124)	(121)	

[a]Average of employment conditions and work time protection.
[b]Average of management participation and plant governance.
*$p < .05$
**$p < .01$
***$p < .001$

policies, employment conditions, nor labor market policies produced large contrasts across the nations, and all attracted high interest from large majorities.

The data collected from each organization about its interests in all nine subfields can also be analyzed to reveal the global spatial structures of each nation's labor policy concerns. The degree to which any pair of subfields is closely related is a function of all organizations' interest orientations. That is, the more similar the profiles are of all the domain organizations' expressed interests in a pair of subfields, the closer those two subfields lie in a spatial representation. Larger social distances between two subfields occur when the organizations express dissimilar levels of interests in both.

As a useful analogy, a social-spatial map is akin to a geographic map. If one calculates all pairs of mileages between N cities and feeds this symmetric $N \times N$ data matrix into a spatial plotting computer program, the resulting printout places the N cities at their correct physical distances from one another. In the same fashion, if a symmetric matrix of pairwise social distances between N social objectives (such as our nine subfields) is calculated and entered into a spatial plotter, the resulting diagram locates each object in terms of its relative social distance from, or proximity to, all the others. The interpretation of either type of map is the same: The farther apart a pair of objects are placed on the map, the greater the distance between them. Where the analogy begins to break down is in the underlying metric used to determine distances in physical and social space. While physical distances can be measured with high precision in a two-dimensional Euclidean space comprised of rectangular coordinates (to the closest kilometer, if not to the meter), standard measuring devices for social distance are not available. Instead, relatively crude procedures for gauging social *similarity* are usually applied, for example, our measure of the extent of equivalence in organizational ratings of pairs subfields. Unlike the linear yardstick distances in geographic surveying, such social-distance metrics may contain sufficient measurement error (noise) that more than two dimensions are necessary to reproduce satisfactorily the underlying social space. Fortunately, multidimensional scaling and plotting computer programs also compute a descriptive statistic, the stress coefficient, which summarizes the amount of error between the observed distance matrix and the distance matrix calculated from the k-dimensional solution (Kruskal and Wish, 1978: 49–52). The closer the stress value comes to zero, the better the fit of the spatial plot to the data.

To calculate the social distances between pairs of subfields in a labor policy domain, we began with an organization-by-subfield matrix ($N \times 9$, where N is the number of organizations), whose cells entries contained the 0–5 levels of interest reported by each row organization about each column subfield. Next, we computed correlation coefficients (Pearson's r) for all pairs of subfields. That is, with the N organizations serving as the number of cases, rs were calculated using each pair of column vectors. The higher a correlation, the greater the similarity between those two columns in the matrix. Next, the square symmetric (9×9) matrix of correlations among subfields was submitted to the ALSCAL (Alternating Least-Squares) nonmetric Euclidean multidimensional scaling solution and plotting routine in SPSS (Schiffman, Reynolds, and Young, 1981). This program iteratively derives a solution for the number of dimensions requested, calculates the coordinate values for each object, plots these points on pairs of Cartesian coordinates, and computes that solution's stress value.

Figures 4.1 to 4.3 display the two-dimensional ALSCAL solutions to the subfield analyses. Their stress values indicate acceptable fits for the U.S. and German matrices (both are below .20), but somewhat higher than desirable for the Japanese. Although the three-dimensional Japanese solution produced a lower stress value, it was not substantively more revealing than the poorer two-dimension fit. So, we assess the two-dimensional plots for all three nations. As an aid to interpretation of these diagrams, we also subjected the same 9×9 correlation matrices to hierarchical cluster analysis (Aldenderfer and Blashfield, 1984), using the average linkage between groups and treating the correlations as squared Euclidean distances. The cluster results allowed us to draw contiguity lines around subsets of the labor policy subfields with the greatest similarity, in the sense that

Figure 4.1. *Spatial distribution of U.S. labor policy subfields: two dimensional solution (stress = .164)*

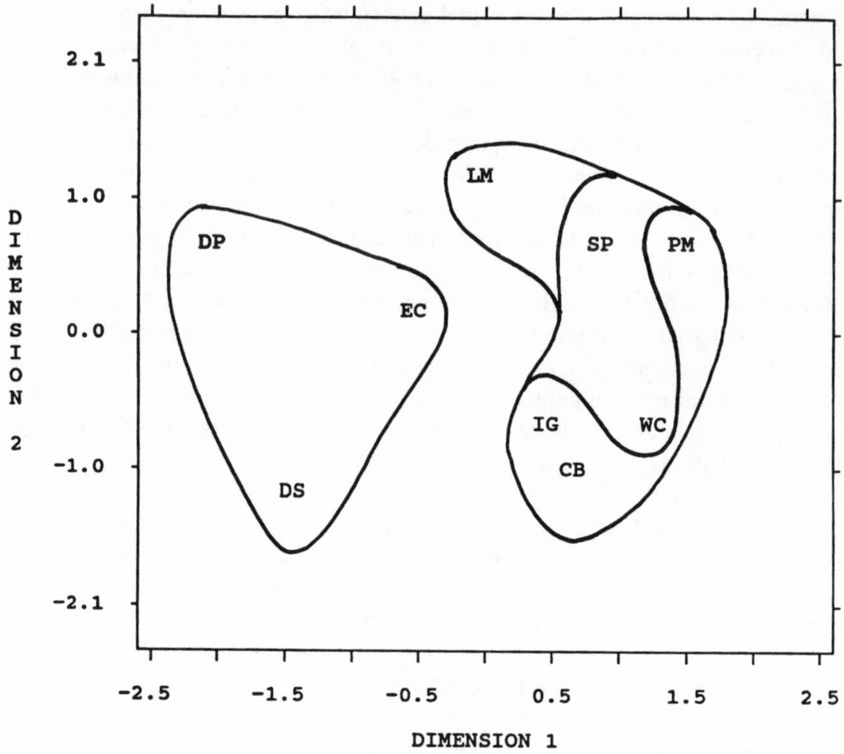

CB = Collective Bargaining
DP = Disadvantaged Populations
DS = Discrimination
EC = Employment Conditions
IG = Internal Governance
LM = Labor Market Policies
PM = Participation in Management
SP = Social Policies
WC = Working Conditions

they could be merged together as "nearest neighbors" because of the small distances between them.

All three nations exhibit a basic polarity between two sets of subfields: (1) three traditional labor-relations subfields (collective bargaining, participation in management, and internal governance); and (2) two subfields with mainly social-welfare content (disadvantaged populations and discrimination). These two clusters appeared as discrete clusters on opposite sides of the three social spaces. Placements of the four remaining subfields varied across nations, suggesting basic cross-national differences in whether organizations conceptualize them mainly as labor-relations or social-welfare problems. In the U.S. and Japan, the employment conditions subfield is located within the social-welfare cluster, but in Germany

Figure 4.2. *Spatial distribution of German labor policy subfields: two dimensional solution (stress* = .141)

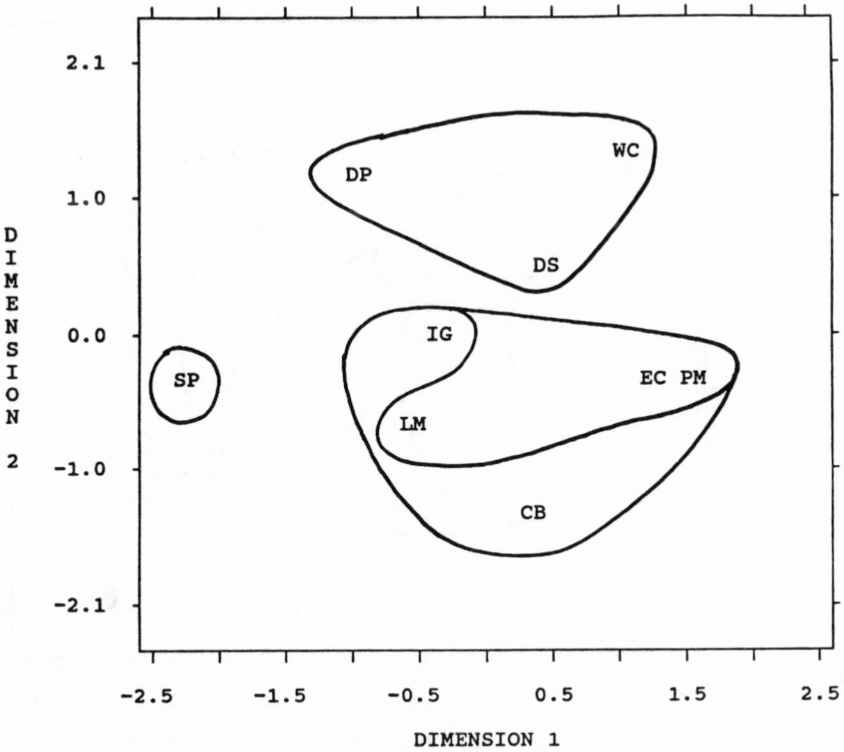

CB = Collective Bargaining
DP = Disadvantaged Populations
DS = Discrimination
EC = Employment Conditions
IG = Internal Governance
LM = Labor Market Policies
PM = Participation in Management
SP = Social Policies
WC = Working Conditions

within the labor-relations sector. Working conditions is placed among the labor-relations concerns in the U.S., but clustered with the social-welfare sector in both Germany and Japan. Labor market policies are connected to the traditional sector in Germany and the U.S., but with the social-welfare subfields in Japan. The social policies subfield was most distinct of all: falling into the labor-relations sector in the U.S. and into the social-welfare sector in Japan and occupying a distinct singleton cluster in Germany. In conclusion, the three nations reveal a basic underlying cleavage between traditional labor market and more recent social-welfare concerns with disadvantaged and discriminated populations. However, cutting across this cleavage are configurations unique to each nation. The origins of these distinctive national patterns lie in the way organizations define their range of pol-

Figure 4.3. *Spatial distribution of Japanese labor policy subfields: two dimensional solution (stress = .255)*

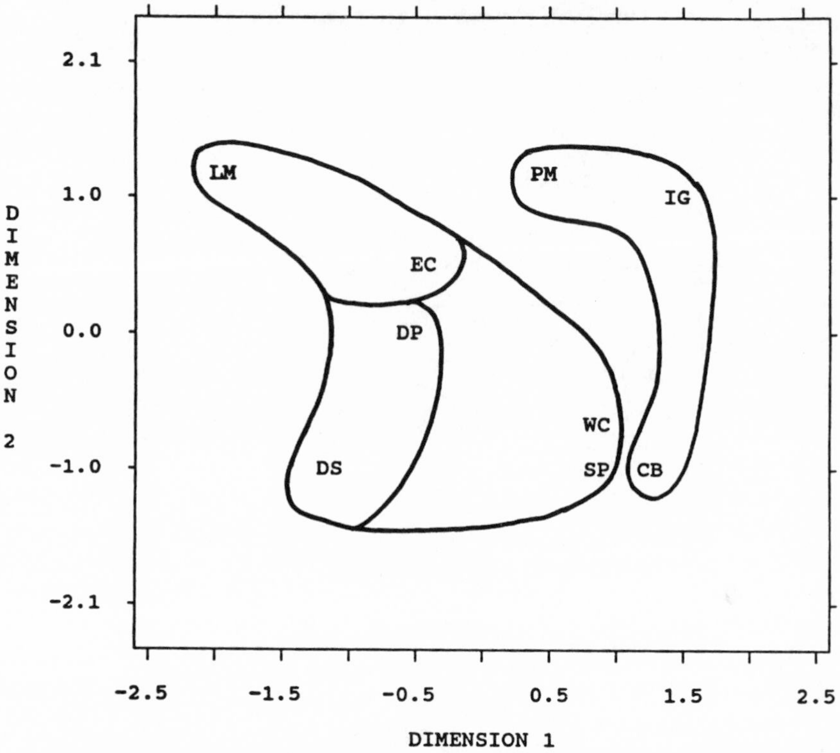

CB = Collective Bargaining
DP = Disadvantaged Populations
DS = Discrimination
EC = Employment Conditions
IG = Internal Governance
LM = Labor Market Policies
PM = Participation in Management
SP = Social Policies
WC = Working Conditions

icy interests, which in turn presumably arise from the historical processes and institutions through which social-welfare matters were sequentially differentiated from narrower labor contract concerns, as discussed in Chapter 2.

ISSUE INTERESTS

The structural diversity of domain policy interests between Germany, Japan, and the U.S. is even more evident when we shift our attention from the subfield to the issue level of analysis. Just as the amount of effort devoted to labor domain policies varies by the type of organization, so does the breadth of organizations' interests in specific domain issues. As described in Chapter 3, we culled many sources to identify 53 American, 45 German, and 51 Japanese issues that were present in those labor policy domains during the 1980s. As a simple measure of the scope of organizational issue interests, we counted the number of issues in which informants reported strong or very strong interests (4 or 5 on the same six-point scale used for subfield interests). Table 4.3 shows the means for the eight basic organization types within each nation. For ease of cross-national comparison, these means are displayed as deviations from the average for all organizations within a nation. For example, to find the U.S. labor union interests, add the +16.4 value for U.S. labor unions to the 20.0 mean of all U.S. organizations. Thus, on average the U.S. unions expressed high interest in 36.4 issues, far more than any other type of American organization. The German and Japanese labor unions also exhibited above-average breadth of issue interests (+9.7 and +3.5, respectively). Other types of organizations with broad high scores include the German states (*Länder*) and the political parties of all three nations. But all other organizations fall at or below their domain's mean interest level. These results indicate that unions and political parties are generalists attending to comprehensive issue agendas, whereas all other organizational types are specialists in their labor domain concerns. As shown by the eta-squares, the range of issue interests among types of organizations differs significantly within each country. But the proportion of variance explained is nearly three times higher in the U.S. than in Japan, with Germany more than twice as high as Japan. In other words, the Japanese organizations tend to resemble one another more in their breadth of issue interests than do either German or American organizations. This greater homogeneity among Japanese labor domain actors may imply greater consensus, or at least a shared perspective, about which organizations should be involved with what issues, consistent with a corporatist explanation, or perhaps only a pervasive reluctance to attend to many policy matters at any time.

To determine the structures underlying organizational interests in labor policy domain issues, we performed both hierarchical cluster and multidimensional scaling analyses on the data for each nation. As with the subfield analyses, a correlation matrix between pairs of issues was calculated using organizations as cases. Hence, the more similar two issues are in terms of attracting the same interest profiles from the organizational audience, the higher their *r*. This matrix was then submitted to both cluster and ALSCAL analysis, choosing five or six clusters and three-dimensional plots, respectively, as the best illustrations. To conserve space, the clusters are summarized in Appendix 3, where complete wordings of each issue item are printed along with the mean organizational interests (using the 0–5 scale in the first column) and the percentage expressing strong or very strong interests (in the second column). (The numbers preceding each issue correspond to their sequence in that nation's questionnaire.) Each cluster is labeled according to the subfields most prevalent among its issue contents.

Comparison of issue clusters across nations is hampered because many issue contents are idiosyncratic to time and place, rather than involving enduring universal matters. For example, German policy issues of disadvantaged populations were concerned mainly with severely handicapped persons, whereas analogous

Table 4.3. *Number of issues with high interests by organization type*

ORGANIZATION TYPE	DEVIATION FROM MEAN INTEREST U.S.	Germany	Japan
Labor Unions	+16.4	+9.7	+3.5
Business Associations	-4.6	-6.6	-3.7
Professional Societies	-6.1	-7.5	-4.4
Public Interest Groups	-3.2	-4.6	-1.4
Federal Agencies	-4.4	-0.7	+0.3
Political Parties	+13.5	+8.1	+12.1
State Governments (Länder)	--	+11.6	--
Advisory Boards (Shingikai)	--	--	-5.3
Mean of All Organizations	20.0	20.6	17.4
Eta^2	.485***	.387***	.172***

***$p < .001$

U.S. and Japanese issues emphasized women and racial-ethnic minorities. Despite such substantive differences, some noteworthy parallels emerged. Traditional labor-management issues such as collective bargaining and internal governance comprised a discernible issue cluster in all three nations. Several social policies – involving retirement and pensions, maternal-paternal leave, health-care – formed distinct agglomerations. Although discrimination issue clusters also appeared, their contents were very heterogeneous: The U.S. cluster included women as well as racial minorities; the German cluster mixed together issues of irregular employment and job training; and the Japanese cluster was narrowly defined by Japanese-Korean and Buraku discrimination.[3] Some unique issues arose in each country, reflecting national concerns of the era: part-time work and store-closing hours in Germany, affirmative action plans in the U.S., and foreign workers in the Japanese labor force.

The global structures of the national issue spaces become much clearer in the ALSCAL analyses of the issue correlation matrices. Figures 4.4 to 4.6 plot the first two dimensions of the three-dimensional solutions, with contiguity lines showing two nested levels of clustering corresponding to the hierarchical clusters in Appendix 3. The main contrast in the U.S. lies between discrimination and disad-

3. The three discrimination items were added to the Japanese questionnaire late in the field period and hence were asked of only 25 of the 122 informants. This small case-base is denoted in the tabular display of Appendix 3 by enclosing their numerical values within brackets.

Figure 4.4. *Spatial distribution of U.S. labor domain issues: dimensions 1 and 2 from three dimensional solution (stress = .166)*

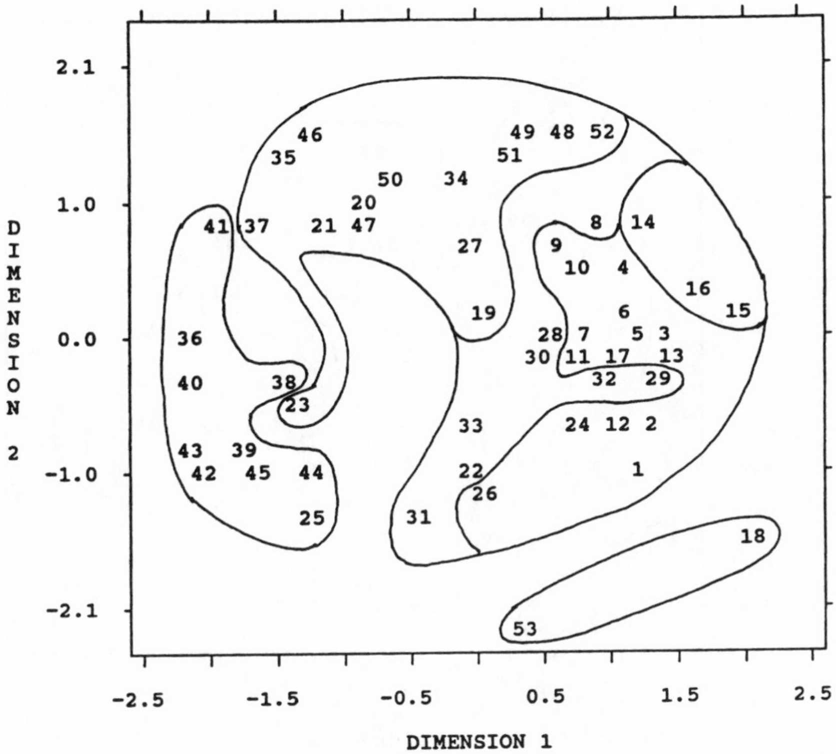

1. Grievance procedures
2. Collective bargaining
3. Right to work
4. Bankruptcy to void contracts
5. Contract givebacks
6. Corporate restructuring
7. Temporary employees
8. Employee stock ownership plan
9. Employees on company boards
10. Employee job responsibility
11. Anti-racketeering statutes
12. Union election procedures
13. Anti-trust violations
14. Employer associations
15. Occupational diseases
16. Safety and health standards
17. Employee assistance
18. Smoking bans
19. Wages and hours
20. Minimum wage law
21. Sub-minimum teen wage
22. Mandatory retirementt
23. Child care
24. Drug testing
25. Promotion, seniority
26. Computer monitoring
28. Pension plan benefits
29. ERISA
30. Social Security reform
31. Women's pension equity
32. Unemployed health care
33. Parental leave
34. Trade adjustment
35. Vocational education
36. Minorities
37. Youth training
38. Older Americans
39. Handicapped workers
40. Women
41. Migrant workers
42. Equal employment
43. Affirmative action
44. Sexual harassment
45. Comparable pay
46. Job creation
47. Immigration reform
48. Import tariffs
49. Plant closings
50. Underground economy
51. Federal aid to industries
52. Environmental regulations
53. AIDS

Figure 4.5. *Spatial distribution of German labor domain issues: dimensions 1 and 2 from three dimensional solution (stress = .194)*

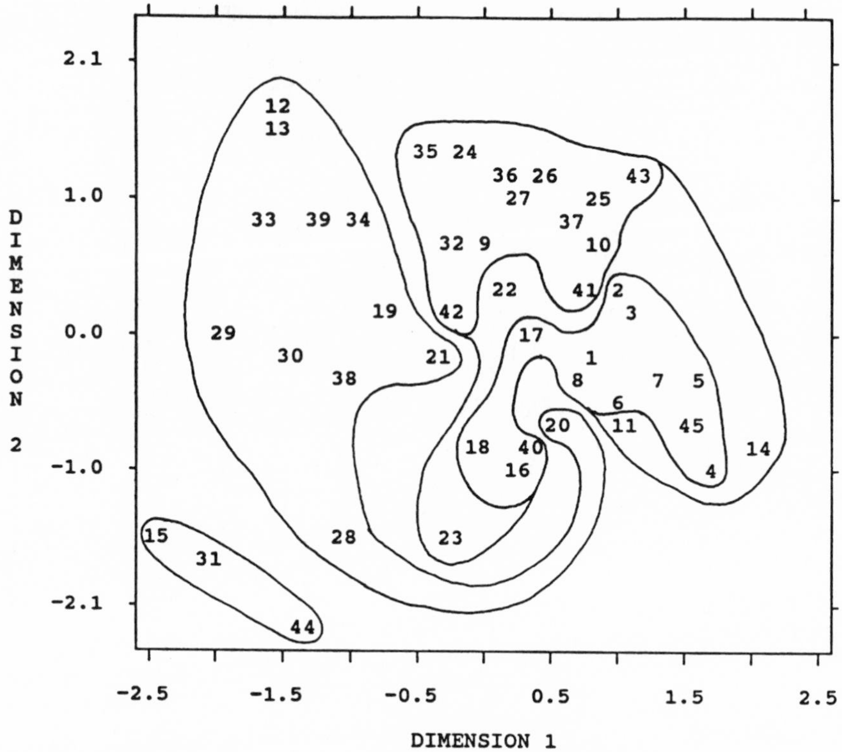

1. Labor Institute neutrality
2. Token strikes in negotiations
3. Lockouts prohibitions
4. Coal and steel industry
5. Enterprise codetermination parity
6. Social plan bankruptcy rules
7. Plant constitution committees
8. Small union minority rights
9. Works council codetermination
10. New technology introduction
11. Association governance law
12. Part-time workers legal rules
13. Limited-work contracts
14. Employees participation
15. Civil servant activity
16. Temporary employment rules
17. Dismissal standardization
18. Renewal of retirement law
19. New technology health risks
20. Bans on dangerous substances
21. Smoking bans
22. Store closing time rules
23. Store service evening
24. Shorter hours distribution
25. Irregular employment hours
26. Sunday, holiday work rules
27. Maximum hours, rest breaks
28. Aged and survivor pensions
29. Training funds, leaves
30. Unemployment compensation rules
31. Social insurance premiums
32. Training dismissal protection
33. Handicapped care openings
34. Handicapped dismissal rules
35. Gender-neutral job ads
36. Women's promotion plans
37. Discrimination proof burden
38. Return of foreign workers
39. Support for ABM-measures
40. Employee quitting rules
41. Unemployment retrenchment
42. Retirement job vacancies
43. Professional training
44. Social insurance cards
45. Labor Court jurisdiction

Figure 4.6. *Spatial distribution of Japan labor domain issues: dimensions 1 and 2 from three dimensional solution (stress = .184)*

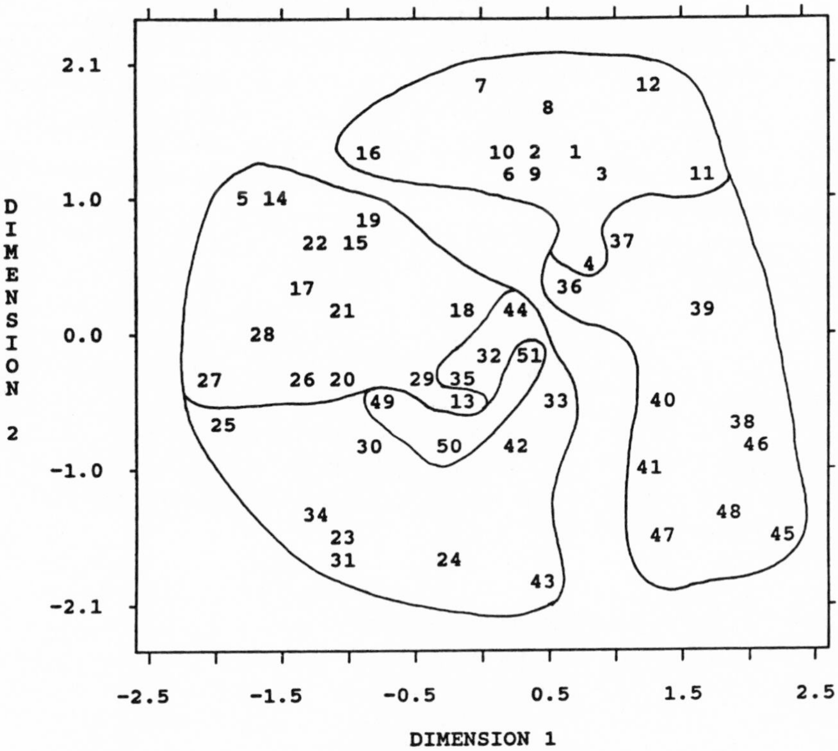

1. Wage standards
2. Hour standards
3. Minimum wage law changes
4. Workers below minimum wage
5. Mandatory retirement age
6. Child care at workplace
7. Promotion, seniority
8. Computer monitoring
9. Radiation, chemicals, disease
10. Safety, healthy enforcement
11. Drug, alcohol abuse help
12. Smoking bans in workplace
13. Unemployment compensation
14. Pension benefits, funding
15. Retiree income guarantees
16. Retiree social security
17. Pension equity for women
18. Unemployed health care
19. Maternal, paternal leave
20. Job change assistance
21. Vocational education
22. Company welfare plans
23. Response to foreign workers
24. Youth unemployment, train
25. Elderly employment
26. Handicapped workers
27. Women workers
28. Equal employ opportunity
29. Sexual harassment
30. Job creation
31. Foreigners in labor market
32. Import tariffs, quotas
33. Plant closings
34. Federal aid to industry
35. Environmental regulations
36. Grievances, mediation
37. Collective bargaining
38. Bankruptcy to void contracts
39. Givebacks, concessions
40. Corporate restructuring
41. Temp employees to avoid contracts
42. Employee stock ownership programs
43. Employee reps on company boards
44. Employee productivity responsibility
45. Prohibit racketeers threat
46. Union election procedures
47. Anti-trust violations
48. Company rights in employer assns
49. Discrimination against workers
50. Promotion of discriminated workers
51. Employment of day laborers

vantaged population issues (on the left) and almost all remaining issues of collective bargaining and working conditions, social policies, labor market policies and job creation and training (top center and right). A two-item cluster involving AIDS and workplace smoking bans appears on the lower right. In the German issue space, the main cleavage separates the social policies cluster (on the left) from all other domain issues (center and right), with a three-item social insurance cluster on the lower left. In Japan, the traditional labor-relations clusters of working conditions, collective bargaining, and governance (on the right) are separated from the social-welfare clusters of social policies, labor markets, and discrimination (on the center and left).

These patterns at the detailed level of domain issues echo the spatial relations found in the subfield analyses just discussed, implying a pervasive structuring of policy concerns by core domain organizations regardless of level of specificity. A strikingly parallel differentiation across all three nations contrasts the traditional labor-relations issues that directly involve workplace management versus the social-welfare issues that deal primarily with the social welfare consequences of the labor market for individuals and groups. However, only in the U.S. did anything approximating the expected rim or circle structure emerge in the issue space. The centers of both the German and Japanese spaces contain a few issues that apparently appealed to diverse organizations: in Germany, retirement job vacancies, smoking bans, store-closing rules, and dismissal standards; in Japan, unemployment health care, import tariffs and quotas, and employee productivity responsibility. Thus, although the sectoring of issues into substantively distinct regions was observed in all three labor policy domains, some German and Japanese issues attracted heterogeneous organizational audiences, thus locating them at the heart of common concerns. These issues have the potential for stimulating policy involvements cutting across the more parochial concerns on which organizations typically concentrate. In addition, the content of these issues seems to symbolize each country's "central" concerns: in Germany, better working conditions; in Japan, productivity conditions.

INTERESTS OF ISSUE PUBLICS

By interchanging (transposing) the rows and columns in a matrix of organizations' interest in policy issues, we can characterize each domain organization according to its profile of interests in all the issues. To the extent that two organizations express similar interests in the issues, their pair of column vectors will be highly correlated. Submitting the $N \times N$ matrix of *r*s to hierarchical clustering and multidimensional scaling analyses, we can investigate the composition and spatial location of the organizations comprising each nation's issue publics. Figures 4.7 to 4.9 display the first two dimensions from the three-dimensional ALSCAL solutions, with contiguity lines for the six-cluster solutions. Although the stress coefficients for these three-dimensional solutions are somewhat higher than desirable, we use these figures because they provide approximate relative loca-

Figure 4.7. *Spatial distribution of U.S. labor issue publics: dimensions 1 and 2 from three dimensional solution (stress = .204)*

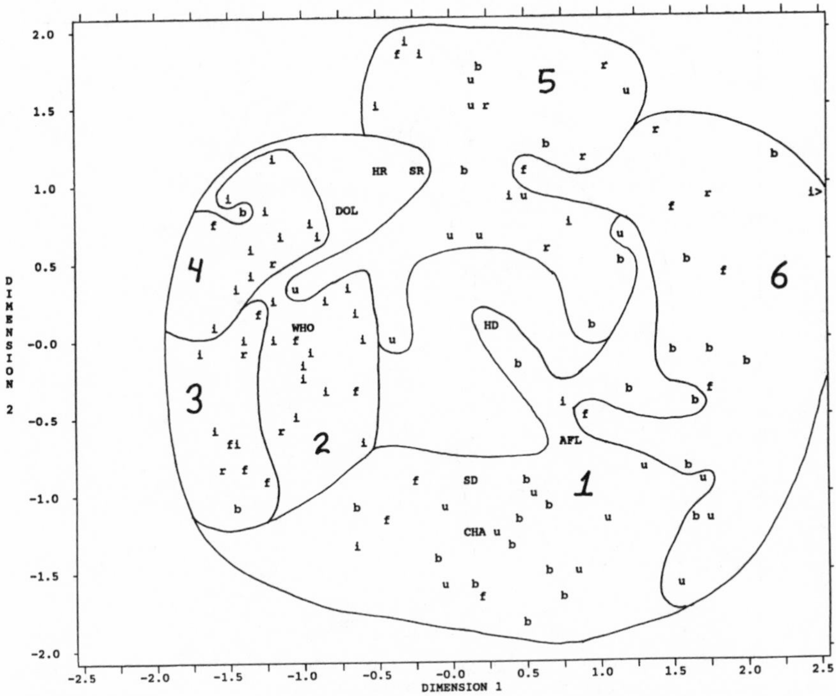

u = labor unions; b = business associations; i = interest groups; r = professional societies; f = federal agencies

tions for the issue public members. The issue public solutions have poorer fits than either the subfield or issue interest analyses primarily because of the large number of interpoint similarities that the multidimensional scaling program must reconcile (about 120 organizations, compared to 9 subfields and about 50 issues). In these diagrams, the individual organizations' locations are identified either by a symbol for their types (e.g., "*u*" for union, "*b*" for business, etc.), or by capital-letter acronyms for the half-dozen most important actors in each domain: the peak labor, business, party, and governmental organizations (see the organization list in Appendix 2 for complete names). Although the clusters have no intrinsic order, we assigned large numerals as labels in the diagrams for ease of reference.

The expected empty center appears in both the U.S. and German diagrams. The first issue public in each nation is a cluster of generalist organizations holding interests in many domain issues. Most of the key organizations fall into this public: in the U.S., the AFL-CIO, the Chamber of Commerce, and the Democratic members of the House and Senate labor committees; in Germany, the three *Bundestag* fractions of the three main political parties (CDU/CSU, FDP, and SPD), the Ger-

Figure 4.8. *Spatial distribution of German labor issue publics: dimensions 1 and 2 from three dimensional solution (stress = .245)*

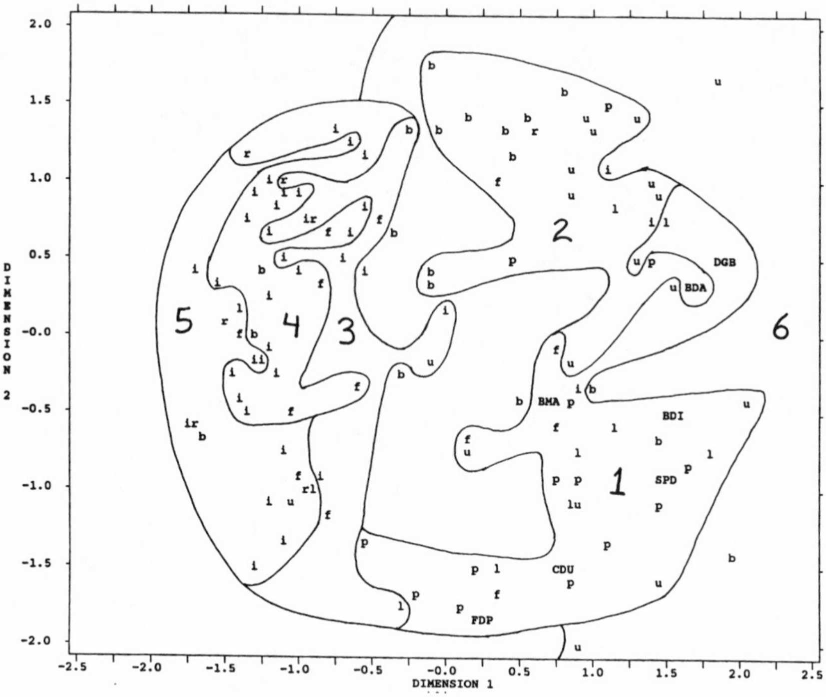

u = labor unions; b = business associations; i = interest groups; r = professional; f = federal agencies; l = state governments (Länder); p = parties

man Trade Union Federation (DGB), the Federation of German Industry (BDI), and the Ministry of Labor (BMA). The remaining key organizations in both nations fall into an adjacent issue public. In the U.S., this second issue public (at the left of the hollow center) contains four major Republican political actors: the Reagan White House, the Department of Labor, and the Republican members of the House and Senate labor committees. In Germany, the only major player not found in the first issue public is the Confederation German Employers Associations (BDA), the peak business association, which resides in the second public at the upper left and virtually on top of the peak union association. The absence of German and American issue publics at the heart of the three-dimensional organizational space implies that no subset of actors expressed interests that minimized their distances to all other organizational interests. Rather, the U.S. and German issue publics occupy a sequence of specialized niches along the rim of the space, suggesting that these domains may lack any central group with a stake in coordinating or mediating among the restrictive policy foci of the narrow issue publics.

In contrast, the center of the Japanese issue public space is solidly filled by the first issue public, with the five other publics orbiting around it. Like its U.S. and

Figure 4.9. *Spatial distribution of Japanese labor issue publics: dimensions 1 and 2 from three dimensional solution (stress = .225)*

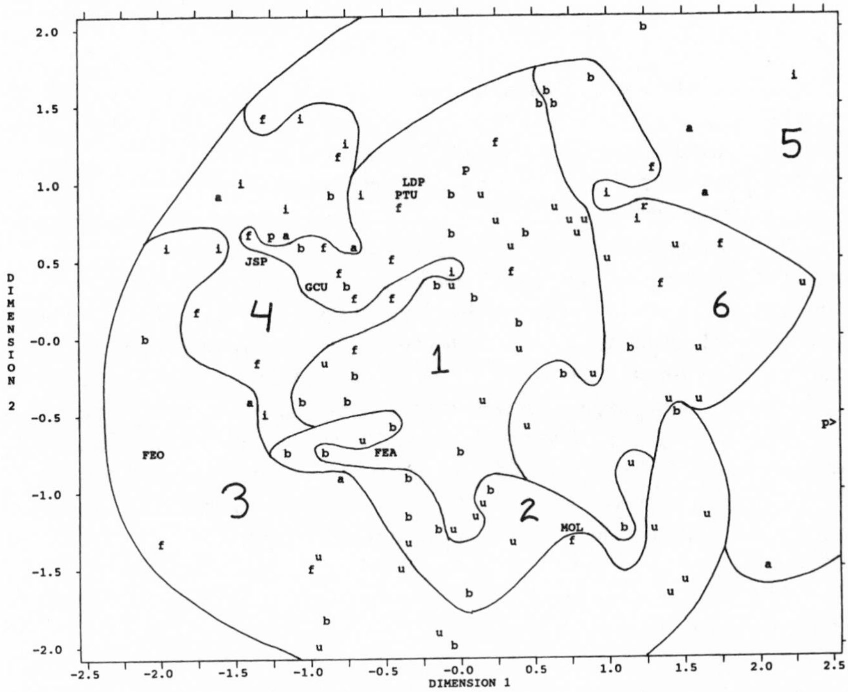

u = labor unions; b = business associations; i = interest groups; r = professional; f = federal agencies; a = advisory bodies; p = parties

German counterparts, this first public is also a generalist cluster. It contains four major political and economic organizations: the Liberal Democratic Party (LDP); the Federation of Employers Associations (FEA); and both major peak labor associations, the Private Sector Trade Union Confederation (PTU) and the General Council of Trade Unions of Japan (GCU). The three remaining key players each occupy distinct issue publics at the left and bottom of the space: the Ministry of Labor in the second, the Federation of Economic Organizations (FEO) in the third, and the Socialist Party (JSP) in the fourth public. Thus, although every issue interest public in the U.S. and Germany seems to be structurally specialized, the core Japanese public expresses interests that are much less divergent from all the other publics. These patterns are consistent both with the more divisive and openly conflicting labor politics of the two Western nations and with the renowned Japanese accommodationist approach (or osmotic corporatist approach [Tsujinaka, 1993]) that deemphasizes differences of political opinion among social actors (Krauss and Ishida, 1989). Indeed, the spatial images are strikingly consistent with the conventional view that Japan has a more consensual political system that do other capitalist industrial democracies. They are also consistent with the recently postulated mechanisms like "corporative management" (Aoki, 1984) on the micro-level and the "network society" (Kumon, 1992) on the macro-level.

CONCLUSION

The policy interests of core organizations in the U.S., German, and Japanese national labor policy domains exhibit common social structures, but with significant variations on the theme. At both the subfield and the issue levels of analysis, the primary cleavage lies between traditional labor-relations concerns (collective bargaining, participation in firm management, and internal governance) and social-welfare matters (discrimination, disadvantaged populations, labor markets). The relative proximity or distance among social policies, working conditions, and employment conditions depends on how these subfields and issues emerged historically during industrial and postindustrial eras and became institutionally accommodated to the political economies of each nation. Despite wide diversity among the three nations in the specific policy topics that were salient during the 1980s, the labor policy organizations differentiated into specialized audiences that were roughly comparable in each country: labor unions and political parties (and the German states) maintained the broadest substantive interests, while business associations, professional societies, federal agencies, and advisory boards each targeted much narrower spans of policy attention. In each domain, the most prominent political, labor, and business actors clustered into one or two core issue publics, while the remaining subordinate publics consisted of less-prominent interest groups. Spatial analyses located all issue publics as specialized sectors on the rim around a hollow center in the U.S. and Germany, but the core issue public solidly filled the central region in Japan.

In their separation into distinct clusters of issues and issue publics, our cross-national labor policy domain comparisons resemble the results of Laumann and Knoke (1987) for the U.S. energy and health policy domains. Like them, we conclude that the appearance of issue clusters and issue publics reflects the overarching constraints of the modern organizational state. This similarity is especially evident for the U.S. and Germany, while Japan exhibits some important divergences from the original model. Governmental authorities and private interest organizations struggle to shape public policies, each pursuing disparate agendas in the legislative, executive, and judicial arenas. Issue publics form seedbeds in which potential alliances among like-minded organizations are nurtured. Because they share similar intense concerns about the same domain policy matters, members of an issue public are predisposed to mobilize on opposing sides of policy events whenever such issues move onto the domain's active agenda. However, the emergence of a core issue public in Japan, a "filled donut hole," indicated a much less pluralistic, less fluid, and more centrally coordinated form of issue orientation than was found in the U.S. and German labor policy domains. Hence, understanding the structure of issue publics and their interests is an indispensable prelude to our investigations of interorganizational exchange networks and participation in policy events in the following two chapters.

5

Policy webs: networks, reputations, and activities

with Naomi J. Kaufman

Several analysts have proposed that state policy-making structures and processes are realizations of networks of resource exchanges among key actors (Heclo, 1978; Lehmbruch, 1984; Wilks and Wright, 1987; Laumann and Knoke, 1987; Broadbent, 1989b; Marin, 1991; Pappi, 1993). These relations are asymmetrical interactions that enable one social actor to affect another's behavior. Peter Marsden articulated a basic goal of such inquiries: "Of particular concern in establishing a link between structure and action is the question of how positions in social structure are transformed into disparities in power among actors" (1982: 201).

We conceptualize the policy networks of the U.S., German, and Japanese national labor policy domains as communication and political support relations among interested organizations that seek to influence public policy decisions. This chapter derives research expectations from the organizational state perspective and from the distinct cultural-historical institutions of the three nations. Next, we examine the global spatial structures of the communication and political support networks among core labor policy organizations, paying special attention to their center and periphery locations. Finally, we use structural equation methods to estimate the relationships of network centralities to organizational reputations and their legislative policy activities.

The struggle over collective decisions involves numerous interactions among organizational state participants, which permits their conceptualization and analysis as networks of exchange relations. Some organizations control scarce political resources that are highly valued by others. Resource-rich organizations typically exchange their resources for the cooperation and support of their exchange partners. Occupancy of central positions within exchange networks allows these core actors to coordinate collective actions aimed at achieving their preferred policy objectives. The emergence of stable networks within a policy domain enhances actors' differential capacities to gain access to resources essential for participating in and shaping policy decisions. Network effects operate independently of these organizations' individual characteristics such as their size or formal authority, which indicate their individual possession of resources. Access to resources and their exchange confers unequal positional advantages, which can be represented as organizations' locations near the centers or on the peripheries of resource networks' social spaces. Actors who are well-connected to important other actors thereby gain important advantages through their access to flows of political resources. Organizations on the network margins, whose ties connect them mainly to other peripheral actors, cannot tap sufficient quantities of quality political resources to participate effectively in collective actions. Thus, organizations occupying the important positions in networks of resource exchanges are more likely to participate in domain activities and to be seen by their peers as consequential in collective policy-making.

As noted in Chapter 1, the resource networks most relevant to our research closely correspond to Knoke's analytic distinction between influence and domination networks (Knoke, 1990b: 11–16; 1992a). *Influence* relationships involve persuasive communications intended to change others' perceptions and beliefs regarding political actions and their potential consequences. Exchanges of information – including scientific-technical, legal, and political knowledge – involve transmissions from one actor to anther without loss of control by the initiator. Indeed, communication is often disseminated widely in efforts to inform a broad audience about one's plans and preferences, both to gain assistance and to discourage opposition.

Domination relationships involve exchanges of sanctions intended to facilitate or restrain others' behaviors in directions desired by the initiator. Transmission of sanctions – including financial and material rewards and public support and legitimation, as well as coercive penalties – often results in the loss of control over those resources by the initiator. Domination typically narrowly focuses on a few selected targets, to the exclusion of many others. In our labor policy analyses, the analytic influence and domination relationships correspond to policy communication and political support networks, respectively. Each network is comprised of dyadic exchange relationships among core domain organizations, generating webs of political linkages that together constitute the social structure of the modern state.

RESEARCH EXPECTATIONS

Dual objectives inspire the analyses in this chapter: (1) uncovering the social-spatial structures of the communication and political support networks among all labor policy domain organizations in each nation, and (2) estimating how the two networks are related to organizations' reputations for labor policy influence and to legislative policy event activities. The next three subsections discuss our expectations and present hypotheses in bivariate format; the fourth subsection presents a causal diagram.

Social-spatial structures

As explained in Chapter 4, social distance is the degree or intensity of interaction among social actors. In a social-spatial map, two actors with frequent and intense direct exchanges should be located near to one another, while pairs having rare and weak indirect exchange relations should be quite distant. If a network of transactions among all pairs of domain organizations is mapped, a basic question is what kind of global configuration can be expected to emerge? Laumann and Pappi (1976: 142) proposed two structuring regularities: (1) the social space will tend to divide into regions jointly occupied by actors sharing similar interests; and (2) those actors playing the most critical coordination roles will tend to locate at the network's center, whereas those with minor roles will be situated in peripheral sectors. When these structuring patterns occur, the spatial diagram resembles a wheel (or, in three dimensions, a sphere), with spokes separating the sectors radiating out to the peripheral rim from a dense hub containing the core elites (an "inner circle" [Useem, 1983] or "central circle" [Moore, 1979]). Such patterns were uncovered in the U.S. for information and resource exchange networks among urban organizations (Galaskiewicz, 1979: 61–90), national energy and health policy domain organizations (Laumann and Knoke, 1987: 242–8), and national labor policy organizations (Knoke, 1990b: 163–71). However, Heinz, Laumann, Salisbury, and Nelson's (1990) study of Washington lawyers' ties to elite persons in four policy domains revealed a "sphere with a hollow core," that is, sharply polarized sectors with no actors able to bridge the empty center. In that analysis, the labor domain was especially polarized between union and business representatives. The researchers surmised that the hollow cores could have resulted from their omission of government officials who might mediate the conflicts and thus bind the domain together.

Consistent with previous empirical findings, we expected center-periphery structures to emerge in each nation's communication and political support networks. Peak labor, business, and governmental organizations would locate predominantly at the network centers, while specialized organizations with similar policy interests would locate in distinct peripheral regions. We also expected that the more central an organization's location in the communication network, the more central it would be in the support network.

Organizational reputations

In all social systems, status, prestige, and power are unequally distributed. Organizations' reputations for consequentiality in national policy domains are likewise unequal, with a handful of actors possessing high reputations and the majority of actors possessing much lower prestige. As peer summary ratings of each actor's perceived standing in the system, such rankings encapsulate both past and prospective capacities to move-and-shake collective affairs (Knoke, 1983), as well as their general visibility through mass media and direct experience. Invidious distinctions may help actors cope with uncertainties in complex markets by providing capsule judgments about competence, trustworthiness, and performance (Shrum and Wuthnow, 1988; Laumann and Knoke, 1987: 152–89; Fombrum and Shanley, 1990; Friedkin, 1993). They may also indicate organizations' abilities to acquire essential resources without compromising their autonomy and power to act independently of their suppliers' and sponsors' interests (Knoke, 1983: 1067). Such collective judgments about reputational orderings often confer "competitive advantage and disadvantage upon conforming organizations within an organizational field" (Fombrum and Shanley, 1990: 234).

Individual and organizational reputations tend to covary positively with their centrality in various resource exchange networks (Boje and Whetten, 1981; Shrum and Wuthnow, 1988; Galaskiewicz, 1979: 143–7). Marsden and Laumann (1977: 217) asserted that "those persons at the center of the network, on whom the peripheral actors are dependent, are the most powerful actors in the system." The process involves subjective perceptions of latent capacities for action: "Network position becomes translated into attributed influence as others attribute to central actors greater potential for establishing coalitions to enhance their political influence" (Boje and Whetten, 1981: 381). Central actors are more salient and visible than peripheral actors, more readily acquire information resources, and "on any given issue are likely to be more active in utilizing" their more numerous or shorter communication channels for conveying their opinions (Friedkin, 1993: 864). And a reciprocal effect may occur as less-powerful organizations seek to establish ties to those they perceive as controlling the critical contingencies in a domain. This relationship is captured in a bivariate hypothesis: The more central an organization's location within a network, the higher its reputation for public policy influence.

Policy event activities

Interest groups and governmental organizations alike strive to influence national policy decisions through a variety of political activities (Knoke, 1986). In the U.S., the rapid growth in national regulatory policies, post-Watergate electoral reforms, and congressional reorganization greatly expanded political access and leverage, attracting many lobbying organizations to Washington. Public interest groups are particularly prone to mobilize their memberships, appeal to the general public through the mass media, launch letter-writing campaigns, and stimulate local lobbying efforts (McFarland, 1984; Gais, Peterson and Walker, 1984; Knoke, 1990a: 208). Schlozman and Tierney listed more than two dozen such techniques used by interest groups with offices in Washington, two-thirds of which were for-profit organizations (1986: 150–1). The most frequent methods were contacting government officials to present viewpoints, testifying at hearings, presenting research reports, and mounting grass roots lobbying efforts. Berry (1984: 149–55) referred to the latter as "constituency lobbying," which involves writing letters, making phone calls, and visits to members of Congress by their constituents. More descriptive accounts indicate that similar influence activities occur in all parliamentary systems (Berger, 1981; Wilson, 1983; Tsujinaka, 1988).

Laumann, Knoke, and Kim's (1985) study of the U.S. energy and health policy domains examined the impact of networks on policy event activities. In their recursive causal model, organizational position in the communication network affected position in the material resource network, and both networks in turn caused organizations' participation in policy events. They found that the network effects differed by domain: Neither network was significant in the energy domain, but in the health domain, the communication effect was more than twice as large as the resource exchange effect. We expect the more central organizations in a network to be more active in seeking to affect policy events.

A causal diagram

Drawing from the bivariate hypotheses we have discussed, Figure 5.1 displays a multivariate recursive causal model that links organizational characteristics, communication and support network locations, and two outcomes – organizational reputations and legislative policy activities. Three sets of predetermined variables are represented at the left. Policy interests are formed exogenously, in the sense that an organization's policy preferences typically reflect its long-standing commitments to specific substantive concerns. Although policy foci can shift in response to changing political circumstances, such changes are less likely to arise from short-term resource exchanges with other organizations than through larger historical trends and internal organizational dynamics. In any event, the time scale of our research is sufficiently short that we will assume organizational interests in labor policy domain affairs remain reasonably stable. Organizational resource capacities encompass material and symbolic advantages that allow organizations to participate in policy-making and attempt to shape collective outcomes. Measures include size and formal organizational structures, which embody a wide array of resource advantages. Organizational type distinguishes among governmental actors with formal authority to make binding decisions on public policy decisions, and such basic private-sector types as labor unions, business associations, and public interest groups whose effects may not be completely captured by other organizational attributes.

In the central portion of Figure 5.1 appear the organizations' centralities in the communication and support networks. To their left, the antecedent variables affect, but do not completely determine, organizational locations in both networks. The basic principle behind these expectations is a cumulative structural advantage: Actors having broader policy interests, larger resource capabilities, and public authority can more easily convert those advantages into proximity to the centers of each exchange network. In other words, organizations that have more, tend to get more; those with less, usually do without. The diagram depicts communication as causally antecedent to support, on the presumption that organizations must first establish contact to discuss common concerns before they can render substantive assistance. Communication is a relatively low-cost relationship that may be sustained between both allies and antagonists. Support, however, is a costly relationship likely to be targeted mainly toward one's policy confederates.

We conceptualize organizational locations in the two networks to require distinct empirical measures. In a policy communication network, actor proximity is

Figure 5.1. *Causal model of relations among organizational characteristics, exchange networks, and reputations and event activities*

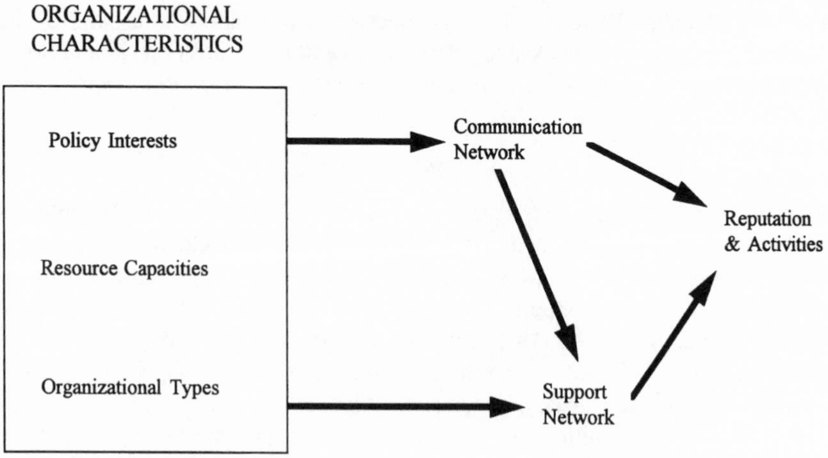

social distance: Two organizations are close to the extent they can directly exchange information, and they are more distant if many intermediaries must connect them. Centrality in a communication network is captured by the number of *paths,* or steps, required to transmit a message from one actor to another. As more intermediaries are required, the connections grow more tenuous and the information grows more susceptible to distortion and disruption. Communication paths may be asymmetric, in that more links may be required for information to go from organization *A* to *B* than vice versa. Path distances are measured by graph-theoretic or cohesion methods that emphasize interorganizational reachability (Alba and Kadushin, 1976). Organizations toward the center of a communication network can more readily contact others directly. Thus they occupy positions requiring few intervening links to bridge the gaps.

In contrast, location in a political support network is best captured by *structural equivalence:* Two actors are equivalent when they compete against one another for access to the same suppliers of scarce resources; and, they are differentiated if they seek support from different sets of providers (Burt, 1987). Structural equivalence may pit subordinate actors in a struggle for the scarce goods and attention from a few suppliers. Such distances are conceptually similar to Marin's (1991: 60–1) "antagonistic cooperation" and to Cook and Emerson's (1978) "negatively connected exchange," which both recognize that exchanges may foster competition as well as cooperation. Structural equivalence is measured by Euclidean *social distance* methods that treat a pair of actors as proximate if they maintain similar patterns of exchange relations with all others in a network (Burt, 1976). The equivalent core organizations allocate support among the same set of claimants. The peripheral organizations, lacking essential resources and thus dependent on core suppliers, are equivalent when they target the same sources of support. In contrast to the *graph-theoretic* approach, actors may jointly occupy a structurally equivalent position without directly exchanging resources among themselves. The measurement section that follows describes how these different conceptualizations of actor proximity are used to identify organizations' network locations.

Finally, Figure 5.1 depicts the two exchange networks as each directly affecting organizational reputations and event activities, net of any effects from the predetermined variables. Again, the structural advantage principle predicts positive relations: The more central an organization's location in an exchange network, the higher its reputation and the more extensive its activities. Because we do not have hypotheses about the relationship between reputations and activities, we analyze them separately later. That is, we estimate two equation systems, the first with organizational reputations as the ultimate dependent variable, the second with event activities as dependent. Although we recognize that reciprocal effects may occur among these four endogenous variables, neither theoretical nor substantive grounds currently warrant specifying and estimating such complex relationships.

Comparing policy domains

Chapter 2 discusses rationales for examining relationships in comparative perspective. Detailed network data permit us to assess whether structural similarities or divergences occur among the three nations. Some institutional theorists (e.g., Boli, 1987; Jepperson and Meyer, 1991), argue that a diffusion of institutional forms across national boundaries promotes strikingly similar social structures among modern states. Likewise, convergence theorists assert that common industrialization dynamics cause institutions to become similar across countries. As a result, the most advanced nations should exhibit marked commonalities in their network spatial structures and the relationships among networks, reputations, and activities. On the other hand, some development theorists argue that institutions are strongly shaped by the historical and cultural legacies of each nation (Eisenstadt, 1973), leading us to anticipate some persistent differences among the U.S., Germany, and Japan.

Japan's state-led, consensus-building concertation of public policy should put its governmental ministries at the centers of both the communication and support networks. Communication ties should be especially important predictors of both organizational reputations and policy event activities. Japan's business and labor sectors are highly organized in associations that participate in corporatist policymaking. The Liberal Democratic Party's continual control of the government from 1955 to 1993 enabled it to orchestrate the important political networks to a much greater extent than in nations where the government alternated parties more frequently. Germany's cooperative federalist state governs a moderately corporatist political economy. These institutions imply extensive ties that pull peak business, labor, and governmental organizations into the centers of both networks. In contrast, the U.S. is usually depicted as a pluralistic and fragmented polity, with relatively little overt governmental coordination of policy actors. Hence, its federal government should be less evident at the centers of either U.S. network. Given the prevailing popular image of Japan as the most heavily "networked" polity and the U.S. as the least, we expect that across various dimensions of network structure (such as density, connectivity, reciprocation, centralization), Japan should rank highest, Germany intermediate, and the U.S. lowest. Similarly, the peak labor, business, and governmental organizations are likely to be most prevalent at the centers of network spaces in Japan, intermediate in Germany, and least in the U.S.

Similar considerations help to generate expectations about national differences that may emerge in the causal model. Reaching consensus about public policies requires prolonged discussion and intense negotiations, with extensive communication and support essential for reaching closure. As the preeminent network society, Japan's labor domain should display stronger connections between network locations, organizational reputations, and event activities. Germany's corporatist arrangements, which emphasize active governmental mediation of labor-business disputes, should also encourage strong connections among these endogenous variables. But the U.S's more laissez-faire approach is likely to produce much weaker effects. Hence, the magnitudes of network effects on organizational reputations and event activities are expected to be highest in Japan, intermediate in Germany, and weakest in the U.S. And the prevalent image of Japan implies that the communication network, so essential to consensus building, should play a more important role in Japan than in the other two countries.

MEASURES

Chapter 4 introduced some of the measures used in the causal analysis that follows. An organization's *subfield interest* score is the number of areas out of nine subfields in which the informant indicated the two highest levels of interest, using the 0–5 scale. Their *issue interests* are factor scores, calculated from the issue loadings on the first unrotated factors emerging from principal components factor analyses for each nation (see Appendix 3 for the item listings). The higher an organization's score, the larger the number of issues about which it expressed strong interests. *Staff size* is the logarithm of the number of persons employed in the organization's governmental affairs office. *Domain effort* is the percentage of the organization's public policy influence effort devoted to the national labor policy domain (see Table 4.1 in Chapter 4). Categoric (dummy) variables were created for each organization type (e.g., labor union, business association).

To identify the domain's *communication network*, respondents were shown a list of their nations' core labor domain organizations and asked for which of the nine subfields their organization most needed policy information from the others. They then checked all organizations from which they received such information. Next, they were asked to check all organizations to which they were most likely to send information (in either the same or a different subfield). A union of the sender network and the transposed receiver network was formed to construct a square, nonsymmetric binary adjacency matrix for each nation. This matrix corresponds to a directed graph, meaning that a communication from organization *i* to organization *j* may be unreciprocated. A matrix entry of 1 indicates that the "row" organization reportedly sends policy information to the "column" organization; a 0 indicates no such directed communication.

Similar procedures were used to measure the domain *support network*. Previous policy domain projects encountered great difficulty in obtaining accurate data on organizations' financial transactions, either because informants did not know the sizes of their contributions or refused to say (Laumann and Knoke, 1987: 193). As an alternative resource measure, we asked informants about receiving public political support:

> Often an organization needs to explain to the public its reasons for a political decision. In these cases, having political support from other organizations can be very important. From which organizations . . . did [your organization] receive such public support in the past?

Square asymmetric binary adjacency matrices were created, in which a "1" entry indicates a row organization reported receiving support from a column organization.

To ascertain *organizational reputation*, we showed informants "a list of organizations that are very active in the national labor policy domain. Please check those organizations that stand out as *especially influential*." No restrictions were placed on the number of choices an informant could make. We measured organizations' reputations by totaling the number of mentions each received from the informants (these are indegrees, the column totals in the general reputational matrix).

Finally, informants were given a list with short descriptions of bills submitted to their national legislatures during the 1980s (25 bills in the U.S., 32 in Germany, 22 in Japan; see Appendix 4). For each event about which an organization expressed interest, a point was given for each of six types of influence activities: (1) participated in formulating the bill; (2) formal contacts with government officials "such as testifying at hearings, serving on commissions"; (3) informal contacts with government officials or nongovernmental organizations; (4) used mass media to publicize the organization's opinion; (5) mobilized members of the organization or the general public to influence the public authorities; and (6) formed coalitions (action sets) to work with other groups. In this chapter we examine only the total involvement of an organization across all events, without distinguishing different patterns of participation among specific events. We defer until Chapter 6 the historical description of each nation's policy-making decisions, with special emphasis on legislative events, as well as the analyses of each event's action sets.

NETWORK RELATIONSHIPS

Table 5.1 displays some basic properties of the two networks. The density of the Japanese communication network (percentage of possible ties) is much lower than that of the German and American networks. (The 38.8% density in the U.S. labor domain is even higher than the 30% densities found in both the U.S. national en-

Table 5.1. *Properties of communication and support networks*

	COMMUNICATION U.S.	Germany	Japan	SUPPORT U.S.	Germany	Japan
WHOLE NETWORK CHARACTERISTICS:						
Density (%)	38.8	28.5	17.0	4.1	4.5	4.9
Connectivity (%)	100.0	100.0	100.0	43.1	52.9	55.3
Path Lengths (%)						
1 (direct)	38.8	28.5	17.0	4.1	4.5	4.9
2	61.2	69.6	79.5	8.7	14.4	17.6
3	.04	.02	3.5	10.8	20.6	19.9
4	-	-	-	10.2	9.9	12.2
5	-	-	-	6.3	2.8	.7
6	-	-	-	1.9	.6	.01
7	-	-	-	.2	.1	-
8	-	-	-	-	.01	-
∞ (no connection)	0.0	0.0	0.0	57.9	47.1	44.7
Dyads (N)	13,572	15,750	14,762	13,572	15,750	14,762
EGO-CENTRIC CHARACTERISTICS:						
Ego-Network Size (N)	54.4	44.1	26.7	9.0	10.3	10.7
Indegrees (N)	45.0	35.6	20.6	4.8	5.7	5.9
Reciprocity (%)	78.3	74.0	73.0	6.0	12.1	11.8
Local density (%)	54.7	52.0	50.0	25.9	22.6	39.4
Organizations (N)	117	126	122	117	126	122

ergy and health domains in the 1970s [Laumann and Knoke, 1987: 217].) This finding seems to contradict the hypothesis that Japan is the network society par excellence. However, all organizations in the three communication networks are fully connected (reachable), with most pairs (dyads) connected through direct or two-step paths. At the actor level of analysis, the mean ego-centric network sizes (total number of unique contacts), indegrees (number of relations received), reciprocity (percentage of mutual dyadic ties), and local density (percentage of ties present within the ego network) all attain their highest values in the U.S. and lowest in Japan, with Germany intermediate, again contrary to expectations. The U.S. evidently displays the most diffuse communication structure, whereas Japan's is more tightly focused, suggesting the targeting of connections consistent with corporatist arrangements.

The political support network presents a much different picture. As expected, the support densities are all sparser than the communication densities, with fewer than five percent of possible ties occurring in each nation. Many dyads (45–58%)

are unreachable by paths of any length, but the Japanese support network exhibits slightly more connectivity than either the German or American networks, consistent with the anticipated ordering. Japan also has the highest means on ego-net size, indegree, and local density (however, only the latter difference is substantial). The U.S. has the smallest values on these indices and on ego-network reciprocity, generally supporting our expectations. Thus, the Japanese labor domain seems to place relatively greater emphasis on its political support network, in contrast to the comparatively stronger attention to the communication network by the two Western nations. This contrast may be due to the stronger institutionalization of Japan's one-party dominant system at the time (with an enduring governing party, LDP, vs. an enduring opposition party, the JSP-GCU [*Sohyo*] bloc). This system encouraged a targeting of connections as well as a strengthening of support connections. This differential importance of the two networks shows up in their effects on organizational reputations and event activities.

To identify labor policy domain organizations' locations in the three communication networks, path distance matrices were computed and submitted to the ALSCAL multidimensional scaling and plotting program. Very acceptable stress coefficients were obtained for two-dimensional solutions in each nation. As in Chapter 4, Figures 5.2 to 5.4 label a half dozen peak union, business, and political organizations with capitalized mnemonics and indicate the remaining organizations by single lower-case letters symbolizing their types. These path distance diagrams' centers are densely filled by organizations having short path distances to the others (i.e., many direct connections), whereas the peripheral regions contain large numbers of organizations whose ties to others are much weaker (i.e., many two- or three-step paths). As hypothesized, the peak organizations in each nation are located close to the communication space centers. Such locations minimize not only the communication distances among these core actors but also their distances to the organizations at the network peripheries. Despite their opposing positions on almost all labor policies, the peak labor and business organizations maintain short (direct) communication linkages to one another, the better to comprehend their opponents' endeavors. The U.S. and German peak organizations lie especially close to the communication network centers, whereas the peak Japanese organizations are considerably more spread out, contrary to our expectation.

Distinct sectors in each communication space are occupied predominantly by specialized private-sector organizations, as hypothesized. Both the U.S. and Japanese domains exhibit sharply demarcated regions, implying that similar types of organizations are more prone to exchange information among themselves. The lower right sector of the U.S. space (Figure 5.2) is occupied predominantly by labor unions, the lower left by interest groups, and the upper sector by business associations. Federal labor agencies are scattered throughout the space, but are close to the center. The Japanese regions are likewise strongly segregated (Figure 5.4): Business associations appear in the left sector, unions are in the lower sector, and the upper-right sector contains most of the governmental agencies and interest groups. The closer clustering of both business and labor in separate sectors implies

Figure 5.2. *Spatial distances for communication among U.S. organizations: two-dimensional ALSCAL analysis of path distances (stress = .142)*

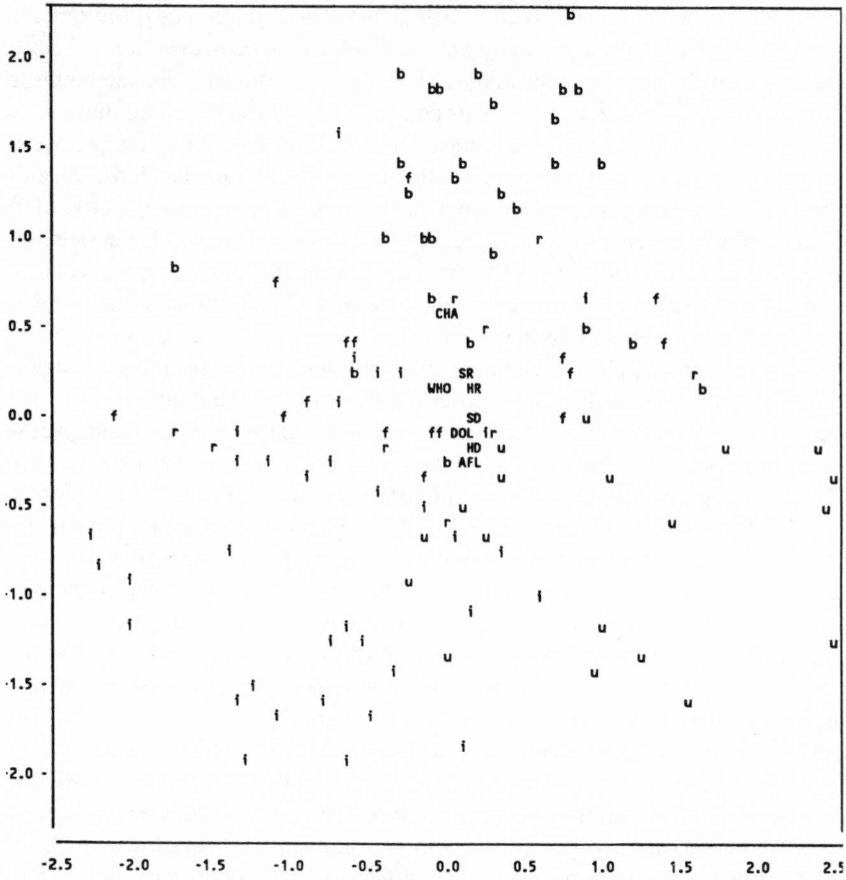

Note: u = Labor unions; b = business associations; i = interest groups; r = professional societies; f = federal agencies; See Appendix 2 for List of Mnemonics

that they communicate extensively among themselves, and not as frequently with outsiders. The greater distance from their respective peak federations indicates that, more than in the U.S., these peak organizations do much of the communicating in the central circle to which the ordinary members are not privy.

In contrast, the cleavages within the German communication space are less clearcut than in either the U.S. or Japan. Although the upper-right sector in Figure 5.3 is occupied mainly by interest groups and professional societies, the remaining peripheral areas contain mixtures of unions, business associations, and state governments (*Länder*). This interlarding of German labor and business organizations implies much smaller social distances between these traditional antagonists than in either the U.S. or Japan. Although both the U.S. and Japan exhibit clearly

Figure 5.3. *Spatial distances for communication among German organizations: two-dimensional ALSCAL analysis of path distances (stress = .138)*

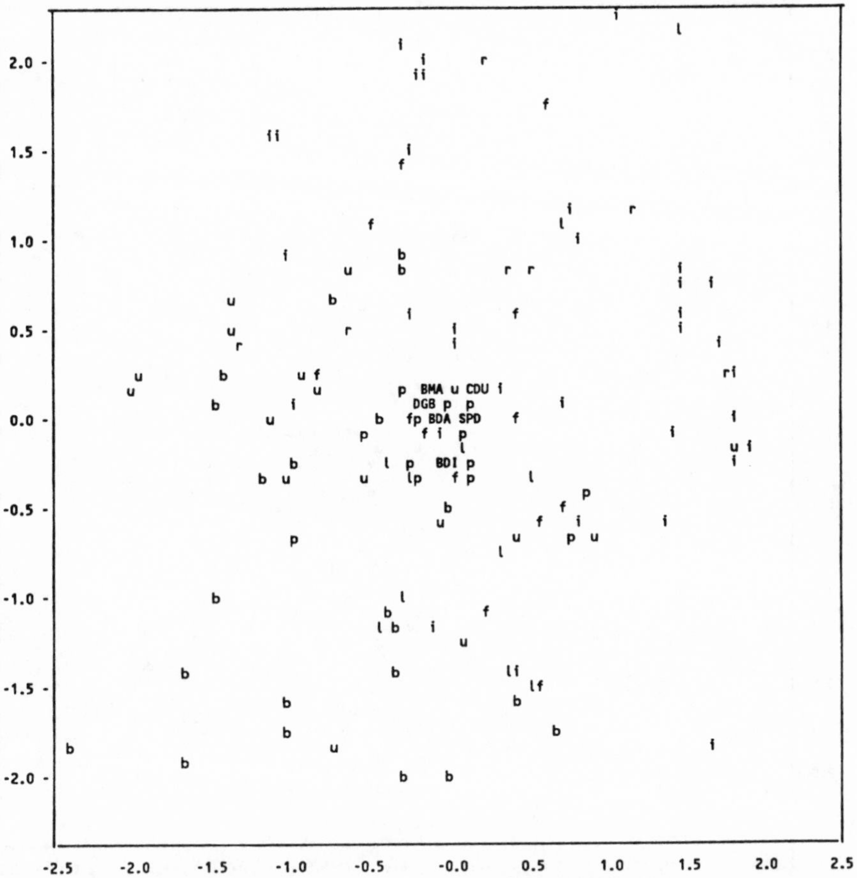

Note: u = Labor unions; b = business associations; i = interest groups; r = professional; f = federal agencies; l = state governments (Länder); p = parties; See Appendix 2 for List of Mnemonics

segregated sectors, the higher density of the U.S. communication network suggests that American organizations may be better connected to other regions than are the Japanese organizations. The sharp segregation of organizational types in Japan is again consistent with a more corporatist communication structure.

To identify structurally equivalent positions in the three support networks, we computed matrices of Euclidean social distances among all pairs of organizations, using the computer program STRUCTURE (Burt, 1989), which were then subjected to multidimensional scaling. For the U.S. and Japan, very acceptable stress coefficients were obtained for two-dimensional solutions, but the German coefficient was much higher (.213), so a three-dimensional solution was estimated (stress = .161). This number suggests that German society is differentiated along more dimensions

Figure 5.4. *Spatial distances for communication among Japanese organizations: two-dimensional ALSCAL analysis of path distances (stress = .134)*

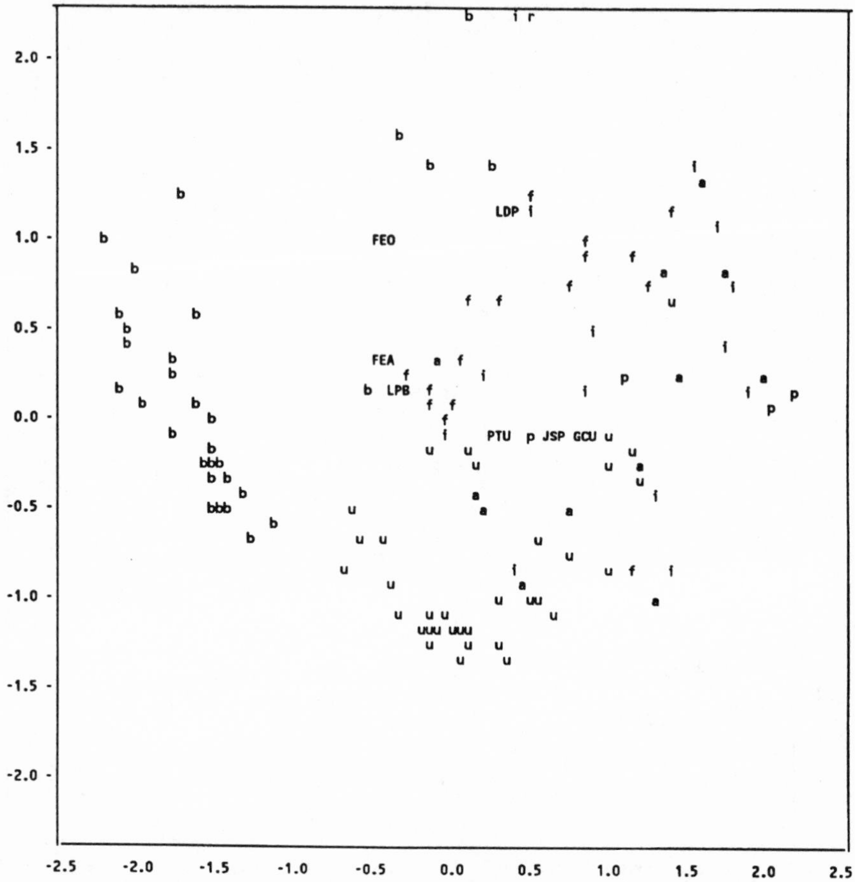

Note: u = Labor unions; b = business associations; i = interest groups; r = professional; f = federal agencies; a = advisory bodies; p = parties; See Appendix 2 for List of Mnemonics

than is society in the U.S. or in Japan, comprising more complex bases of political alliances. (Figure 5.6 plots only the first two dimensions from this solution.)

These global patterns contrast markedly with those of the communication networks.[4] Although densely populated centers appear in all three diagrams, their occupants are not peak organizations but are primarily the isolates who neither give political support to nor receive it from other organizations. Instead, the peak labor, business, and political organizations that are the primary support providers are lo-

4. To improve diagram legibility, extreme outliers were moved into the edge of the graph by changing all very large coordinate values to ± 3.00. These modification affected no more than five organizations in any figure.

Figure 5.5. *Spatial distances for resources among U.S. organizations: two-dimensional ALSCAL analysis of Euclidean distances (stress = .156)*

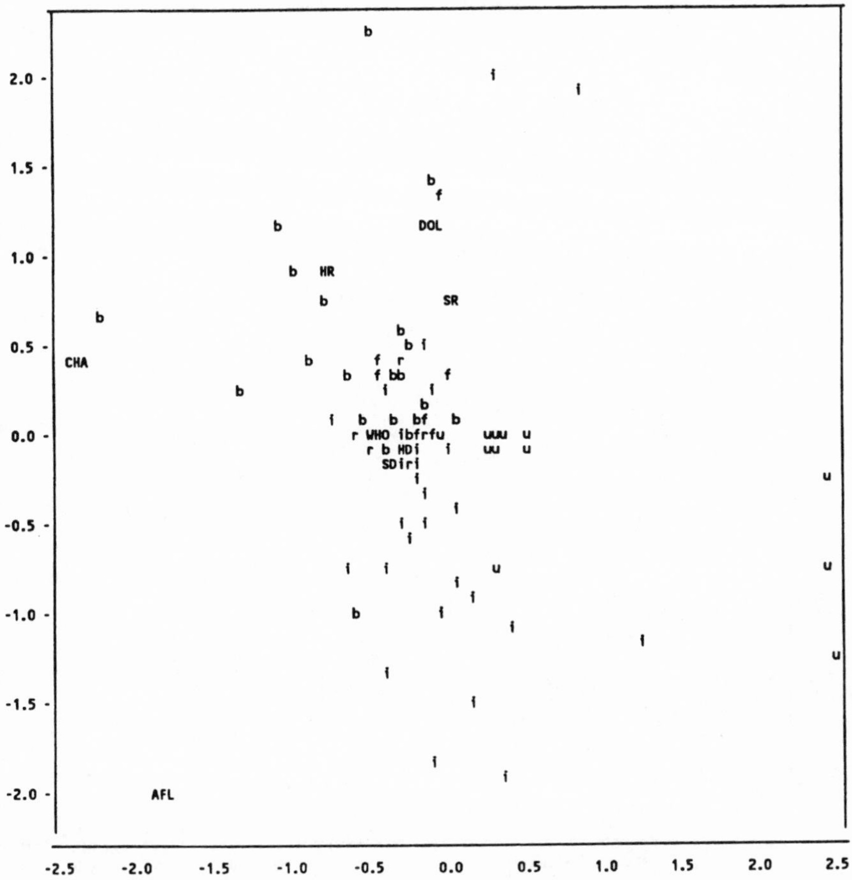

Note: u = labor unions; b = business associations; i = interest groups; r = professional societies; f = federal agencies; See Appendix 2 for List of Mnemonics

cated in widely separated areas toward the peripheries. Thus, the U.S. Chamber of Commerce occupies the far left side of Figure 5.5, while the AFL-CIO appears at the bottom left. Similarly, the German Trade Union Federation (DGB) falls at the upper left of Figure 5.6, while the Confederation of German Employers Associations (BDA) and Federation of German Industry (BDI) are at the bottom. In Figure 5.7, the two main Japanese political parties are located on extreme opposite sides of the support space: the conservative Liberal Democratic Party (LDP) at the upper left and the Japan Socialist Party (JSP) at the lower right. The two major employer associations – the Federation of Economic Organizations (FEO) and Federation of Employers Associations (FEA) – are pulled toward the LDP and the

Figure 5.6. *Spatial distances for resources among German organizations: three dimensional ALSCAL analysis of Euclidean distances (stress = .161)*

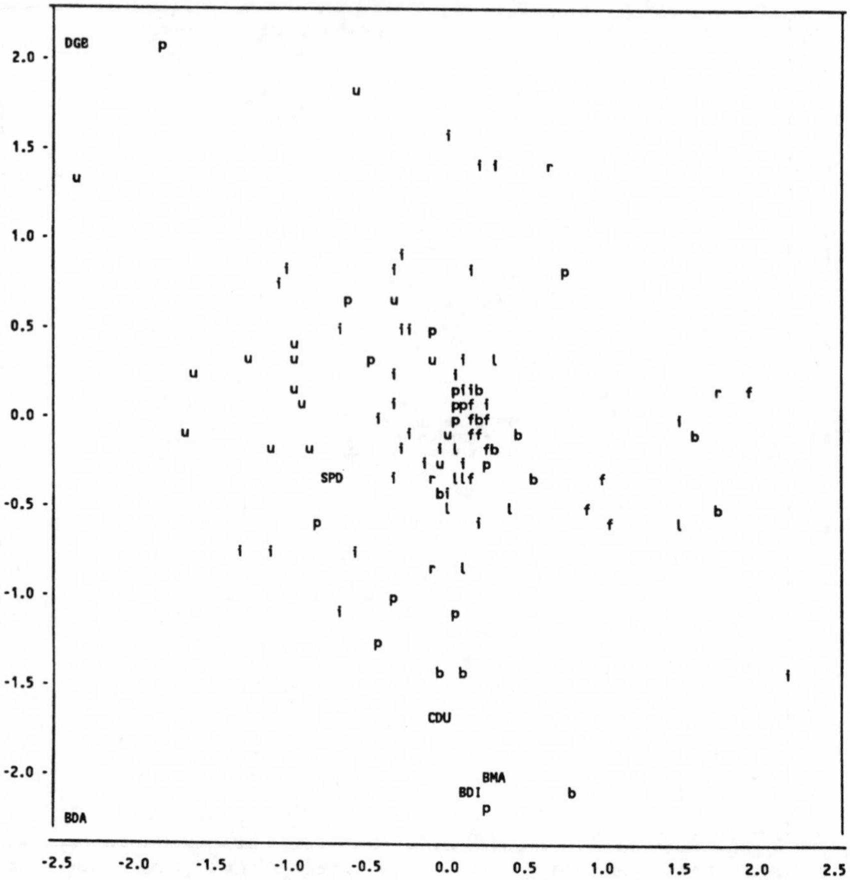

Note: u = labor unions; b = business associations; i = interest groups; r = professional; f = federal agencies; l = state governments (Länder); p = parties; See Appendix 2 for List of Mnemonics

Ministry of Labor's Labor Policy Bureau (LPB) whereas the two major labor unions – the General Council of Trade Unions (GCU) and Private Sector Trade Union Confederation (PTU) – are attracted toward the JSP.

The three nations' support patterns arise because support seekers target distinct sources. The peak business associations, labor unions, and parties extend political assistance only to those domain actors who share their policy preferences. No business organizations ever support labor unions, nor do the central labor federations provide political sustenance to employer associations. Parties succor only their distinct constituencies, and interest groups receive support only from those providers with whom they share policy objectives. Thus, in contrast to communication, the support network is fragmented among disjointed segments of unique

Figure 5.7. *Spatial distances for resources among Japanese organizations: two-dimensional ALSCAL analysis of Euclidean distances (stress = .117)*

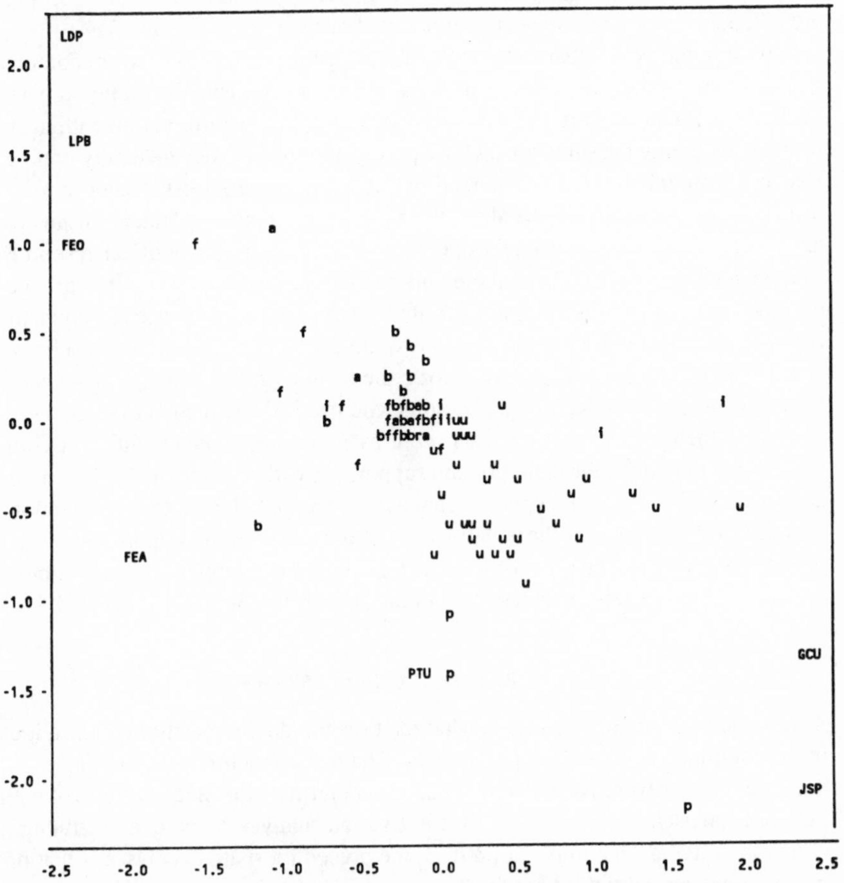

Note: u = labor unions; b = business associations; i = interest groups; r = professional; f = federal agencies; a = advisory bodies; p = parties; See Appendix 2 for List of Mnemonics

providers and their claimants.

The major governmental ministries and political parties also occupy diverse sectors within each country's support network. In the U.S., the White House (WHO) and the Democratic congressional labor committees (HD and SD) are pushed into the center of Figure 5.5, because they, like many lesser organizations, are not major sources of political support. The Department of Labor (DOL) and the two Republican labor committees (HR and SR) fall farther from the center, but still distant from both the AFL-CIO and the Chamber of Commerce (CHA), suggesting their patronage of distinctive clienteles. Germany's ruling Christian Democratic Union (CDU) and the Ministry of Labor (BMA) are both close to the two peak employer associations (BDI and BDA) in Figure 5.6, whereas the opposition Social Democratic Party (SPD) is pulled more toward the peak labor federation (DGB). As major support providers, the Japanese political parties, JSP and LDP, as well as the Ministry of Labor (LPB), occupy polarized locations in Figure 5.7, adjacent to their respective union and business constituents.

Although the peak organizations' locations in Figure 5.5 to 5.7 seem contrary to expectations, their occupancy of disparate regions reflects the highly targeted nature of political support. Organizations exchange policy information with many sources, including organizations whose policy preferences they generally oppose. Hence, communication is widespread because key players readily choose to inform other key domain players about their arguments, plans, and intentions in policy fights. But supporting one's opponents with sustaining political resources follows a different logic. Giving aid and comfort to an enemy is counterproductive and simply untenable. Consistent with the structural equivalence principle, the major suppliers of public support occupy quite distinct locations in that exchange space. These peak support providers form the focal points of demands and claims from specialized supplicant organizations who need public recognition and legitimation of their policy efforts. Thus, in contrast to the single center within the communication networks, the labor domain support networks contain multiple centers, each occupied by its distinct peak organizations that pull dependent organizations into their orbits. None of these national configurations offer support for our expectations that peak labor, business, and governmental organizations are more prevalent in the Japanese centers than in the centers for Germany and the U.S.

STRUCTURAL EQUATION ESTIMATES

A basic question in this chapter is what relationship do organizations' centralities in the communication and support networks have with their reputations and event activities? To answer this question, we seek to determine the unique effects of both networks on each outcome, using the multivariate analysis technique of structural equation systems. One implication from the preceding spatial analyses is that organizational centralities within the two networks should be measured by contrasting methods.

For the structural equation model in Figure 5.1, the centrality measure for the communication network is based on betweenness, whereas the centrality measure for the support network is based on prominence. *Betweenness* measures the number of times an organization occurs on a geodesic, that is, the shortest path distance between two organizations in the system (Freeman, 1977, 1979). Thus, the higher an organization's betweenness score, the greater its potential for mediating or disrupting policy communication. Betweenness scores for each organization in the communication matrix were calculated using the UCINET program (Borgatti, Everett, and Freeman, 1992). A betweenness centralization measure also exists for the network as a whole. The Japanese communication network is far more centralized (23.8%) than either Germany's (5.1%) or the U.S.'s (2.6%), consistent with expectations. Despite its much lower communication network density, once the centralized pattern of the ties is taken into account, Japan is revealed as the strongest "integrated network" polity among the three nations. That is, the Japanese peak associations and governmental organizations are the specific targets of narrowly focused communication, whereas communication is far more diffusely broadcast in Germany and the U.S..

Prominence (also called "power" or "prestige") measures the extent to which an organization provides support within the network (Bonacich, 1987; Knoke and Burt, 1983). The more support an organization gives to others, the higher its prominence. Prominence scores for each organization in the support matrix were calculated using the STRUCTURE program (Burt, 1989).[5] The organization with the highest prominence within each nation's support network is used as the numeraire for setting the scale of relative prominence (i.e., its prominence score is set equal to 1.0). These most-prominent organizations are the AFL-CIO in the U.S., the German Labor Union Federation (DGB), and the Japan Socialist Party (JSP). (Only in Japan did the opposition party, not the peak labor federation, rank as most prominent. This contrast is consistent with conventional impressions that the Japan Socialist Party has a much stronger dependence on labor unions than do the socialist parties of other advanced, capitalist, industrial democracies [Ishida, 1961: 80–4].)

The two network centrality measures exhibit only marginally significant covariation in the U.S. and Japan (r = .23 and .22, respectively), and moderate covariation in Germany (r = .36). These patterns offer meager support for the hypothesis that the more central organizations in the communication network are also more central in the support network. Rather, organizational locations within each network appear to reflect unrelated processes.

Structural equations for the causal model were estimated using LISREL (Jöreskog and Sörbom, 1989). In these specifications, the effects of the exogenous variables (LISREL gammas) were not constrained to equality across nations, but the effects among the endogenous measures (LISREL betas) were tested for equality among every pair. Only those parameters that did not differ significantly across nations were constrained to equality in the final estimates reported here. The model for organizational reputations produced an excellent fit ($x^2 = 3.60$, $df = 3$, goodness of fit index = 1.000), and the model for event activities was almost as good ($x^2 = 5.87$, $df = 4$, goodness of fit index = .998). Because we did not offer explicit hypotheses about the effects of the seven exogenous variables, we do not display their coefficients.

The parameters of greatest substantive interest are the effects among the three endogenous variables, corresponding to the paths at the right side of Figure 5.1 (communication, support, and either reputation or activity). Figure 5.8 displays the common metric values for the completely standardized solutions (i.e., path coefficients), which permit comparisons of variables measured on different scales. For the organizational reputation model, these three effects are identical for the U.S.

5. Because calculating aggregate prominence scores for a nonsymmetric matrix involves finding the left-hand eigenvector, a unique solution is possible only up to a scalar.

Figure 5.8. *Standardized path coefficients among networks, reputations, and event activities (Other exogenous effects not shown)*

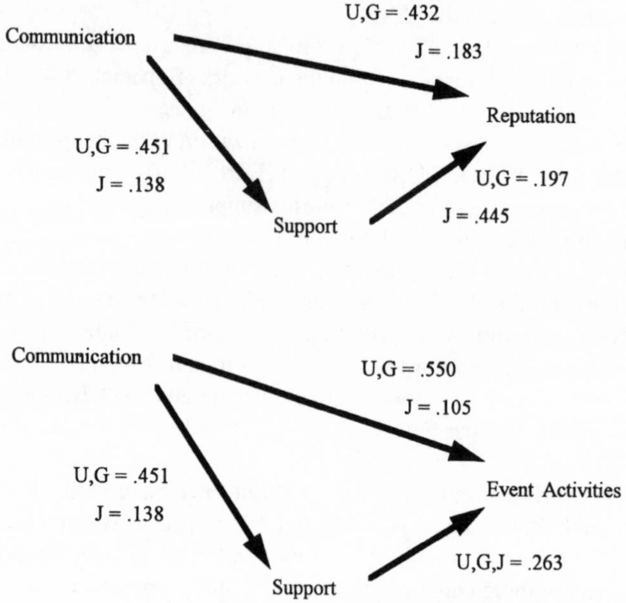

and Germany, whereas those for Japan are completely different (top of Figure 5.8). The direct effect of communication centrality on support centrality is more than three times as large in the U.S. and Germany as in Japan (.451 vs. .138). These two networks exert contrasting impacts on organizational reputations. In the U.S. and Germany, the direct effect of communication (.432) is more than twice as large as the support effect (.197). The pattern for Japan is almost exactly the reverse: The support effect (.445) is more than twice the communication effect (.183). This unique result can be interpreted as reflecting a "twist" in Japanese labor unions in the 1980s. As discussed in Chapter 2, on the one hand the private labor unions led by the PTU and *Rengo* strengthened their ties to the LDP, the economic federations, and other major interest groups. But until the formation of *Rengo* in 1987, or at the very latest, *Rengo's* absorption of the GCU (*Sohyo*) in 1989, the Japanese labor movement was represented by the GCU. The GCU had a stronger tie to the JSP, especially through support networks. This twist may mean that, despite their high communication levels, the private unions' reputations were much lower than those of the public-sector unions.

The indirect effects of communication on reputation through support are small and roughly the same for all three nations (.089 in the U.S. and Germany, .061 in Japan). Comparing the causal models for event activities across nations reveals the same basic patterns (bottom of Figure 5.8). The direct effect of communication on activity is more than twice as large as the effect of support in the U.S. and Germany (.550 vs. .263). And the Japanese pattern again is exactly the opposite, with the support path over twice as large as the communication path (.263 vs. .105). In this model, the small indirect effects of communication on event activity through support are somewhat stronger in the U.S. and Germany (.112) than in Japan (.036).

In sum, the two structural equation models show that, controlling for antecedent attributes, the more central an organization's locations in both the communication and the support networks, the higher its reputation for public policy influence and the greater its public policy event activities. Because all endogenous path values could be constrained statistically to equality between the U.S. and Germany, we found partial support for the expectation that the causal relationships are identical across those two nations. However, the unique and contrasting path coefficients for Japan also partially supported an alternative hypothesis, that network centrality effects on organizational reputations and activities are highest in Japan. More precisely, political support comprises the most critical network in Japan, whereas communication is much more determinative for the two Western nations.

CONCLUSION

Our analyses provide some answers to questions about the linkages among network structures, organizational reputations, and policy event activities. Unlike Heinz et al. (1990, 1993), we found no evidence of empty centers ("hollow cores") in these elite networks. In all three domains, the communication and support exchange spatial structures had clearly identifiable regions occupied by the peak business, labor, and political organizations. However, the spatial locations of these peak actors varied markedly across the two types of networks, presumably reflecting dissimilar interactor social distance processes. In each nation, all the peak organizations jointly occupied a single center in the communication space, with the secondary actors pushed into specialized sectors on the peripheries. But in the political support space, the major support-providing organizations occupied distinct and distant positions, adjacent to their specific claimant organizations. We attribute these divergent social organizational patterns across networks to a common dependency of all actors on informative policy discussions regardless of their sources' policy preferences, but an extreme (and obviously rational) unwillingness to provide sustaining resources that could help opponents to win policy fights. These divergent functions of communication and support resources offer compelling evidence for maintaining conceptual distinctions among networks and for measuring interorganizational relations with different techniques – specifically, by graph-theoretic and structural equivalence methods.

The causal model estimates of the two networks' effects on organizational reputations and legislative event activities disclosed remarkably consistent effects among these endogenous variables. Centrality in the communication network is modestly related to centrality in the support network, more strongly in the U.S. and in Germany than in Japan. Communication centrality more strongly affects reputations and activities than does support centrality in the U.S. and Germany. The Japanese pattern is exactly the opposite – political support centrality is far more important than communication centrality in explaining Japanese labor domain organizations' reputations and activities. The greater centralization of support in Japan implies that the relationship comprises the key political network. The virtual identity of the U.S. and Germany suggests an underlying similarity within these two Western polities, whereas Japan's markedly different pattern implies the durability of unique historical experiences and institutional arrangements. We touched on these contrasts in our analysis of the Japanese "twist," or lack of key actors in communication activities and political support activities, and the impact of stronger institutionalization support networks during the long one-party dominant system. Thus, we find evidence consistent with both the institutional homogenization (for the U.S. and Germany) and the persistent difference perspectives (for Japan) on comparative political systems, at least at the level of national policy domains. Because our data captured social organization in a relatively brief period, spanning less than a decade, we cannot determine whether, since the end of World War II, the U.S. and German networks converged from disparate antecedents, nor whether the Japanese networks exhibit any propensity toward or away from the Western pattern.

Our results carry important implications for the larger state – civil society debate and particularly the organizational state approach. Fundamentally, we find the boundary between state and society blurred in all three polities. In each labor policy domain the peak private-sector organizations were located at the core of the communication exchange network, enjoyed high organizational reputations, and engaged in extensive policy event activities. Although final legal authority over public policies is clearly vested in the legislative, judicial, executive, and regulatory agencies of the state, our analyses underscore the folly of treating these organizations in isolation from the larger pressure-group system forming their political environment. Substantial interpenetrations between state and civil society occur both through formalized activities, such as consultation and advising, and through pervasive informal channels that comprise the lobbying game. However, variations on this theme are evident across states, with the U.S. the most pluralistic and Japan the least.

Collectively, the interorganizational communication and support relations constitute the political networks that our crude network measures can only begin to adumbrate. The pivotal role of network dynamics in the organizational state explanation of policy-making augurs well for continuing to develop this analytic framework. Communication and support relations in these systems of cooperative and competitive actors substantially shape both reputations and behaviors in similar fashion. The next chapter probes in greater detail into the organizations' participation in legislative policy events.

6

Fighting collectively: action sets and events

We continue to investigate labor policy domain events, turning to the social structure of organizations' interests and their participation in specific legislative bills debated during the 1980s in the Congress, *Bundestag*, and Diet. After briefly reviewing the major policies that arose in each legislature, we examine the advocacy circles and action sets that formed around each event. The results set the stage for further inquiries into the dynamics of collective decision making on legislative events in Chapter 7.

LEGISLATIVE EVENTS OF THE 1980s

Because business interests dominated policy-making during the Reagan, Kohl, and Nakasone governments, legislation favoring labor and minority group interests had a difficult time reaching the national agendas. In the U.S., despite decades of divided presidential and congressional government, Republican control of the Senate in Reagan's first six years thwarted any serious effort by organized labor and its allies to push for progressive social legislation. In Germany and Japan, where the parliamentary form of government assured a basic unity between executive and legislative branches (see Appendix 1), no major challenge to conservative interests could arise. Consequently, labor politics of the 1980s was a matter of negative changes rather than major upheavals from the labor side. In some cases, conservative political actors took the offensive along with business against labor, justifying their attacks by neoliberal ideologies of "administrative reform" or deregulation. They further justified this offensive by the need to respond to globalization, trade liberalization, and the information society. The following subsections summarize the major legislative initiatives; thumbnail chronologies of the specific legislative proposals analyzed in this chapter appear in Appendix 4.

The United States

A 1980 electoral tidal wave swept out Jimmy Carter, turning the presidency over to an ideologically committed right-winger backed by a 53–47 Republican margin in the Senate. Labor policy was "not a top priority for Ronald Reagan," according to a White House policy aide (personal communication, June 1988). "We had no agenda to expand or modify labor law; there was no consensus to do things differently." A Republican staffer on the House Education and Labor Committee commented, "There was a vacuum in the labor field, especially in the Senate under [then-chair Senator Orin] Hatch. Nothing for organized labor could move because of the stalemate." Just after Reagan took office, the federal air traffic controllers' union (PATCO) went on strike over the controllers' stressful working conditions and low pay. Reagan responded by immediately firing all the strikers, banning the union, and replacing the fired controllers with nonunionized workers, thus setting the tenor of labor-business conflict and distrust throughout the 1980s. With the president's primary attention focused on cutting income taxes on the wealthy and on expanding defense spending, no major labor legislation initiatives were likely to come, either from the Department of Labor or from the Congress. Because the Republican majority of the Senate Labor and Human Resources Committee could bottle up any Democratic proposals, "Sometimes you win simply by not losing," as the presidential aide explained.

Most of the low-key labor policy action that did occur early in the decade was focused on tidying up loose ends. With the Social Security system facing a deficit by 1983, a presidential commission recommended the biggest overhaul in the system's funding since the program began in 1937. Payroll taxes were raised, cost-of-living increases were delayed for six months, and taxes were imposed on high-income recipients. In 1986 the mandatory retirement age of 70 years was abolished for all workers except police, firefighters, and college professors. Several modifications were attempted in the sweeping Employment Retirement Income Security Act (ERISA), which had been passed in 1974 under President Nixon. Although this law did not require employers to provide pension plans, it set minimum vesting standards for those who did, excluding credit for workers who were under 25 years old, or who had less than 10 years continuous work, or the spouses of workers who died before retirement. Hearings were held on such matters as coverage of public employees, civil suits about wrongfully denied benefits, and penalties for pension plan abuse by labor union officials. However, only two major regulatory changes were implemented. In the 1984 presidential election year, a rare coalition of the Reagan Administration and women's rights groups pushed through relaxed vesting standards that made it easier for women to qualify for pensions with less continuous service, starting at age 18, and to receive some benefits if a deceased spouse were vested. In 1987, after the collapse of the U.S. steel industry threatened the Pension Benefit Guarantee Corporation's ability to insure bankrupted private pension funds, the White House and Congress agreed to raise premiums and tighten default standards in order to place the bailout organization on a tighter fiscal footing.

Another bipartisan reform effort was the restructuring of federal job-training programs. The troubled Comprehensive Employment Training Act (CETA), which had once subsidized more than 700,000 local government jobs for low-income persons, was replaced just before the 1982 elections by a training-only program.

The Job Training Partnership Act (JTPA), the major legislative effort of Senators Ted Kennedy and Dan Quayle (who later became George Bush's vice president), restricted support services beyond direct job training and gave primary control to state governments with a greatly expanded role for private businesses in operating local programs. The Reagan Administration staunchly opposed job creation bills, even during its early term in the depths of the worst post – World War II recession. The Republican-controlled Senate successfully blocked three House Democratic efforts to revive Depression-era public works programs for youths and dislocated workers. Once the recession was over, special long-term unemployment compensation was also terminated.

Labor's prospects brightened when the 1986 elections gave the Democrats a 55–45 majority in the Senate, breaking the congressional stalemate. Senator Kennedy took over as chair of the Senate Labor, Welfare, and Education Committee, bringing to the committee a much more activist agenda than his predecessor. He collaborated with labor, women's, and minority group organizations to craft a set of proposals "based on decent jobs for every worker and decent workers for every job," according to his staff director (personal communication, June 1988). This agenda went beyond conventional labor issues to encompass family matters that were preliminary to labor force entry. One component started with children, including prenatal care, immunization, child care, and basic education; other components embraced medical care, job training, and minimum wages for their parents.

During the 100th Congress (1987–8), several of these bills began emerging from both chambers' committees, despite certain opposition from the White House and from the business community spearheaded by the U.S. Chamber of Commerce and the National Association of Manufacturers. An occupational identification and notification bill proposed a Risk Assessment Board within the Health and Human Services Department to warn employees about exposure to dangerous substances in their workplaces. The Reagan Administration opposed the bill on the grounds that its procedures were unworkable, would be expensive to enforce, would be subject to a slew of lawsuits, and were duplicative of warning mechanisms existing in the Occupational Safety and Health Administration (OSHA). Although the House passed its version in 1987, the Senate debate bogged down in fights over parliamentary procedure. Still unable after four attempts to obtain the 60 votes necessary to limit debate (cloture), the Senate majority leader abruptly pulled the bill from the floor in March 1988. It was never resubmitted.

Two other major partisan fights also broke out during the 1988 election season, resulting in much posturing by both parties. The House and Senate passed an omnibus trade bill that included pro-labor provisions requiring companies with more than 100 employees to give at least 60 days notice before closing a plant or laying off at least one-third of its work force. Opposed by business groups on the grounds that it was anticompetitive and would discourage new-firm creation, it was vetoed by President Reagan in May 1988, despite strong public opinion favoring some form of worker protection. The plant-closing provisions were then put into a separate bill, and enough Republicans joined the Democrats to create veto-proof majorities in both chambers. Reagan allowed the bill to become law without his signature, allegedly to put an end to "political shenanigans" on the issue. However, Republicans were more successful in blocking the Family and Medical Leave Act of 1986, which was supported by labor, women's rights, and health organizations. It would have required employers to give unpaid time off to employees who were parents of newborn babies or who had serious family medical problems. The Reagan Administration supported business objections that mandated leaves would give companies little individual flexibility. Passage of a scaled-down version of the bill was delayed until 1989, at which time President Bush's veto was sustained in the House. Not until Bill Clinton assumed the presidency in 1993 was family leave finally implemented.

Labor was more successful on two bills late in the Reagan Administration. Bipartisan support assured a 1988 ban on the use of polygraph (lie-detector) tests as a condition of private-sector employment, exempting only government agencies and firms that dealt in security services, national security, and controlled drugs or where employers had a "reasonable suspicion" of a worker's involvement in a crime against the company. Greater controversy surrounded the effort to increase the minimum wage, which had been stuck at $3.35 per hour since 1981, despite substantial inflation during the decade. The labor-Democrat coalition pushed for a jump to $4.55, phased in over three years. Citing studies predicting that higher minimum wages would eliminate many small business jobs, the Reagan Administration steadfastly opposed any change. Instead, it campaigned unsuccessfully for a sub-minimum, or "training wage," that would allow a lower starting wage for teenagers. The impasse ended only in 1989, when, following an earlier veto, President Bush agreed to a compromise that boosted the minimum wage to $4.25 per hour over the next two years, in exchange for providing a lower three-month training wage for new employees between the ages of 16 and 19 years, with expanded earned-income tax credit.

In conclusion, the U.S. labor legislation of the 1980s revolved around three basic questions: How generous a social-welfare safety net should be erected for labor force participants – social security, pension equity, bankruptcy bail-outs, and child care? How extensively should the government modify the labor market through job-training programs, vocational education, immigration controls, job creation, and wage standards? And how intrusively should the government regulate workplace practices such as health risks, plant closings, union busting, and employee screening? Conspicuously absent from the legislative agenda throughout the Reagan era were efforts to deal with racial and sexual discrimination in the employment transaction. Although equal opportunity legislation had prohibited discrimination in 1963, the struggle over interpretation and enforcement continued (Burstein, 1985). However, by the 1980s the center of action had shifted from the legislature to the judiciary, where the Supreme Court decided several landmark cases involving hirings, promotions, pay equity, and layoffs. But, because we did not collect comparable data about the judicial arenas of Germany and Japan, we cannot investigate the role of litigation in shaping national labor policies.

Germany

In the fall of 1982, Helmut Kohl was elected as chancellor of the Federal Republic. His election came in the middle of the legislative period, which had begun when the Social-Liberal Coalition – consisting of the Social Democrats (SPD) and the Free Democrats (FDP) – won a big electoral victory. However, the two coalition partners could no longer agree on any basic principles of economic and labor policy. In Germany, as in the U.S., conservative, or neoliberal, ideas gained wider public acceptance during the 1980s, mainly under the influence of so-called strategy papers on a new economic and labor policy written by influential Christian Democratic and liberal politicians and by some academics. Graf Otto Lambsdorff, an FDP leader and minister of economics in the Social-Liberal Coalition, published one of the most influential papers on September 14, 1982. He proposed policies that finally could be implemented only by a coalition of the Christian Democratic Union/Christian Social Union (CDU/CSU) with the FDP. One could say that his strategy paper gave the final impetus to the FDP's switch of coalition partners, resulting in the formation of a Conservative-Liberal government headed by Kohl. The main thrust of Lambsdorff's paper was directed against such new Social Democratic reform projects as improved worker protection, shorter working hours, and stricter regulation of overtime work. His positive proposals can be characterized as neoliberal; for example, he advocated job-sharing models and more flexible implementation of protection laws for disadvantaged groups (Zachert, 1984: 177).

One year later, when the new coalition had already started to formulate bills believed to implement its ideas, Haimo George, chair of a working group on labor and social policy of the CDU/CSU parliamentary party, formulated some "Personal Initiatives" in support of deregulating German labor law. Responding to a request from Chancellor Kohl, the CDU/CSU prime minister of Lower Saxony published ten theses on policies to fight unemployment. During more than a decade of CDU/CSU – FDP coalition government, these ideas continued to play a role in discussions about the attractiveness of Germany for industrial capital investments. The arguments of neoliberal economists and the diagnoses of progressive social scientists normally go in opposite directions. On the one side, the main reasons for the high unemployment rate in Germany are seen in its high wages, especially the extra employer payments for the social security system; in the mandatory benefits that are paid to former employees in the case of plant closings; and in the generally rather rigid regulations of German labor law, which hinder a flexible response of enterprises to new economic conditions. On the other side, the advantages of the German system of codetermination are stressed. This system supposedly gives plants great internal flexibility when workers have to accept new positions to which the plant work council has agreed. In the U.S., by contrast, the work rules are much more rigid when they are built into collective bargaining agreements with unions. Thus, U.S. flexibility can be achieved only externally, via layoffs – that is, ultimately, through more flexible labor markets (Erd, 1989: 143–4, and the literature cited therein).

The Kohl government followed the neoliberals' policy recommendations. But in the early 1980s a balanced budget had highest priority. The major austerity measures built into the Budget Supplementary Law of 1984 (*Haushaltsbegleitgesetz*) only continued what the Social-Liberal government had begun. The high national deficit had been a main issue in the 1980 federal election campaign. One problem was that when unemployment increased, the government could no longer finance additional programs of the Labor Ministry's Federal Unemployment Agency to subsidize jobs and vocational training. Thus, the Schmidt government had already been forced to cut back these programs even though left-wing Social Democrats and unions opposed such austerity measures. Although the Kohl government was only continuing this policy, it did so with more decisiveness and greater consequences, because balancing the budget was its higher priority. Hence, the possibilities for an active labor market policy were heavily curtailed. The Federal Unemployment Agency is responsible for both unemployment benefits and an active labor market policy. When it must pay more in unemployment benefits due to a rise in the unemployment rate, it has less money with which to fight high unemployment through active labor market measures. These cross-purposes are seen as a major fault of this system (Webber, 1987: 74–85; Schmid, 1990: 250).

Although the unemployment rate remained rather high, the Kohl government's efforts to balance the budget were relatively successful, so deficit spending could essentially be reduced. Although conservative governments usually have fewer problems than social democratic ones in curtailing social benefits, the 1982 change in government was not a major turning point in German labor market policy. Compared to the U.S., Germany exhibits a relatively high consensus across party lines on the basic instruments of an active labor market policy (Schmid, 1990: 251). A recent corroboration of this thesis, which was originally meant to interpret the change in the governing coalition in the early 1980s, could be observed during the German reunification process, when the Kohl government began to use standard labor market policies to fight the negative consequences of introducing market economics into the former East Germany.

What was new in the Kohl government's labor market policy, as opposed to the policy of the Social-Liberal Coalition, was some deregulation of the rigid German labor laws. Kohl's argument was that more flexibility would bring higher employment rates. The most important law in this respect was the Employment Assistance Law of 1985 (*Beschäftigungsförderungsgesetz*), which, for example, made it easier to hire employees only for a certain period of time. Normally in Germany labor contracts are supposed to be without time restrictions, making employee layoffs very difficult. This interpretation is a guideline for most labor court rulings. Because of both this and mandatory social benefits for plant closings (introduced in the 1972 Works Constitution Law [*Betriebsverfassungsgesetz*]), management's discretionary power in labor relations is rather small. Neoliberal economists have interpreted this limitation as a "modernization tax" on business (Soltwedel and Bothe, 1990: 140).

The evaluation of deregulation policy in this area was very controversial. The governing parties and employers were convinced that a more flexible labor law would have a positive impact on the employment rate. Laws like the Employment Assistance Law were intended to weaken the highly protected position of German employees only in exceptional situations and then only temporarily, without having a major impact on the substance of labor protection laws (for this interpretation, see Wlotzke, 1985). The Social Democrats and the unions disagreed with this interpretation, doubting that these positive effects would really occur. They feared a neoliberal counterrevolution (Kastendiek and Kastendiek, 1987: 179), or at least a counterreformation, in German labor law (Zachert, 1984) that could touch the core of the labor law to the detriment of employees.

Even this clear conflict over deregulation did not hinder the collaboration in labor market policy between the Kohl government and its so-called social partners, that is, unions and employer organizations. Both participated in a meeting at Chancellor Kohl's invitation to reach an agreement on vocational education for the unemployed, publicly labeled a "qualification offensive" (*Qualifizierungsoffensive*). The CDU/CSU – FDP coalition parties tried to implement these policies quickly, initiating bills only three weeks after that meeting. These policies were included in the seventh amendment to the Work Assistance Law (*Arbeitsförderungsgesetz*) and brought improvements in vocational-training programs, such as subsidies to unemployed workers participating in these programs. Naturally this bill attracted a large majority, with private industry prominently supporting this active labor market policy. Employers favored these measures because they calculated that such programs could help to secure a high level of skilled workers in the near future. Some leftist groups argued that these programs were too heavily influenced by employers, who were not really interested in ameliorating the conditions of the truly disadvantaged, such as unskilled workers and unemployed women (Schmid, 1990: 250).

Overall, relations between the Kohl government and the unions remained rather tense throughout the first full legislative period (1983 to 1987). They disagreed on the austerity policy detrimental to social benefits, on deregulation policy, and on the best measures for fighting unemployment. The government wanted to fight unemployment by restricting the labor force with measures such as offering early retirement and inducing foreign workers to return voluntarily to their home countries. The Kohl government began its program as early as 1983: A law to promote voluntary emigration by foreign workers was enacted late in 1983, and special regulations for early retirement were enacted in the spring of 1984. The unions, foremost among them the Metal Workers' Union, argued that fewer weekly working hours would be the best remedy for high unemployment rates. However, not all member unions of the peak labor association, the German Trade Union Federation (DGB), agreed that a shorter work week would be the best solution. A movement to shorten the work week from 40 to 35 hours without cutting back wages began in 1984 when the Metal Workers' Union and the Union of Printers struck for this goal. They finally compromised with the employer organizations on an average 38.5-hour work week, although they had to accept greater flexibility at the plants, which were allowed to vary the work week in the range of 37 to 40 hours.

One consequence of this strike was a proposal to change a paragraph in the Work Assistance Law that allowed the unions a very flexible strike strategy. The Metal Workers' Union applied what it called the "mini-max strategy." Lean production within and multiple interdependencies between firms involved in the same production line enabled unions to go on strike with minimum effort. That is, they could strike in only a few central plants and still achieve a maximum impact because production would not be possible at any of the other plants connected to the central ones by their multiple interdependencies. Laid-off workers would be entitled to unemployment benefits from the Federal Unemployment Agency if they were employed in the same industrial branch but not in the same region as the union that had started the strike. One additional condition for unemployment benefits was that the unions in the other regions not demand exactly the same improvements as the unions in the region where the strike began (Webber, 1987). The president of the Federal Unemployment Agency was convinced that he could stop the payment of unemployment benefits to laid-off workers in the same industry in the other regions. He argued that the unions were using the unemployment agency to pay for the consequences of their strike. But courts in Bremen and Hesse ruled that the president was not allowed to stop those payments because the unions did not demand exactly the same improvements in all regions (Mückenberger, 1986: 174).

Employers interpreted these court rulings as one-sided privileges for the unions and contended that the state's neutrality in labor strikes was no longer in force. The political answer to this judicial interpretation was to change the controversial Paragraph 116 in the Work Assistance Act. The new paragraph would enforce the Federal Unemployment Agency's neutrality during strikes by explicitly forbidding the agency to remunerate laid-off workers if their plant had been indirectly affected by a strike in another region within the same industrial branch. The fight over amending Paragraph 116 grew rather heated in the fall and winter of 1985 and the spring of 1986. And the German public became involved because media coverage was broad and intense. The intense opposition to the amendment may have been stimulated by the fact that this fight did not seem hopeless from the start. The employees' caucus within the CDU/CSU parliamentary party seemed to reject the deterioration of the union position during strikes. Nevertheless, after the original proposal was corrected in some minor details, the CDU employees' caucus finally supported the bill. Following this amendment's enactment in early 1986, the controversy ended somewhat abruptly.

One consequence of the labor strife could be detected in the federal election of January 1987. The CDU/CSU lost voters, especially workers who returned to the Social Democratic Party, which they had left in the early 1980s (Pappi, 1990: 23–4). Still, the CDU/CSU – FDP coalition again won a parliamentary majority in the 1987 election. As is common practice in Germany, the coalition partners formally agreed on a set of policies that they wanted to implement in the upcoming legislative period. This special agreement contained no section on labor policy, but labor policies were embedded in the sections on economic, social, and labor market policies. The coalition partners wanted to continue their deregulation policy and agreed to establish an advisory council on the best measures to use to strengthen the international competitiveness of the German economy through more flexibility in German labor law. In this context, one plan was to mitigate regulations concerning store-closing hours and at least allow shops and offices to remain open to the public during one evening per week. The Free Democrats asked that a special representative of middle-management employees be included in plant work councils. The coalition agreed that work councils had to be informed when management planned to introduce new technologies, but they opposed giving the council a veto over the introduction. The very favorable position of the unions in the codetermination law concerning the coal, iron, and steel industries was maintained in the law enacted in 1988. Regarding labor market policy, improved support of certain target groups was to be reached mainly through amendments to the Work Assistance Law. The coalition partners also sought to evaluate the consequences of the Employment Assistance Law.

In conclusion, the second Kohl government, installed in 1987, continued the labor market policies begun when the CSU/CSU – FDP Conservative-Liberal coalition first came to power in 1982. It was successful in this respect because the federal government was supported by the state governments (*Länder*) in the Federal Chamber (*Bundesrat*), which was controlled by the state prime ministers from either the Christian Democratic Union or the Christian Social Union. Thus, the Kohl government enjoyed a double majority during this period, the necessary majority in the *Bundestag* and the very helpful additional majority in the Federal Chamber. However, the second legislative period saw much less labor policy controversy than did the first period. Highly controversial bills like those involving the austerity program, the budget, or the strike paragraph were missing. The austerity measures were so successful that the federal budget was almost balanced, and tax cuts seemed a strong possibility. The Kohl government thought that the available labor law instruments had a positive effect on the employment level even if the unions denied this (e.g., Adamy, 1988). Therefore, the sunset of the 1985 Employment Assistance Law was deferred to the end of 1995. The main conflict in Germany between the government and the opposition parties switched to the broad social policy domain, especially the health system, which lies outside our definition of the labor policy domain.

Japan

In the 1980s there were two underlying lines that determined labor policy legislation in Japan: administrative reform and structural adjustment. The latter smoothed the process of social transformation and reduced international friction. Both lines combined to transform labor policy as well as labor politics.

When in the general policy speech in the fall of 1980 the Suzuki cabinet declared administrative reform to be its primary policy goal few would have predicted its broad and deep impact on both policy and political structure. This reform adopted the slogan "Clearance of Post-war Policy and Politics in Japan" during the Nakasone cabinet (1982–7) and became very effective. At the beginning of his term, Prime Minister Zenko Suzuki was in a weak position due to being elected amid severe factional politics between the pro-Tanaka and anti-Tanaka factions. He was not regarded as an able-enough politician to trigger such a drastic change (Masumi, 1988: 450).

Prime Minister Suzuki succeeded Mr. Ohira, who died during the 1980 election campaigns for the House of Representatives and the House of Councillors. Ohira's death brought an epoch-making victory to the LDP, which recovered from its narrow margin situation in both houses (it received 284 in the HR out of 512 total seats, an increase of 36 seats). The LDP led by Ohira had been terribly defeated in the previous election just several months before because of its intention to introduce the general consumption tax in 1979. This had taught the LDP that a tax-rise reform must be accompanied by rather severe administrative reforms, cutting expenses, and streamlining and rationalizing government organization.

Despite this cautious start, however, "administrative reform politics" institutionally lasted more than a decade, from 1981 to 1993, including the Special Advisory Council for Administrative Reform (*Rincho*, 1981–3) and the three Advisory Councils for the Promotion of Administrative Reform (*Gyokakushin*, the 1st: 1983–6, the 2nd: 1987–90, the 3rd: 1990–3). The administrative reform atmosphere dominated Japanese politics, similar to neoliberal reform in other advanced countries, especially between 1981 and 1986 (Otake, 1994: 19). After the rise of tax reform in 1986, it was gradually pushed aside by tax politics and later by the electoral reform politics of the 1990s.

The *Rincho* Council was created in 1980 by a law approved by all but the Japan Communist Party. It consisted of nine formal members: three from business, two from labor, and one each from the bureaucracy, local government, journalism, and academia, respectively. It also mobilized more than 100 bureaucrats and ex-bureaucrats (Rincho-Gyokakusin OB-kai, 1991). Because the *Rincho* and *Gyokakushin* councils submitted reports to the prime minister more than twice a year and each report promoted a bundle of legislation and cabinet decisions, the councils kept exceptionally high prestige as well as the continuous attention of the mass media.

In addition to the councils being a unique arena outside of the Diet, administrative reform was characterized by a unique and complicated set of political actors: Prime Minister Nakasone (recruited from a minor faction in the LDP by former-PM Kakuei Tanaka); Toshio Doko, a charismatic business leader and former head of the Federation of Economic Organizations; the chair of the *Rincho* and the first *Gyokakushin* councils; labor unions from the public sector (anti-reform) and private sector (pro-reform); a supportive business community; and powerful bureaucrats. This set of actors ensured its implementation.

Although "building the welfare society with vitality" and "contribution to the international society" were the stated slogans throughout the reform process (Rincho-Gyokakusin OB-kai, 1991), in practice this meant the structural reform of Japanese society as a whole and alteration of the postwar structure of social-labor policy. This reform was implemented, for instance, through the enactment of the Elderly Insurance Law in 1982 and through the revisions of the Employment Insurance Law and the National Health Insurance Law in 1984 and the Labor Standard Law in 1987. It was also implemented through the privatization of the two biggest public corporations, the National Railways in 1986 and the Telegram and Telephone Public Corporation in 1984. Both of these public corporations should be given careful attention, because their labor unions had been the key driving actors in the leftist *Sohyo* movement. The reforms also encouraged the cabinet to freeze the salaries of public servants for a couple of years by ignoring recommendations from the Personnel Authority and to reduce the national government's budgetary burden by any means.

This kind of "successful" performance could not have been achieved without political leadership and maneuvering in strategy as well as in tactics. In this context, integrated business leaders, corporatist labor leaders in the private sector, and the Nakasone leadership should be mentioned as major contributors.

Business was very quick to respond to the trend. To support Mr. Doko, five major business organizations, including Nikkeiren (FEA), Keidanren (FEO), Keizai Doyukai, the Japan Chamber of Commerce and Industry, and Kansai Economic Federation, formed the Five Members Committee for Promoting Administrative Reform in 1981 and conducted a strong campaign for administrative reform without a tax rise (Masumi, 1988: 452; Kanbara, 1986: 15–22). "Without a tax rise" was critical for the business side. Therefore, when the new tax, a kind of consumer tax, was proposed by the Nakasone cabinet in 1986, the solidarity of business started to erode (Otake, 1994: 286–95).

A situation of divided labor was considerably complicated at the time (Tsujinaka, 1987; Oomi, 1994; Shinoda, 1989). After the turning point in 1975 (mentioned in Chapter 2 and caused by restraint in wage hikes in the 1975 wage-bargaining round and by public-sector labor's loss of the "strike for the right to strike"), the cleavage between public and private labor deepened. It became critical when, in 1977, *Sohyo* (the old national federation primarily based on public-sector labor unions) was reluctant to pass the Law Concerning Temporary Measures for Displaced Workers in Specified Depressed Industries, which was eagerly desired by both business and private labor unions (Oomi, 1994). One year before, the private-sector labor unions had formed a consultative body, the Trade Union Conference for Policy Promotion, which accelerated their unification movement outside of *Sohyo*. Then, in 1982, they created the Japanese Private Trade Union Council. In 1987 this became *Rengo* (the Japanese Private Sector Trade Union Confederation). In 1989, after absorbing *Sohyo*, this body became the Japanese Trade Union Confederation (Tsujinaka, 1993). The private labor unions promoted the administrative reform by allying with business and government, but the public-sector labor unions were strongly against it because they were targeted to be disarmed and disintegrated. Therefore, the struggle for leadership in the labor movement was one of the important contexts behind the politics of administrative reform.

Despite electoral victories in 1980 and 1986, in both the House of Representatives and the House of Councillors, the vulnerability of the Liberal Democratic Party concerning its social bases was becoming clear. A sense of impending crisis compelled the party to seek new sociopolitical alliances. This weakness made the LDP give added significance to labor policy. Functioning as the sole governing party since its establishment in 1955, the LDP had enjoyed long Diet dominance. Between 1976 and 1980, again between 1983 and 1986, and from 1989 on, however, the LDP suffered losses in the size of its Diet majority, making its management and control of the Diet more difficult. The LDP's traditional allies – farmers and small-to-medium-size company owners – were shrinking as a proportion of the electorate. This forced the LDP to cultivate new constituencies. Employees in general became their major target as a clientele. Actually, the LDP had started approaching the leaders of labor unions in big companies during the late-1970s, and this strategy became overt in the 1980s (Tsujinaka, 1987). The LDP and these union leaders ultimately became latent allies in the process of administrative reform and in practical industrial and labor policies aimed at helping workers.

This leadership aspect aside, the national budgetary situation was becoming critical. The first Oil Shock of 1973 induced a recession accompanied by a revenue shortfall of 35 percent. Facing financial difficulties, the cabinet issued deficit bonds. The total amount skyrocketed annually until 34 percent of the 1979 national budget came from bond sales – a rate more than twice that of other advanced countries. In 1981 the balance of national bonds was 82 trillion yen and the growth rate of debt service in the national budget was around 25 percent per year (Masumi, 1988: 451). Although the government had to solve the problem by budget cuts, this was made difficult by the rigidity of budget allocation items, each defended by interested ministries and other parties (Campbell, 1977). The easiest way to solve the deficit problem was to increase tax revenues. The government (let by the Ministry of Finance) first tried tax reform in 1979 under the Ohira cabinet, introducing an indirect tax and strengthening enforcement of the taxation system. However, popular reaction against this move by the swing voters ("buffer players") produced a loss of votes for the LDP and an increase for the opposition, especially for the Japan Communist Party (Kabashima and Broadbent, 1986). This electoral loss compelled the government to alter its policy direction away from taxation and toward reducing expenditures. As a result, when Yasuhiro Nakasone became director general of the Public Management Agency in 1981, he proposed public administrative reform as a primary cabinet goal.

Yasuhiro Nakasone, the leader of a smaller faction in the LDP at that time, became prime minister in 1982 after the sudden resignation of Zenko Suzuki. He was supported by the pro-Tanaka faction coalition. As a weaker leader in the LDP, Nakasone, in order to get his programs through, had to utilize the mass media and attract and mobilize non-LDP actors like intellectuals, journalists, and even private union leaders and opposition parties. As a place to enlarge, cultivate, and rearrange networks useful for his maneuvering, the administrative reform areas (*Rincho* type councils and their supplementary staff organizations) provided a favorable opportunity.

Nakasone successfully appeased the Clean Government Party (CGP, or *Komeito*, a Buddhist party and the second largest opposition party in the 1980s) and the Democratic Socialist Party (DSP), officially supported by *Domei*, the second largest labor national center until 1987. Nakasone allied himself to the New Liberal Club (NLC, a splinter conservative party) and finally absorbed it after the historic 1986 triumph in both houses' elections. Nakasone's "informal" alliance tactics with the CGP and DSP helped to pass "confrontational" bills, such as revision of the Employment Insurance Law in 1984, three laws of privatization for the Japan Telegram and Telephone Public Corporation in 1984, the Manpower Dispatching Business Law in 1985, and eight laws concerning privatization of the Japan National Railways in 1986 (Iio, 1993: 284; Hosei Daigaku Ohara Shakai Mondai Kenkyusho, 1982–92).

Other bills of the period were not directly related to administrative reform. From the late 1970s on, the government consciously promoted systemic policies for structural adjustment, encouraging changes in industry and labor to keep Japan maximally competitive. For that purpose, it first enacted the Law Concerning Temporary Measures for Displaced Workers in Specified Depressed Industries (1977) and a similar law covering workers in depressed areas (1978). These laws were revised in 1983 and 1987, along with related competitiveness policies for unemployment insurance, retirement from small- and medium-size businesses, new minimum wage standards, and worker retraining. Most of these revisions went through long hearing and consultative processes with related actors, including labor unions and business associations, before the direct drafting process of the bills (Shinoda, 1989; Oomi, 1994; Ohara Shakai Mondai Kenkyusho, 1982–90).

Despite its numerous problems, Japan adjusted and performed better than other advanced countries. But its very success caused consequent conflict with those nations. A rising tide of exports brought trade friction and high appreciation of the yen on international exchange markets. Foreign nations criticized the Japanese government for the nation's overheated economy, while Japanese labor unions pushed for changing the economy by increasing domestic demand. The government responded with a comprehensive plan to accomplish this task, the Maekawa Report in 1986. The report argued for stimulating more domestic demand, such as by increasing employment, and for reforming working conditions. This plan led to policies for increasing investment in public works and for reducing working hours and working days (Ohara Shakai Mondai Kenkyusho, 1987: 434). In the same context, the Labor Standard Law was revised in 1987, and the National Holiday Law in 1985. United Nations International Year campaigns for fairness and equity for women and for the handicapped created international pressures that supported the passage of laws designed to help women employees as well as the handicapped.

The high appreciation of the yen relative to the dollar had an epoch-making effect on Japan. During the 1980s, after the Plaza Accord in 1985, the yen's value increased from 260 to 120 yen to the dollar. This change elevated Japan's status in the international system and generated domestic demands for industrial adjustment. On the one hand, a stronger yen promoted the penetration of Japanese businesses into foreign countries. On the other hand, it forced Japanese export companies to reduce still further their costs and to rationalize their endeavors. Later, a large number of foreign workers rushed into the Japanese labor market, causing a new type of labor problem. The government's adjustment policies, reviewed earlier, tried to smooth this shift.

These policy achievements, besides boosting real economic performance, helped the Nakasone cabinet to last four years and eight months. This was the longest cabinet duration since 1972, and the cabinet had one of the highest levels of popular support. After the 1986 LDP triumph in both houses' elections, Nakasone overruled the party's ban on a third re-election as the president of LDP. He was regarded as seeking a presidential type of prime minister role, due to his method of advisory council-oriented policy-making and utilization of the mass media. He dared to extend his policy reform strategy to the area of education in 1984 and, finally, to the area of new taxes after the 1986 election, but he had made the tactical mistake of promising not to adopt a "large indirect tax." Thus, he was forced to resign in 1987. The tax reform was finally achieved by the Takeshita cabinet, but only at great cost, the demise of the cabinet.

In conclusion, the period that we are analyzing in the survey was that of an offensive by neoliberal conservatives, personified by Nakasone, who successfully allied themselves with new forces like private labor unions. Under this trend, the opposition shifted toward the realist position. Thus, even the Japan Socialist Party adopted a New Declaration in 1986 in which it finally renounced its stance as a "class party." Despite this adjustment, opposition strength stagnated or even declined, especially that of the JSP. Japanese labor legislation in the 1980s involved two impressive structural changes regarding politics and policy. Most conspicuously, policy change created a variety of laws in the name of administrative reform. As a whole, these laws contributed more to the structural adjustment of society in order to increase its productivity and to the vitality of business than they did to the betterment of the individual citizen's living standard. These changes, however, as well as the involvement of many actors in them, seem to have laid the groundwork for coming changes in the political arrangement of Japanese society. These political changes can be observed to start in 1989, just after our survey period.

ADVOCACY CIRCLES AND ACTION SETS

At the systemic level, the central research questions for this chapter are: Do similar structural configurations among organizations and events occur in the three nations' labor policy domains? If so, what are the forms of global opposition network structures among advocacy circles and among action sets across legislative events? The sources of our hypotheses are the empirical results of previous organizational state analyses (especially Laumann and Knoke, 1987) and the additional conceptual extensions described in Chapter 1. We anticipate that opposing advocacy circles would have formed on most legislative bills, because the selection process emphasized major conflicts that pitted the interests of labor, capital, and other special interest groups against one another. We cannot predict whether majorities of the labor domain organizations would also join every event's advocacy circles. However, we expect that small proportions of any advocacy circle, perhaps only a minority of its member organizations, would create an action set for any given bill. The costs of fighting collectively on events are generally too high for most organizations to pay repeatedly across all the domain events about which they might express policy positions. Thus, advocacy circles are likely to involve broader ranges of more marginally committed organizations than are action sets, which require greater commitments of time and effort from organizations that join.

Organizations participating in both advocacy circles and action sets might be very selective about those events in which they become involved. Their enduring policy interests likely constrain both their preferences on particular events and which action-set partners they join. For example, business associations would rarely team up with labor unions to support the same policy event outcomes. Political parties and governmental agencies would usually align themselves with their traditional political constituents; that is, business interests with the U.S. Republican Party, German Christian Democratic Union, and Japanese Liberal Democrats; labor interests with the U.S. Democratic Party, German Social Democrats, and Japanese socialists. Thus, the coalitions assembling around different policy events are not random configurations, but tend to attract members from within limited subsets of candidate organizations. We expect the structural patterns at the global level to reveal moderately polarized opposition networks. That is, while opposing blocs of advocacy circles and action sets would tend to exhibit considerable within-bloc overlap, enough variation should occur to prevent coalitions from being identical over all events.

Further, given the difficulties that most organizations have in sustaining intense involvement in many events, the organizational state perspective does not anticipate finding a single coordinating subset of organizations involved in every legislative fight. Instead, it implies that spatial representations of the global opposition networks for advocacy circles and action sets should display an empty central region. In other words, no coalition for a given event would draw its organizations from opposing sides of other events and thus mediate domain disputes. Rather, we expect to find distinct clusters of opposing advocacy circles and action sets arrayed in distant locations of the opposition network space. Such spatially dispersed patterns imply that neighboring coalitions consist of substantially overlapping members who consistently agree on policy objectives while disagreeing with the positions taken by the coalitions occupying other regions of the policy space.

At the organizational level, our basic research goal is to identify the factors that explain an organization's participation in action sets. We expect the chief predictors to be (1) the breadth and intensity of an actor's interests over the range of policy domain issues and (2) the availability of organization resources – financial and material assets, influence reputations, network locations. Because participation entails costs, more resources allow an organization to participate in more action sets.

For the most part, the organizational state implies that the relationships described would generally be supported in all three national labor policy domains. That is, markedly similar patterns should emerge in the global opposition networks of advocacy circles and action sets, in the factors that produce action sets, and in organizational decisions to join them. If differences are observed, they should reflect the different national histories and institutional arrangements discussed in Chapter 2. For example, although a polarization between labor and business interests is expected to structure the major cleavage lines in all domains, we believe that such divisions would be stronger in the U.S. because its bitter historical conflicts would prevent cooperative ties in areas of common concern, whereas the more proactive roles of governmental ministries and political parties in both Germany and Japan would more effectively mitigate these conflicts and reconcile opposing interests. Given Germany's and Japan's stronger traditions of activist party factions, political actors (government agencies and parliamentary parties) would tend to be more involved with action sets in both countries than in the U.S. Thus, we generally anticipated that the research hypotheses we have sketched would receive robust support from all three cases but that important national differences would still occur.

MEASURES

The selection of 25 U.S., 32 German, and 22 Japanese labor bills from the 1980s was described in Chapter 3, and their chronologies appear in Appendix 4. During the interviews, informants indicated their organization's level of interest in the proposed legislation and whether the organization took a position on the bill (for, against, both sides, or not interested). For those taking the pro, con, or "both" position, brief activity histories were recorded, including "forming coalitions with other groups." Informants also named the organizations they had worked with on each bill. For each event, we identified the complete memberships of all event publics, advocacy circles (pro, con, both), and action sets (also pro, con, and both, and classified according to which organizations took the leading roles, using both self-descriptions and nominations by other informants). The analyses that follow use both the frequency counts and the membership information for these social formations.

As described in Chapter 5, independent variables include organizational reputation, communication betweenness, issue interest, and dummy variables for organizational type. *Political capacity* is an index that counted one point for organizations having each of the following components: (1) staff to monitor labor policy, (2) staff to "gather systematic technical data," (3) in-house legal counsel, (4) a public relations person or unit, (5) a program "designed to activate persons in local areas . . . to lobby their own Congressmen and Senators on labor issues," and (6) an "associated political action committee."

EVENT PUBLICS AND ADVOCACY CIRCLES

Table 6.1 presents the number of U.S. organizations classified as event publics, advocacy circles, and action sets for each of the 25 legislative bills (policy events). Tables 6.2 and 6.3 display similar information for the 32 German and 22 Japanese policy events. Attention to events was more concentrated in Germany and the U.S. than in Japan. Even when organizations expressing "very little" interest were counted as event public members, most policy events attracted a minority of the American and German domain organizations: Only in 5 of the 25 U.S. policy events did half of the 117 domain organizations express any interest; in Germany, only 3 of the 32 policy events attracted interest from more than half of the 126 organizations. However, 11 of the 22 Japanese events saw event publics consisting of half or more of the 122 organizations, suggesting a far greater saliency of Japanese labor events. This result is partly explained by the inclusion of some broader cases, such as the tax reform bills in Japan. Twelve U.S. events and most (66%) German policy events attracted one-third or fewer of the domain organizations to the event public. In contrast, just 4 of the Japanese events drew such scant attention.

In all three countries, most event public members were also advocacy circle members. Large majorities of the domain organizations that expressed some interest in an event also stated a position on that event (see the means at the bottom of the "pro," "con," and "both" columns of Tables 6.1–6.3). Across all the events, the U.S. organizations formed 47 advocacy circles; the German organizations created 75 circles; and the Japanese organizations generated 53 circles. For most bills, many more organizations favored the bill's passage than opposed it. Japanese and German organizations were very likely to create "both positions" advocacy circles on a bill, whereas only negligible numbers of U.S. organizations straddled the fence (no U.S. "both" circles occurred). These findings suggest similar national patterns of attention to events in labor policy domains, again with the Japanese labor domain organizations participating at much higher rates.

ACTION SETS

The final columns in Tables 6.1 to 6.3 display the numbers of organizations constituting the actions sets for every legislative event. The column headings refer to the main organizations that led each coalition. In the U.S., these leaders were the AFL-CIO (23 action sets), the Chamber of Commerce and National Association of Manufacturers (14), or other organizations (11). In Germany, the coalition leaders were the German Trade Union Federation (DGB; 22 action sets), the Confed-

Table 6.1. *Numbers of U.S. organizations participating in event publics, advocacy circles, and action sets for 25 labor policy domain legislative events*

POLICY EVENT	EVENT PUBLIC (N)	ADVOCACY CIRCLES PRO	CON	ACTION SETS* AFL-CIO	COC-NAM	OTHERS
2. Black Lung Benefits	27	16	5	3+		
3. CETA & JTPA	69	43	21	8+	19+	9-
5. Union Pension Fraud	29	9	8	6-		
6. Public Employee Pensions	34	20	5	9+		
7. Automobile Domestic Content	33	21	10	18+	6-	
8. ERISA Benefits Recovery	15	6	--			
9. American Conservation Corps	31	19	7	7+		
10. Mine Safety Cooperation	19	15	4	3+		
11. ERISA Pre-1974 Benefits	28	15	5	9+		
12. Public Works Compensation	47	34	8	13+		
13. Garment Homework Limits	30	11	18	13-	4+	3+
16. Vocational Education Renewal	45	40	--	4+	3+	11+,3+
18. ERISA Pension Spousal Equity	42	30	6	10+	4+	4+
19. JTPA Summer Remedial Education	45	34	4	5+		
20. Teenage Sub-Minimum Wage	55	22	29	15-	10+	
23. Immigration Reform	50	24	16	11+	6-	3-
24. American Boxing Corporation	7	5	--			
28. Occupational Risk Assessment	62	25	32	17+	18-	5-
29. Parental & Disability Leave	76	41	28	22+	15-	7+,5-
30. Minimum Wage Increase	64	35	20	25+	8-	5-
31. 60-Day Plant Closing Notice	62	30	29	21+	20-	5-
32. Bankruptcy Benefit Suspension	34	22	5	10+		
33. Double-Breasting by Companies	48	20	23	10+	19-	
35. Polygraph Ban	46	30	10	15+	4-	
36. PBGC Premium Increase	38	35	3	8+	8+	
Mean	41.4	24.1	13.5	11.4	10.3	5.5

* Position in favor = + Position against = −
AFL-CIO = American Federation of Labor-Congress of Industrial Organizations
COC-NAM = Chamber of Commerce, National Association of Manufacturers

eration of German Employers Associations (BDA; 13), or 16 coalitions led by other organizations (including action sets that took both sides on the event). Three major Japanese action sets were headed by the Japan Private Sector Trade Union Council (1982–7) and the Japanese Private Sector Trade Union Confederation (1987–9) (PTU; 9 coalitions), the General Council of Trade Unions of Japan (GCU; 21), and the Japan Federation of Employers Associations (FEA; 20), with other organizations creating nine additional action sets. The column entries indicate the number of organizations belonging to each action set and the position taken by the action set. For example, for event 3 in Table 6.2, the "36−" in the DGB column means that 36 organizations led by this peak union association opposed passage of the entitlement reductions bill; the "12+" in the BDA column means that employers' association led 12 organizations favoring the bill; and the

Table 6.2. *Numbers of German organizations participating in event publics, advocacy circles, and action sets for 32 labor policy domain legislative events*

POLICY EVENT	EVENT PUBLIC (N)	ADVOCACY CIRCLES PRO	CON	BOTH	ACTION SETS* DGB	BDA	OTHER/ BOTH
1. Labor Court Jurisdiction	11	--	7	--	4-		
2. Illegal Employment	14	8	4	--			
3. Entitlement Reductions	85	23	39	15	36-		12+,10
4. Remigration of Foreign Workers	42	24	7	5	4-		9+
5. Early Retirement	69	40	14	6	28+	6-	
6. Stricter Sunday Work	46	19	12	9	13+	5-	6
7. Bankruptcy Law Reform	26	11	9	3		4-	
8. Deregulate Work Protection	46	22	14	8	9-	12+	
9. Employment Opportunities Act	92	47	29	8	24-	35+	3
11. Limits on Public Servant Earnings	27	16	5	3			5+,5-
12. Extend Unemployment Payments	45	38	--	--	18+		
13. Anti-Gender Discrimination	37	22	9	--	6+	3-	
14. Farmers' Social Benefits	11	10	--	--			4+
15. Reduction of Overtime Work	19	7	8	--			
16. Improve Vocational Education	41	27	4	5	11+#	11+#	
18. Employment of Handicapped	54	26	10	14	6-	12+	10
20. Fed. Employment Agency Neutrality	58	30	21	5	20-	22+	
21. Extend Co-Determination Rights	39	22	11	--	18+	5-	
22. Vocational Training Act	17	13	--	3			3+
23. Farmers' Social Insurance	11	8	--	--			3+
25. Mothers' Annuity Insurance	53	30	10	7			19+
26. Labor Participation in Management	32	19	8	--	11+		
27. Worker Savings Promotion	24	17	--	3		8+	
28. Illegalize Employee Lockout	28	12	10	3	6+		
29. Part-Time Worker Protection	26	15	4	--	8+		
30. Restrict Leasing of Workers	18	10	5	--	6+		
31. Steel Industry Co-Determination	35	24	7	--	13+		
32. Amend Work Promotion Act	51	20	14	14	11-	7,11+	
33. Represent Youth on Work Councils	36	25	6	4	11+		
34. Social Insurance Registration	27	19	--	--			9+
35. Age Limit for Doctors' Licenses	33	14	14	--			11+,10-
36. Amend Work Council Act	51	17	20	10	14+/3		9+
Mean	37.6	20.5	11.6	6.9	12.7	10.8	8.0

*Position in favor = + Position against = − Took both sides = unsigned
DGB = German Trade Union Federation BDA = Confederation German Employers Associations
# DGB and BDA in same action set

unsigned "10" in the last column means that 10 organizations formed a third action set that favored some portions of the bill and opposed others (this action set was led by the Union of German Retiree Insurers).

In all three nations, action sets that formed around legislative events were less common, and the average number of organizations participating in them was much smaller, than their corresponding event publics and advocacy circles. Fewer than

Table 6.3. *Numbers of Japanese organizations participating in event publics, advocacy circles, and action sets for 22 labor policy domain legislative events*

POLICY EVENT	EVENT PUBLIC (N)	ADVOCACY CIRCLES			ACTION SETS*			
		PRO	CON	BOTH	PTU	GCU	FEA	OTHERS
0. Old Age Insurance	65	28	31	-	3-	7-	12+	
3. Depressed Industry Employment	52	44	-	3	14+#	14+#	14+#	
5. Unemployment Insurance Reform	52	28	12	3		5-	6+	
6. National Health Insurance	71	26	34	6		10-	9+	
7. Privatize Tobacco Monopoly	29	18	6	-		4-		
10. Privatize Telephone & Telegraph	42	21	11	3		8-	5+	
11. National Pension Reform	65	32	18	4		6-	6+	
12. Small Industry Retirement Funds	29	26	-	-		4+		
13. Occupational Training Reform	37	31	-	-		3+	3+	
14. Equal Employment Opportunity	85	53	21	8	3+	5+	9-	6+,4-
15. Temporary Employment Agencies	66	33	19	5		5-	8+	
16. Citizen's Holidays	62	46	5	6	5+	5+	3+	
17. Elderly Stable Employment	68	52	7	-	3+	4+	5+	5-
19. Workers' Disaster Insurance	46	28	8	4		3-	7+	
24. Privatize National Railway	61	34	16	4		8-	5+	4-
26. Elderly Insurance Premiums	62	14	42	3	4-	9-	6-	
27. Retail Sales Tax	78	29	37	4	3+	6+	3+	6+,5-,4-
28. Salaried Workers Savings Promotion	43	37	-	-		3+	3+	
29. Handicapped Employment Reform	44	34	5	-			4+	3-
30. Regional Employment Development	29	23	-	-		3+	3-	
32. Reduce Work Week to 40 Hours	81	48	22	3	5+	7-	9-	5+
33. Consumer Tax	93	39	43	3	10-	7-	11+	
Mean	57.3	32.9	19.8	4.2	5.6	6.0	6.6	4.7

* Position in favor = + Position against = –
PTU = Japan Private Sector Trade Union Confederation
GCU = General Council of Trade Unions of Japan
FEA = Japan Federation of Employers Association
# PTU, GCU, and FEA in same action set.

half of the organizations in the average event public joined an action set. However, at least one action set was formed for all except two U.S. policy events and for all but two German events. Only one Japanese event had fewer than two action sets, whereas one (event 27, the sales tax defeat) saw six unique coalitions arise. However, the average Japanese coalition (with 5.6 organizations) was barely half as large as those in Germany (10.7) and the U.S. (9.7). The three most common patterns across events were labor and business action sets on opposite sides of the same event (10 U.S., 10 German, and 11 Japanese events); a labor union action set unopposed by a business action set (occurring for 9 U.S. and 10 German events, but only for one Japanese event); and separate union and business action sets on the same side (4 U.S. and 6 Japanese events). Action sets involving joint leadership by both labor and business organizations were extremely rare. None occurred

Figure 6.1. *Spatial distances among U.S. action sets: three-dimensional ALSCAL analysis of simple matching coefficients (stress = .179)*

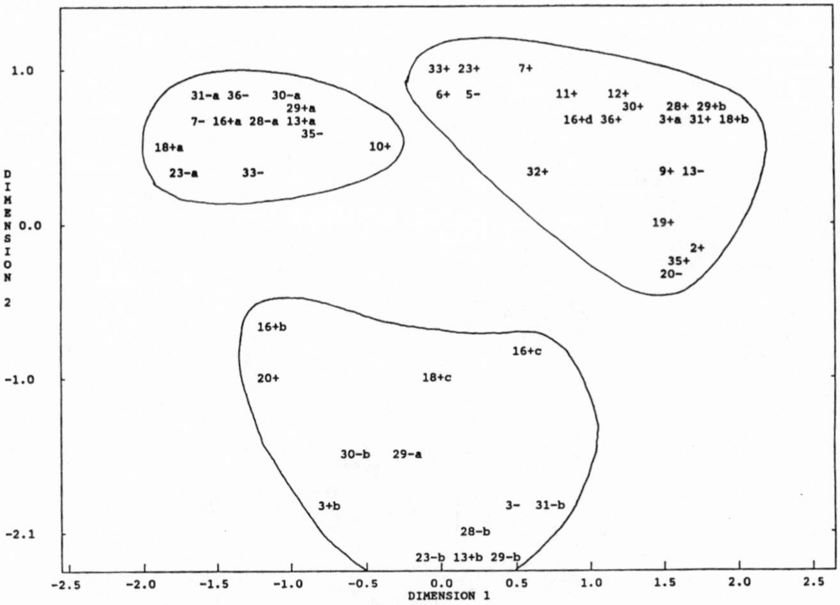

Note: Numbers refer to policy events listed in Table 6.1; + = favored passage of bill; – = opposed passage of bill.

in the U.S., and only one such alliance appeared in the German (event 16, the professional education improvement bill) and Japanese domains (event 3, the depressed industries and regions bill). Several of the 15 German action sets that were led by other organizations (including those taking "both" positions) also included some labor and business organizations, reflecting the German proclivity for playing to both sides of the audience. The Japanese "other" action sets consisted mostly of business associations or labor unions that chose not to work with their respective peak associations. In sum, in all three labor domains, although many cleavages appear between labor organizations and their business opponents, the majority of events exhibited less polarized patterns. In about a third of both the German and Japanese policy events, other distinctive action sets emerged.

The spatial structures among action sets are apparent in Figures 6.1 to 6.3. These diagrams display the first two dimensions from ALSCAL analyses (see Chapter 4), where the similarity measure is the simple matching coefficient (SMC), the number of organizations common to a pair of action sets. The closed lines (contiguity circles) around groups of action sets were determined through a hierarchical cluster analysis of the SMC data. Action sets with many overlapping members were clustered together, whereas action sets having few members in common were located in widely distant clusters. The U.S. opposition network structure was fairly

Figure 6.2. *Spatial distances among German action sets: three-dimensional ALSCAL analysis of simple matching coefficients (stress = .207)*

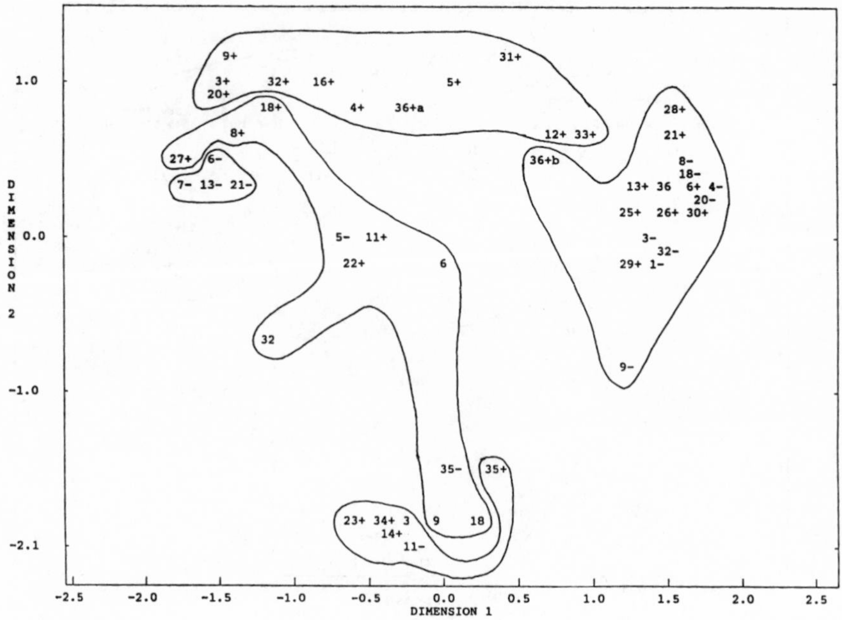

Note: Numbers refer to policy events listed in Table 6.2; + = favored passage of bill; − = opposed passage of bill; no sign = took both sides on bill.

simple, consisting of three widely separated clusters (some policy event numbers include letters to distinguish several action sets sharing the same preference, for example, event 16). For the U.S., the first dimension reflected a business (on the left) versus labor (on the right) split, while a second dimension, running from labor issues to general social issues, differentiated the business and labor action sets at the top from other coalitions at the bottom. Three large clusters appeared: 13 business action sets in the upper-left corner; 22 labor action sets in the upper-right corner; and 13 heterogeneous action sets consisting mostly of Reagan Administration agencies, vocational education supporters, women's organizations, and a few union and labor groups in the lower center. These odd couplings do not indicate political affinity so much as a strong differentiation from the labor and business centers of gravity. A break-away union action set, (3−), that opposed other unions on the CETA-JTPA bill also appeared in the bottom cluster, as did the business action set favoring that bill (3+).

The German opposition network map was more complex, consisting of five clusters with intertwined pseudopods. A business-labor split was discerned along the first dimension, whereas a second dimension of partisan versus nonpartisan issues contrasted business and labor action sets at the top with others at the bottom.

Figure 6.3. *Spatial distances among Japanese action sets: three-dimensional ALSCAL analysis of simple matching coefficients (Stress = .173)*

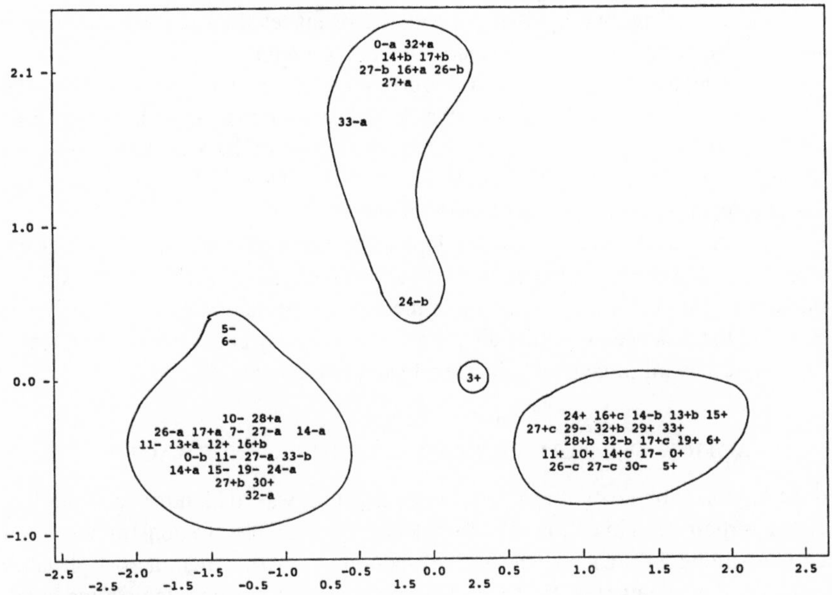

Note: Numbers refer to policy events listed in Table 6.3; + = favored passage of bill; − = opposed passage of bill; no sign = took both sides on bill.

Sixteen of the 18 action sets in the rightmost cluster were dominated by the unions. Similarly, the small cluster of four action sets on the upper lefthand side were business led, as were 5 of the 11 action sets in the long vertical cluster running from the top to the bottom of the diagram. The remaining 6 action sets in this cluster, as well as the 6 in the bottom cluster, were led by other organizations. Finally, the cluster at the top bridging the business and labor sectors contained 11 action sets, three (on the left) led by the Confederation of German Employers Associations, 6 (on the right) led by the German Trade Union Federation. In its middle was event 16+, a jointly led coalition. All bills at the top of the space were initiated either by the government or by the coalition partners in parliament. The farther to the right bills were located, the more they were supported by the unions. The more to the left, the more the bills were supported by business groups. The lefthand side of the diagram was more densely populated than the righthand side, indicating the conservative nature of the Kohl government. All events in the top cluster had plus signs and were enacted into law, indicating the proactive role of the Kohl government in labor policy. The role of the veto coalition opposing union – Social Democrat bills was more pronounced in the small group of four action sets led by the peak employers association on the left side (events 6−, 7−, 13−, and 21−). The German organizations that took both sides on the government-initiated bills seldom formed action sets. The clusters in the middle and bottom of Figure 6.2 were composed of bills supported or opposed by organizations outside the basic labor-business division. Thus, the global image of the German national labor policy domain was one of sprawling alliances, smaller distances between opponents, and much less polarization than occurred in the U.S. domain.

The Japanese action set image in Figure 6.3 was somewhat simplified by the failure of any organizations that took the "both" position to form action sets. Three widely separated clusters emerged: at the top, a bloc of 10 action sets in which the peak Japan Private Sector Trade Union Council/Confederation played the central role; at the lower left, a second cluster of 24 action sets in which the peak General Council of Trade Unions of Japan was the main participant; and at the lower right, 24 action sets led by the peak Japan Federation of Employers Associations. A singleton cluster, consisting of the 14-member action set on event 3, was located in the exact center of the diagram. It was the only event that attracted joint participation by all three peak labor and business organizations.

ACTION SET PARTICIPATION AND INFLUENCE TACTICS

At the organization level of analysis, our central task was to identify variables that predict participation in action sets. As a dependent variable, we constructed an index that summarizes each organization's action-set involvement across all labor domain policy events (the 25 U.S., 32 German, and 22 Japanese legislative bills). For each bill, an organization was scored +1 if it joined an action set, 0 if it had an interest in that bill but did not join an action set, and −1 if it had no interest in the event. The scores for the different events were then summed. The unstandardized regression coefficients in Table 6.4 reveal that in all three nations, organizations having a wide range of labor domain issue interests were very likely to have joined action sets on many events. That is, the larger an organization's stake in diverse domain issues, the more coalitions it would join in its efforts to affect legislation on these topics. Organizational reputation also had significant positive effects in each nation, meaning that organizations enjoying reputations as especially influential actors in the labor domain were much more likely to work with others in many legislative battles. Greater political capacity was associated with greater action-set participation both in the U.S and Japan, but not in Germany. Thus, larger organizational resources fostered greater involvement in two of the three nations. Although the regression coefficient for betweenness centrality in the policy communication network was positive in all equations, it failed to reach statistical significance in any nation. Labor unions in all three countries were considerably more likely than other organizations to join coalitions (7.98 more action sets in U.S. than nonunion organizations, 5.16 more in Japan, and 3.77 more in Germany; these differences were not significant). Japanese business associations were also more likely to participate in action sets than were other types of organizations. Together, these three equations accounted for between a quarter of and

Table 6.4. *Regression of action-set participation on independent variables*

INDEPENDENT VARIABLES	U.S.	GERMANY	JAPAN
Constant	-27.72*** (2.32)	-30.83*** (1.85)	-24.34*** (2.50)
Issue Interest	1.68*** (.40)	2.40*** (.37)	1.45*** (.25)
Organizational Reputation	.11** (.05)	.06* (.03)	.09* (.04)
Political Capacity	1.10** (.47)	-.04 (.39)	1.33** (.53)
Communication Betweenness	1.69 (1.51)	.74 (.75)	.11 (.34)
Labor Union	7.98*** (2.16)	3.77* (1.91)	5.16** (1.96)
Business Association	--	--	7.14*** (1.87)
R^2 (adjusted)	.542***	.456***	.261***

* $p < .05$ ** $p < .01$ *** $p < .001$
Note: Numbers in parentheses are standard errors.

half the variance in the numbers of action sets to which labor domain organizations belonged. Thus, additional explanatory variables remain to be discovered.

Political organizations employed a varied repertoire of tactics in their attempts to affect the outcomes of legislative events. Especially noteworthy modes were appeals in the electronic mass media, computerized direct mail (McCarthy, 1983; Godwin and Mitchell, 1984), constituency-legislator linkages, and heavy reliance on conventional lobbying practices such as congressional-hearing testimony and personal contacts (Schlozman and Tierney, 1983). Public interest groups were particularly prone to mobilize their memberships, to appeal to the general public through the mass media, to launch letter-writing campaigns, and to stimulate local lobbying efforts (McFarland, 1984; Gais, Peterson, and Walker, 1984; Shaiko, 1991). A national sample of nonprofit associations found that slightly more than half the organizations made their positions on national policy proposals "known to the federal government" (Knoke, 1990a: 208). Constituency lobbying and personal contacts with federal officials and their staffs ranked as the two most common influence tactics. In contrast, corporations tended to work through law firms, consulting or public relations firms, or other institutional representatives (Salisbury, 1984; Laumann, Knoke, and Kim, 1985; but see Loomis, 1983, on the Chamber of Commerce's grass roots politicking). The greater availability of members or money as resources undoubtedly explains the choice among alternative influence tactics.

During our interviews with the labor domain organizations, we asked informants to recall for each event whether their organizations had performed any of five types of influence tactics (although seven items were posed in the Japanese interviews, only five were common on the U.S. and German questionnaires). These tactics were

Participated in formulating this proposal or suggested alternatives.

Formal contacts with government officials, legislature, or courts, such as testifying at hearings, serving on commissions, or filing friend of the court briefs.

Informal contacts with government officials, legislature, or non-governmental organizations.

Using mass media to publicize your organization's opinion about the event.

Mobilizing members of your organization or the general public to influence the public authorities.

Table 6.5 displays the percentages of organizations using each influence tactic, aggregated across all legislative events. (Note that each organization contributed an observation to these data for every event in which it expressed some interest; thus, the case base for the percentage calculations was the organization-event.) Significant differences occurred across the three countries for each tactic: German organizations were much more likely to formulate policy alternatives and to use mass media appeals; the Japanese organizations were much less likely to engage in both formal and informal lobbying contacts, use mass media, and mobilize their grass roots members. The mean number of tactics used per legislative event was highest in Germany (2.60 of five tactics), lowest in Japan (1.53 tactics), and intermediate in the U.S. (2.27).

CONCLUSION

In the U.S., Germany, and Japan, most national labor policy fights are orchestrated and conducted primarily through action sets, which are the basic social organizational units of political operations. These arrangements are often formally institutionalized practices, for example, the AFL-CIO member unions' Monday morning strategy sessions at its Washington headquarters, or the U.S. Chamber of Commerce's nine-page directory listing its "formal, informal, and ad hoc coalitions" that are "issue oriented, work together to share information and coordinate resources, and serve as rallying centers to achieve public policy results helpful to the business community" (Chamber of Commerce of the U.S., 1988: 2). The advocacy

Table 6.5. *Influence tactics used by interested organizations for all events combined*

Influence Tactic	U.S.	Germany	Japan	η^2
Formulate policy alternatives	44.4	63.0	50.7	.021***
Formal contacts with government	60.9	58.6	45.5	.020***
Informal contacts	61.4	61.5	22.5	.148***
Use of mass media	38.6	49.5	15.6	.095***
Mobilize members	35.0	30.7	19.0	.193***
Mean number of tactics used	2.27	2.60	1.53	.093***
N of organization-events	(1,220)[a]	(1,240)[a]	(1,718)[a]	

[a]Many organizations are included several times because they participated in many events.
*** $p < .001$

circle and action-set patterns were strikingly similar in the three nations at both the system and organization levels. However, the fine-grained evidence points to some divergences that may have arisen from differing institutional contexts.

Labor and business associations often took opposite sides on policy events, and almost never collaborated in leading the same action set. Several German events were characterized by coalitions taking "both positions" on bills, apparently from customary appeals to diverse constituencies. Whereas German and Japanese business groups and labor unions occasionally worked together, their U.S. counterparts remained bitter antagonists across many policy fights. With the exception of one Japanese event, coordinating central coalitions did not emerge in these domains. Instead, great social distances opened up between opposing hemispheres, indicating that advocacy circles and action sets form substantively disjoint clusters across all domain events. The U.S. domain was considerably more polarized between unreconciled labor and business organizations, reflecting its long history of divisive class conflict. The absence of any trusted mediator in this domain was underscored by informants' spontaneous comments, which revealed pervasive and long-standing distrust and animosity between U.S. labor and business interests.

In contrast, a more accommodationist stance prevailed in German and Japanese labor policy-making, growing out of their more institutionalized sharing of quasi-public authority by both business and labor. A substantial number of German action sets were created and led by professional societies and other nonlabor, nonbusiness interest groups. The Japanese system was characterized by a recurrent split between the two peak labor associations. Most often U.S. professional societies and public interest groups were only junior partners in one of the labor or business coalitions. In all three countries, federal ministries and agencies also occasionally participated in action sets. However, the German and Japanese parliamentary parties were more conspicuous than the U.S. legislative committees as collaborators in partisan fights. These contrasts perhaps reflect a divergence in formal institutional structures between parliamentary and presidential systems, or between "responsible party" and entrepreneurial political systems.

We assumed that self-interest was a major driving force behind coalition formation. As reflected in the regression equations, organizations that saw their interests at stake in many event outcomes participated frequently in action sets. Influential organizations were more likely to participate in such coalitions, perhaps to reinforce their continuing capacity to shape event outcomes. Political resource capacity also played a modest role in favoring involvement in action sets in the U.S. and Japan. In Germany, lack of resources apparently was no barrier to involvement in collective action. Although strategic positions in communication networks exerted no net impacts on activation, network connections were nonetheless critical factors for political mobilization in each domain. Advocacy circles and action sets could not form without extensive accessibility among potential members. The high densities of policy information linkages in all three domains assured that almost all compatible organizations could be connected in one or two steps.

Peak business associations and labor federations were the major policy event players in all labor domains. However, sufficient variation occurred in the composition of advocacy circles and action sets across events to rule out recurrent monolithic opposition blocs. Both labor unions and business associations were selective in the battles they chose to fight. In no country was the national labor policy domain as fragmented among highly diverse, nonoverlapping pressure groups as depicted by a pure model of pluralist contention. Rather, a hybrid form was evident, perhaps a "class pluralism" in which capital and labor interests form a basic skeleton to which a dappled skin of occupational, professional, ethnic, gender, and racial interests must conform. The presence of several German and Japanese action sets that were independent of business and labor may indicate a further post-pluralist development toward corporatist structuring of the political arena. Such evolution seems unlikely for a U.S. labor domain whose fault lines have solidified in an early-twentieth-century confrontational mode.

Contemporary analyses cannot address all important questions about the modern organizational state. Understanding why the German and Japanese patterns of the 1980s appeared to be more accommodationist while the U.S. structure seemed to be more antagonistic would be enhanced through longitudinal observation of domain polarization spanning several decades. Crystallized opposition structures may signal a reduction of previous conflict intensity as core players come to accept and operate within routine rules of the policy game. Further, ignoring the connections between policy elites' actions and unrest in the larger society exaggerates the self-contained image of national policy domains. Future work should complement our results by developing both the historical and noninstitutional contexts of current systems. Having shown that advocacy circles, action sets, and opposition networks are useful analytic tools for capturing the interorganizational structure of policy events, our next chapter attempts to explain the outcomes of policy fights.

7

Exchange processes

with Thomas König[6]

In 1989 the U.S. Congress passed the first minimum wage hike in a decade, from \$3.35 to \$4.25 per hour over two years. The act also included a lower three-month "training wage" for teenagers. A more generous wage increase proposed by labor unions was defeated through hard lobbying by the Minimum Wage Coalition to Save Jobs, whose partners included the U.S. Chamber of Commerce, major corporations and small businesses, and 150 trade associations. The National Federation of Independent Businesses mobilized its half-million members to deluge their representatives with letters and telegrams describing the potential job losses in each congressional district. President Bush's earlier veto of a higher rate bill had forced the compromise that gave business firms a lower pay scale (CQ Almanac, 1989). The outcome of this policy fight illustrates the substantial impact of organized interest groups on national political economies. Explaining how organizations affect public policy decision is the ultimate objective of this chapter.

We confine our research to the impact of interest groups in civil society on legislative decisions. We realize that the relative importance of the national legislature in the total policy-making system varies from nation to nation. For instance, in Japan the ministries have a much stronger hand in making the content of legislation than do the departments in the U.S. And the Japanese ministries also have greater latitude in creating regulations and interpreting laws. Therefore, focusing our comparisons just on legislative politics produces a somewhat unbalanced analysis. However, in each nation, the legislature made the final decision on the majority of the events for which we collected data, suggesting that the legislature is the central policy arena of each country, to which the full panoply of other powerful actors attend and whose decisions they seek to influence. Accordingly, the legislative arena is the best, indeed the only, directly comparable institution among the three nations. Hence, a detailed examination of legislative bills comprises an appropriate locus for cross-national research.

6. The final version of the paper on which this chapter is based was first presented at the International Sunbelt Conference, 1993, in Tampa, Florida: Thomas König and Franz Urban Pappi, "Political Decisions and Private-Public Influences in Policy Domain Networks: An Access Model for the Analysis of Collective Decisions in the American and German Labor Policy Domain."

We investigate the passage of labor bills, conceiving labor unions, business associations, parliamentary parties, and governmental agencies as actors with interests in their collective outcomes. These policy actors partially control the decisions, but the control they possess may not necessarily fit their preferences. Organization *A* may be interested in bill 1, which is partially controlled by organization *B*. If *B* is interested in bill 2, which is controlled by *A*, an exchange of control between the two actors would guarantee higher satisfaction or interest realization for both. Political exchange is more than a vague metaphor for social interaction. Parliamentary logrolling exemplifies the concept's realism. But a wide gap exists between a simple instance of binary political exchange and the type of generalized exchanges postulated by models of economic transactions involving numerous participants in a perfect market.

In this chapter, we develop an institutional access exchange model and apply three versions to estimate the supply and demand for control of labor policies in the American, German, and Japanese national legislatures. These models measure the values of legislative bills and the power of actors to affect their outcomes. We assess each model's ability to predict accurately those collective decisions.

A MODEL OF POLITICAL EXCHANGE

From a normative democratic viewpoint, collective decision making through voting and through political exchange appear to be strange bedfellows. Choosing between motions in a committee or among candidates in an election is often normatively assumed to be done by "sincere" voting. That is, an actor's vote presumably corresponds directly to her true preferences among the available alternatives. If the other voters' ranked preferences on three or more motions are known, sophisticated voting may guarantee a stable collective choice. In such cases, a voter should not regret casting a sincere first ballot because, anticipating the defeat of her most preferred motion, she would have voted for her second preference to avoid victory by her least-desired motion (see Brams, 1975; Mueller, 1989).

Political exchanges enable voters to improve their interest satisfaction with decision outcomes when they compare their stakes on several motions in which they hold voting rights. A legislator may trade her vote on a bill that is least salient in order to gain critical support for a bill having much more importance to her. Creating a majority vote for the more-salient bill has higher utility for the legislator than does majority support for the less-salient bill. Thus, a legislator justifies casting an insincere vote for the unimportant bill on the grounds that she thereby increases her overall utility by ensuring the passage of her more salient bill. Of course, an increased utility occurs only when the vote trading actually results in the necessary majority in favor of the preferred bill. Otherwise, the legislator's vote for the nonsalient bill is wasted.

Insincere voting can be justified by mutual utility gains made by the parties involved in the vote trading. But the nontrading legislators cannot remain indifferent to vote exchanges because those trades may impose external effects (utility losses) on the nontraders, who otherwise would be better off. The legislators who support a bill suffer utility losses if the vote trading turns their expected majority into a minority. The losses among the nontraders may outweigh the utility gains made by the vote traders, thus lowering the overall net welfare in the legislature. This vote-trading paradox occurs whenever the collective welfare of a committee or legislature engaged in bilateral logrolling results in gains by the vote traders being outweighed by losses among all other actors, not counting the instability of the solutions reached (Brams, 1990: 191–206). For example, vote trading may produce tax loopholes and pork barrel spending on public works for which a minority benefits at the expense of large cumulative losses by the majority. Thus, the individualistic justification of logrolling is problematic, not to speak of caveats from a normative democratic viewpoint.

Despite these normative problems, James S. Coleman tried to design a vote-trading model to overcome problems of instability and cyclical voting (Coleman, 1971, 1973a). His initial idea was to treat the right to vote as partial control of an event. The legislators each have one vote for every bill, which they may exchange like commodities. Because this assumption makes no sense for discontinuous decision rules, where additional votes lose their value once a simple majority has been reached, Coleman stipulated a probabilistic decision rule: A bill's collective outcome becomes the "yes" or "no" preference of a randomly selected legislator. Following such a procedure, legislators can meaningfully trade their votes, irrespective of the aggregate yes and no votes. Legislators favoring a bill can raise the probability of a positive collective outcome by trading their nonsalient votes for pledges of support on their salient bill. Coleman's probabilistic decision rule thus turns the partial control of an indivisible event into "full control of a portion of the consequences" (Coleman, 1986: 117).

Not surprisingly, few researchers saw a vote-trading model built on a very exotic decision rule as useful for legislative studies. And Coleman did not improve his original model in his later *Foundations of Social Theory* (1990). On the contrary, he discussed at great length the problems of the partial control concept with respect to decision rules, concluding, "Thus, it is evident that a system in which the only events are those under collective control and the rights to control the outcomes take the form of votes cannot be analyzed through minor modifications of the linear system of action" (1990: 868). Coleman focused on systems in which divisible resources are exchanges and collective decisions with binary outcomes must be made simultaneously. First, the actors' power derives from demands for their individually possessed resources. Second, the actors' interests in the indivisible events can be multiplied by their power to compute effective demand. The result is an allegedly perfect system in which "all power, in no matter what form, is used in arriving at the social choice," the choice with the highest effective demand giving the social optimum (Coleman, 1990: 863). Coleman's original model was successfully applied several times in more-or-less modified versions to predict collective decisions by community elites or national policy domains. In common, these applications had relatively broad concepts of political resources, comprising more than voting rights, so that exchanges made sense even when the decision rule was only vaguely conceptualized. We next review these applications before introducing our own institutional access model.

APPLICATIONS OF MODIFIED EXCHANGE MODELS

The precondition for barter, a primitive form of exchange, is a double coincidence of interests among a pair of actors. Actor *A* is interested in a resource bundle, *K1,* which is possessed by actor *B.* In turn, actor *B* is interested in another resource bundle, *K2,* which actor *A* offers to him. In a perfect market, these inter-actor dependencies are transformed into a dependence of all actors on the market, or the clearinghouse, where the supply of and demand for commodities are balanced by a specific price that completely clears the market and leaves all actors satisfied with their exchanges. Coleman took this microeconomic model as his starting point, substituting divisible resources for commodities. The first diagram in Figure 7.1 displays a schematic representation of Coleman's original exchange model with its two basic elements, actors and events. These elements are related by the actors' interests in the events and by the actors' control over the events. With resources, control turns into simple possession or more complicated property rights. Because the actors' interests drive the system, we display all subsequent exchange models as starting with these interests. We assume a closed system, in the sense that an actor's entire interests are distributed across the set of events. Thus, every actor's interests must sum to 1.0. And, because every event is completely controlled by the system actors, the actors' control over an event also sums to 1.0.

To predict collective decisions in a German community elite system, Peter Marsden and Edward Laumann (1977) proposed the most straightforward exchange model modification (see diagram 2 in Figure 7.1). That project asked about elites' political resources, so they could construct a control matrix – a square array showing the relationship of every system actor to every other actor – that indicated the proportion of every resource held by each actor. Empirical measures of event interests were also available, although the consequentiality of the resources had to be estimated. This new component of the control relationship was no longer measured directly but was decomposed into two parts: possession of a resource and its consequences for the collective decision of a particular event. Marsden and Laumann assumed that an empirically measured network of community affairs discussions could be used to estimate the interest dependencies among the actors. With this assumption, they estimated the resource consequentialities for each collective decision. They argued that "the network of discussion of community affairs among the elite thus defines the pattern of resource interchange between actors, i.e., the overall 'balance of trade' between actors in the Coleman model" (1977: 216).

Even if Marsden and Laumann's interpretations were valid, the problem remains whether interest dependency is indeed a direct indicator of actual resource

Figure 7.1. *Basic and modified exchange models*

1. Coleman's Original Exchange Model

	are interested in ---------------->		are controlled by ---------------->	
Actors $j=1,...n$	x_{ji} <----------------	Events $i=1,...m$	c_{ij} <----------------	Actors $j=1,...n$
	consequences		control	

$\Sigma_i x_{ji} = 1.0$ $\Sigma_j c_{ij} = 1.0$

2. Marsden/Laumann's Resource Possession Model

	consequences		impact		control	
Actors $j=1,...n$	<---------- x_{ji}	Events $i=1,...m$	<------- f_{ik}	Resources $k=1,...r$	<------- c_{kj}	Actors $j=1,...n$

3. Laumann/Knoke/Kim's Resource Deployment Model

	interests		effective		deploy	
Actors $j=1,...n$	<----------- x_{ji}	Events $i=1,...m$	<---------- a_{ih}	Actors $h=1,...n$	<--------- c^*_{hj}	Actors' Resources $j=1,...n$

4. Laumann/Knoke/Kim's Resource Mobilization Model

	interests		effective		control	
Actors $j=1,...n$	<-------- x_{ji}	Events $i=1,...m$	<-------- a_{ih}	Actors' Resources $h=1,...n$	<------- c^*_{hj}	Actors $j=1,...n$

5. Marsden's Influence Model

	influence		consequences		control	
Actors $j=1,...n$	<-------- q_{jh}	Objects $h=1,...n$	<---------- y_{hi}	Events $i=1,...m$	<------ c_{ij}	Actors $j=1,...n$

exchanges among actors. If a system is already in equilibrium, interest dependencies still exist among actors, but they do not induce further exchanges (see Kappelhoff [1993: 161–3] for this critique of Marsden and Laumann). Kappelhoff proposed to use excess demand as an indicator of exchange possibilities. Excess demand is measured as the difference between an actor's effective demand for control of an event and the value of the actor's control held before exchange. But regardless of how community affairs discussions are measured, the fact remains that network data only estimate system parameters that are not directly measured.

The network itself is not a crucial part of the modified model. Pappi and Kappelhoff (1984) found suitable direct measures of interest dependencies, allowing them to compute all model parameters without reference to network data.

Other exchange models relied more directly on network relations, using them as an explicit model component. Laumann, Knoke, and Kim (1987) used resource exchange networks as indicators of the control matrix, in contrast to influence models where networks function to modify the interest component. If a resource exchange network serves as a component of the control matrix, actors play a double role: controlling other actors and as objects of control. Our institutional access model uses the term "agents" to designate when actors are the objects of control.

One can argue that these alternative models were driven, not by the interest of actors in events, but by the actors' derived interests in those agents who effectively decide events in which the actors are interested. The Laumann-Knoke-Kim model used a resource exchange network to estimate the control relations resulting from exchanges and not as a measure of original control. But they encountered the same problem as Marsden and Laumann, because they lacked a measure of agents' effectiveness in the collective decisions. In their application, Laumann, Knoke, and Kim made the same assumption as Taylor and Coleman's (1979) first application of the original Coleman model to a sociometric network: Before exchanges are made, every actor has control only over herself. This assumption means that an agent's effectiveness is identical with its power. This identity is not a disadvantage of the modified model, but it limits the type of data suitable for estimating the model parameters.

Laumann, Knoke, and Kim proposed two concepts of agent control (see diagrams 3 and 4 in Figure 7.1). Their first version, a resource deployment model, was that a set of powerful actors deployed their resources to effective agents so that resources given to the agents reflect the first actors' power. Their second version, a resource mobilization model, was that the agents already possess resources that the powerful actors then activate for their own purposes. In the resource mobilization model, an actor becomes more powerful as it more effectively mobilizes its agents' resources. Empirically, both aspects of agent control seem to have occurred in the U.S. health and energy policy domains (Laumann, Knoke, and Kim, 1987: 366–8. For similar results in the German labor domain, see König, 1992: 145–79).

Influence models, on the other hand, may be interpreted as modifications of Coleman's original model that builds a network into the interest component. Coleman experimented with sociometric applications of his model (Taylor and Coleman, 1979) and later developed a concept of psychic investment in other actors (Coleman, 1986: 121–2). Following Mead's distinction between an active self ("I") and an object self ("me"), he conceptualized network actors in this dual role. Actors could exchange resources with other "object actors" in whom they have made psychic investments. If one accepts that actor *A*'s psychic investment in actor *B* is a prerequisite for a possible influence by *B,* a model of psychic investments can be interpreted as an influence model. The exchange of control over events is driven not by the actors' own interests in the events, but is influenced by the object actors. Marsden (1981) developed such an influence model, which distinguished between object actors' intrinsic interests in events and extrinsic interests resulting from the influence of controlling actors (see diagram 5 in Figure 7.1). He argued quite explicitly that "the notion of extrinsic interest summarizes a disaggregation of the concept of interest into two components, intrinsic interest and influence" (1981: 1214). Depending on behavioral assumptions about what actors actually exchange, the Laumann-Knoke-Kim mobilization model could also be interpreted as a type of influence model.

Stokman and Van den Bos (1992) criticized Laumann-Knoke-Kim's use of a resource exchange network to measure control. They argued that the approach fails to take into account the direct effectiveness of actors. Agents are effective in deciding events due to their voting power, whereas actor power in the Laumann-Knoke-Kim model derives from the control of effective agents: " . . . the interests of actors with direct effectiveness for controlling valued events, do not directly contribute to the value of events unless they themselves have control over other efficacious actors" (1992: 227).

Stokman and Van den Bos raised an important issue in using network data: how to treat the power matrix's main diagonal. In most applications, the diagonal is either undefined or left empty, because asking somebody how much she exchanges with herself normally makes no sense. When a resource exchange matrix is treated as a control matrix, the problem becomes how to measure self-control, that is, an actor's control over herself in the role of an agent. Although Stokman and Van den Bos raised this very important issue, they missed the mark as an objection to the model's theoretical rationale. Agents cannot use power for their personal advantage. Indeed, agents are conceptualized as instruments who act solely on behalf of the actors. But each actor is simultaneously an agent and, to the extent that it has self-control, an actor thus can realize its own interests through its role as an agent. Laumann, Knoke, and Kim included public (governmental) actors among the set of all actors without treating them only as agents. Thus, the objection that their model shows "an extremely instrumentalist view of the state" (Stokman and Van den Bos, 1992: 227) makes sense only concerning the concrete application of the model and cannot be accepted as a valid argument against its theoretical foundations.

Stokman and Van den Bos decomposed the unified Coleman model into a two-stage model of collective decision making: (1) an influence stage in which all actors influence each other during one or more influence rounds; and (2) a decision stage when only the actors having the authority to make binding decisions actually vote on the events or bills on the basis of their extrinsic preferences, that is, on their preferences as influenced by the other actors during the first stage. Because Stokman and Van den Bos were well aware of the vote-trading problem and the limited applicability of exchange models for divisible resources to the problem of collective decisions, they could not just apply Marsden's influence model and remain within the family of models discussed thus far. The constraint arises from the fact that, in Stokman and Van den Bos's application, control is really measured by voting power. The strongest point in their argument concerns this voting power concept, which is much clearer than the vague idea of agent effectiveness in the Laumann-Knoke-Kim model.

AN INSTITUTIONAL ACCESS MODEL

This section extends the Laumann-Knoke-Kim model by making a clear separation between actor and agent roles and by accepting the Stokman-Van den Bos argument for a stricter definition of voting power. Our institutional access model differs in three respects from the resource deployment and mobilization models discussed in the preceding section:

(1) We make a clear distinction between public and private actors in policy domains. Public actors have the authority to make binding decisions, and therefore they play the double role of actors and agents.
(2) Accepting Stokman and Van den Bos's critique of the vague concept of effectiveness of agents for events, we construct an authority, or voting power, matrix, relying on our understanding of the legislative processes in the three countries.
(3) We solve the problem of self-control by empirically emphasizing that the only exchanged control is the access actors have to the agents. The voting power matrix is not seen as a component of control, but rather as a component of interest, because the system is driven by the derived interest of the actors in effective agents.

Readers interested in the technical details of the institutional access model should refer to this chapter's appendix, which describes it in formal matrix algebra expressions. Although we occasionally use this notation in the main text, we endeavor to discuss the model's essential features in a primarily verbal form that is more accessible to a general audience.

We call it an institutional access model because our delineation of the authorities to whom access is sought comes from an understanding how institutions function to reach collective decisions and because access to decision makers is the crucial, divisible resource that can be exchanged (König, 1993: 604). What is most important to understand is that access is not event-specific, but it is policy domain-specific. Thus, at any time a given policy domain is characterized by a single access matrix that does not vary across events but that optimizes the actors' access to effective agents.

What consequences does this access have for the agents' decisions? Every agent's voting power is fixed and cannot be exchanged. The agents are not conceived of as targets of influence processes who really can change their preferences concerning particular events. Here we adopt a narrow conception of influence as a means of persuasion (Parsons, 1967: 366–71). We conceive of agents as merely the instruments of the actors, in the sense that the agents decide each event stochastically as a result of the biased influences of the actors having access to them. Thus, Coleman's probabilistic decision rule has not been built into the agents' voting behavior. The advantage of this assumption is that it does not require any agent commitments that would allow the actors to influence them. In such an exchange system, a broker can give a third party access to an effective agent without having been initially influenced by this third party. A broker simply passes along arguments to an agent without necessarily accepting these arguments as his own. Thus, brokers act more like lawyers in an intermediary position between two parties than as friends of both parties who try to manipulate closure within an opinion system.

MEASURING CONTROL VIA ACCESS

At first glance, measuring actors' access to agents would seem to be an easy matter of posing direct questions about networks. But the organizational informants do not have our analytic distinctions between organizations playing the dual roles of actors and agents in their minds. Many informants may claim to enjoy access to effective public agents. Yet when they try sending messages, they often discover those presumed channels are useless because the intended recipients pay little attention. Therefore, we decided not to measure access by a simple direct network question but to measure access indirectly, by treating information exchanges as empirical realizations of access possibilities.

Information is allegedly the most general resource in a policy domain. If no valuable information were exchanged, actor *A* could hardly be imagined to have access to agent *B*. Although some information is broadcast freely in policy domains, the organizations to whom such generalized information is sent will not necessarily make the best judgments about which subset of agents actually grants access to the sender. Hence, we first asked each informant about the policy domain subfield for which the organization needs outside information. Then, we asked which organizations provided that information. Next, we asked analogous information-supply questions. Each informant first told us in which domain subfield the organization could provide valuable policy information to others, and listed all the organizations to whom this information was sent. We used these responses to construct a confirmed information exchange network. A report by organization *A* that it sends information to organization *B* is accepted only when organization *B* confirms that it receives information from organization *A*. Thus, this confirmed communication relation is not symmetric, although several empirical links do confirm that some exchanges occur in both directions. Therefore, whether the information senders are placed in the rows or the columns of the resulting matrix does make a difference.

According to the logic of the resource deployment model, the resource senders control the receivers. In the labor domain study, this resource is valuable labor policy information, for which the receivers have a strong demand. When organization *A* provides a resource that organization *B* needs, *B* depends on *A* more than the other way around. Judging from the way the network questions were asked, our data are more compatible with the deployment model than with the mobilization model.

Figure 7.2. *The confirmed information exchange matrix (E)*

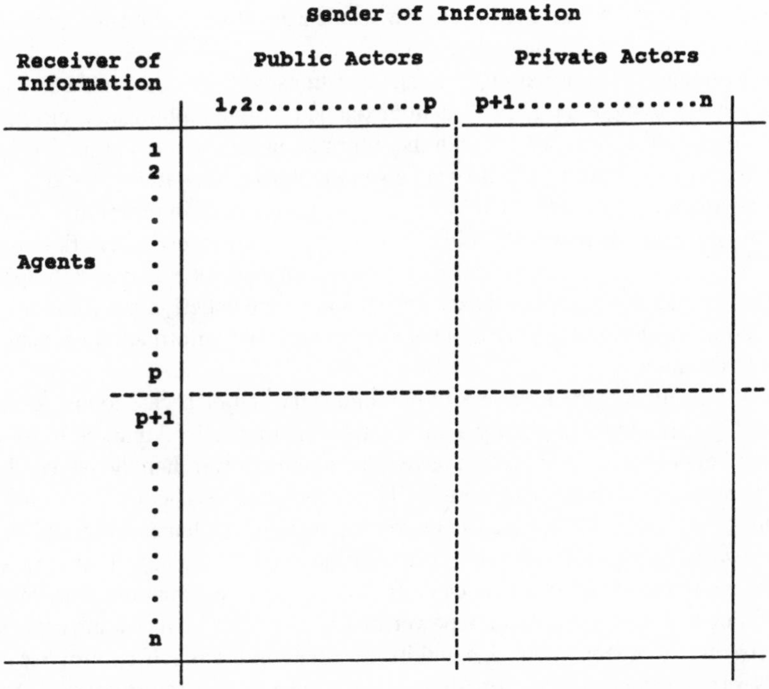

Sender of Information
Receiver of Information
Public Actors
Private Actors
1,2............p
p+1..............n
Agents
1
2
p
p+1
n

Meaning of main diagonal: number of actors to whom column actor sent information that was not confirmed by respective receivers.

Standardization of E: $n_{kl} = \dfrac{e_{kl}}{\sum_{l} e_{kl}}$

The confirmed information exchange network generates a square matrix with main diagonal entries of zeros (see the schematic form in Figure 7.2). To construct a control matrix from this network, we must first solve the problem of self-control, then standardize the matrix and come to terms with the indirect control problem. Finally, we must rearrange the matrix to separate the public actors from the private actors.

We measured each agent's self-control by the number of organizations whose information sendings were not confirmed by that agent. Agents get many more offers of information than they need, and we interpreted the number of such unacknowledged transmissions as an indicator of an agent's independence or self-control. As the informant for the German Labor Ministry and Social Affairs explained, the ministry does not need outside information, so none of the information sent to the ministry was confirmed. Accepting this answer at face value results in the German Labor Ministry possessing a perfect self-control of 1.0, because all entries in the exchange matrix are row-standardized (including the unconfirmed sendings in the main diagonal).

Although the information exchange questions were asked from the perspective of the deployment model, we cannot exclude possible mobilization mechanisms. Actors could control agents with the information they receive or, phrased differently, with the information they are able to mobilize. This ability could be backed up with other resources, such as political support offered in return for valuable information. Because we used only the confirmed information network to measure control, the access model's exchange component may not be completely specified. This limitation sometimes makes understanding the underlying logic of the mobilization model more difficult, where only confirmed information exchange data are available.

The latent construct we seek to measure is the actors' access to the agents. The deployment model implicitly assumes the logic of a sellers' market, in which the suppliers of scarce information have more market power than the buyers. Indeed, any buyer who can afford to refuse all offers possesses self-control. The mobilization model inverts this logic to a buyers' market, in which the buyers (information receivers) occupy the more powerful positions. Hence, organizations possess self-control to the extent that they can afford not to send information to organizations willing to accept such offers. A powerful deployer has a high sending capacity, because many organizations demand its information. It has self-control because, in its role as a receiver of information, it is less dependent on the offers made by other actors. A powerful mobilizer has a high receiving capacity because many organizations try to target it, whereas in its role as a sender, the mobilizer depends less on the others's use of its valuable information. A powerful mobilizer is a "sink" within an exchange system, whereas a powerful deployer is a "source" of value. Because the specific questions we asked stressed more the sellers' market perspective, they are better suited to the deployment model. However, an empirically unanswered question is whether the mobilization or deployment model better operationalizes the access that political agents grant to public and private actors.

A comparison of the self-control values generated by the deployment and mobilization models for the U.S., Germany, and Japan reveals few systematic differences, although overall the mobilization values seem slightly higher. The most remarkable finding is that, in the U.S., the House Democrats and the Senate Republicans are quite open to information sent to them, but have complete self-control according to the mobilization model. That is, because they can afford not to send any information to the outside, they act as sinks of influence peddling. For six of the eight years covered by the American project, the Republican Party held a majority in the Senate while the Democrats controlled the House of Representatives. Without overinterpreting these measures, one could argue that the majority parties are the main gatekeepers in the U.S. Congress. But by serving as information sinks in a legislative system with abundant information, these parties can close off themselves to control by outside mobilizers. In parliamentary systems such as Germany and Japan, similar obstruction would be much more difficult to achieve, because even a majority party must remain open at least to other public actors, above all to the ministries and the cabinet. The German Labor Ministry's claim earlier not to need any outside information could be strongly interpreted as indicating that the German system is closer to a sellers' market. Information sent is used to control the receivers, while self-control indicates an ability to reject information offers.

Before interpreting the standardized confirmed information exchange matrix as a control matrix, we must consider the possibility that control is possible not only through direct linkages but also indirectly through brokers. A system without brokerage has the disadvantage that only a subset of actors directly controls agents. In Germany and Japan, many claimant organizations lack direct access because only the peak business and labor organizations can communicate their member organizations' interests to the core public agents. In network terms, these member organizations can reach the agents only through indirect paths of length two or three. Empirically, the confirmed information exchange networks in each national labor policy domain are weak components. That is, the organizations can gain access to one another only by disregarding the direction of their connections. However, the access model's control matrix is no longer identical to the square matrix. Instead, it is reduced to a smaller rectangular matrix, where the subset of public actors serving as agents define the rows of the matrix, and all private and all public actors are located in the columns. The unconnected organizations in this rectangular matrix would remain disconnected even under equilibrium conditions.

Thus, we must come to terms with the problem of brokerage. Does it make sense to assume that brokerage processes occur in these legislative systems, in the sense of a go-between organization that passes on valuable information from an actor to an agent? We concluded that limited brokerage should be built into our access mode, by allowing only a single middle actor and no paths longer than two steps. Thus, direct access still carries a greater weight than do such indirect ties. Details of this modification are reported in the chapter appendix. If an organization decides to play the broker role, it should be aware that its self-control may diminish because it passes on arguments to agents that do not necessarily represent the broker's own interests. This constraint is no problem for a private organization, because its self-control is not taken into account in the final model. But, public actors may also act as brokers, even when that role reduces their possible interest satisfaction due to lower self-control values. Although public actors could have been excluded as brokers, we decided not to treat them differently from private actors in this respect.

DIRECT AND REVEALED INTERESTS

This section introduces a measure of organizations' interests in policy events, then discusses differing conceptualizations of basic parliamentary and presidential decision-making processes. Our analysis focuses exclusively on collective decisions about legislative bills. Laumann and Knoke (1987: 17) defined policy events as occurring "when a concrete proposal for authoritative action is placed before a decision making body." Strictly speaking, the bills themselves are not events, but decisions about bills by committees or other collective decision-making bodies are policy events. Chapter 3 briefly describes how the labor policy events were selected and Appendix 4 provides chronological summaries for each nation (those bills are numbered according to their sequences in the questionnaires).

We distinguish between organizational preferences and interests in a bill. An organization's preference is measured as a simple dichotomy, that is, in favor ("pro") or against ("con") the bill. In general, an organization expresses greater interest in a bill when the utility difference between a positive and a negative collective decision on that bill is higher. We asked informants whether their organizations had any interest in a bill. If the organization had no interest, its direct interest in the bill was coded as 0, and it was asked no further questions about that event. For an expression of any interest in a bill, we asked how strong was that interest and recorded the informant's response from very strong (5) to very little (1) interest.

A second interest measure, revealed interest, encompasses organizational actions taken to influence the legislative outcome. If an informant stated that the organization had a direct interest in an event, she was asked what the organization had done to try to influence the outcome. Possible tactical actions included: participating in formulating the policy, formal contacts with governmental officials or legislators such as testifying at hearings or serving on commissions, informal contacts with officials, using mass media to publicize the organization's opinion, mobilizing members or the general public, and forming coalitions with other groups (see Table 6.5 in Chapter 6). We interpret these actions as "revealing" the actual interest of an organization in a political event.

Generally, one would anticipate a high correlation between the two interest measures because the 0 entries are matched (an organization with no interest in an event was not asked about influence activities). However, the covariation may differ if only those events are considered for which actors have shown at least some interest. Then, we hypothesize that the revealed interest measure would better indicate an organization's overall interest in events than would the direct interest. This difference should be especially evident for bills initiated by opposition parties in parliamentary systems. Although such proposals may address important issues, participants know that those proposals are very unlikely to be accepted by a legislature dominated by the governmental party or coalition. In general, we expect positive correlations, which we interpret to mean that organizations really spend their scarce resources when they have an interest in a legislative bill. After corroborating this interpretation, we shall rely on the simpler direct interest measure to estimate our institutional access model.

Tables 7.1 to 7.3 list the legislative bills of the three nations, with the means of the direct and revealed interests of the actors (see Appendix 4 for detailed descriptions and dates of all the bills). The legislative periods covered by these events are the 97th to 100th U.S. Congresses; the 10th and 11th *Bundestags* (Federal Diet)

Table 7.1. *Direct and revealed interests of U.S. organizations in legislative events*

EVENT	MEAN DIRECT	MEAN REVEALED
2. Black Lung Benefits	0.8	0.6
3. CETA & JTPA	2.6	2.3
5. Union Pension Fraud	0.3	0.5
6. Public Employee Pensions	1.1	0.8
7. Automobile Domestic Content	1.2	1.0
8. ERISA Benefits Recovery	0.6	0.2
9. American Conservation Corps	0.9	0.4
10. Mine Safety Cooperation	0.7	0.4
11. ERISA Pre-1974 Benefits	0.8	0.4
12. Public Works Compensation	1.4	0.9
13. Garment Homework Limits	1.0	0.9
16. Vocational Education Renewal	1.6	1.3
18. ERISA Pension Spousal Equity	1.4	1.1
19. JTPA Summer Remedial Education	1.6	0.8
20. Teenage Sub-Minimum Wage	2.0	1.4
23. Immigration Reform	1.9	1.6
24. American Boxing Corporation	0.2	0.1
28. Occupational Risk Assessment	2.5	2.2
29. Parental & Disability Leave	2.7	2.2
30. Minimum Wage Increase	2.4	1.9
31. 60-Day Plant Closing Notice	2.5	2.2
32. Bankruptcy Benefit Suspension	1.0	0.7
33. Double-Breasting by Companies	1.7	1.3
35. Polygraph Ban	1.5	1.2
36. PBGC Premium Increase	1.4	1.0

[1]Range 0 to 5, with 5 = very strong interest, 0 = almost none.
[2]Range 0 to 6, number of influence activities mentioned.

of the German Federal Republic; and the periods after the so-called Japanese double election of 1980 (of both the House of Representatives and the House of Councillors [see Pempel, 1992: 17]), after the separate elections for both chambers in 1983, and after another double election in 1986. These legislative periods are important, because the political parties' fortunes at elections and at the start of new governments strongly influence the legislative agendas and the policy cycle. Only Japan experienced continuing stable political conditions during the 1980s, with the Liberal Democratic Party enjoying its uninterrupted reign begun with its founding in 1955. (Although the LDP engaged in coalition tactics in 1983 with a small splinter party, the New Liberal Club, that group was absorbed by the LDP three years later.)

In the U.S., the 97th Congress beginning in 1981 marked a break from its predecessor, with the Republican President Reagan succeeding the Democratic Carter Administration while his party also won a majority in the Senate. At the 100th Congress in 1987, the Democrats regained the Senate majority. In Germany, the

Table 7.2. *Direct and revealed interests of German organizations in legislative events*

EVENT	MEAN DIRECT	MEAN REVEALED
1. Labor Court Jurisdiction	0.4	0.2
2. Penalties for Illegal Employment	0.4	0.3
3. Budget Reductions for Entitlements	3.0	2.5
4. Remigration of Foreign Workers	1.4	1.0
5. Early Retirement	2.3	1.8
6. Stricter Rules for Work on Sundays	1.5	1.0
7. Bankruptcy Law Reform	0.8	0.5
8. Deregulation of Work Protection	1.5	1.2
9. Employment Opportunities Act	3.1	2.3
11. Limits on Public Servants' Extra Earnings	0.8	0.6
12. Extend Unemployment Payments	1.5	1.0
13. Anti-Gender Discrimination	1.2	0.6
14. Farmers' Social Benefits	0.4	0.4
15. Reduction of Overtime Work	0.7	0.3
16. Improvement of Vocational Training	1.3	0.9
18. Notice of Employment for the Handicapped	1.8	1.3
20. Neutrality of Federal Employment Agency	2.1	1.7
21. Extend Co-Determination Rights	1.3	0.8
22. Vocational Training Act	0.5	0.4
23. Farmers' Social Insurance	0.4	0.3
25. Mothers' Annuity Insurance	1.8	1.2
26. Participation of Labor in Management	1.1	0.7
27. Promotion of Savings Formation by Workers	0.8	0.6
28. Illegalize Employee Lock-Out During Strikes	0.9	0.5
29. Protection of Part-Time Workers	0.9	0.5
30. Restrictions on Leasing of Workers	0.6	0.3
31. Labor Participation in Steel Industry Management	1.2	0.8
32. Amend Work Promotion Act	1.8	1.4
33. Work Council Representation of Juveniles, Trainees	1.2	1.0
34. Social Insurance Registration	0.9	0.6
35. Age Limit for Physicians' Licenses	1.1	0.6
36. Amend Work Council Act	1.8	1.3

[1]Range 0 to 5, with 5 = very strong interest, 0 = almost none.
[2]Range 0 to 6, number of influence activities mentioned.

10th *Bundestag,* starting early in 1983, was the first full term of the coalition government of the Christian Democratic Union/Christian Social Union and Free Democratic Party led by Chancellor Helmut Kohl, after the break up of the Social Democratic Party–FDP coalition in the fall of 1982.

In the U.S., the Democrats, after winning back the majority in the Senate, also tried to win back policy leadership, although this initiative is usually the preserve of the president. But, the Reagan Administration had not been very active in the labor policy domain. The only major labor legislative effort during Reagan's first term was termination of the Comprehensive Employment and Training Act (CETA) and its replacement by the Job Training Partnership Act (JTPA). The 1982

Table 7.3. *Direct and revealed interests of Japanese organizations in legislative events*

EVENT	MEAN DIRECT	MEAN REVEALED
0. Old-Age Insurance	2.4	1.2
3. Depressed Industry Employment	1.8	0.8
5. Unemployment Insurance Reform	1.7	0.7
6. Nationalize Health Insurance	2.4	1.1
7. Privatize Tobacco Monopoly	0.9	0.5
10. Privatize Telephone and Telegraph	1.6	0.6
11. National Pension Reform	2.2	1.0
12. Small Industry Retirement Funds	0.9	0.4
13. Occupational Training Reform	1.3	0.6
14. Equal Employment Opportunity	2.8	1.3
15. Temporary Employment Agencies	2.2	0.9
16. Citizen's Holidays	2.0	0.4
17. Promotion of Stable Employment for the Elderly	2.3	0.7
19. Workers' Disaster Insurance	1.5	0.7
24. Privatize National Railway	2.3	1.0
26. Higher Contributions for Elderly Insurance	2.2	1.0
27. Retail Sales Tax	3.1	1.8
28. Salaried Workers Savings Promotion	1.3	0.4
29. Handicapped Employment Reform	1.4	0.5
30. Regional Employment Development	1.1	0.4
32. Work Week Reduction to 40 hours	3.1	1.5
33. Consumer Tax	3.7	1.9

[1]Range 0 to 5, with 5 = very strong interest, 0 = almost none.
[2]Range 0 to 6, number of influence activities mentioned.

JTPA, which kept only the job-training elements from its predecessor program, received the highest interest level of all labor bills during Reagan's first six years in office. Only after the Democrats began introducing major labor legislation in the 100th Congress, did the domain actors' interest and activity levels again rise. Major Democratic initiatives included the 1987 High Risk Occupational Disease Notification and Prevention Act, the Parental Leave and Disability Act, and the Minimum Wage Increase Act. The proposed Plant Closing Act in its original Democratic formulation would have required mandatory advanced notice of plant closings. Viewed in terms of expressed interest levels from late 1981 to the middle of 1987, one gets an impression of some activity at the beginning, followed by a rather quiescent period, until a rise in the interest levels beginning in early 1987.

The German interest pattern differed insofar as the new coalition government of CDU/CSU and FDP introduced major labor policy proposals shortly after its first inauguration in 1983. The highest organizational activity level was triggered by the fiscal austerity measures of 1983, which restricted some social entitlement programs and cut back salaries for public servants (see event 3 in Table 7.2). Shortly after this bill, the government introduced the Employment Opportunity

Act into parliament in an effort to deregulate German labor law. The new law made it possible, for instance, to hire workers only for a certain duration and thus was supposed to circumvent the normal termination notices that employers had found difficult to apply successfully. From 1985 to the end of the period under investigation, German labor policy-making grew more routinized, attracting only medium to low interest levels.

In Japan, the bills drawing most attention from labor domain organizations were scattered more evenly across the period under investigation, suggesting the more stable conditions of governing in this country. The two bills with the highest activity and interest levels pertained to new consumer taxes that would have fallen outside of the labor domain as defined for the U.S. and Germany (see events 27 and 33 of Table 7.3). Because the debates about the taxes were framed to increase the burden on employees and other social groups (besides increasing tax revenues), these bills were presumably relevant forms of labor policy. The Japanese organizations also showed above-average interest in a bill reducing the work week to 40 hours (event 32) and in a bill forbidding discriminatory treatment of women in the labor force albeit also loosening the work protection of women (event 14). Major social policies such as old age and health insurance attracted higher interest than policies that affected small groups like the handicapped, as was also the case in the other two countries. The privatization of formerly state-owned companies, including the Japan National Railway and Japan Telephone and Telegraph, was part of the labor policy domain because these changes transformed the legal status as well as the political position of the labor movement and the party positions of more than half a million workers. This change weakened socialist public-sector union power. Therefore, the left wing of the Japan Socialist and Japan Communist parties bitterly opposed these bills as "union-busting" efforts. On the other hand, through this change, the workers in these companies obtained the right to strike, which had been one of the most controversial issues in Japanese industrial relations.

Overall, the revealed activity levels seem lower than the direct interest measure in Japan, whereas both measures seem roughly comparable in the U.S. and Germany. This difference appears in the correlations of the two measures across all events: The value is highest in Germany ($r = 0.98$), followed by the U.S. ($r = 0.97$), but a bit lower in Japan ($r = 0.93$). These correlations are aggregate values. Mean correlations computed for individual organizations produce the same rank ordering, with lower values: $r = 0.84$ in Germany, 0.82 in the U.S., and 0.67 in Japan. As previously mentioned, such high correlations are partly an artifact that no interest also means no activity. Defining the zero interests and zero activity levels as missing, the two measures are only moderately correlated in the U.S. ($r = 0.43$), a little bit lower in Germany ($r = 0.35$), and much lower in Japan ($r = 0.24$). This lower value for Japan indicates that many Japanese organizations allow and rely upon their peak federations to carry out real political pressure activities. The two measures are sufficiently similar to indicate that actors with direct interests also spend their resources to influence the event outcomes. Therefore, in the institutional access model, we use only the direct interest measure.

The model requires a direct interest measure that is standardized across all events. That is, each organization's relative interest is computed as its interest in an individual event divided by the sum of all its direct interests. The crucial decision here is whether to treat the periods under investigation as a single interval or to decompose each period into its separate legislative terms (König et al., 1993). Because we postulate that actors seek access to agents, and because we rely on a general policy network rather than on policy specific networks, we decided to treat the entire investigative period as one interval. This operationalization can be further justified with the argument that the overall power balance did not change dramatically during these periods in the three countries. Conservative governments remained in power, so organizational efforts to gain access did not require major strategic changes.

Although the amount of interest an organization has in a specific event and the derived interest it has in a particular agent define the model's purposive component, these elements are insufficient to predict a legislative bill's outcome. We must also know the actors' preferences in favor of or opposed to the specific bill. Space limitations prevent us from showing the preferences of all actors for all bills in the three nations. Some insights can be gained, however, by comparing the preference profiles of the peak labor unions and business associations. According to organizational reputations, in the U.S. the most powerful union was the AFL-CIO and the most powerful business association was the Chamber of Commerce of the U.S. In Germany, these roles were played by the German Trade Union Federation (DGB) and the Confederation of German Employers Associations (BDA), respectively. In Japan the peak business organization was the Japan Federation of Employers Associations (FEA). The peak labor union with the highest reputation was the Japan Private Sector Trade Union Confederation (PTU), not the General Council of the Trade Unions of Japan (GCU). The GCU was still independent at the time of our study, but it soon disbanded and was absorbed by the PTU in 1989. The GCU originally was closely aligned with the Japan Socialist Party, and its members were "most public sector unions including militant leadership of railway . . . unions . . ." (Anderson, 1992: 38). As mentioned in Chapter 2, the 1980s saw the labor movement initiative shift from the GCU to the PTU, concluding with the integration of both federations. In 1982, the PTU's forerunner, the PTUC formed as a consultative council rather than as a national center. The PTU was established in 1987 as an alternative center to the GCU, during the latter part of our field period.

In addition to the policy preferences of these peak organizations, Tables 7.4 to 7.6 list the initiators of each bill and the final outcomes (passage into public law or rejection). Thus, we can determine whether the most powerful labor and business organizations usually agreed with the government in their labor legislation preferences.

Table 7.4. *Initiators, peak labor and business organization preferences, and outcomes of U.S. legislative events*

EVENT	INITIATOR[1]	PREFERENCE[2] AFL	COC	OUTCOME[3]
2. Black Lung Benefits	A	+	0	+
3. CETA & JTPA	A,C	+	+	+
5. Union Pension Fraud	S	-	+	-
6. Public Employee Pensions	H	+	0	-
7. Automobile Domestic Content	H	+	-	-
8. ERISA Benefits Recovery	H	+	-	-
9. American Conservation Corps	C	+	0	-
10. Mine Safety Cooperation	A	+	0	-
11. ERISA Pre-1974 Benefits	H	+	0	-
12. Public Works compensation	S	+	0	-
13. Garment Homework Limits	A,S	-	+	-
16. Vocational Education Renewal	C	+	+	+
18. ERISA Pension Spousal Equity	C	+	+	+
19. JTPA Summer Remedial Education	C	+	+	+
20. Teen Sub-Minimum Wage	A	-	+	-
23. Immigration Reform	C	+	-	+
24. American Boxing Corporation	H	0	0	-
28. Occupational Risk Assessment	C	+	-	-
29. Parental & Disability Leave	C	+	-	-
30. Minimum Wage Increase	C	+	-	-
31. 60-Day Plant Closing Notice	C	+	-	+
32. Bankruptcy Benefit Suspension	C	+	-	+
33. Double-Breasting by Companies	H	+	-	-
35. Polygraph Ban	C	+	+	+
36. PBGC Premium Increase	A,C	+	0	+

[1] A = Administration; H = House of Representatives (with Democratic majority); S = Senate (with Republican majority until event 24); C = Congress
[2] + in favor of bill; − against; 0 no interest
[3] + bill became public law; − bill failed

The adversarial character of labor policy is readily apparent from the numerous disagreements between labor and business concerning the legislative events. Measured in this way, the conflict between business and labor was higher in Germany than in the U.S. or Japan. Starting with Germany in Table 7.5, remarkably the DGB and the BDA never agreed about any of the 32 bills (0 percent). Of course, in some cases both peak organizations were not at all interested or one held a clear preference while the other was uninterested. Of the 12 German bills where the DGB and BDA took opposing sides, the business position prevailed in 10 cases. For the 25 U.S. bills, as shown in Table 7.4, the Chamber of Commerce and the AFL-CIO held the same position on five proposals (20 percent), all of which were enacted into law. Of the 12 U.S. bills on which the AFL-CIO and Chamber of Commerce took opposing sides, the labor and business preferences each prevailed six times.

Japan exhibited the highest agreement level between the most powerful union (PTU) and the most powerful employers' organization (FEA). They reported the

Table 7.5. *Initiators, peak labor and business organization preferences, and outcomes of German legislative events*

EVENT	INITIATOR[1]	PREFERENCE[2] DGB	BDA	OUTCOME[3]
1. Labor Court Jurisdiction	L	-	0	-
2. Penalties for Illegal Employment	L	0	0	-
3. Budget Reductions for Entitlements	R	-	+	+
4. Remigration of Foreign Workers	R	-	0	+
5. Early Retirement	R	+	0	+
6. Stricter Rules for Work on Sundays	O	+	-	-
7. Bankruptcy Law Reform	O	+	-	-
8. Deregulation of Work Protection	L	-	+	+
9. Employment Opportunities Act	R	-	+	+
11. Limit Public Servants' Extra Earnings	R	0	0	+
12. Extend Unemployment Payments	R	+	-	+
13. Anti-Gender Discrimination	O	+	-	-
14. Farmers' Social Benefits	R	0	0	+
15. Reduction of Overtime Work	O	0	0	-
16. Improvement of Vocational Training	R	0	+	+
18. Employment of Handicapped	R	-	0	+
20. Federal Employment Agency Neutrality	R	-	+	+
21. Extend Co-Determination Rights	O	+	-	-
22. Vocational Training Act	R	0	0	+
23. Farmers' Social Insurance	R	0	0	+
25. Mothers' Annuity Insurance	O	+	0	-
26. Participation of Labor in Management	O	+	-	-
27. Worker Savings Promotion	R	-	+	+
28. Illegalize Employee Lock-Out	O	+	0	-
29. Protection of Part-Time Workers	O	+	0	-
30. Restrictions on Leasing of Workers	L	+	0	-
31. Steel Industry Co-Determination	R	+	-	+
32. Amend Work Promotion Act	R	-	0	+
33. Represent Youth on Work Councils	R	+	0	+
34. Social Insurance Registration	R	-	0	+
35. Age Limit for Physicians' Licenses	L	+	0	-
36. Amend Work Council Act	R	0	-	+

[1]L = State government through *Bundesrat*; R = Government or coalition parties in *Bundestag*; O = Opposition parties in *Bundestag* (SPD, Greens)
[2] + in favor of bill; − against; 0 no interest
[3] + bill became public law; − bill failed

same policy preferences for 10 of the 22 bills (45 percent) and took opposing positions on only five proposals. For the seven remaining bills, the PTU (and PTC) was not interested, but the FEA held a definite position. When both business and labor agreed, their preference prevailed in seven of the 10 cases. The PTU position won in three of the five bills with opposition. The level of disinterest by the peak Japanese labor organization is astonishing compared to the U.S. and Germany, whose peak labor federations were far more opinionated about labor policy than were their peak employers associations. Especially remarkable, the PTU expressed no interest in the privatization policies of the Japanese government.

Table 7.6. *Initiators, peak labor and business organization preferences, and outcomes of Japanese legislative events*

EVENT	INITIATOR[1]	PREFERENCE[2] PTU	PREFERENCE[2] FEA	OUTCOME[3]
0. Old-Age Insurance	G	-	-	+
3. Depressed Industry Employment	G	+	+	+
5. Unemployment Insurance Reform	G	0	+	+
6. Nationalize Health Insurance	G	-	+	+
7. Privatize Tobacco Monopoly	G	0	+	+
10. Privatize Telephone and Telegraph	G	0	+	+
11. National Pension Reform	G	0	-	+
12. Small Industry Retirement Funds	G	+	+	+
13. Occupational Training Reform	G	+	+	+
14. Equal Employment Opportunity	G	+	-	+
15. Temporary Employment Agencies	G	0	+	+
16. Citizen's Holidays	G	+	-	+
17. Promotion Stable Elderly Employment	G	+	-	+
19. Workers' Disaster Insurance	G	+	+	+
24. Privatize National Railway	G	0	+	+
26. Higher Elderly Insurance Premiums	G	-	-	+
27. Retail Sales Tax	G	+	+	-
28. Salaried Workers Savings Promotion	G	+	+	+
29. Handicapped Employment Reform	G	+	+	+
30. Regional Employment Development	G	+	+	+
32. Work Week Reduction to 40 hours	G	0	+	+
33. Consumer Tax	G	-	+	+

[1]G = governmental or majority party (LDP) bills
[2] + in favor of bill; − against; 0 no interest
[3] + bill became public law; − bill failed

However, if we recognize the delicate and transitional position of the PTU (1987–9), and especially of its forerunner the PTC (1982–7), the puzzle will be partly solved. Because, as we mentioned earlier and in Chapter 2, for most of the period covered by our project (1982–8) the legitimate national center of the Japanese labor movement was occupied by the GCU, not by the PTC or PTU. The 1980s were literally an era of transition, or, equivalently, an era of competition over labor initiatives by two groups. Despite its dominant position, the GCU was degraded day by day under the neoliberal offensive of the conservative government, as well as under the policy-participatory offensive by the private labor union leaders. Thus, if we take GCU as the labor center, the analysis would be drastically different. Although such an analysis can show another aspect of Japan related to the 1960s and 1970s, we preferred to focus on the emerging aspects of Japan in the 1980s.

To return to interpreting the results, the PTU/PTC could not play any role nor show any interest in many events because of their delicate strategic and tactical considerations. On the other hand, the GCU, which was destroyed by the government's privatization policies, exhibited a clearly antigovernment position. The

GCU led action sets concerning 21 of the 22 legislative events. Of the 19 events where both the GCU and FEA mobilized action sets, the GCU and FEA opposed one another 11 times. Clearly, the shift of the labor movement initiative from GCU to PTU in the late 1980s signaled a shift of power toward Japanese business.

Concerning the initiators of the bills, proposing new legislation in both the U.S. and Germany is not a privilege of the presidential administration nor of the majority parties, but is explicitly used by all members of the U.S. Congress and also by the German opposition parties. But the intentions of different initiators of new legislation may differ between a presidential system lacking strict party discipline in Congress and a parliamentary system where opposition-party success normally means a change in government. Among the 32 German events, all bills initiated by the government or the coalition parties (CDU/CSU-FDP) in parliament ultimately succeeded in becoming enacted laws. This outcome is not always self-evident in the German system, because the Federal Chamber (*Bundesrat*) has a veto right over some legislation (see Appendix 1). During the period under analysis, the majority of state governments (*Länder*) in the *Bundesrat* were led by prime ministers of the CDU or CSU and thus were not in opposition to the federal government. *Bundesrat* members also have the right to initiate legislation, but only one of the five bills introduced by a state government was finally successful (event 8). None of the nine legislative initiatives by the opposition parties gained majority support, as everybody could easily anticipate from the outset. Opposition parties normally use their right to initiate legislation as a strategy to gain public attention and to mobilize their policy supporters, sometimes forcing the governing parties to respond with bills of their own.

For the U.S., we distinguished among bills initiated by the Administration, by the House, by the Senate, and by both chambers of Congress. Formally only members of Congress can initiate legislation, so an Administration typically must send its proposed bills to a ranking member of Congress belonging to the president's party. We coded a bill as congressional if it was introduced in both houses of Congress. When a bill was introduced only in one chamber but did not reach the other chamber, we coded it either as a House- or Senate-initiated bill. Such bills usually attracted the least interest from the domain organizations, and such bills, of course, never became public laws. All House bills had support from the AFL-CIO, which was not necessarily true of Senate bills during the 1981–6 period when the Republican Party was the majority. After the Democrats regained the Senate majority in the 1986 elections, all congressional bills were supported by AFL-CIO, but most were opposed by the Chamber of Commerce. The Chamber never opposed any bill initiated by the Reagan Administration.

In Germany, the peak labor association (DGB) supported eight of the nine bills initiated by an opposition party (normally by the Social Democrats), expressing no interest for only one (event 15). Of the 18 bills initiated by the German government, the peak employers' organization (BDA) normally either gave support or expressed no interest. Only in three instances – extending unemployment payments (event 12), steel industry codetermination (event 31), and work council amendments (event 36) – did the employers' organization oppose a government proposal. On the other hand, the DGB more often opposed than supported the government's proposals.

Except for one bill (event 16), the Japan project selected only government legislative initiatives, which were all expected to become public laws because of the Liberal Democratic Party's parliamentary dominance. In every case where a bill proposed by opposition parties was opposed by the ruling party and the ministries, it never passed in its original form. At best, they served to modify ministerial-ruling party bills (Richardson and Flanagan, 1984: 363). In fact, the majority of Japanese parliamentary bills were introduced by the prime minister, representing bills initiated by the ministries. The ruling LDP initiated far fewer bills, and the opposition party even fewer. In only one case, the 1987 retail sales tax bill (event 27), did the government fail to gain the necessary majority vote in the Diet. This defeat of the government was caused by dissenting LDP members and was considered a quite unusual outcome at the time. That dissension anticipated the 1993 ouster of the LDP after 38 years of uninterrupted single-party governance.

One may question whether a complicated exchange model can be meaningfully applied to situations like Japan, where almost all legislative decisions are clear from the beginning, or in the German case, where governmental initiatives regularly become law and opposition party initiatives are routinely defeated. A model would appear unnecessary for predicting these outcomes. Only in the U.S., with its perennially divided government, does the application of a model to assess its predictive power seem to make much sense. But we stress here that a model's predictive accuracy, which of course is normally a "post-diction," is not our primary objective. Rather, we seek to explain the internal dynamics of decision making in complex collective action systems. Hence, we use model predictions only as a validity check on our ability to represent these dynamics accurately. If a model predicts events correctly, then we can use such derived concepts as the power of the organizations, the value of the events, or the comparison of the exchange in equilibrium with the original exchange matrix as valid measures to describe a national labor policy domain. But, before attempting that validation, the next section introduces our final building blocks, three versions of the decision-making authority matrix.

AUTHORITY TO MAKE BINDING DECISIONS

Organizational participation in the policy formulation and decision phases of the policy cycle has the unequivocal goal of influencing the outcome of a collective decision. Normally organizations intend to affect the substantive content of policies. Thus, domain actors seek access to effective agents who possess authority to make binding decisions. In the strictest sense, effectiveness is best operationalized as the voting power of legislative actors to enact laws. We consider power to be an actor attribute, that is, as an ability to control effective agents. For our model to be completely consistent with game theories (e.g., Holler and Illing, 1991), voting power measures should be translated as effectiveness. But, because power measures like the Shapely-Shubik index are well-known in the social sciences, we cannot completely avoid using the term voting power in discussing the authority matrix.

This section considers three versions of the authority matrix: a legislative model with a strict voting power definition; a policy leadership model that additionally takes into account rights or expectations to initiate or block legislation; and a party government model that excludes the opposition parties as agents. These models differ first in their delineation of the agents and second in the concrete voting power entries in the authority matrix.

The *legislative model* takes into account only those agents with formal voting power to pass legislation. Institutional rules differ, of course, concerning which agents have formal voting power in various political systems. Here we are bound to maintain the crucial assumption of our approach, that all the consequential actors in a national policy domain are corporate actors, not individual persons. This assumption also holds for public actors and, therefore, for the agents. Consequential public actors are parliamentary parties and executive branch agencies, such as the ministries with jurisdiction in the labor policy domain in Germany and Japan and the White House and some departments in the U.S. For both parliamentary systems, an assumption that political parties act as unitary actors is quite realistic because they usually obey the norm of strict party discipline in voting on bills. Party discipline carries far less weight in the U.S. presidential system, because the executive branch depends less on permanent majority support in the Congress than is the case in parliamentary systems. We are well aware that postulating unitary parties in each congressional chamber is a very strong assumption, but party discipline in Congress during the Reagan era was higher than in the 1970s (Schneier and Gross, 1993: 199–201) and was higher in labor policy than other domains.

For the U.S. legislative model, the only actors possessing voting rights are the Democrats and the Republicans in the House of Representatives and the Senate, plus the president because of his right to veto legislation (see Appendix 1). Because we are examining the labor policy domain, we decided to include the parties in the relevant committees, that is, the House Committee on Education and Labor and the Senate Committee on Labor and Human Resources. The Democrats and the Republicans within these committees are treated as agents of their respective parties in Congress. The presidency is also represented not by a person, but institutionally, by the White House Office.

The voting power of these five agents could be derived from game theoretic power indices (König, 1993: 351–4). Applying these indices to the U.S. "tricameral" system of House, Senate, and presidency is inconclusive because the crucial problem of how to weight these three independent collective deciders has not been convincingly resolved. Treating the members of Congress as individuals, the Shapley-Shubik power index of the president is 0.162 and the Banzhaf index is 0.038, whereas another measure making somewhat different assumptions results in an index of 0.77 for the president (see Brams, 1990: 228–42). In this situation, we used an ad hoc procedure that first divided the total voting power of 1.0 into equal thirds for the three voting units (House, Senate, White House), then weighted by the percentage of seats held by each party within a unit. This procedure gave the Republican president one third of the total voting power (0.334). The House Democrats received a fraction between 0.186 and 0.204 depending on their congressional strength, and the House Republican proportion ranged from 0.147 to 0.129 (with the two parties always summing to 0.333). The most important change during the period under investigation occurred in the Senate in 1987 when the majority position changed from Republican to Democrat. Before that switch the Senate Republican voting power varied between 0.177 and 0.183 across three Congresses while the Democrats' share ranged from 0.156 to 0.150 (again their sum was 0.333). After the 1986 election, the Senate Republicans' voting power fell in the next Congress to 0.150 and the Democrats' rose to 0.183.

In Germany, the right to make the final legislative decision depends on the type of bill, that is, mainly on whether the 10 German states (*Länder*) are involved in implementation. When the states are excluded, the *Bundestag* has undivided formal voting power, but when the states are involved, the *Bundesrat*'s consent is necessary. The corporate actors within the *Bundesrat* are the state governments, with their voting share constitutionally fixed in rough proportion to the population of each state. In the *Bundestag,* the parliamentary parties are well organized as fractions, each with a board of parliamentary leaders, one of whom is normally responsible for labor policy. Because this leader is not identical to the ranking member of the party within the Labor Committee of the *Bundestag,* we decided to include both the parliamentary parties in the *Bundestag* and the party members of the Labor Committee as separate actors. The legislative model treats only the parliamentary actors as agents and allocates their voting power according to the proportion of seats held. During the two legislative periods spanning the seven years under investigation, four German parties were represented in the *Bundestag*. In the 10th *Bundestag* the share of the CDU/CSU was 0.490, falling to 0.449 in the 11th *Bundestag* after 1987; the SPD share likewise fell from 0.388 to 0.374; the FDP's share increased from 0.068 to 0.093; and Green Party sharing also rose from 0.054 to 0.085. These figures apply just to bills decided only in the *Bundestag*.

When the *Bundesrat* had to give its consent, we applied the same principle as in the U.S.: The *Bundestag* and *Bundesrat* each receive one half of the total voting power of 1.0, and the proportions within both chambers are allocated according to party strength. Thus, half the voting power is distributed among the ten German states. The four largest states – North Rhine-Westphalia, Bavaria, Baden-Wuerttemberg, and Lower Saxony – each received a voting power of 0.061; next followed three states with 0.049 (Hesse, Rhineland-Palatinate, Schleswig-Holstein); and finally three small states had a voting share of only 0.037 (Bremen, Hamburg, Saarland). Because state governments are directly represented in the *Bundesrat* (see Appendix 1), state election results have no impact on state shares in the *Bundesrat,* although they obviously have consequences for the party composition of a state government.

Japan, in contrast to the U.S. and German federal systems, has a unitary central government. All three nations separate their legislative powers. Japan's Diet is divided into a House of Representatives and a House of Councillors (see Appendix 1). After World War II, Japan adopted a parliamentary cabinet system characterized by a fusion of power between the majority in the legislature and the cabinet. The cabinet is collectively responsible to the Diet, which has the right to elect the prime minister, who then appoints his cabinet ministers, a majority of whom must be Diet members. This bicameral system more closely resembles the British Parliament than it does the U.S. Congress, in the sense that Japan's House of Representatives is superior to the House of Councillors in designating the prime minister and in passing laws in instances of disagreement between the two chambers. Given the House of Representatives' dominance and party discipline within both chambers, we used the proportion of Representative seats to indicate each party's formal voting power. The Liberal Democratic Party enjoyed absolute majorities during the study period: Its formal voting power was 0.58 for the first legislative period (1980–2), 0.52 for the second period (1982–6), and 0.60 for the third period (1986–9). Other parties shared the minority of parliamentary seats, with the Japan Socialist Party's voting power ranging between 0.17 to 0.23, and the Democratic Socialist Party, the Clean Government Party, and the Japan Communist Party shares ranging between 0.05 and 0.11 across the three periods. The House of Councillors was excluded because we assumed that the party councils formulated common labor policy for both chambers. Keep in mind that the authority matrix for the legislative model is practically a vector because few differences in voting power occurred between legislative periods under study. Hence, variation in the agents' formal voting power across periods is generally very small.

The legislative model takes into account only formal voting power in the final legislative decisions. To influence outcomes, many actors adopt a *policy leadership model,* seeking to influence the agency or party initiating and drafting the bill. Initiators and drafters most clearly act as legislative policy leaders when they are expected to block bills formulated by rival factions. In many parliamentary systems, a cabinet or individual ministers perform the policy leadership role. The ministerial policy leadership model characterizes the German system very well. Japan also exemplifies this pattern, but the problem is to distinguish between the leadership roles performed by a ministry's political head and by its bureaucrats. Our study cannot distinguish among actors within ministries because ministries are treated as unitary corporate actors. But we know from other sources that the career bureaucrats who staff the ministries, and not the politically appointed cabinet ministers, formulate and present the vast majority of parliamentary bills (Richardson and Flanagan, 1984: 347).

The German federal ministers lead their ministries quite independently from the cabinet and surely not "at the pleasure" of the chancellor (see Appendix 1). The chancellor has the authority to create new portfolios and change old ones and to appoint the ministers, but in coalition cabinets this latter power is limited by the coalition partner. Once the ministers are appointed, they take charge of their departments. The ministers and the chancellor form the cabinet, a strictly collegial body that gives ministers equal voting rights. Formally, only the cabinet has the constitutional right to initiate bills, not the chancellor nor any single ministry. Of course, many bills are drafted within a particular ministry or by sets of ministries among which one is the *primus inter pares.* Almost all bills initiated by the cabinet or by the *Bundestag* coalition parties are actually drafted by the ministries. The ministers also perform a gatekeeper role for bills initiated by the opposition parties or by state governments within the *Bundesrat.* In the latter case, the bills are introduced to the *Bundestag* with an evaluation of the federal government, so the policy leadership of the cabinet and the de facto leadership roles of the ministers in their specific policy domains are even institutionally supported. The main actors complementary to the ministries in the parliament are the corresponding committees and the parties within these committees. Therefore, in the policy leadership model we enlarged the set of German agents by including first the ministries in charge of the specific event and second the party actors within the Labor Committee of the *Bundestag.*

The literature on the German governmental system often emphasizes that the most important entry points for private interest groups to influence legislative outcomes are the ministries drafting the bills. Following this argument, in the German policy leadership model the ministries active on a bill were assigned one half the voting power. The other half was equally divided between the parliamentary parties in the *Bundestag* and the parties in the Labor Committee. If the Federal Chamber had to give its consent, the sum of the voting power of the state governments was one-quarter and the sum of the legislative actors was also one-quarter, keeping the ministries' power share constant at one-half. Within the *Bundestag,* the Labor Committee, and the *Bundesrat,* the voting shares for the policy leadership model were computed following the same principles as in the legislative model.

The policy leadership model for Japan is even simpler than that for Germany because we differentiated only between the Diet as a whole and the ministries with jurisdiction for labor policy. Here again the voting share of all ministries together was fixed at one-half, and the other half was divided between the legislative parties. This weighting roughly corresponds to the ratio of cabinet (bureaucratic ministry) to Diet member bills in the 1975–9 Diet (Richardson and Flanagan, 1984: 347).

The U.S. government differs from the two parliamentary systems because the role of Congress is so much greater in drafting and initiating legislation. The only additional actor we took into account was the Department of Labor. We scrutinized all bills with respect to active involvement by the Reagan Administration, that is, by the White House Office and the Department of Labor. If the labor department was involved, it received a voting share of one-sixth, with another one-sixth going to the White House. If the department was inactive, then the White House Office received the same voting power as it did in the legislative model (0.333). This allocation seems justified irrespective of the White House's actual involvement, since its final veto power must always be taken into account. The voting powers of the four congressional actors remained unchanged from the legislative model.

A comment seems appropriate about why the U.S. president plays a key policy-making role, whereas neither the German chancellor nor the Japanese prime minister appears in the policy leadership model. This difference lies in the German ministers' and the Japanese career bureaucratic vice-ministers' independent statuses concerning policy-making within their portfolios. In contrast, U.S. department secretaries clearly serve "at the pleasure of the President." The U.S. president's policy leadership is far greater than any comparable functions of the German chancellor and Japanese prime minister. The president stands at the center of public expectations about governmental legislation, and he addresses public issues in his presidential program and his state of the union addresses. The right to veto legislation empowers the president as a third collective decider in the U.S. legislative process. The president is directly elected by the people, which confers on the presidency a legitimacy independent of the Congress. Although all comparisons between the German chancellor and the U.S. president do not reveal a much stronger presidential role – the chancellor's organizational power to create new ministries exceeds the president's dependence on Congress in this respect – excluding the German chancellor from the labor policy domain is justifiable because ministerial power is heavily concentrated in the Labor Ministry or in other ministries depending on legislative content. Given this shared ministerial responsibility for particular bills, the German agents' voting powers vary greatly across events.

A third version of the authority matrix is the *party government model.* This majority coalition model derives from the policy leadership model with one major modification: The opposition parties are no longer treated as agents. For the German and Japanese parliamentary systems, that means the opposition parties are eliminated as legislative actors. Their voting power within each decision-making body is entirely assigned to the remaining agents. In Japan this change results in a power share of 0.50 for the Liberal Democratic Party; the other half is allocated equally among all ministries having at least some responsibility for labor policy. Lacking detailed information about specific ministry involvement in every event, we assumed that they equally shared this responsibility.

Agents in the German party government model included only the parliamentary parties of the CDU/CSU-FDP coalition in both the *Bundestag* and the Labor Committee and the state governments led by prime ministers of the CDU or CSU. The opposition Social Democratic and Green parties were excluded, as were state governments with SPD prime ministers. In the investigative period, the CDU/CSU-FDP coalition enjoyed majorities in both legislative chambers. The power shares assigned to the German ministries remained the same as in the policy leadership model, and the coalition parties' and state governments' powers were evenly divided between those actors because the logic of the minimal winning coalition is that the coalition partners have equal power. That is, when one party leaves a coalition, it no longer enjoys a majority.

Party government in the U.S. is more difficult to designate because the concept does not fit a presidential system as well as it does a parliamentary system. But the president may be considered the leader of his party whose success depends on support from his party's members in Congress. When the president's party holds a majority in both chambers, a proactive presidency can pass major legislation if party discipline obtains (e.g., Lyndon Johnson's Great Society). But the Reagan presidency was a situation of divided government, with Democrats always controlling the House and also the Senate during Reagan's final two years. During such circumstances, party government is often reduced to a reactive coalition in which the president's vetoes are sustained by his congressional party's ability to prevent overrides of the veto. The Republican Party at least held this important blocking position during the Reagan era. Thus, the U.S. party government model was identical to the policy leadership authority matrix after removing both the House and the Senate Democrats as agents. Their voting power was added to the respective Republican Party voting power; that is, both House and Senate Republicans were assigned a voting power of 0.333. The president received either the remaining one-third or shared this proportion equally with the Department of Labor. Keep in mind, however, that the U.S. party government model under divided government is a veto coalition and not a proactive ruling party model as obtains in Germany and Japan.

PREDICTING EVENT OUTCOMES

Accurately predicting event outcomes is only one goal in applying the institutional access model. Another advantage of examining alternative models is that several derived measures can yield new insights into policy-making processes. Of course, only derived measures from models that really predict the event outcomes and that do not seem misspecified should be considered. Each model's predictive power can best be evaluated by comparison to a simple baseline model. We first analyze such a baseline model, then compare its outcomes with the institutional access models' predictions. Table 7.7 summarizes all comparisons to be discussed.

The informants reported their organizations' interests in an event and whether they held a position for or against the bill. The simplest prediction of legislative outcomes is whether the public agents' preferences sum to a positive or a negative outcome. That is, we use the agents' formal voting powers according to the legislative model to see whether parliamentary majorities in Germany and Japan, and the U.S. Congress and president, favored a bill or opposed it. This baseline model does not take into account that agents do not completely control themselves but are open in differing degrees to outside influences. A prerequisite for a positive outcome is support by the necessary majorities in each chamber, which are not allowed to disagree. But an interest level of zero (no preference) by one out of the necessary public actors is acceptable.

A major disadvantage of the baseline model is that not all public actors expressed interest in every event. Thus, information about the agents' preferences is

Table 7.7. *Predicted legislative event outcomes with different institutional access models*

MODEL	U.S.		GERMANY		JAPAN		
	Correct	Incorrect	Correct	Incorrect	Correct	Incorrect	Inap.
Agent Preferences Model (Baseline)	20	5	26	6	13	-	9
Legislative Deployment Model	15	10	21	11	21	1	-
Legislative Mobilization Model	16	9	20	12	22	0	-
Policy Leadership Deployment Model	14	11	27	5	20	2	-
Policy Leadership Mobilization Model	16	9	23	9	22	0	-
Party Government Deployment Model	16	9	32	0	22	0	-
Party Government Mobilization Model	20	5	29	3	22	0	-

missing for those events. The outcomes for 9 of the 22 Japanese events could not be predicted because the preference of the Liberal Democratic Party in the Diet was unknown. (We could assume its support for those government [i.e., cabinet] bills, because of the consultation system between the bureaucracies and the LDP Policy Affairs Research Council; see Appendix 1). Although the Japanese Diet system gave the opposition some substantial functions, it cannot be denied that the LDP was the only decisive actor in parliament because it held an absolute majority. If the LDP was not interested in a bill (despite formal recognition), then the baseline model could not predict its outcome.

In the two other nations, the situation was a bit better because several agents were needed to create the necessary majorities. In Germany the two coalition parties (the CDU/CSU and the FDP) had to agree and, when the Federal Chamber's consent was necessary, the majority of the *Bundesrat* also had to agree. To predict the baseline model outcomes, we followed two rules: (1) in the *Bundestag* one actor's preference would suffice if a coalition partner had no interest; and (2) in the *Bundesrat* only one CDU/CSU state government favoring or opposing a bill would suffice if all others had no interest in the bill. If the coalition partners expressed opposing preferences (one in favor and one against the bill), then a negative outcome was predicted, as was also the case if only one opposition party that lacked a necessary majority favored a bill. These baseline model decision rules correctly predicted the outcomes of 26 of the 32 German legislative events.

In the U.S. the baseline model decision rule was that the majority party in the House (the Democrats), the majority party in the Senate (the Republicans until 1987, and then the Democrats), and the president all had to favor a bill to predict a positive outcome. If any of these three necessary preferences was absent, then either a positive or a negative outcome was predicted, depending on whether the expressed preferences favored or opposed the bill. If either two or all three agents had no interest in a bill, or if either one of the necessary majority parties or the president opposed it while another agent favored passage, then a negative outcome was predicted. Applying these rules correctly predicted 20 of 25 U.S. event outcomes.

These baseline predictions for each nation are now compared to the predictions made by six versions of the institutional access model. These six variations were created by crossing two dimensions: (1) the three forms of the authority matrix (legislative, policy leadership, party government); and (2) the two types of actor control (deployment of information, mobilization of agents' information). Overall, the party government mobilization model made the best outcome predictions for all three nations, whereas the legislative mobilization model's predictions were actually worse than those of the baseline model. Before commenting on the specific results, we must mention one disadvantage of the legislative model. As discussed in the chapter appendix, by assuming identical agent voting powers for all events, the legislative form of our institutional access model produces a baseline mechanism that takes account only of agent effectiveness, while completely removing organizational interests in the bill from the logic of the exchange process.

The policy leadership model fares better in Germany, which provided very good data on the involvement of the different ministries in drafting legislation. We also had the contrast between bills where the consent of the Federal Chamber was needed and those where this consent was not required. Thus, the German authority matrix contained most variance between rows, that is, between the agents' voting power for the different bills. The German labor policy domain therefore offers many incentives for exchanging access to different types of agents. The policy leadership model clearly makes better predictions in Germany than does the legislative model. Substantively, we interpret this result as showing the importance of the German ministries in drafting or blocking legislation. Of course, the ministries are controlled by the coalition parties and not by the opposition, so we get a perfect prediction of all 32 bill outcomes for the party government model, combined with the deployment logic of access. Keep in mind that, for all three types of access matrices, the deployment form always fits the German data slightly better than the mobilization form. This improvement is primarily due to the high self-control of the federal Labor Ministry in the deployment model.

The institutional access model did not improve the predictive power of the U.S. baseline model. Within each type of authority or voting power model, the mobilization mechanism of control fit the data better than did the deployment mechanism. The role of the German Labor Ministry for the deployment model found a parallel in the roles played by the House Democrats and Senate Republicans in the mobilization model. These agents were the majority parties of their respective chambers for most bills during the investigation period. Both agents had a self-control of 1.0 in the mobilization model. The institutional access version that predicts the U.S. event outcomes at least as well as the baseline model is the party government mechanism combined with the mobilization control. We mentioned earlier that, for divided governments, the logic of a party government model is a veto coalition. And indeed, all five U.S. bills that were incorrectly predicted by the policy leadership deployment model were bills initiated either by the Republican majority in the Senate or by the Reagan Administration (events 5, 10, 12, 13, 20; see Table 7.4). In every case, the model predicted a positive result, but the actual outcome was negative. Thus, the deployment version of the policy leadership model overestimated the president's ability to influence the votes of individual congresspersons who do not belong to his party. We were unable to model these subtle decision processes because our research design assumed unitary party actors in Congress.

For Japan, the mobilization version of the legislative model readily predicted all 22 events correctly. This result is not surprising given the selection of only government bills and the LDP's absolute majority in the Diet. The only advantage of applying this model to the Japanese data is that we now can predict the outcome of all 22 events, not just the 13 bills in the baseline model. But even for the Japanese case we could compute some derived measures to gain further insight into the logic of collective decision making.

DISCUSSION

One important problem for the institutional access model is whether the actors gain control through deploying their own information or whether they gain control through the mobilization of the agents' information. In discussing these two mechanisms for actor access to agents, we hypothesized that the U.S. system better exemplified the mobilization process, whereas the German system corresponded more closely to the deployment logic. This hypothesis was supported by the different predictive powers of the two access forms in those nations. The success of the mobilization model for the U.S. is astonishing, because the questionnaire was originally formulated from the deployment model perspective. Of course, the actors' control of agents in equilibrium differs little for the two forms of access, especially in Germany and Japan. Computing the final control of the agents across the actors between the respective elements of the control matrices of the mobilization and the deployment models results in correlations of at least 0.90 in Germany and Japan. In the U.S., a big difference occurred between the equilibrium control computed according to the mobilization and deployment models. The correlations for the U.S. agents ranged only between 0.40 and 0.50. We interpret this contrast as a substantial corroboration of our hypothesis that in the U.S. actors gain control over the agents when they can mobilize the agents' policy information. The mobilization model not only yields better predictions for the U.S. legislative outcomes, but these predictions are really based on a different control distribution in equilibrium.

The power of individual organizations in a second derived measure deserves comment. For each nation, we computed derived power scores using the model that best predicted the event outcomes. These models were the party government model in the mobilization version for the U.S., the party government model in the deployment form for Germany, and the mobilization version of the legislative model for Japan. A very general conclusion is that the public actors who also play the role of agents are the most powerful actors in all three systems. This result clearly arises from these organizations' very high levels of self-control, especially in instances of self-control equal to 1.0, for example, the Labor Ministry in the deployment model in Germany. This public actor alone holds almost one-third of the total system power. All other German actors, even the public actors, lag far behind the Ministry of Labor. Thus, organizational power is very sensitive to very high values of self-control by certain public actors. When the public actors were omitted, the correlation between this derived power measure and organizational reputations (see Chapter 5) revealed that participants' attributions of general influence in the labor policy domain differed substantially from the actors' power gained through access to effective agents. These correlations were 0.56 in Germany, 0.53 in the U.S., and slightly lower in Japan. In general, reputational perceptions tend to overestimate the impact of private interest groups, whereas the institutional access model accords more power to political actors who are not agents.

Of course, one could argue that this interpretation was not unanticipated, because it was already built into the internal logic of the institutional access model.

Yet even granting some validity to this objection, the institutional logic was not foreordained to produce good predictions of the event outcomes. One problem with the institutional access model is ambiguity about the origins of the public actors' event preferences. These preferences could be extrinsic decisions that are reached after the influence processes of the private interest groups have their impacts. Then, we would overestimate the power of the public actors because part of their power actually should be allocated to those private actors most able to influence them. On the other hand, one might imagine that the public actors need high self-control because they have publicly committed themselves to groups of voters. Thus, they cannot be completely open to influence attempts by powerful interest groups. Overall, the big advantage when applying the institutional access model is that now we better explain the outcome of legislative bills by taking into account not only the manifest actions of the public actors but also the effects of private actors' arguments in favor of or against certain bills. The confirmed information exchange network (or a similar network of access channels between actors and agents) contains crucial information on the linkages between private and public actors. Important conceptualizations of the political system, such as corporatism and pluralism, can be stated as concrete hypotheses about the access structures. But theorists of interest intermediation typically pay little attention to the underlying mechanisms of collective decision making inside the modern state. Our organizational state approach clearly builds these mechanisms into the authority matrix, combining with the access network to explain a large majority of legislative event outcomes.

Future extensions of the institutional access model should pay greater attention to measuring the public actors' self-control. Our operationalization was a start, but because self-control was such a sensitive element in the model, developing a more precise measure is critical. And the model itself could be improved by treating the agents not as mere reactors to random arguments presented by the actors, but as thoughtful, strategic policy entrepreneurs. However, combining rational actors with rational agents in the same model will require major innovations by the next generation of political exchange analysts.

APPENDIX TO CHAPTER 7

Basic matrix algebra notation

The interest matrix **X** is standardized row-wise, with the amount of interest that the actor in row *j* has treated as a fixed sum of 1.0:

$$\Sigma_i X_{ji} = 1.0$$

In the same way the total amount of control over event *i* across all actors is fixed:

$$\Sigma_i c_{ij} = 1.0$$

Model presentations always start with the interests of the actors, and therefore, all standardizations are computed row-wise. Thus, even when using the original labels of the relations between the system elements, which would make sense only with a backward reading, matrices are not transposed so that column-wise standardizations result.

The central behavioral assumption is that actors allocate their resources proportional to their interests in the events, thereby reaching an equilibrium after exchange. The value of an event (v_i) equals the effective demand within the system and power of each actor (p_j) equals the value of his or her control over resources. This microeconomic exchange model is applicable to vote trading under the strong assumption that actors' preferences for or against a bill (y_i) are irrelevant for an exchange to occur. Only the intensity of interest, or volume of relative interests, matters. Actor *j*'s volume of interest in event *i* is designated by x_{ji} and the direction of interest by y_{ji} (where + means "pro" and − means "contra" an event). The volume of interest equals the absolute (unsigned) direction of interest:

$$x_{ji} = |y_{ji}|$$

Subsequent modifications of this original exchange model decompose either the control or the interest relations. All modifications intended to improve the model's applicability in large collective decision systems rely on information about networks among the actors.

The institutional access model

The basic relationships in this model are represented by the following schema:

	are interested in		are decided by		are controlled by	
Actors	⟶	Events	⟶	Agents	⟶	Actors
$j = 1,2..n$	$\mathbf{X}_{ji}$	$i = 1,2..m$	$\mathbf{A}_{ik}$	$k = 1,2..p$	$\mathbf{K}_{kl}$	$1 = 1,2..n$

The derived interest of actors in agents can be defined as:

$$x'_{ik} = \Sigma_i \, x_{ji} \, a_{ik}$$

Following Coleman, the behavioral assumption of the model is summarized in the Cobb-Douglas utility function:

$$U_j = \Pi_j \, k_{kj} \, e^{x'_{jk}}$$

Thus, the actors try to gain better access to those agents who are most effective for realizing their interests.

The basic data to estimate the system parameters are the interest matrix **X,** the authority or decision-making matrix **A,** and the control matrix **K.** This information suffices to compute the actors' power, the agents' effectiveness, and the events' values. Actor power is the ability to gain access to effective agents:

$$p_j = \Sigma_k e_k k_{kj}$$

Agent effectiveness is voting power for valuable events:

$$e_k = \Sigma_i v_i a_i k$$

Finally, event values are defined by the interests of powerful actors, or the effective demand for control of an event:

$$v_i = \Sigma_j p_j x_{ji}$$

Exchange in this system is possible only with respect to the actors' access to the agents, that is, exchange continues within the **K** control matrix until an equilibrium (**K***) is reached. In this model, **K** is no longer a square actor-by-actor matrix, but it is rectangular because the agents are a subset of the *N* system actors. Following the assumptions, the equilibrium condition is defined as follows:

$$p_j \Sigma_i x_{ji} a_{ik} = w_k k^*_{kj}$$

Brokerage relations

Indirect access through a single middle organization is first added to a standardized direct control matrix, **N,** which is then truncated to create the rectangular control matrix, **K.** This formula shows how the control matrix of the deployment model is computed:

$$k_{kl} = (n_{kl} + \sum_{h=1}^{N} n_{kh} n_{hl}) / 2$$

The mobilization model would use an analogous direct control matrix, **M.** These two networks, **N** and **M,** both have self-control values in the main diagonal for all actors, not just for the agents. The resulting control matrix (**K**) is one of the three basic building blocks for our institutional access model. In contrast to the Laumann-Knoke-Kim model, the agents comprise only a subset of the domain organizations and the empirical information exchange matrix is assumed not to measure exchange at equilibrium, but to measure control of the agents before exchange occurs. The exchange process is driven by the derived interest of actors in agents and results in an access matrix in equilibrium, **K***. The other two model components are the matrix of nondirectional interests in events ($|\mathbf{Y}| = \mathbf{X}$) and the authority or decision-making matrix (**A**).

The legislative mobilization model

One disadvantage of the legislative mobilization model is that agents' formal voting power remains constant for each event within a legislative period, with the partial exception of Germany when the Federal Chamber had a role in some bills. Actors' strategies for gaining access to the agents did not take into account their interests in single events, but only considered the agents' voting power or effectiveness. If an authority matrix would contain identical rows, that is, if the voting power were exactly the same for all events, then the derived interest of the actors in the agents is given by the product of organizational interests (matrix **X**) times agent authority (matrix **A**). Because matrix **A** really is only a vector and the sum of the interest levels is 1.0 for all actors, the measure of the actors derived control over the agents is identical to the agents' effectiveness. In our applications, the rows of the **A** matrices differ (except in the German case) only because the agents' voting power changed slightly between the legislative periods. This study design effect should not end up in a major strategy of the actors to exchange their access to an effective agent of an early period for access to an effective agent in a later period. A better research design would have applied the model to specific events that were all chosen within a single legislative period, at least as far as the legislative model is concerned.

8

Power structures

with Willi Schnorpfeil

This final empirical chapter weaves together the diverse strands of the preceding analyses into a comprehensive fabric: the power structures of the three national policy domains. Specifically, we combine three types of interorganizational relationships – the communication exchanges (Chapter 5), organizational reputations (Chapter 5), and action-set coalitions (Chapter 6) – to reveal the multiplex patterns connecting core and peripheral clusters of actors identified by equivalent ties to one another. These relationships among positions jointly define the structures through which power is generated and distributed among actors (Knoke, 1981: 275). Any power structure analysis must build on two types of theoretical premises: first, the conceptualizations of power from which the important dimensions of power relationships can be derived; and second, the theoretical perspectives that can be used to interpret the resulting structures. Concerning the first problem, we rely on a network concept of power and use blockmodel analysis to generate images of basic power structures. Regarding the second problem, the organizational state's contrast to pluralist and corporatist concepts of power relations guide our interpretations of the power structures.

Within national policy domains, organizations formulate, collectively decide, and implement binding policies. The people involved in public policy-making apply conventional definitions of domains, which often coincide with the jurisdictions of legislative committees or state ministries. Participants perceive that problems, issues, and solutions belong to a domain because of certain substantive similarities (Burstein, 1991), even if the political actors realize that they have some discretion in framing matters to fit into a variety of domains. The next section discusses the two theoretical premises, the problem of power structure dimensions and how to measure them with power networks.

POWER NETWORKS OR POWER IN NETWORKS?

Conceptualizing power in a network context can take two different paths. One possible approach is to search for power networks in which the content of relations linking network actors can be interpreted as a power measure. The other possibility is to conceptualize power as a latent dimension of all networks or at least of those with asymmetric or directed relations. The best example of the first approach is a reputational measure where all system participants report whom they believe to be especially powerful or influential in the system (see Chapter 5). Another example is a resource dependency network that is interpreted as the reverse view of a power network by power dependency theory. In the second power structure approach, the content of the relation is less important than certain formal properties that indicate that "one social actor exerts greater control over another's behavior" (Knoke, 1990b: 3). A classic example is Homans's discussion of small-group interactions where "the more popular members tended to receive the most interactions" (Homans, 1974: 180). Homans insisted that the volume of received interactions is not a simple effect of the actor's popularity or esteem, but measures his power from possession of a scarce reward. "That is, power and not approval is the fundamental variable determining the rank order of the members of the group in the number of interactions they receive" (Homans, 1974: 182).

Now, the labor policy domains of large nation states are not simply enlarged versions of small groups, even if we hear sometimes of cosy triangles as parts of them. Thus, one may seriously question whether the findings about small-group status and power can be extrapolated to large systems consisting of corporate actors. We favor such an extrapolation if, and only if, the theoretical rationales underlying the explanations apply in both cases. An exchange theory explanation built on rational choice premises does fulfill that condition. Rational actors, both as individuals and as corporate actors, try to realize their interests consistently. Small groups and policy networks differ in another respect of great importance to a power structure analysis. Beyond the agenda-setting stage, all further steps in the policy cycle depend heavily on institutional rules. Policies in the form of legislative bills are obviously a very good instance because a parliament must make the final collective decision. Whereas behavior in small groups is mostly subinstitutional, policy-making in the legislative arena is highly institutionalized, given that only certain actors have the right to make the final authoritative decision.

The right to make binding decisions for a collectivity presupposes a certain degree of institutionalization. In this chapter we propose a definition of power that assumes institutionalized relations among social actors. It is the ability to achieve one's objectives in collective decisions. We thus agree with Parson's concept of power as the "generalized capacity to secure the performance of binding obligations by units in a system of collective organization" (1967: 308). By stressing the collective aspect of power we go beyond the merely dyadic view, where, in Weber's words, power is the ability of one actor "to carry out his own will despite resistance" (1947: 152). Within the institutionalized policy domain settings, a single actor is able to achieve its objectives in collective decisions, either directly in an authority role or indirectly through access to the authorities.

What does the distinction between authority and access mean for power in networks? Access is, of course, a basic network idea. One actor has access to another if it can use its direct or indirect contacts to obtain a hearing for its policy proposals. Investigating who has power via access to the authorities should be easy once all the actors with authority are identified (i.e., organizations with legitimate ability to make binding decisions, such as legislatures, courts, and executive agencies). But we want to delineate domain power structure using only network relations and not an individual actor's characteristic, such as whether an actor possesses formal authority. Otherwise, we would need only to divide a network into the subset of authorities and the subset of private actors and then compute the densities within this fourfold table. Instead, we want to derive the power structure solely from network information. We argue that, in institutional settings like policy networks, authority is a scarce resource to which powerful actors must have access in order to reach their objectives in collective decisions. We do not treat the authorities as separate entities outside the set of policy actors, but as specific roles played by a subset of actors we call *public actors*. The *private actors* are, then, those policy domain participants without an authority role. Because private actors can gain access to public actors through intermediaries (brokers) who are also private actors, and because public actors can also improve their power position through their access to other public actors, a bipartite network of just the contacts between public and private actors would not suffice. Furthermore, playing an authority role cannot be used as an attribute to separate the two sets of actors.

MEASURING RELATIONSHIPS

Having decided to examine a full network that includes all domain actors irrespective of their authority roles, our next question is how to construct a matrix that optimally measures power in networks. One general problem with exchange networks is that the commodities or resources exchanged can be very different. We agree in general with Cook's (1990: 120) doubts about the meaningfulness of the concept of directionality of ties in exchange networks. Nevertheless, some imbalances may be built into actual exchange networks, especially if more than one potential power resource is taken into account. For example, valuable policy information may be exchanged for other valuable information, but also traded for other influence resources, such as legislative votes or political money. To obtain a complete picture of the multiple, hidden power dimensions in exchange networks, an analyst would have to enumerate completely the important power resources and their prices or exchange rates. In addition, one should try to gather data on exchange offers that were *not* accepted by the more powerful organizations. Because we lack the necessary information about these aspects of exchange networks, we draw instead on three relations whose aspects we examined in preceding chapters: organizational reputation attributions, information exchanges, and action-set coalitions.

First, the network of *organizational reputations* captures a salient power structure dimension. Recall from Chapter 5 that informants were asked to designate all other organizations that they saw as "especially influential" in the labor policy domain in general. In our preceding analyses of these responses, we examined only the total number of mentions an organization received from its peers ("votes received") as an indicator of its reputation. In other words, the more influential an actor is perceived to be within the labor policy domain, the higher its column total within the nominator-by-nominee matrix. This chapter further analyzes the organizational reputation question, preserving the pattern of mentions made and received within the full reputational matrix. In the standard matrix representation of a network, the initiators of relations are placed in the rows and recipients appear in the columns. In the reputational matrix, a "1" means that the informant for a row organization reported the column organization as being especially influential. Thus, the more influential organizations have many 1s in their columns, whereas those with meager reputations have sparser entries. The reputation network is not a social exchange network, in the sense of summarizing information on actual exchanges or interactions. Rather, it is a purely perceptual network. It serves both to identify those actors believed to be powerful and to remedy some pitfalls of misspecifying the exchange relations described next.

A second power structure dimension is captured by the *access network.* In this matrix, the actors granting access are in the rows and the actors seeking access appear in the columns. Because the column actors enjoying better or broader access should be the more powerful ones, we cannot rely solely on the column actors' claims about those organizations to which they have access. Ideally, their responses should also be cross-validated by the respective row actors. Therefore, we constructed a matrix of "confirmed information exchange" to derive the latent access dimension of power networks. We operationalized granting and enjoying access as the intersection of receiver and transposed sender ties so that receiving valuable information by the row actor has to be cross-validated by sending valuable information to this actor by the respective column sender. Not all information exchanges in a policy domain consist of valuable items in high demand by the other actors. Much information is broadcast freely to all system participants. To distinguish valuable from more-or-less freely distributed information, recall from Chapter 5 that informants reported about one of nine labor domain subfields where their organizations sought important policy information that only other organizations could provide. They were then asked which organizations gave them this type of information. Thus, we could conceptualize the focal actors as organizations demanding valuable information and who therefore depend on other domain members to provide this highly demanded information. A complementary relation is the information-supply connection. Again, organizations designated one subfield in which they provided information valued by other actors, then mentioned those organizations to which they sent this information. Consequently, a valid entry in the constructed confirmed information exchange matrix means that *both* the sender and the receiver agreed on the existence of that relationship. For example, if political party *A* reported receiving policy information from union *B,* this tie was assumed to occur only if union *B* also reported sending valuable information to party *A.* The interpretation of a 1 in the access matrix is that the confirmed information senders have access to the receivers of this policy information.

Using both organizational reputation and access network matrices, we can identify a core cluster of labor domain organizations that all system participants perceive as especially influential. These organizations jointly occupy the center of the confirmed information exchange network, in the sense that they send and receive valuable information from other positions. Nevertheless, if nothing were known about the interests of the organizations in this central position, one may doubt whether they actually constitute a unified ruling caucus. Do they usually agree on public policies, or are they divided into two or more opposing subgroups concerning their policy preferences? Whenever one operationalizes the power concept as an ability to achieve one's objectives in collective decisions, one must also guard against the possibility that an actor appears powerful only because it shares policy preferences with the really powerful actors. But merely sharing a common policy preference during a policy-formulation phase cannot guarantee an ultimate outcome favorable to organizations free riding on the real power players. These small-fry often must negotiate compromises and concessions until the final collective decision can be reached. Less-powerful organizations can protect themselves from utility losses by building coalitions with other actors who share their preferences concerning a particular policy. Therefore, we constructed a third power structure matrix, an *action-set network.* As defined in Chapter 6, action sets are coalitions whose partners hold the same outcome preference on a legislative bill and who work together on that event. The action-set matrix is symmetric (that is, corresponding rows and columns are identical), with 1s meaning that a given pair of organizations worked together to influence the outcomes of two or more bills. Hence, organizations having larger row (and column) totals were involved with more coalition partners than were organizations having sparser entries.

By jointly analyzing the three power structure dimensions – organizational reputation, access network, and action-set network – we come close to operationalizing Emerson and Cook's power dependence theory. That is, actors obtain power to the extent that others depend on them to supply desired resources. To accomplish this objective fully, we would have to interpret the reputation network as a resource dependence matrix wherein reputational differences indicate power imbalances. These inequalities can be overcome either by network extension ("increasing the number of alternative suppliers of valuable resources") or by coalition formation (Cook, 1990: 221). But interpreting a nonmutual reputation mention as an indicator of resource dependency overemphasizes the dependence aspect. Reputational attributions may simply indicate the informants' judgments as neutral observers of the system. Thus, we adopt a conservative strategy of interpreting the organizational reputation matrix at face value, that is, as the insiders' views of the labor policy domain power structure.

TYPES OF POWER STRUCTURES

Organizational influence reputations, confirmed policy information transfers, and cooperation in action-set coalitions serve as the three relational building blocks for our power structure analysis of the three labor policy domains. Organizations exhibiting similarly patterned relations with others across these networks will be put into a common cluster. Thus, this procedure condenses the original $N \times N$ binary networks into much smaller matrices, which can be interpreted as compact images of the domain power structure. These images depict the power structures insofar as the three original relational matrices contain data measuring power networks and power in networks. We turn here to the question of what types of power structures might indicate which types of interest intermediation exist in a policy domain.

The literature on interest intermediation in policy domains offers an abundance of analytic types that are difficult to reduce to a few key dimensions. In addition to the main theoretic archetypes of pluralism and corporatism, many subtypes have been proposed, for example, pressure pluralism, liberal corporatism, or such variant types as Parentela-systems and clientelism. Some authors pay special attention to the implementation phase in the policy cycle, whereas others also take into account the policy formulation and decision-making stages. Because our research focuses on the latter two phases, we pay special attention to the roles postulated for parliamentary parties in comparison with the administrative bureaucracy.

To facilitate our task of summarizing the basic typological features of interest intermediation, we focus only on the polar power structure types of pluralism and corporatism. Based on the results of the preceding chapters, we depict the labor policy domain as a basically polarized system: Business organizations and labor unions are normally found in confrontational coalitions that favor or oppose specific legislative policies. The problem for democratic systems is how to overcome this inherent class-based polarization. For pluralists, cross-cutting cleavages function as an integrative mechanism. Corporatists argue that the peak organizations representing each class negotiate compromise policies, with the help of the state, to avoid political stalemate. To the extent that one class coalition routinely dominates the authorities, we might call it a "class" system. What network structures do these theoretical arguments imply? One should expect to find signs of cross-cutting cleavages in a coalition network, but one may doubt whether a crude measure of action-set cooperation could detect less-intense cooperation occurring across class lines. We anticipate that the coalition network will primarily exhibit a fundamental cleavage between business and labor. More fine-grained aspects of the power structure should be visible within the information exchange network. Therefore, we now summarize the three major network implications of the pluralist and corporatist images in terms of access patterns between private interest groups and public authorities.

Two types of access

In the pluralist world view, private and public actors play quite different roles in policy domains. Private interest groups try to gain access to those political parties and ministries comprising the governing center whose task is to make the final collective decision on legislative proposals. The interest groups with greater access to this governing center are better able to reach their policy objectives. But neither the governing center nor those interest groups enjoying better access will exaggerate their successes because, according to the democratic majoritarian principle, the opposition party is the potential alternative government. Therefore, opponents will not be completely isolated in the communication structure. Concerning the information exchange network, public organizations in the governing center should be the major recipients of valuable information. They are less inclined to send information to the private actors, who must accept a binding policy once an authoritative decision is made.

In the corporatist world view, the private interest groups' access to public actors is balanced by the public actors' access to the peak business and labor organizations. These peak associations become responsible for delivering their respective rank-and-file members' acceptance of the negotiated policies. Some corporatists argue that the government, especially the labor ministry, is a coequal bargaining partner with business and labor. The legislature merely endorses the solutions reached through the labor ministry's negotiations with these contending private interest groups. However, if one leaves aside very narrow policies targeted toward specialized clienteles and pays attention to policies having broader impacts, the legislative parties no longer appear so passive. Rather, active parliamentary participation and consent is essential for an effective "concertation" of economic and labor policies. Lehmbruch (1984) even argued that close cooperation by a party with a social class base, especially a labor party with strong union ties, is a basic characteristic of every corporatist system.

Sector-internal communication patterns

If a corporatist system is basically a bargaining system, then it will function optimally only when the number of negotiating organizations is small. Because each actor participating in the deal will have veto power over the outcome, the necessary compromises can be reached more effectively where fewer negotiators are involved. Hence, the presence of peak business and labor organizations is a necessary precondition of corporatism. However, such peak organizations must entertain de facto monopolies of interest representation within their respective sectors (Schmitter, 1977). Our matrix of confirmed information exchanges for the respective labor and business sectors can be expected to reveal whether their peak organizations indeed play such centralizing roles in relation to the other organizations. If corporatist orchestration occurs, we expect a clear center-periphery communication pattern. The peripheral organizations should exchange information with the peak associations, but the peripheral actors will not be linked among themselves. If this pattern does not occur, a pluralist system of interest intermediation is more plausible.

Composition of the governing center

In classical pluralism, the different roles played by public and private actors lead us to expect that the boundaries between state and civil society will not be blurred. The governing center should mainly be composed of public actors that are the major targets of influence attempts by the private-sector actors. Whether this center, the most powerful position to which private actors seek access, really emerges is another question. The political center may also conceivably be an instrument manipulated by powerful civil societal groups. In contrast, the governing centers of a purely corporatist system might be composed of all the powerful actors, irrespective of sector. These core organizations may interact more closely with one another than they do with their respective rank-and-file members.

With these three guiding principles, we can test the hypothesis that Germany exhibits more corporatist policy-making in the labor domain, at least compared to the U.S., which is unanimously evaluated as more pluralist. And we shall compare the power structures of these two nations with that of Japan, about whose system of interest intermediation more disagreement exists (Lijphart and Crepaz, 1991), but which has been characterized as "corporatism without labor" (Pempel and Tsunekawa, 1979).

ORGANIZATIONS AND NETWORKS

We begin with an overview of interorganizational relations in the U.S., Germany, and Japan. First, we elaborate the organizational typology developed in Chapter 3. Then we describe three basic relationships within the conventional public-private categories.

Classifying organizations

Because of our focus on legislative policy formulation that ends in an authoritative decision on a proposed bill, we expect parliamentary actors to play a crucial role in labor policy domains. Identifying these sets of public actors turned out to be a difficult task that could be fulfilled only after close readings of each national constitution. The right to vote in a legislature is given only to individual persons. But legislators may be organized collectively along party lines, so these party groups in parliaments and in legislative committees are the corporate actors that really count. Of course, such party structuring makes much sense in parliamentary systems like Germany and Japan, where the parliamentary parties may be meaningfully treated as unitary actors that build executive and legislative coalitions. Even in the U.S. Congress, parties are allegedly a good first approximation if one decides not to treat only individual representatives and senators as the consequential actors. For the U.S. labor policy domain, the four important party actors are the Republicans and Democrats belonging to the respective House and Senate labor committees. In the Japanese parliamentary system, only the parties are treated as unitary actors without making a distinction between the House of Representatives and the House of Councillors in the Diet. This decision was realistic because the Liberal Democratic Party (LDP) had absolute majorities in both houses during the 1980s period covered by our investigation. In Germany, during the 1980s prior to reunification, four political parties were represented in parliament. Because parliamentary parties are very important, they are considered to be unitary actors in addition to their members in the respective labor policy committee of the *Bundestag.*

Delineating the public actors within the executive branch was similarly problematic. In the U.S., only the president has a formal constitutional role in the legislative process, through his veto power. Although the U.S. White House Office was included as the head of the administration, the German chancellor and the Japanese prime minister were excluded because the labor ministries have much more autonomy in steering labor policy. These ministers owe their formal policy-making roles to the right of the cabinet to initiate legislation. Even the U.S. federal departments significantly represent the administration vis-à-vis Congress. Thus, including the labor ministries along with other executive branch organizations that deal with labor legislation makes sense in all three countries.

A unique public actor category, absent in both the U.S. and Japan, is the German state government (*Land*), which sends its delegates to the second chamber, the *Bundesrat.* The state governments vote on about 60 percent of the German legislative bills. Their participation is mainly justified by the states' role in implementing those policies. Therefore, the state governments had to be included as a separate category in Germany. Japan also has a special public actor category with no equivalent in the other two nations. These are the ministerial advisory boards (*Shingikai*), which are generally prescribed by the National Government Organization Law. Their role is to submit final reports after the research, examination, and evaluation of policy proposals. Advisory boards generally serve as unitary corporate organizations, not as collective deciders like a parliament composed of other corporate actors, which must be decomposed into its constituent political parties as unitary organizational actors.

Identifying the private corporate actors in the three national labor policy domains is much easier. Labor unions and business associations are, of course, the most significant types. Other important organizational types present in all three nations are the professional societies and the so-called public interest groups. Among these are welfare associations, as well as associations of disadvantaged groups in the labor market, or peak organizations of cities and counties. In the U.S., public interest law firms are also included in this category as nonmembership groups and national associations of state actors like the National Governors' Association. This latter type of state actor is absent as a German lobby organization, because the states are directly represented in the *Bundesrat.* But in both Germany and Japan, peak organizations for local communities' interests are represented in this category, as they are in the U.S.

Finally, Germany and Japan have a category between the private and public sectors, the major social insurance institutions covering old age pensions, health care, and unemployment. They are constituted in Germany as public law corporations with mandatory membership and the right of self-government. Union and employer representatives normally cooperate in their boards of directors, giving these institutions a corporatist flavor. Because the members' dues and employer contributions are regulated by law and can be compared to taxes for the mandatory members, the term "parafiscus" is sometimes used (Tiepelmann and van der Beek,

Table 8.1. *Organizational reputations by type of organization*

ORGANIZATION TYPE	MEAN INDEGREES U.S.	Germany	Japan
Labor Unions	40.8	36.7	18.5
Business Associations	27.1	31.1	13.0
Professional Societies	18.7	30.0	[a]
Public Interest Groups	22.9	41.7	14.0
Mandatory Insurance Associations	--	48.2	12.3
Ministries	37.1	64.2	33.3
Political Parties	77.5	38.4	41.4
Länder	--	43.5	--
Shingikai	--	--	33.2
Overall Mean Indegrees	30.8	41.8	20.4
Network Density	0.275	0.345	0.178

[a]Only one organization; classified with PIGs

1992). Many social insurance bodies are organized at the regional level, and in this capacity they collaborate with the national peak organizations. The peak social insurance associations behave as any other interest group does in seeking to influence public actors on behalf of their members and staff. Because the members' organizations implement social insurance policies decided by the state, we keep them separate from conventional private interest groups in Germany. Almost without exception in the U.S., and for the majority of cases in Japan, insurance organizations are wholly private voluntary associations that do not act as special administrators in implementing state policies.

Describing relationships

Describing the network densities, indegrees, and outdegrees among different types of organizations gives an initial overview of these power structure dimensions. The summary is preliminary in the sense that the organizations are not clustered according to similar power relations with one another, yet it retains descriptive value for the conventional private-public actor typology.

Starting with the organizational reputation network, Table 8.1 displays the nine organizational types' rankings (in network terms, their indegrees: the number of

Table 8.2. *Confirmed information exchanges by type of organization*

ORGANIZATION TYPE	MEAN INDEGREES U.S.	Germany	Japan
Labor Unions	13.2	5.4	5.6
Business Associations	9.9	5.7	3.7
Professional Societies	9.4	5.6	[a]
Public Interest Groups	9.6	6.8	2.9
Mandatory Insurance Associations	--	12.0	1.8
Ministries	14.1	9.6	7.2
Political Parties	30.3	14.4	11.4
Länder	--	8.1	--
Shingikai	--	--	2.4
Overall Mean Indegrees	11.7	8.3	4.9
Network Density	0.104	0.069	0.042

[a]Only one organization; classified with PIGs

times an actor was mentioned as "especially influential" in the labor policy domain in general). The mean network density is highest in Germany (34.5% of choices made, with an average 41.8 "votes" received per organization), intermediate in the U.S. (27.5% of choices, 30.8 votes per organization), and lowest in Japan (17.8% of choices, only 20.4 votes per organization). The ministries enjoy reputations for influence that are substantially above the average in each nation. However, the legislative parties differ markedly: Both the U.S. and Japanese party organizations enjoy the highest reputations, but the German party mean is below the average. In interpreting these figures, one should keep in mind that average power reputations may conceal much heterogeneity within categories containing a few major and many minor players. This situation occurs for the German political parties, which included many parliamentary factions and committees of the opposition Social Democrats and Greens. Hence, we would be premature to conclude that political parties are not very important in the German labor policy domain, at least relative to the German ministries.

Turning next to the access (confirmed information exchange) networks, a first impression of Table 8.2 suggests that the chief communication targets in all three national labor policy domains are political parties and ministries. These two categories receive the highest indegrees, followed in the U.S. and Japan by the unions

Table 8.3. *Participation in action-set coalitions by type of organization*

ORGANIZATION TYPE	MEAN INDEGREES U.S.	Germany	Japan
Labor Unions	.632	.691	.106
Business Associations	.307	.105	.150
Professional Societies	.022	.076	[a]
Public Interest Groups	.023	.137	.000
Mandatory Insurance Associations	--	.244	.000
Ministries	.050	.256	.000
Political Parties	.000	.191	.000
Länder	--	.311	--
Shingikai	--	--	.000
Overall Network Density	0.085	0.112	0.029

[a]Only one organization; classified with PIGs

and in Germany by the mandatory social insurance associations. Note that the overall densities for confirmed communication are much lower than the organizational reputation networks and considerably below the unconfirmed communication ties analyzed in Chapter 5. The commonalities across the three nations give the impression that comparisons using this network can be very meaningful.

Finally, Table 8.3 presents the action-set coalition network in somewhat different fashion. Here the entries refer to the density of coalition partners chosen from *within* each organizational category. For example, in Germany 69.1 percent of the labor unions were linked to one another by collaboration in two or more event action-sets. The U.S. figure was almost as high, at 63.2 percent, but barely one-sixth of the Japanese unions formed such coalitions. This disparity does not mean that action sets were less important in Japan, but rather that more unions surrendered their activism to their representative peak associations and initiated little direct action. The German public actors – the state governments, political parties, and ministries – all participated in coalitions at above-average rates. In contrast, coalitions formed in the U.S. and Japan arose mainly within the union and business sectors, not across organizational types. That difference may stem from formal coalitions being a more preferred device in legislative systems that rely on coalition governments to promote policy preferences than in either parliamentary systems like Japan built on absolute majorities, or presidential systems like the U.S., which do not require a coalition to elect the governmental head. It also suggests that the state takes a more neutral position in the U.S. and Japan. The overall mean densities of the three action-set coalition networks are relatively sparse, roughly comparable to the confirmed communication ties, but notably lower than the reputational networks.

BLOCKMODEL ANALYSES

We seek answers to two questions: Which organizations have structurally similar relations in the three networks, so that we may cluster them together into common positions? And, what do the connections among those positions reveal about the underlying power structures of the three labor policy domains? Defining a power structure as the patterned relations that generate and distribute power among actors (Knoke, 1981: 275) only narrowly captures power in networks. That definition fails to tap the symbolic aspects of power networks reflected in organizational reputations. We included this dimension as a precaution against misspecification of power models, because we assume that insider perceptions of power and influence are an important component of the power structure.

Blockmodel analysis is a quantitative method for reducing the complexity of relations and perceptions in multiple networks of actors. Details of the technical procedures are available from several sources (e.g., Knoke and Kuklinski, 1982; Wasserman and Faust, 1992). In very general terms, starting with multiple actor-by-actor binary networks, a blockmodel analysis either clusters actors into positions or clusters their relations into roles. We chose the former approach because it promises to yield better results for large networks. (We used the CONCOR algorithm, which allows for differing weights applied to the three original networks [Arabie, Boorman, and Levitt, 1978].) Our blockmodel analyses searched for structurally equivalent organizations, that is, organizations that maintained the same or very similar patterns of ties to the other organizations across all three networks. The original network data were then partitioned into eight subgroups, each containing organizations that occupy structurally similar positions within the three-network power structure. We label these groupings as "positions," or "blocks." The interorganizational relations within and between these blocks may be represented as *digraphs* (directed graphs), in which the links between two positions (represented as letters) are depicted by arrows emerging from the sending block and pointing at the receiving block. A tie between blocks, indicating a powerful relationship between the organizations in those blocks, is considered to exist only if the density of relations within or between positions exceeds the overall mean density of the respective network. A block with a high density of ties among its members is represented by enclosing its letter in a circle.

To combine the three networks in one blockmodel analysis, we had to make assumptions about their relative importance for the overall structure. We assumed that the confirmed information exchange matrix measures the most important power dimension. An organization's position within the power structure is determined in part by both information sent and information received. From the way the questions were asked, the information receivers are supposedly dependent organizations because they claimed to need the information that is provided by the senders. Technically, both the rows and the columns of the confirmed communication matrix must be taken into account. By contrast, the action-set coalition matrix is symmetric – both parties are included twice – the columns and rows contain the same data. We decided to count these data only once, that is, to take into account only the row vectors. Hence, the coalition network received only half the weight of the theoretically more important confirmed information matrix. Finally, the organizational reputation matrix is an asymmetric network; its rows are the respondents and its columns are the organizations receiving mentions as especially influential actors. Correlating a pair of rows, which are the responses of two organizations, measures the extent to which those two organizations chose the same organizations. Thus, the higher the correlation, the more the two organizations agreed on who is influential. However, to correlate a pair of columns would use not just two organizational responses, but the choices made by all organizations in the system. Hence, the higher this correlation, the more similar the domain organizations' perceptions of the two target organizations' influence. This approach is the "constituency perspective," which views sets of organizations naming others as powerful actors as a constituency of the two column actors (Laumann and Knoke, 1987: 169–88). In addition to that interpretation, we also argue that only this column perspective represents a systemic view of the policy domain, whereas correlating the rows yields mainly the local perspective of the two respondents. Such local perceptions of reputations contain too much noise for a systemic interpretation. Because the entries in both the confirmed communication and the coalition networks are always based on at least two respondents' answers, they have high validity. We decided to include only the columns of the organizational reputation matrix in the input data for CONCOR. Thus, the confirmed communication matrix received half the total weight in the solution, while the action-set coalition and influence reputation matrices are each weighted one-quarter.

Although blockmodel analyses aim to represent the original networks in highly condensed forms that involve only a few positions or blocks, determining an optimal number of blocks is relatively difficult. The CONCOR algorithm is a divisive procedure which progressively splits the universe of actors into more and more subgroups, each containing fewer and fewer actors (Breiger, Boorman, and Arabie, 1975; Schwartz, 1977). We used a version of CONCOR (Mitchell, 1983) that calculates a goodness of fit measure (*b*) developed by Carrington, Heil, and Berkowitz (1980). After each division, *b* measures the discrepancy between the resulting within- and between-block densities and an ideal-typical pattern where some block densities are 1.0 and all others are 0. Because the fit to the ideal-typical pattern improves as the number of blocks increases, the change in fit relative to the matrix size can serve as a criterion for selecting an optimal number of blocks.

A global measure of *b* simply adds all the *b*s for the separate matrices. Because our goal aim is to compare the U.S., German, and Japanese power structures, our conclusions would be affected by making separate decisions about the optimal solution for each nation. For example, a German four-block solution might depend mainly on the coalition network, whereas the Japanese solution could be based more on the reputational data. Therefore, we concluded that the global *b* would not serve as the best measure of blockmodel fit. Instead, we examined the separate *b*s for the three matrices, looking for a solution in which the sequence of the separate *b*s was the same for all three countries. This result occurred for the eight-block solutions. In each country, the action-set coalition network had the highest *b*, the confirmed communication network had the second highest *b*, and the reputational network ranked last. Thus, the perceptual dimension of the power structure is not only theoretically but also empirically downgraded relative to collective action and information exchanges.

We expected that the coalition network would primarily structure the main diagonal of the blockmodel, bringing together actors with similar interests in the labor policy domain so that the internal block densities are very high. Coalitions could be formed on several legislative bills about which we asked the respondents to give us information. A second expectation was that the reputational network would mainly structure the columns of the data matrices. That is, we expected overall agreement within each policy domain about who are the powerful actors, so the column blocks will contain either high densities or very low densities (in a dichotomous representation, either 0s or 1s). The fine-grained details of the power structure then would appear in the confirmed information exchange network. This hypothesis is justified insofar as both pluralist and corporatist expectations about power structures are formulated primarily in terms of access to key policymakers, which we measured by information exchange.

POWER STRUCTURES IN COMPARISON

Eight-block solutions for three networks in three nations are already rather complex and not easy to interpret comparatively. Because two of the three networks are weighted less than the third, and because both the action-set coalitions and organizational reputations are rather simple, we concentrate on interpreting the digraphs for the confirmed communication networks. The sequences among the eight blocks, ordered by their average reputations, is indicated by labeling the positions with letters: *A* stands for the most influential block, *B* for the next most powerful position, and so on. Two positions whose members are extensively linked in the coalition network are identified either (1) by using a capital letter for the more-powerful block and a lower-case letter for the less-powerful coalition partners, or (2) by using the same capital letter with numerical subscripts when members of the two blocks occupy adjacent ranks in the reputational hierarchy. In the digraphs, directed arrows indicate that confirmed policy information was sent between blocks, and circles indicate within-block exchanges at above-average rates. Double-headed arrows mean that high information flows were approximately balanced in both directions. For imbalanced information exchanges, two arrows of varying thickness reveal which position sent more to the respective re-

Figure 8.1. *Confirmed information exchange among eight positions in the Japanese power structure*

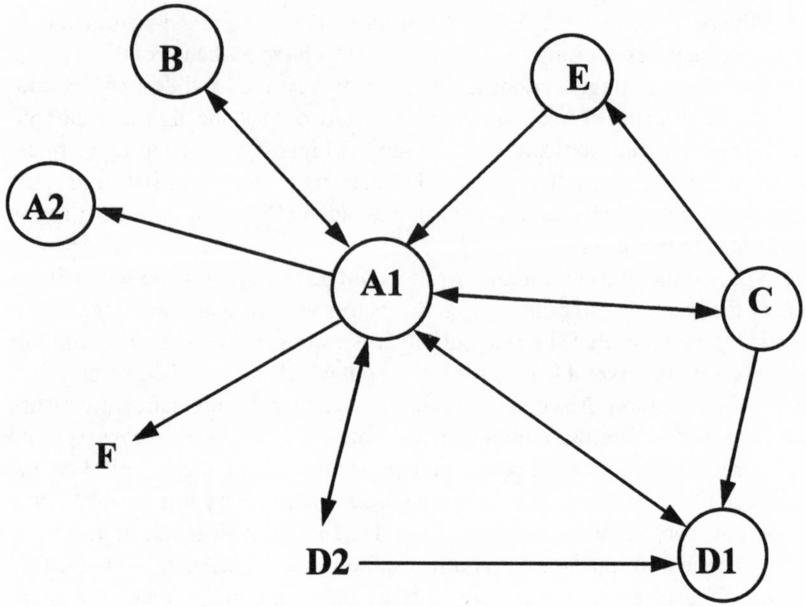

cipient. Imbalanced information flows to positions occupied by the public actors is one important characteristic of pluralist interest intermediation.

The Japanese confirmed communication digraph, in Figure 8.1, reveals a simple structure: a single position (*A1*) maintains direct links with the other seven positions, four of which have balanced information flows in both directions, two of which indicate outflows, and only one of which exhibits a one-sided inflow to the center. This most powerful central position is occupied by all the important players in labor policy-making, including the Liberal Democratic Party, the Ministry of Labor and other key ministries, the major advisory councils, five of the most important business organizations (including the Federation of Economic Organizations and the Federation of Employers Association), and the two peak union associations – the Japan Private Sector Trade Union Confederation (*Rengo:* PTU) and the General Council of Trade Unions of Japan (*Sohyo:* GCU). Although the GCU was absorbed (formally integrated) within the PTU in the fall of 1989, and our field research took place in the spring of 1989, the joint location of GCU and PTU in *A1* is remarkable. The labor unions led by the GCU had, unlike the PTU, been considered the major opponents of the LDP and business organizations like the FEO and FEA. The second most powerful block (*A2*) consists of numerous employers' organizations that frequently form coalitions with the political and business organizations in the governing center. The third block (*B*) contains health, welfare, and social insurance ministries and interest groups whose main tie to the

Figure 8.2. *Confirmed information exchange among eight positions in the German power structure*

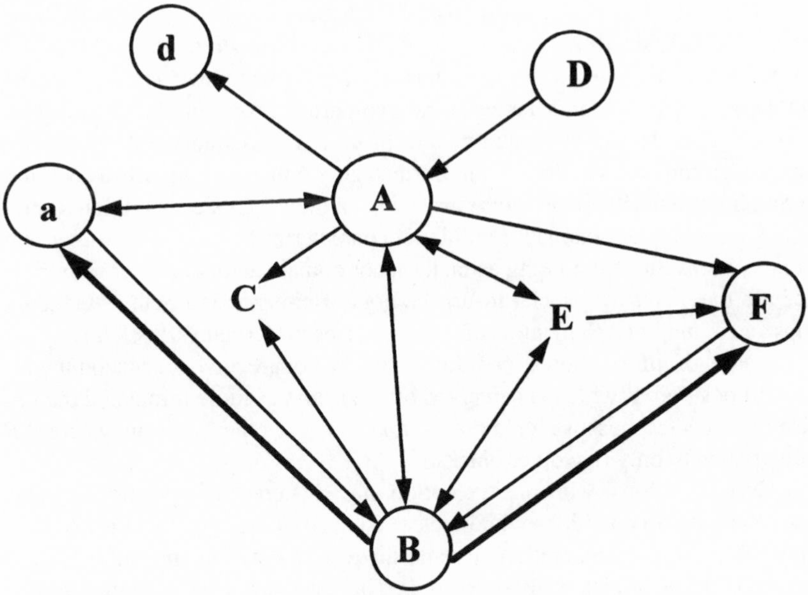

system is its above-average communication to and from the center. Low-ranked positions *E* and *F* are comprised, respectively, of very specialized ministries with their advisory boards and of business associations.

The Japanese labor unions are scattered among three blocks (*C, D1,* and *D2*). Although these three positions communicate among themselves and with the center, their coalition leaders (the peak union federations, GCU and PTU) appear to have been an integrated part of the governing center dominated by the LDP-business coalition. However, *D1* may be an incipient rival to the *A1* center: It attracts more above-average communication ties than the other positions, and it contains the Japan Socialist Party Policy Council.

To summarize, the Japanese system can best be described as a consensus system and a shared information system where the peak labor federations are integrated participants within the governing center, despite (or perhaps because of) the "creative conservatism" of the LDP government (Pempel, 1982). Overall, rather than simply dominating labor, such a system might be able to negotiate policies among all important sectors of the society, with the brokerage of the dominant Liberal Democratic Party and the Ministry of Labor (Allison and Sone, 1993). Unfortunately, at the eight-block level of analysis, we cannot resolve this question.

In Germany, two rival labor policy centers are evident in Figure 8.2. The most powerful position (*A*) contains the major public actors of the governing center, including the parliamentary party of the CDU/CSU, this party's members on the Labor Committee of the *Bundestag,* and the important ministries, above all the Labor Ministry. Block *A* also includes the peak business associations (the German Industry Association and the Union of German Employers), which are close allies of the CDU/CSU. The second most powerful position, *B,* contains the political allies of the CDU/CSU, that is, mainly the liberal Free Democratic Party (FDP) and the peak organizations of the health system. So the German power structure seems to reflect a division of labor between the two partners forming the federal governing coalition. This complicated pattern may be a consequence of the usually complex German politics. That is, the German government is normally a coalition government, a majority in the *Bundesrat* being an important side condition to successful governing. German labor politics is characterized by an influential group of organizations that are missing as major labor domain actors in other countries: These are the mandatory social insurance organizations acting both as claimant groups and as major implementors of social policies in Germany. Block *B* is as frequent a target of information as position *A,* that is, both receive four incoming arrows. But position *A,* which is perceived by the actors as more influential than *B,* is also more central because it maintains links to every other position, whereas *B* is directly tied to only five other blocks.

All German unions, with one exception, are clustered into position *D.* This block cooperates in coalitions with block *d,* comprised mainly of welfare organizations. The Social Democratic Party and three state governments led by Social Democratic prime ministers also occupy *D.* Thus, we now see that in the German communication pattern, *B* is not in opposition to power center *A,* but this role is played by the Social Democrat–union sector *D.* The German system would be corporatist if, like Japan, a close alliance had occurred between the governing center *A* and block *D.* However, during the period under investigation, such an alliance was not practiced. German society is thus more polarized into two well-organized sectors, business and labor, than is Japanese society. But the German state does not play a central unifying role with the peak associations of both sectors, as does the Japanese state. Their divergence indicates that the parties comprise the political core in Germany, whereas the ministries form the core in Japan. The German political cleavage was possible because the governing coalition enjoyed a double majority, the essential majority in the *Bundestag* and the very helpful additional majority of *Länder* headed by the CDU/CSU prime ministers in the *Bundesrat.* These state governments are all located in block *a,* which cooperated in coalitions with center block *A.* Finally, positions *C, E,* and *F* are composed, respectively, of the Green Party, specialized business associations, and, in *F,* mandatory social insurance organizations. Because the German power structure is further complicated by the presence of mandatory social insurance organizations and the necessity of coalition governments, we label it the architecture of complexity. This system's most difficult task is to organize the corporate actors that are either closely affiliated with the respective governing parties or responsible for implementing domain policies. The Social Democratic Party cooperates closely with the outsiders of this arrangement, but of course it has some access to the governing center.

Figure 8.3. *Confirmed information exchange among eight positions in the U.S. power structure*

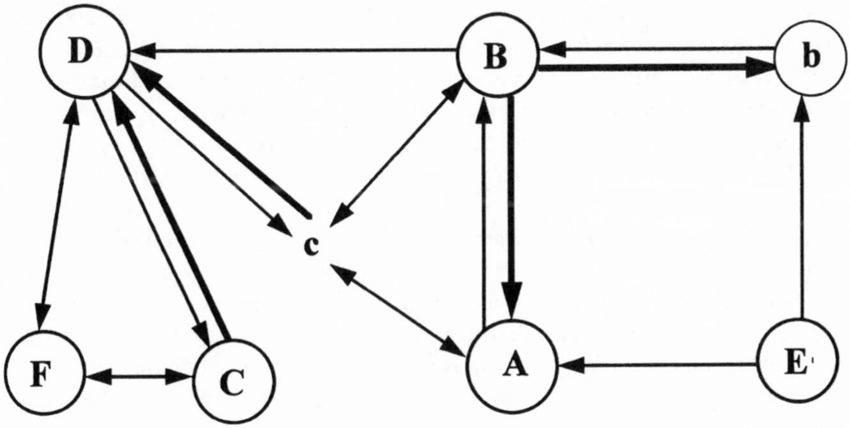

The U.S. labor policy domain in Figure 8.3 resembles the German power structure insofar as its governing center also faces rival positions in the confirmed communication network. Center block *A* consists of a large group of public actors, including the White House Office, the Department of Labor, and Republicans on the House and Senate labor committees. In addition, it contains some peak business organizations closely aligned with the Republican Party, such as the Business Roundtable and the National Association of Manufacturers. But block *B* also clusters some of the most powerful business organizations outside of the governing center, in particular the Chamber of Commerce of the U.S. Position *B* was a major claimant group in the labor policy domain during the Reagan era. A second major rival of *A* in the communication structure is block *D*, which combines the Democratic members of the House and Senate labor committees with minority groups, such as the NAACP and National Urban League, and urban interests such as the National League of Cities. This rival position is less powerful than the governing center: It ranks not second but only fourth in the influence reputation hierarchy. But block *D* has even greater centrality than block *A*. It is the target of information sent by four other positions (from *B;* from *C*, the union block including the AFL-CIO; from *c*, comprising mainly public interest groups; and from *F*, primarily women's interest groups). Like block *B*, block *A* receives direct communications from just three blocks (from *B;* from *c;* and from *E*, a cluster of insurance associations and health interest groups). Further, *D* functions more as a communication hub than does *A*, because two of its four incoming flows are strongly unbalanced compared to one such arrow targeting position *A*. Most importantly, in contrast to Japan and Germany, these U.S. opposition blocks (*A* and *D*) do not maintain direct ties to one another. With one exception, all labor unions occupy the same block (*C*). Its coalition partner, namely block *c*, is largely composed of public interest groups, particularly the national associations for counties, governors, and state legislatures. Note that *c* comprises the only indirect link in both directions between the two rivals, *A* and *D*.

In sum, during this era of divided national government, the wide communication gulf between a Republican Administration and a Democratic Congress is a salient feature of the U.S. power structure. The congressional Republicans are incorporated into the governing center together with the White House Office, whereas the congressional Democrats constitute a discrete and distant opposition. The American power structure can best be described as a class-polarized system with political integration. Business interests and labor interests take opposing sides, with clusters of organizations heavily targeting a political center split along party lines. Because the Democrats held the majority in the House of Representatives throughout the Reagan era and regained the Senate majority at the end, the unions enjoyed much better access to parts of the public sector than did either the German labor unions under conservative regime holding majorities in both federal chambers, or Japanese labor unions as an informal partner of the LDP-led governing center.

CONCLUSION

Comparing the three nation's labor policy domains, what are the more general interpretations we can reach beyond empirically accurate descriptions of the power structures at a given moment? One general conclusion is that public actors play a very important role in all three domains. Election outcomes, which determine party control of the national legislatures and the administration, are crucial for understanding interest intermediation and authoritative decision making within these domains. For Germany, one would anticipate that the power structure changed substantially when the Social Democratic state governments gained the majority in the *Bundesrat.* In Japan, at least a possible rival to the governing center consists of some unions and the Socialist Party. But, with the demise of the GCU, this likelihood grew increasingly remote. A more likely scenario is that the LDP's subsequent loss of majority standing in the Diet will massively rearrange party politics, and, hence, the national power structure. In the American case, we would have expected relatively little change in the power structure after President Clinton's election in 1992 gave the Democrats control of the Administration as well as of both congressional chambers. Although the U.S. communication structure probably would become somewhat more centralized, no major claimant group would risk cutting its ties to an opposing party that might win presidential office in the future. But the 1994 election results, giving the Republicans control over both congressional houses for the first time in 40 years, undoubtedly are transforming the U.S. power structure in major ways in anticipation of the impending presidential election.

9

Variations on a theme of organizational states

We launched our investigation of the national labor policy structures and processes of the U.S., Germany, and Japan from the organizational state approach. By imposing a single research design involving nearly identical measurement, data collection, and analysis procedures, we sought to eliminate any variation attributable to methodological techniques. Hence, if cross-national differences *were* observed, we should interpret them as genuine. Nothing in our analytic or empirical approach necessarily constrained either differences or similarities from emerging. Indeed, the chief advantage of conducting rigorous comparative research lies in its capacity to sort out unique from common elements in a manner inaccessible to investigations of one nation.

As may already be evident from the preceding chapters, we discovered certain broad similarities, but also many important differences. Distinctive policy-making structures characterize the U.S., Germany, and Japan. Although they belong to the same genus, each is a distinct species; or, to switch to a musical metaphor, the national organizational states reflect variations on a theme. These variations arose in distinctive institutional histories that continue to be played out on the contemporary stage. But they also exhibit new, previously unnoticed aspects. These new aspects surfaced and became apparent during our investigations of the interorganizational influence networks. The organizational state leads to images of structure built up from those empirically measured relationships. Accordingly, existing theoretical models, derived mainly from institutional styles of analysis, cannot be expected fully to capture or describe the structures and systems that surface from the organizational state approach. What is now needed is a new set of explanatory models that will more fully capture the subtle differences among the world's competing capitalisms. This book constitutes one modest step in that direction.

The following section reviews the major results from our comparative analyses of the three national labor policy domains. Next we show how three distinctive types of political systems emerge from these results, representing unique conjunctions of formal policy-making institutions with informal power networks. We conclude with a discussion of the promises and pitfalls of comparative research in contemporary social science and future directions for organizational state studies.

REVIEW OF RESULTS

The state clearly constitutes the formal locus of collective decision making that affects the larger civil society within which it is embedded. It is the only institution possessing sufficient resources, authority, and legitimacy to make and implement hard choices among available alternatives and to enforce these outcomes – in the form of legislative, judicial, and regulatory acts. Our organizational state conceptualization, along with most other approaches in political science and sociology, assumed that a full understanding of state behavior requires analysts to take into account many participants who are not formally part of the state apparatus. That is, the key policy actors included not only formal governmental agencies but also those so-called private-sector actors with the capacity to participate in formulating and influencing collective policy decisions. The organizational state perspective identified their roles in decision making by examining political relationships among core policy domain organizations. The approach analyzed national political systems through a focus on formal organizations, not on individual persons or social classes. This level of analysis was justifiable because individuals usually exert meaningful influence over policy debates as representatives of organized interests rather than to further their personal stakes in the conflict (Heinz, Laumann, Nelson, and Salisbury, 1993). Furthermore, our initial search for key policy actors yielded formal organizations. The results, however, do bear importantly on questions of larger social organizational patterns.

The distributions of types of organizations, identified in the three national labor policy domains by equivalent criteria, provided us with some initial material for meaningful comparisons. Chapter 3 showed that the main types of actors – government, business, and labor – were similar in the three societies (Table 3.2). However, they were present in differing frequencies. In addition, certain types of organizational actors were unique, indicating qualitative differences among the nations. Japan had the highest proportion of labor and business associations, while Germany had the lowest. Japan had by far the fewest professional societies and public interest groups, while Japanese organized labor and business seemed to perform the vast majority of functions within civil society. In contrast, the U.S. and German systems left more room for public interest activism and, in Germany, for the additional organizations of the mandatory social insurance system. The different number of government actors in the three countries reflected differences between the political systems as well as our decisions about how fine-grained actors, such as parties or ministries, should be decomposed into their constituent parts in order to encompass the set of consequential independent actors. Within the national state, the U.S. and Japan focused more on the executive branch, whereas political party contention played a bigger role in Germany. However, the nature of executive branch leadership differed greatly between the U.S., with its presidential system and fragmented bureaucracies, and the two parliamentary systems led by cabinets and strong executive ministries.

Issue publics, the set of all organizations exhibiting similar profiles of interest in the entire range of domain policy issues, provided the fertile ground on which political actors grew. If the large majority of organizations expressed no interest in a given policy issue, that issue may have had a hard time getting realized. Earlier U.S. research found a donut or hollow-core pattern of interest distribution among organizations, indicating that no organization took a generalist's interest in all issues. We wondered whether this donut image would hold again for the U.S. and whether it would also appear in Germany and Japan.

Our investigation, spanning nearly decade-long conservative eras in each nation, discovered about four dozen general labor policy issues that gained some attention. These issues fell within nine basic subdomains (10 in Germany). The issues showed the same basic cleavage between labor relations and social policy concerns in all three nations.

A basic business-labor cleavage underlay the U.S., German, and Japanese labor policy domains, as revealed not only in the contemporary issue public data but also in historical labor domain developments (in Chapters 3 and 7) and in interorganizational spatial patterns (Chapters 4–6). This sharp class conflict between labor and capital was evident in the oppositional social organization of each nation. In the U.S., this striking gulf delimited the regulation-intervention policy preferences advocated by organized labor and its minority-group allies and the market-sovereignty approaches favored by large corporations and their small-business confederates. But, in Japan, the cleavage revealed a different ideological division, between the protection of union benefits advocated by leftist labor and the bureaucratic-industrial cooperation advocated by conservatives. In Germany, the divide was less evident, mainly because the actors most interested in social policy were careful not to be drawn into the class divide of classic labor issues.

All the nations exhibited a gradient in the breadth of organizational policy interests, with some organizations more narrowly focused than others. On average, German and U.S. labor domain organizations spent about 51 percent of their total policy effort on labor domain affairs, but Japanese organizations devoted a slightly smaller proportion (43%; see Table 4.1). A majority of organizations in all three nations expressed high levels of interest in only a few issues and subdomains. Organizational attention to most policy events (legislative bills) was even more restricted. Few bills roused a majority of organizations to action. But this pattern of interest was more extreme in the U.S. and Germany than in Japan. Spatial representations of the U.S. and German issue publics exhibited hollow-core or donut patterns, whereas a number of organizations crowded into the center of the Japanese issue public space (Figures 4.7–4.9). These images indicated the absence of any potentially coordinating group in the first two nations but the possibility that some Japanese organizations could play the generalist role of trying to oversee and mediate the whole domain (including the LDP, PTU, GCU, and FEA). Thus, Japan's central issue public would enjoy greater capacity for and interest in centralized coordination.

Confining our data collection to the most prominent national organizations did not predetermine which specific actors would occupy the key power positions within each labor policy domain. As described in Chapter 3, applying a visibility-activity criterion to each nation yielded a wide range of key organizations: labor unions, business associations, professional societies, public interest groups, advisory boards, governmental agencies and ministries, political parties, and legislative committees. Thus, each policy domain comprised all types of organizations, reflecting the broad spectrum of policy interests within those civil societies.

Within these highly select populations, we found clear hierarchies, as revealed in Chapter 5. In each nation, only a few organizations – consisting of a few peak labor and business associations, labor ministries, political parties, and legislative actors – jointly occupied the central positions in the webs of communication and support networks. These core actors typically combined comprehensive perspectives on domain affairs with broad constituency mandates, public legitimation, and power resources that enabled them to fight policy battles simultaneously along several fronts. Consequently, they enjoyed the highest reputations among their peers as politically influential domain organizations. But many organizations that were central in one network were not so central in the other; that is, the two centralities were not strongly correlated. This low covariation indicated a disjuncture between information-rich organizations and support-rich elites that revealed important distinctions among the three nations, as will be explained.

In contrast, by their lack of resources and broad interests, the more specialized actors – public interest groups championing minority causes, professional societies defending narrow turfs – engaged in only episodic actions. Hence, they were pushed into the peripheral positions of the labor domain, from where they had to seek alliances with the core organizational movers-and-shakers if they hoped to leave any imprint on the specialized issues about which they were most concerned.

We asked our organizational informants to identify the most influential organizations in the labor domain. The results of that influence reputation question yielded a somewhat different hierarchy in each nation. Among the top 15 choices, government ministries occupied eight slots in Japan, but only two each in the U.S. and Germany. Conversely, political party groups and public interest groups were more prevalent in the U.S. and Germany than in Japan. Already, this distribution began to paint pictures of a state-centric tendency in Japan, but greater political party emphasis in both the U.S. and Germany.

Information exchange forms the basis for political action in every system. The existence of direct communication links enabled the labor domain organizations to anticipate one another's behaviors and to coordinate their actions. In Japan, only 17 percent of the organizations directly exchanged information, as compared to 29 percent in Germany and 39 percent in the U.S. In a communication network, the shorter the number of linkages necessary for a pair of organizations to exchange information, the closer they were situated in spatial representations. Among the three communication network patterns (Figures 5.2–5.4), the most influential German organizations clustered most tightly at the spatial center, with the top U.S. actors almost as tightly clustered. The Japanese center was a little more dispersed. The three centers differed more in their membership. The U.S. and German centers were similar in containing all the contending political party groups plus the business and labor peaks. But the Japanese center contained mainly the government organizations (7 of 16), the business peak federation mandated and responsible for the labor domain (FEA), and the more docile of the two peak labor federations (PTU). The Japanese center excluded the political parties (LDP and JSP), as well as the leftist, oppositional labor peak federation (GCU), and the generalist business peak federation (FEO). The Japanese center thus represented a bureaucratic intermediation of communication: The peak associations mediated communications from the civil society and worked directly with the specialist government agencies to discuss labor policy, without political party interference. In turn, the Japanese government agencies located between the business and labor peaks and brokered their information flow. In contrast, in the German center, the peak business and labor federations located adjacent to one another, indicating close direct communication of crucial policy information. Accordingly, the German state did not play a major brokerage role among these federations. And in the U.S. center, the congressional Republicans and the White House mediated for the Chamber of Commerce, while the congressional Democrats and the Department of Labor mediated for the AFL-CIO and other important labor unions. Hence, a party-based brokerage of communication among interest groups and social classes characterizes the U.S.

Political support, in contrast to information exchanges, indicated the willingness to put one's reputation on the line to back up an ally. Organizations did not extend support to their enemies, even if they might trade information with them. Fewer organizations provided this more expensive resource to others. The spatial images, reflecting these highly differentiated patterns among givers and recipients, located the support providers at the edges of the support network spaces and the nonclaimant organizations at the center (Figures 5.5–5.7). The Japanese support network was polarized between the left labor peak on one side and the business peak on the other. The Ministry of Labor shared close support with the general business federation and the conservative political party. The more policy-oriented PTU union federation was located closer to the business peak (FEA) than to the left union federation and the Japan Socialist Party. This alignment indicated that the FEA and the PTU supported one another in reaching compromises within an otherwise highly polarized polity. The German support network resembled the Japanese image, in that the labor and business peaks located in widely separate areas, implying that they did not offer direct political support to one another or work out compromises. No moderate union or business peak federation bridged the support gap in Germany, and the state nestled close to business. This pattern was noteworthy, given the German communication structure. Both the German and Japanese systems excluded support for the oppositional labor group. In this regard, the U.S. support network implied a state that took a more balanced stance. The business and labor peak federations were not so polarized and the Department of Labor sat at a greater remove from both sectors.

Overall, we found that the more central an organization was in either the communication or the support network, the higher was its reputation for being influential in labor politics. Similarly, the more central organizations were also more active in attempting to influence the outcomes of legislative policy events. These relations held for all three societies. However, we found national differences in the relative importance of the two networks. We surmised that the political support network would be more related to organizational reputation in party-competitive societies like the U.S. and Germany and that the communication network would be more important in a consensus-building society like Japan. To our surprise, the opposite turned out to be the case (Figure 5.8). Evidently, political actors in the U.S. and Germany felt more able to initiate action on their own, if they only had the requisite policy information. But in Japan, information was much less important than was the provision of political support by peak federations.

Legislative fights were structured around action sets, groups of organizations that shared preferences on specific policy events and worked together to affect their outcomes (Chapter 6). The fundamental labor-capital conflict comprised the main axis around which other policy disputes were socially organized, but it did not impose a rigid framework into which all significant policy domain conflicts were squeezed. Although the peak labor and business associations led most action sets, their specific composition varied markedly across nations. Several German action sets were led by professional societies and other nonlabor, nonbusiness interest groups. German and Japanese action sets were more likely than those in the U.S. to include political parties. An unreconcilable labor-business antagonism seemed most apparent in the U.S., whereas a more accommodationist stance was evident in Germany and Japan. Given the numerous, narrowly specialized, organizational interests just noted, very few issues and events instigated enduring, broad opposition groups. Hence, in all three nations, large social distances were evident between opposing action sets. Most importantly, no overarching group emerged that was capable of bridging these gulfs. Many legislative conflicts were limited in scope, drawing participation by relative handfuls of organizations, rather than replicating large polarized blocks across event after event. Consequently, action sets tended to have short lives, with different coalitions assembling around the peak business and labor associations for each new legislative fight.

The ability to affect collective decisions in national labor policy domains was differentially distributed among organizations. Gaining access to other powerful actors was the critical factor, whether considering perceptual or behavioral dimensions of power. As we already mentioned, organizational centrality within the policy communication and political support networks explained reputations for general influence, conceptualized as subjective reputations for influence (Chapter 5). Similarly, when political power was conceptualized as the ability to affect the outcomes of legislative bills (Chapter 7), organizational power depended on an ability to gain access to those public agents possessing the formal authority to decide policy events.

An institutional access approach revealed that a critical determinant of organizational power was exchange of control in the form of actors' access to agents. To explain why some proposed bills became laws and others failed, we modified a political exchange model to take into account the unique institutions of each national legislature (Chapter 7). Building on previous models, the crucial exchange relationship was the organizations' linkages to decision-making authorities. We distinguished between actors who expressed interest in legislative bills and the agents (public authorities) who formally decided those bills, keeping in mind that an agent was also an actor if it expressed a preference for a legislative outcome. The access model involved control, as confirmed communication ties between organizations and public authorities; interest, as the proportion of an organization's total effort concentrated on influencing a bill's outcome; and authority, as constitutionally designated rights to make binding legislative decisions.

We compared six versions of the institutional access model (three forms of authority relationships by two forms of control) to predictions of the bills' outcomes by a baseline model that relied only on the public agents' policy preferences. The versions yielding the most accurate predictions were the party government model with the deployment logic of access for Germany; the party government model with a mobilization logic of access for the U.S.; and the mobilization version of the legislative model for Japan. In each case, the most powerful actors in a nation were the public authorities who also played the role of agents, primarily by maintaining a high level of self-control. Thus, explaining collective decisions in the national labor policy domain required taking into account both the informal networks of policy communication among organizations and the formal structures of legislative institutions, a theme that we elaborate in the next section.

A power structure is a stable arrangement of relations among social positions, jointly occupied by actors with similar relations to other positions, that generates and distributes power in a social system. Three basic types of interorganizational relationships jointly defined the U.S., German, and Japanese labor domain power structures (Chapter 8): organizational imputations of reputed domain influence; loosely knit, fluid action-set coalitions across events; and access network, consisting of confirmed communication links to allies and antagonists. Based on blockmodels produced by hierarchical cluster analyses, the three domains exhibited distinctive power structures at the eight-position level of aggregation.

The Japanese power structure was the simplest: a single center, comprising most of the important players (Liberal Democratic Party, Ministry of Labor, and peak labor and business associations), maintained direct communications links with the other seven positions. The Japan Socialist Party was separated from the main center. The other positions kept few ties to one another. This image resembled the classic definition of corporatism, in which a core group dominates the other sectors (Schmitter, 1977), with labor playing a much weaker role, as indicated by its split among three blocks.

Germany's power structure involved two centers coalesced around the two political parties that formed the Kohl coalition government. One center contained the Christian Democratic Union, the Labor Ministry, and peak business associations. The second center consisted of the Free Democratic Party and peak health associations. Together they maintained strong ties to the Christian Democratic *Länder* governments and the mandatory social insurance associations. The main opposition center contained the Social Democratic Party and the labor unions. The separation of labor from the Greens and public interest groups weakened potential opposition power. This power structure image was more consistent with a pluralistic system that deemphasizes labor than with a form of state corporatism in which the labor groups and their party would not have comprised a separate position.

The U.S. power structure was best characterized by the fundamental class cleavage noted earlier. It had two rival powerful positions, a Republican Party–business block and a Democratic Parry–minority-urban block. Because of constitutional separation of powers in the U.S. system, both blocks continued to exercise authority under the conservative Reagan Administration. They lacked direct communication ties to one another, exchanged information only through the public interest groups. The Republican-business position maintained close ties with another business organization position and to insurance and health associations. The Democratic position developed close ties with labor and women's groups positions. This extreme polarization persisted in large part because each structural position had some chance to influence labor legislation.

As with the institutional access models, we observed that each nation's political institutions partially shaped its characteristic power relationships. In the Japanese and German systems, a dominant party or coalition appointed a prime minister and virtually controlled the passage of all legislation. Under these circumstances, opposition coalitions had little hope for significant influence. But under the U.S. separation of powers allowing the presidency and both congressional chambers to be controlled by different parties, maintaining strong opposition blocks in society made much political sense. The executive and legislative authorities retained the ultimate constitutional right to enact or defeat policy proposals. However, in all three political systems, the potential for electorally inspired shifts in party control meant that the legislative and executive authorities must exercise their rights through close consultation with and support from powerful groups in the civil society. In the 1980s, such power resided more often with business than with either organized labor or public interest groups. Thus, the modern state and civil society were inextricably bonded into comprehensive, if patterned, biased, and shifting, policy webs.

The struggles between labor and business that erupted in the 19th century took on very different meanings at the end of the 20th century, as institutional solutions or stalemates accumulated in the three advanced capitalist, industrial democracies. The labor-business cleavage still cut across many issues, making an enduring consensus about appropriate policy solutions difficult in most instances. But the three nations managed to work out different compromises. They all granted some basic legitimacy to mediating institutions, such as the U.S. National Labor Relations Board, the German mandatory social insurance associations, and, in Japan, such cross-sector consultative forums as the Industry-Labor Consultation Committee (*Sanrokon*), the Social Economic Council of Citizens, and many advisory councils. These institutions tempered the intensity of the conflicts by representing the interests of both employees and employers. But beyond that, the solutions occurred within very different distributions of power, leading to very different forms of participation and legislative outcomes.

In light of our empirical results, the different policy outputs produced by the three systems in the 1980s began to make more sense. The Reagan Administration's jump into deep debt and mild cutbacks on labor and social policy reflected the authority stalemate between two powerful centers in the state and in society. Given this stalemate, conservative politicians took the easy route of distributing new benefits, such as tax cuts to the wealthy and fat contracts to military contractors underwritten by federal loans from Japanese and other investors. Imposing greater costs by cutting labor and welfare benefits was more difficult, because the opposition possessed blocking power. The Kohl government was based on a coalition of parties with ties to the mandatory social insurance associations, so it could not make deep cuts in social spending. It had neither the strength nor the will to upset the moderately corporatist, codetermination arrangements of business and labor that had proved beneficial to both groups. The Nakasone and subsequent Liberal Democratic Party regimes in Japan, however, faced no other effective contender for power, at least from outside the LDP (although the situation inside the party became increasingly complicated). So they were able to push through policies that radically cut back government expenditures and severely damaged the power of the leftist, opposition labor unions and their political party.

INSTITUTIONALIZATION OF POLICY DOMAINS

The results of our comparative labor policy domain analyses necessitate some revisions in our initial view of the organizational state as it applies to policy-making in the national labor domains of Japan, Germany, and the U.S. By identifying the key policy domain actors and relationships, and by showing how these elements combine in nationally distinct patterns, the organizational state approach yields important insights into policy-making. The analytic framework and the network methods were indispensable for generating rigorous accounts of structural divergences among the three nations. Neither informal networks nor formal political institutions alone suffice to explain labor policy-making; only their combination can paint full portraits of the varieties of modern organizational states.

We agree with Peter Ordeshook's observation:

> The new institutionalism, although motivated by theoretical results derived from the rational choice paradigm, is less an attempt at synthesizing economics and political science than it is an effort at recombining behavioralist research with more traditional concerns of political science. (Ordeshook, 1990: 25)

Such institutions as bureaucratic authority, electoral procedures, legislative committees, executive agencies, policy agendas, and voting rules constrain actors' preferences and perceptions, but participants' actions also reshape these contexts.

The central significance of these formal political institutions grew increasingly apparent to us during our analyses of both the exchange models estimated (Chapter 7) and the power structures (Chapter 8).

The institutionalization processes shaping the social structures and political activities of national policy domains encompass formal and informal dimensions. Formal political institutions are ultimately enshrined in constitutions that specify the formal authority of office, who may participate in collective decisions, and how those decisions can be properly made, as supplemented by procedural rules governing those institutions' quotidian affairs (see Appendix 1). These historical documents express distinctive national ideologies about the proper arrangement of power among political entities. Hence, they are fundamentally cultural assertions concerning the essential norms of national political life. But the practices of actors both implement and defy them. The U.S. has the world's oldest written constitution, derived from the Lockean laissez-faire liberalism of an agrarian society. It encapsulates a checks-and-balances division of power among the national executive, legislative, and judicial branches that is intended to limit the state's encroachment on individual rights in an increasingly pluralist, multicultural society. The American constitution's provision for a separately elected president and Congress planted the potential for divided and grid-locked government that has been plaguing the U.S. for a generation. The current German and Japanese constitutions were heavily influenced by U.S. Occupation authorities. But neither emerged tabula rasa from thin air. Both were grounded in the strong communitarian cultures of their ancient, ethnically homogeneous societies. Although both nations adopted parliamentary systems in their constitutions, their actual manifestations took distinct turns. Japan preserved an integrated central state bureaucracy (with competing decentralized divisions, bureaus, and ministries) under the unitary state system with a bicameral legislature. Germany opted for an increased federalization that gave the subnational states a major role in national affairs and fostered the need for coalition governments. Hence, the constitutional potential for a split between the executive and legislative branches of the national state, as well as for turnover in the dominant party regime, was least for Japan, somewhat greater for Germany, and highest for the U.S..

The informal institutions of national policy domains arise from the web of interactions connecting state authorities to those organizations in the civil society that can effectively demand participation in public policy debates. Although lacking the constitutional legitimacy of governmental institutions, such informal configurations are indispensable to explaining the dynamics of policy disputes. Through information exchanges, coalition formation, and attributions of influence reputations, these policy participants jointly forge a national power structure that serves simultaneously as opportunities for and constraints on the pursuit of collective outcomes. Thus, as with formal constitutions, the policy networks effectively express cultural norms about appropriate political strategies, tactics, and actions. Constitutional edicts are relatively rigid and usually change at a glacial pace, although the electoral rules they impose may allow for rapid change in party

Figure 9.1. *Typology of national labor policy domains as combinations of formal and informal institutions*

		INFORMAL INSTITUTIONS (POWER STRUCTURES)	
		Multiple Centers	Single Center
FORMAL INSTITUTIONS (CONSTITUTIONS)	Presidential System	Contentious USA	Autocratic
	Parliamentary System	Collaborative GERMANY	Coordinated JAPAN

domination. Electoral coalitions among political parties also exhibit greater plasticity in response to shifting circumstances. Policy players constantly importune instrumental ties that they believe will further their policy interests. However, these alliances are channeled by embedded patterns of social networks. These linkages are not randomly patterned; rather, they are hemmed in by past histories of collaboration and antagonism, by current conditions of trust and distrust, and by anticipation of future costs and benefits from available alternatives.

Each nation's informal institutions helped shape its distinctive concentration or dispersal of power. Japan presents the most unified configuration, with a single center jointly occupied by the peak governmental, political, labor, and business organizations. All other positions revolve around this single center of political gravity. In contrast, the informal power structures of both Germany and the U.S. consist of multiple centers of power. One center is comprised of the conservative political parties controlling the national governments in the 1980s in alliance with key business associations. One or more opposition centers are arrayed around the liberal or socialist party and their labor union and minority interest group partners.

We contend that the formal and informal dimensions of political institutions must be jointly considered in order properly to characterize national differences among the three policy domains. Figure 9.1 displays the covariation of formal and informal institutional dimensions as a cross-tabulation of two dichotomies. Four basic types of domains are generated, three of which are represented by the nations in our study. The U.S. presidential system is vulnerable to frequently divided executive-legislative government, such as occurred under Reagan in the 1980s. Because some interest groups' policy preferences could be satisfied simply by preventing their opponents from gaining ground, no efforts need to be attempted to reach an accommodation among disputants. Here, distinct power centers are occupied by bitterly contending rivals who seek to displace one another in the policy-making center by ousting the political party controlling the national executive and legislative branches. We label this type of policy domain *contentious,* reflecting the deep-seated and often antagonistic nature of American labor relations. The contrasting type occurred in Japan: a *coordinated* policy domain where a single power center arose in a parliamentary system assuring unity of legislative and executive organs. The Liberal Democratic Party's generations-long domination of Japanese national politics meant that all major claimants would have to seek inclusion within the single power center or risk being totally shut out of any say in national policy decisions. By the time of our research, the peak Japanese labor federations, especially the PTU, clearly tried to play an integrated role within an umbrella grouping, coexisting with business interests. This fact is in sharp contrast with the conventional image of Japanese labor. Labor changed from its previous strategy of allying with opposition political parties like the JSP and DSP, which could never win control of the Diet. However, this broad embrace may have proven to be too inclusive for the LDP to sustain, possibly contributing to the political "cell-division" that ultimately eroded that comprehensive party in the 1990s.

A third type is the *collaborative* policy domain, represented by Germany's multiple power centers within a parliamentary system. The critical contrast with Japan is the absence of a dominant German political party, meaning that control of the government requires a coalition of parties. Major interest groups enjoy privileged access to their "natural" political coalition partners, but all major players avoid becoming overly dependent on a single power holder. Hence, a strategy of keeping the lines of communication open, of subduing antagonism, and of cooperating with opponents when feasible, is more practical in Germany than in either the U.S. or Japan. The result is a more fluid and collaborative political culture in Germany.

Our study did not include a case of the fourth type of policy domain. This type combines the formal institutions of a presidential system with a single power center in the informal institutions. We label it an *autocratic* policy domain, because it seems likely to concentrate effective policy-making in the hands of the presidential party and to manipulate the support of subordinate interest groups. Only if no plausible split between the executive and legislative parties were feasible would such an authoritarian arrangement be likely to arise or to persist. Perhaps empirical instances of an autocratic domain are France under President de Gaulle immediately following his creation of the Fifth Republic and the *caudillismo* of Juan Peron's Argentina.

WHITHER COMPARATIVE RESEARCH?

As in most social research specialties, no single overarching perspective predominates today in comparative sociology and politics (Øyen, 1990; Wiarda, 1991). Encompassing grand theories have yielded to middle-range explanations, reflecting the fragmentation of intellectual endeavors. Comparative research on the modern state has become a congeries of competing models and paradigms, whose prospects for synthesis into a reunified approach are dim. Such conventional concepts as "tradition-modernization" and "development" acquired a pronounced Western bias that fell from fashion as the world grew increasingly multipolar. With the decline of Western hegemony in numerous spheres – military, economic, political, cultural – a plurality of approaches to the state has proliferated. Ironically, the end of the Cold War, bringing the collapse of a viable communist paradigm, has only served to accelerate these centrifugal forces. Still, rich terrain for study remains in the unique histories and institutions of the world's nearly two hundred nations. A wider spectrum of substantive and theoretical issues among the world's diverse competing capitalisms has displaced the classical debates over market-versus-command economies and democratic-versus-totalitarian politics. Explaining the proliferation of new political-economic "species" has moved to the forefront.

In the present intellectual climate, prospects for the universalizing social science championed by earlier generations of scholars now appear unrealistically optimistic:

> By "universalizing social science" we mean something like "valid in space and time," meaning a social science transcending geography and history with all that implies of structural and cultural diversity. This would go beyond comparisons of societies with one another in space and over time. It would also include theories about how they interact synchronically and how they transform diachronically – a giant task, in other words, but modern social science is working at it with equally giant data banks. (Galtung, 1990: 107)

The alternative individualizing strategy searches for the causes and conditions of a given society's specific sociopolitical formations (Tilly, 1984: 81). This mode of theory construction seeks to identify the distinctive pathways through which sociopolitical structures and processes arise, persist, destabilize, and transform into their successors. An account applicable to nation *A* may differ dramatically from the explanation suitable for nation *B*. Rather than forcing all phenomena to fit into the same Procrustean bed, the individualizing strategy generates ideographic interpretations for one case that may have little relevance for the next case. The unanswered question remains whether a variation-finding theory might ultimately be constructed that could explain these particular cases as the result of changes in a limited set of relationships among key variables.

The alleged irreconcilability of universalizing and individualizing social science poses a false dichotomy, implying that only one comparative research methodology can produce correct knowledge. A more fruitful dual strategy combines both nomothetic and ideographic tacks, with the latter providing the essential grist for the former's mill. The most urgent requirement is for comparative researchers to broaden the scope of states investigated using equivalent measures and rigorous methods. The three organizational states examined in this book comprise an extremely narrow subset, the world's most highly developed political economies. The interaction of formal and informal institutions on collective decision making may be important just among these states. Only by replicating the research design across the full range of modern states – one-party regimes in Latin America, military governments in Africa, socialist societies in Asia – can we determine the parameters of this explanation. Because of exceptional requirements in time, money, and expertise, such a project could not be lightly undertaken nor easily accomplished. Given the enormous diversity of histories, institutions, and cultures within this population, we would be surprised were the relationships identified as significant for the most advanced capitalist democracies also to prove relevant for all other societies. But by identifying those nations where such relationships pertain and those where they are missing, we could begin to delimit the boundaries of the organizational state perspective. And, in the current situation of stridently competing claims, that small advance would be a significant achievement.

Concerning the theory of democratic states, from the organizational state perspective, we developed an institutional access model that seeks to explain legislative policy decisions in large systems comprising both public and private actors. We postulated that the underlying variables that affect collective decisions are identical in democratic systems. The weights of different actors and the substantive outcomes of the decision process differ. However, this difference arises from *varying policy preferences* of the consequential actors and from different *institutional restraints* on the typical actors within each policy domain. Actors' consequentiality in a policy domain depends partially on the actors' access to the authorities and partially on the institutional delineation of authority roles. Some actors are privileged to the extent that they are able to play the double role of actors and agents in authority positions. Identifying these mechanisms through detailed analyses of three cases demonstrated considerable progress compared to the empiricist approach, in which empirical generalizations must be uncovered through the control of third variables. Although we could present results from only three comparative case studies, we were able to identify some common properties among them. These three nations' importance as on-going democratic experiments strengthens the implicit argument for the generalizability of our results. One could label our strategy the comparative model–guided case study approach.

FUTURE ORGANIZATIONAL STATE RESEARCH

Comparative analyses with a historical dimension are integral to expanding our knowledge about policy domains. Our projects were essentially cross-sectional snapshots taken during relatively stable eras, when conservative governments aspired to few labor policy initiatives. Without a longer time frame, we have no way to determine how typical or exceptional are these relations. The dynamics of a mature policy domain may differ substantially from configurations in formative periods. Longitudinal research is necessary to sort out changes that occur within a stable system from changes in the system itself. Three directions for investigation are possible. One course extends analyses backwards toward the creation of new policy domains, using archival evidence to reconstruct the formative impacts of technology, demography, political entrepreneurship, and public media. Of special concern are how the initial social construction of social problems and the propagation of proposed policy solutions generate a new policy domain that becomes distinct from existing fields. For example, how did special education develop as a policy area separate from education and social welfare? A second direction follows an existing contemporary policy domain forward into the future where stagnation, collapse, or revitalization may occur. The U.S. space exploration domain's 40-year history may serve as the paradigmatic case of early successes supplanted by failure, drift, and an uncertain prospect. Finally, a third approach seeks to anticipate the emergence of an entirely new policy domain, which is then tracked over the coming years. Perhaps the worldwide revolution in telecommunications, although already underway for at least a decade, best exemplifies this strategy.

The collective fates of domains and their participants are intertwined in the larger societal and political affairs of the nation and, increasingly, the world. The twin tasks for policy domain researchers involve filling in the details of their structures and processes, while connecting them to the surrounding contexts. The challenges lying ahead can be distinguished into direct challenges of the organizational state approach and broader challenges of comparative research in this area. Among the first, the following four tasks seem to be especially important:

- Extending the organizational state approach to other policy domains in other times and places. Comparing the policy-making structures and processes of other domains will extend our understanding of interdomain variability within as well as across countries. It will also provide valuable data for contextualizing policy-making.
- Mapping the important formal institutions and their interrelations across macro-, meso-, and micro-levels of analysis. Researchers need to understand both the constitutional and actual (procedure) operations of these institutions in relation to informal connections that link political actors. In the decision-making model, our study examined their interaction only for legislative decisions. But many other institutions of the organizational state remain to be investigated systematically, particularly those in the regulatory and judicial arenas.
- Discerning the micro-dynamics of network processes in the informal state institutions. Our static measures could not capture the fluid, mutable character of exchanges and collaborations among domain participants. Their temporal sequences must be identified and tracked if we are to realize the full potential for network analysis to explain policy domain behaviors.
- Reconciling the exchange and coalitional logics of collective decision making. In the exchange model, the actors are supposed to exchange access to agents with other actors irrespective of their possible policy disagreements. In pluralistic systems, with overlapping memberships across event-specific action sets, corporate actors are pragmatic enough not to repudiate profitable bargains because of ideological restraints. Forming action sets with like-minded actors does not supersede the exchange processes. This situation may only occur in extremely polarized systems with nonoverlapping domainwide action sets.

The next three challenges go beyond the aims that we set for ourselves in this study. They are relevant for the context of comparative policy network studies:

- Uncovering the role of experts in policy formation. Persons skilled in scientific, technical, legal, and financial evaluation are constantly consulted by policy advocates for ammunition to bolster their policy preferences. Yet, we know very little about how ideas interact with political power to shape the course and outcome of policy fights.
- Giving the cultural dimension its due. How are prevailing political cultures – beliefs, convictions, ideologies, even theologies – manifested in the institutional-structural relations of policy domains? Now that Marxism is exiting the historical stage, does the central

struggle around the globe pit the democratic ideal against the bureaucratic-authoritarian reality?

- Discerning the cross-national linkages among policy domains. The United Nations' increasing military, social, and political functions are just recent phenomena in an evolving international system of states whose full implications remain unclear. In this global village, proliferating intergovernmental organizations, multinational corporations, and transnational professional societies provide many avenues for the interpenetration of national states. These supranational entities convey new cultural norms and institutional practices that may promote greater homogeneity among nations, but they may also foster diversities and tensions whose consequences await careful social science analysis.

The opportunities for theoretical and empirical advances abound. The choices among explanatory perspectives proliferate, as do the varieties of data. By demonstrating the utility of the organizational state approach as applied to three national labor policy domains, we believe we have made a significant contribution to the scholarly armamentarium.

Appendix 1

Legislative procedures in three nations

This appendix provides brief descriptions of the formal legislative institutions of the U.S., Germany, and Japan during the 1980s. These synopses are intended to provide readers with a handy guide to the key players and basic procedures by which proposed bills become laws. In describing Japan, we put an accent on comparison with the U.S. and Germany. For greater detail, readers may consult specialized works, such as Oleszek (1989) and Davidson (1992) for the U.S.; Edinger (1986) and Hancock (1989) for Germany; Thaysen, Davidson, and Livingston (1990) for a U.S.-German comparison; Richardson and Flanagan (1984), Mochizuki (1982), Iwai (1988); and Kojima (1979) for Japan; Nohon Kokusai Koryu Senta (1982) for a U.S.-Japan comparison; Hikaku Rippo Katei Kenkyukai (1980) for Japan in comparative perspective.

THE UNITED STATES

The U.S. Constitution of 1789 established the federal government's basic framework on principles of limited central power, the tripartite separation of powers among judicial, executive, and legislative branches, and checks-and-balances among these arenas. The president and vice president are elected to four-year terms with a majority of Electoral College votes (that is, a plurality of citizens' votes in a state gives a presidential candidate all that state's electoral votes, equal to the number of its senators plus representatives). Subject to congressional approval, the president appoints the heads of executive departments and federal agencies (his cabinet secretaries), whose responsibilities are to administer the government. The president also nominates and the Senate confirms new federal judges and members of the nine-justice Supreme Court, whose function is to interpret the constitutionality of laws passed by the Congress.

The bicameral U.S. Congress consists of a 100-member Senate (two members from each state) and a 435-member House of Representatives (the size of each state delegation is proportional to its population, as determined at each decennial census). All representatives are elected for two-year terms in November of every even-numbered year, as are one-third of the senators for six-year terms. Thus, each biennium comprises a numbered Congress, whose formal terms begins at noon on

January 3rd of odd-numbered years. For example, the 100th Congress held its session during 1987–8. Bills introduced during a given congressional term must be enacted during that period, or they automatically die and must be reintroduced at the next Congress.

Legislative procedures constantly evolve, but always involve decentralized power and multiple decision points. Both the House and Senate have elaborate committee systems designed to deal with different types of policies. Committee composition reflects party lines, with the chair and majority of members from the party holding a majority of the chamber seats. Complex policy issues are divided into smaller subissues that are parceled out among committees, which may further break down issues and assign them among their subcommittees. Frequently a bill falls under the jurisdiction of several committees, creating fragmented decision making. For example, several House and Senate committees consider some aspects of labor policy. Most bills work their way slowly through the legislative process, subject to delay, defeat, or modification at each stage. Strategically located committees, factions, and individuals may shape proposals if they can garner majority support. Thus, advocates of a particular bill must build several successive majorities at each critical decision point before the bill becomes law.

A representative introduces a bill by handing it to the House clerk, who puts it in a box called the "hopper." To introduce a bill in the Senate, a senator first gains recognition from the presiding officer. If any senator objects, introduction is postponed one day. Bills written by the executive branch are usually introduced by the chair of an appropriate congressional committee. Peterson (1990: 165) estimated that about 15% of a presidential administration's bills are drafted in the White House, 75% in the cabinet departments, and 10% by other agencies. Introduced bills are designated by HR in the House and S in the Senate, followed by a number.

In most cases, introduced bills are referred to the appropriate standing committees (21 in the House, 16 in the Senate). Jurisdiction is based on precedent, statute, and formal committee mandates as defined by House and Senate rules. (The exceptions are private bills, designed to benefit individual persons, which are referred to the committees designated by their sponsors.) A bill is "read for the first time" when referred to a committee and placed on its calendar. The majority of introduced bills do not pass beyond this point, as failure of a committee to act on a bill is equivalent to killing it.

If a committee chooses to act, the next step involves soliciting testimony from government departments and agencies, expert witnesses, interest groups, and even ordinary citizens. The chair may assign the bill to a subcommittee for further study and hearings, or it may be considered by the full committee. Hearings can be public, closed, or both. After considering a bill, a subcommittee reports to the full committee its recommendations for action and any proposed amendments. Following this report, the full committee votes on its recommendation to the House or Senate. This procedure is called "ordering a bill reported." Most reports call for favorable action by the chamber, since a committee can effectively kill a bill by simply not reporting it out.

The committee's staff prepares a written report describing the bill's purposes and scope, any committee revisions, proposed changes in existing laws, and usually the views of executive branch agencies. Committee members opposing a measure may include dissenting opinions in the report. The committee usually "marks up" (proposes amendments to) the bill. If changes are substantial and complicated, the committee may order a "clean bill," which contains the proposed amendments. The original bill is then set aside and the clean bill is reported to the chamber floor.

After a committee reports out a bill, the originating chamber must approve, alter, or reject the committee's amendments. Bills are brought to floor debate in an orderly sequence. The Senate majority leader, in consultation with the minority party leader and others, schedules bills for debate by placing them on the Senate's calendar. If a bill is routine, it must await its turn. If the matter is urgent, the bill can be taken up immediately either by unanimous consent or by a majority vote of the senators. In the House, priority is granted if a "special rule" is obtained from the Rules Committee, upon request from the committee chair, members, and sponsors. Resolutions to provide a special rule specify how long the bill may be debated and whether it can be amended from the floor. If floor amendments are banned, the bill is considered to be under a "closed rule," which permits only members of the reporting committee to alter the language, subject to chamber acceptance. When a bill is debated under an "open rule," amendments may be offered from the floor.

Duration of the House debate depends on whether the bill is discussed by the House proper or whether it is sitting as a Committee of the Whole. Time is either allocated by a special rule or set to one hour per member. In the Committee of the Whole, time agreed for general debate is equally divided between proponents and opponents. After general discussion, the bill is read section by section for amendments, with five minutes debate given to each side per amendment (which can be extended by unanimous consent and for pro forma changes). Senate debate is unlimited until unanimous consent to conclude occurs. A "filibuster" (parliamentary delaying maneuvers by opponents) can be stopped only with a successful motion for "cloture," requiring a three-fifths majority of the entire Senate.

The Senate may cast an untabulated voice vote, a standing vote (division), or a recorded roll call to which members answer "yea" or "nay." The House also uses voice and standing votes, but roll calls were replaced in 1973 by an electronic voting device. A teller vote is used only in the House, where members file up the center aisle past counters, who reveal only the totals. A one-fifth quorum can demand that individual members' votes on amendments be reported publicly. After a bill has been amended, a motion can be entertained to send it back to committee. If passed, a bill is removed from the calendar, usually signaling its death. If the motion fails, the bill then is "read for the third time," and a vote on final passage is taken. If a majority votes for the bill, it is formally passed by the chamber.

After a bill is passed in one chamber, it goes to the other, which may take action, ignore it, or work on its own version. Often, the second chamber makes only minor changes acceptable to the first house, thus routing the bill to the president.

When the second chamber significantly alters a bill, the measure is usually "sent to conference." Unless both chambers agree to conference, the bill dies.

Conference participants, appointed by the presiding officers of the two chambers, are usually senior members from the committees that managed the bill. The conference members seek to maintain their chambers' version while discussing the other house's amending actions. In reconciling the two versions, new legislative language is not supposed to be written. But many bills achieve compromise only after a new language is provided. Members generally agree to concessions only to the extent they feel their chamber will accept the compromises. Sometimes conference participants return to their respective chambers to obtain instructions about proposed changes.

Once the conference reaches agreement, a written conference report incorporating their compromises is sent to each chamber. House and Senate approval of the conference report is approval of the compromise bill. After a bill is passed in identical form by majorities of both chambers, it is first signed by the Speaker of the House and then by the President of the Senate. Next, it goes to the White House for the president's decision.

Constitutional checks-and-balances allow the President to veto a bill passed by Congress, but also stipulate how Congress may override a veto. The president must take action on any bill sent by Congress within ten days of its passage (not counting Sundays). To approve a bill, the president signs, dates, and usually writes the word "approved" on the document. Presidents often sign major legislation at formal ceremonies held in the White House rose garden with central congressional figures in attendance. Federal laws are numbered corresponding to the Congress in which they pass. For example, PL 100-334, prohibiting bankrupt firms from suspending life and health insurance benefits, was signed by President Reagan on June 16, 1988, the 334th public law of the 100th Congress.

If the president does not sign a bill into law within ten days while Congress remains in session, it is enacted without his signature. But, if Congress adjourns before the ten days expire and the president fails to sign, it does not become law; this method is the so-called pocket veto. A president vetoes a bill by refusing to sign it within ten days and sending it back to Congress with a message stating his reasons. If Congress takes no further action, the bill dies. However, Congress can override the veto if two-thirds of a quorum (a majority) in each chamber vote to do so by roll call. If a presidential veto is overridden in both houses, the bill becomes law; otherwise it is dead.

GERMANY

On May 8, 1949, the parliamentary council in Bonn adopted the Basic Law (*Grundgesetz*), or provisional constitution, which established the legal-institutional basis for the Federal Republic of Germany. It provided for a "democratic and social federal state" to ensure long-term political stability and rule of law. The Federal Republic is organized according to a mixture of principles. A complex checks-

and-balances system of dual popular sovereignty and states' rights at various levels of government is intended to prevent the concentration of governmental powers. The constitutionality of federal and state laws is judged by the Federal Constitutional Court (*Bundesverfassungsgericht*), consisting of two senates of eight judges each, elected for 12-year terms, half by each chamber of the federal parliament.

The upper chamber of parliament, the Federal Council (*Bundesrat*) is a very peculiar institution with roots in former German governmental systems. It functions like a second chamber for some bills (*Zustimmungsgesetze*) which will become enacted law only with its consent. Before German unification, it consisted of ten states (*Länder*), represented by their governments, with the number of votes varying from 3 to 5 according to state population (the four Berlin delegates were nonvoting before reunification in 1989, since that city remained legally under Allied occupation). Each delegation votes as a bloc on instruction from the state government. The *Bundesrat's* jurisdiction covers reviews of proposed legislation affecting the interests of the 10 states plus Berlin (expanded to 16 *Länder* after reunification). The government of a single state has the right to initiate bills, but it first needs a majority of votes in the *Bundesrat,* and this bill has then to be introduced into the parliament by the cabinet which has to add its comments.

The lower chamber of the German parliament, the Federal Diet (*Bundestag*), is the major legislative institution, with the additional function of electing the chancellor and controlling the government. Before unification, it had about 500 representatives, directly elected every four years by enfranchised citizens aged 18 years and older (the 22 Berlin deputies had restricted voting rights). A "five-percent clause" stipulates the minimum popular vote necessary for a party to enter parliament. The *Bundestag* is internally organized with a presidium or executive committee, consisting of a president and four vice presidents, and a 23-member Council of Elders, which plan the agenda and daily activities of the chamber. Each party represented in the *Bundestag* forms a "fraction" or caucus for planning party strategy and enforcing party unity. Party representatives are assigned to working groups for various legislative issues. A committee system corresponds to the federal ministries, with members assigned by party leaders in proportion to their party's strength in the chamber. In the 11th legislative period (1987–90) the *Bundestag* had 21 standing committees.

A joint sitting of *Bundestag* and *Bundesrat,* the Federal Convention (*Bundesversammlung*), is an electoral college meeting every five years to choose the federal president by majority vote. The president is formally the head of state, but plays no policy-making role, as he is required to accept all decisions of the parliament and courts. His role is largely ceremonial and symbolic, with moral connotations.

Political leadership in the federal government (*Bundesregierung*) is institutionally supported by a strong chancellor, who is not chosen by popular election. The chancellor (*Bundeskanzler*) is the only cabinet officer elected by the *Bundestag,* for a four-year term by an absolute majority of votes from a coalition of parties.

The chancellor chooses his ministers and has the power to create new portfolios and change old ones without parliamentary approval. The ministers are in charge of their departments which they direct independently and not "at the pleasure" of the chancellor. And the cabinet, ultimately, is a strictly collegial body with equal voting rights of the ministers. The cabinet has the constitutional right to initiate bills, not the chancellor or the single ministers. But, before a cabinet bill is introduced into parliament, the *Bundesrat* has the option to give its comments on the bill within six weeks, which then must be sent to parliament along with the bill.

The majority of the *Bundestag* and the federal government act in unison to initiate and pass the legislation necessary for the policies on which the coalition parties have agreed, normally in a written coalition contract. The opposition parties are unable to pass their bills, except in rare cases when the vote in parliament is not governed by strict party discipline, due to a joint decision of the coalition leaders. In these cases, the bills will have been initiated by members of parliament. Generally speaking the rights of legislative initiative are clearly ranked among the three institutions: *Bundestag,* cabinet, and *Bundesrat.* The *Bundestag* has highest priority in the whole legislative process. Five percent of its members or a single parliamentary party can initiate bills which are sent to committees after a first reading in a plenary session. One of the committees has primary responsibility for writing a report for the parliament which comes to a definite decision in a second or third plenary session. Because government bills are first referred to the *Bundesrat* for its opinion, one can therefore argue that the cabinet ranks second concerning its constitutional rights of legislative initiative, whereas the *Bundesrat* ranks third, since its bills are introduced to parliament only via the cabinet with its mandatory comments.

When a bill reaches the *Bundestag,* the Council of Elders reviews and submits it to preliminary vote by the entire chamber. If the bill passes this first reading by majority vote, it is assigned to the appropriate committee for deliberation and modification. Hearings may be held at which testimony from government officials and others is given. When a committee majority approves a bill, it then returns to the *Bundestag* for the second and third (final) reading. After it passes the lower house, and the *Bundesrat* approves (*Zustimmungsgesetze*) or does not object (*Einspruchsgesetze*), the bill is sent to the appropriate cabinet ministry for countersignature. Next, the federal president signs it and the bill becomes law on publication in the Federal Registry.

Following German constitutional doctrine, only the *Bundestag* has the right of the final legislative decision. But whether this decision becomes an enacted law depends on fulfillment of additional conditions. To understand the logic of the *Bundesrat's* two types of veto, one has to take into account the character of the division of labor between the German Federal Republic and its member states. Under the German system, the federation has far-reaching jurisdiction over all major policy domains except mainly education, whereas the states are charged with implementing most federal laws. And, whenever a law has to be implemented by the states, the *Bundesrat* is given full veto power. When its majority votes against a bill passed by parliament, the Committee of Mediation, consisting of members of both chambers, can be asked to negotiate a compromise which has to find an explicit agreement by both institutions if the *Länder* are involved in its implementation (*Zustimmungsgesetze*). In all other cases, the *Bundesrat* has only a suspensive veto which can be overridden by a majority of the *Bundestag*.

One could stress different aspects of the legislative process in models which are supposed to grasp the power-generating mechanisms of the three institutions and their acting parts. We briefly discuss three possible models. The first model focuses completely on the formal voting power of the parliamentary parties in the *Bundestag* and the state governments in the *Bundesrat.* Since party discipline in voting is the rule, the parliamentary parties can be treated as corporate actors in the same sense as the state governments in the *Bundesrat.* The voting power of the parties or states in their chamber can be measured with indices like the Shapley-Shubik value for coalition building. When the consent of the *Bundesrat* is not required, the *Bundestag* parties have full powers; when the consent is required, the *Bundestag* parties and the state delegates share the power in equal parts. This first model will be labeled the voting power model.

A second model takes into account the right to initiate legislation in addition to formal voting power. This policy formulation and decision model stresses the policy leadership of the ministers. Most of the bills which finally became enacted law are initiated by the cabinet. There are no formal power measures available for this purpose. We therefore use an ad hoc procedure and give the ministers whose portfolios are related to the content of a bill half of the formal voting power. We are assuming at the same time that the *Bundesrat* is not able to play the role of a policy leader.

Our third model is a party government or coalitional model. The opposition parties and the state governments with prime ministers of the opposition party are supposed to have a power of zero. Only where the state governments of the opposition party have a majority of votes in the *Bundesrat* would the *Bundesrat* power share be assigned to them and not the states with a prime minister from a coalitional party at the federal level.

JAPAN

The Japanese Constitution of 1947, enacted by the Allied Occupation with its intention of democratization and demilitarization, was totally changed from the previous Meiji Imperial Constitution of 1890. Under the Meiji Constitution, which was an amalgam of absolute monarchy (Emperor sovereignty) and parliamentary cabinet system, the executive branch enjoyed extensive decree powers in law-making as well as in law implementation in the name of the Emperor. The 1947 Constitution, which was influenced by the U.S., introduced principles involving the people's sovereignty, representative democracy, and local autonomy. However, its political institutional model was that of the United Kingdom as a parliamentary cabinet system in the unitary (not federal) state. Its legislative structure is close to that of the Federal Republic of Germany, which has a mixture of U.K.-type cabinet and U.S.-model committee systems (Hikaku Rippokatei Kenkyukai, 1980: 5,329).

The 1947 Constitution established three separate organs: a legislative branch consisting of two houses, an executive branch led by a parliamentary cabinet, and a judiciary branch with the Supreme Court. They check and balance each other in complex ways: The Diet (parliament) appoints the prime minister, who in turn appoints the cabinet; the cabinet can dissolve the House of Representatives (the lower house of the Diet); the Supreme Court determines the constitutionality of any laws or other official acts; and the cabinet appoints Supreme Court judges.

The Diet has two chambers, the House of Representatives (HR) and the House of Councillors (HC). They are quite similar, each consisting of elected representatives, with substantially equal power and responsibility for lawmaking and investigation of the government. Both have standing committees (18 in the HR and 16 in the HC) corresponding to the national ministries, several special committees, and parallel legislative procedures. They differ in composition and in electoral system. The HR has 511 members elected from 130 medium-sized electoral districts (2 to 6 representatives per district) every four years unless the chamber is dissolved earlier. The medium-sized electoral system was replaced by single representative district electoral system with bloc-level proportional representation in 1994. On average, dissolution occurs every 2.5 years. The HC has 252 members with terms of six years, with half the councillors elected every three years. The councillors get elected by two procedures: 152 are elected from 47 prefectural districts having one to four councillors, and 100 are chosen in a national election, by majority method until the 1980 election and by proportional method after the 1983 election. In an example of gerrymandering, or the increasing imbalance of voting power between the countryside and urban areas, the votes required to elect a single representative to the HR range from 50,000 in rural areas to 300,000 in urban areas in the 1980s. This underrepresentation of the urban constituency usually gave the LDP and some JSP members, with their stronger rural support, a distinct advantage over other parties that counted on urban support.

The most important difference between the two chambers is that an HR decision has superiority over that of HC in the following cases: the designation of the prime minister, the passage of a law in case of disagreement between the houses, the submission of and decision on the budget, and the ratification of treaties. However, since the passage of a law contrary to an HC decision requires a two-thirds majority in the HR, the HR and HC are quite equal regarding lawmaking.

Because the Diet (HR and HC) "shall be the highest organ of state power, and shall be the sole law-making organ of the State" (Art. 41), laws can be enacted by passage through the two houses. The promulgation of laws by the Emperor based on the cabinet's advice as a matter of state is a ceremonial procedure, just the same as other acts by him as a symbol of the state. The Supreme Court, despite having authority to rule on constitutionality, has rarely used the authority, making the procedure a sort of formality. It has often referred to "judicial passive-ism" and "government action theory" to justify its attitude. The Joint Committee of Both Houses, held when both houses differ on a decision, was not held between 1953 and 1989 because the Liberal Democratic Party (LDP) or conservative coalition kept its majority in both houses (Abe, Shindo, and Kawato, 1990: 20).

Political leadership in the Japanese national government was complicated by the division of formal institutional structures established by the Constitution and informal substantial structure under the predominant party system by LDP from 1955 to 1993 (Richardson and Flanagan, 1984: 330–4). Formally, the prime minister is as powerful as the chancellor is in Germany and is vested with the power to choose and change any ministers in the cabinet. This wide range of authority is substantially very close to that of the president in other countries (Kobayashi, 1972: 650). Under the parliamentary cabinet principle, the majority of cabinet members as well as the prime minister must be members of the Diet, and all cabinet members must be civilians. Since the establishment of the Constitution, all prime ministers have been elected from among the members of the HR. Despite the position's "huge and strong" authority, however, the prime minister has been constrained both internally and externally by such informal factors as factional politics within the LDP, bureaucratic expertise and sectionalism, opposition party resistance based on consensus-oriented rules and tactics in the Diet, and the power of the mass media. The cabinet led by the prime minister acts as a collegial body and can initiate bills (cabinet bill) as well as implement laws as its own primary function.

In contrast to their U.S. counterparts, Japanese legislators do not have extensive staffs to conduct research and prepare bills. Until 1993, they had only two staff persons funded by the state. Their party organizations lacked the capability to compensate for this, unlike some of the European parties. Consequently, the legislators, mainly the LDP politicians, rely heavily on ministerial officials for such services. The officials actually prepare all the cabinet bills, budgets, and treaties submitted to the Diet by the cabinet. All ministerial officials are professional career bureaucrats with considerable expertise in their fields. In addition, the Japanese ministries have developed a wide variety of "third sector" organizations, such as advisory councils, study groups, research consortia, public corporations, and foundations. These bodies act as their "social roots," channeling information, demands, and signals from the society to provide the materials for legislation (Muramatsu and Tsujinaka, 1992: 222–5).

Before a bill is submitted to the Diet, the officials in charge of the relevant ministry submit a draft to the leaders of the dominant party in the Diet. Until it lost control of the HC in 1989, the LDP controlled both Diet chambers, thus exercising enormous influence over revising the content of proposed laws, according to electoral needs and the objections of special interest groups. Within the LDP, the Policy Affairs Research Council (PARC), with subdivisions corresponding to the ministries, has been the core organ of policy deliberation. Japanese parties are highly disciplined, and tend to vote as a bloc following their central headquarter's decisions. Hence, even with a thin majority of seats, the LDP had exercised considerable control over Diet legislation. However, aside from having recruited many of its leading figures from ex-ministerial bureaucrats, the LDP usually respected the general policy indications laid out by the bureaucracy, because they shared the same perspective on policy matters.

After the cabinet convokes the seasonal Diet session based on the constitutional statute, each chamber must determine its own composition: chamber chairs, committee chairs, committee memberships, and so on. When the LDP controlled the majority of seats in both houses with a large margin, it appointed all the committee chairs, mostly from its own ranks. With its loss of absolute power in both houses, in the era of nearly equal powers in the 1970s (Krauss, 1984), this practice started to change toward the accommodation of opposition parties.

The Diet session is divided into three types: the ordinary session (150 days), the extraordinary session, and the special session for the designation of the prime minister after the general election. The lengths of the extraordinary and special sessions as well as the length of an extension of the ordinary session are decided by the will of both chambers – customarily, a unanimous decision by parliamentary factions (political parties within the Diet). Bills introduced in a session automatically die unless they pass the Diet during that session.

Formally, bills submitted to the Diet come from three sources: the cabinet, individual Diet members, and Diet committees. Before submission, the House Legislative Bureau scrutinizes the drafts of both member and committee bills, and the Cabinet Legislative Bureau examines the cabinet bills. On average, about 150 bills are submitted to the Diet each year (Ooyama, 1993: 120). This figure is comparable to that for European countries, but very small compared to that of the U.S. (more than 5,000). Cabinet bills, written by the ministries, comprise about 75% of the bills every year. Members and committees submit another 25% each year. During the era of LDP dominance, cabinet bills were very successful, with about 80% passing on the first attempt. The remainder were modified, resubmitted, and then usually passed to become law. Accordingly, the success rate of cabinet bills was approximately 96% (Mochizuki, 1982: 93–5; Ito, 1989: 141). But less than 20% of the member and committee bills became laws, not a very successful record. These figures are very similar to those of West Germany, where annually, out of 150 bills submitted, 70% were cabinet bills and most of them successfully passed (Ooyama, 1993: 120).

Submitting a member bill requires the approval of more than 20 representatives in the HR or more than 10 councillors in the HC. Bills influencing the budget plan require the approval of more than 50 representatives or 20 councillors. Accordingly, the party executive must approve the bills sponsored by its members. Therefore, not legislators, but parties actually submit member bills. Committee bills are presented in the appropriate Diet committee after approval by the respective party Diet Affairs Committee. This requires all parties to consent (Kishimoto, 1982: 69). Therefore, only committee bills supported by all or most of the parties can pass the Diet to become law.

Following submission of a cabinet or member bill, the chamber chair consults with the Steering Committee and refers it to the appropriate committee. Sometimes a special committee is designated to review a bill based on a Diet law or on both houses' rules. Committee bills can skip this review process. Committee review is not open to public scrutiny, except for the press and for persons recognized by the chair. Before or during the review, with the steering committee's agreement, the sponsors may be asked to explain the reason for the bill to a plenary session of the Diet.

The committee review process begins with the bill's initiator explaining its reasons. Questions and answers from the floor follow this explanation. For cabinet bills, in place of cabinet ministers, other ministerial officials can testify as government committee members and explanatory members. These include the director general of the respective bureau in the ministry or agency and the director of the respective division. Ministries have their own liaison offices in the Diet to support this process. Even in the Diet, bureaucrats perform important roles, just as they do in West Germany (Hikaku Rippokatei Kenkyukai, 1980: 134). A debate and a vote follow the Q & A period. About 25 percent of all bills are amended before the vote. Half of the amendments concern simply the date of enforcement (Mochizuki, 1982: 100–103).

During the review process, the committee may also hold public hearings, including the dispatch of members to the respective local areas and local public hearings. This hearing process has limited significance in Japan compared to in the U.S., and to in Germany since the late 1960s (Abe, Shindo, and Kawato, 1990: 19). Except for budget deliberations and some crucial bills recognized by the chair, hearings are not obligatory. Because the speakers at any hearing are recommended by their parties, they generally just repeat the party's claims and so inspire little interest.

After committee review, the bill goes to the plenary session of the Diet. The plenary session is open to the public. A session requires attendance by at least one-third of the Diet members, and it may decide a bill with a majority vote of the attending members. In case of a tie, the chamber chair can cast the tie-breaking vote. Bills are decided by either approval or denial. Some bills are not decided, and thus are dealt with either as an incomplete deliberation (that is, withdrawn) or as a continued deliberation (to be deliberated again in the next session). The plenary session is generally held by the consent of the Steering Committee but sometimes, in the case of controversial bills, by the chair's authority.

During a plenary session, the committee chair in charge of the bill first makes a report about the deliberation and debate by the parties and then takes the vote. In very rare cases, the chair also conducts a question and answer session before calling the vote. There are three methods of voting: a voice vote, a standing vote, and a recorded roll call vote. The latter method is used for a highly disputed bill. Sometimes, similar to filibustering in the U.S., the opposition members use "slow-down tactics" (in Japanese, literally "walking at a cow's pace tactics") in order to delay or prevent action by the Diet. After a bill is passed in one Diet chamber, it is sent to the other house to face the same procedure. Because individual Diet members do not break party discipline, the fate of a bill can be almost automatically predicted by the party positions on it. Thus the plenary session becomes a formality.

There are some important characteristics of Japanese legislative process recently elaborated in comparative perspective (Mochizuki, 1993; Iwai, 1988; Ito, 1989). Borrowing the concept of "viscosity" from Jean Blondel, Mochizuki (1982) focused on the ability of the legislature, especially of the opposition, to block, delay, or alter the government's legislative proposals. This is especially important in the Japanese case because under the long LDP dominance, the Diet as well as the opposition parties had been considered impotent – a rubber stamp or at most a ratifying mechanism. Mochizuki emphasized the norms and institutional structures of the Diet which contributed to the viscosity of the parliamentary process: a decentralized committee system, the unanimity norm on procedures (opposition participation in determining the agenda and time table), the system of short deliberative sessions, and the bicameral nature of the Diet.

Based on Mochizuki's observations as followed by some Japanese scholars, the significance of the Diet in comparative perspective is obvious. The HC as a second chamber is more important than those of Germany, the U.K., and France. Regarding the committee system, its autonomy is strong enough against the executive branch to place it in the same rank as the system in Germany. The most important feature is "time politics," caused by the combined effect of the session system and the unanimity norm. Japan stands virtually alone in having a multiple session system and a discontinuity of sessions which can easily kill the life of bills (Mochizuli, 1982: 63). In addition, time constraints are more severe because of (1) the long recess of the ordinary session in December and January; (2) the recess custom in committees other than the budgetary committee during the period of its deliberation; and (3) the fixed weekday deliberation custom, with only two days available for each committee deliberation (Ito, 1988: 135). As a result, fewer than 12 days out of the 150-day-long periods for the ordinary session are available for each committee deliberation. In the same way, only 50 days, totaling 50 to 80 hours, in a year are spent for the plenary meeting. These figures are extremely short, even compared to those of Germany (70 days, 450 hours) and not to mention those of the U.S. (150 days, 1,000 hours) (Ooyama, 1993: 120).

In sum, Japanese legislative policy-making proceeds in four arenas: pre-Diet, extra-Diet, within-Diet, and non-Diet. Negotiations in these four arenas involve combinations of key institutions and actors: the Diet, the ministerial bureaucracies, the LDP (composed of leaders, PARC and policy groups named "zoku [tribe]," and backbenchers), the opposition parties (same composition as for the LDP), and interest groups. Under strict time constraints imposed by complex institutional customs, the Diet process acts hurriedly within the available time. Thus the within-Diet arenas have limited function regarding deliberation. In the middle of this process, the Diet Affairs Committee of each party and the Steering Committees in both houses play important roles in negotiations. Through the negotiation, the government and the opposition seem to be rather cooperative in law-making despite the confrontational appearance of their ideologies. This can be shown in the higher rate (on average, 70–90%) of agreement with cabinet bills by the opposition parties, and in the higher rate (10–20%) of substantial revision of cabinet bills by the government to accommodate the opposition. Under the one-party predominant situation, substantial deliberation mainly occurred in the pre- and the extra-Diet arenas, where PARC, *zoku* policy experts, bureaucracies, interest groups, and even the opposition parties and movements did matter in respective ways. The Diet was primarily functioning more as a checking, criticizing, and legitimating mechanism than as a deliberative body. Although the opposition was sometimes more effective in criticizing the implementation of law rather than in making law (Kakizawa 1982: 211), their capacity to revise bills using the institutional leverage of time politics seemed to be increasing in the 1980s.

Appendix 2

Labor policy domain organizations by type

Code	Symbol	Name
		UNITED STATES
Labor unions		
1	ACTW	Amalgamated Clothing & Textile Workers Union
2	AFGE	American Fedn of Government Employees
3	AFL	American Fedn of Labor-Congress of Industrial Orgs
4	AFE	American Fedn of State, County, Municipal Emp
5	AFT	American Fedn of Teachers
6	CWA	Communications Workers of America
7	IAFF	Intl Assn of Fire Fighters
8	IAM	Intl Assn of Machinists
9	IBT	Intl Brotherhood of Teamsters
10	ILGU	Intl Ladies Garment Workers Union
11	ILWU	Intl Longshore & Warehouse Union
12	IUOE	Intl Union of Operating Engineers
13	OCAW	Oil, Chem, & Atomic Wkrs Intl Union
14	SEIU	Service Employees Intl Union
15	UAW	United Auto Workers
16	UE	United Elec Radio & Machine Wkrs of America
17	UFCW	United Food & Commercial Wkrs Intl Union
18	UMW	United Mine Workers
19	USW	United Steelworkers of America
Business associations		
20	AAI	Alliance of American Insurers
21	ABA	American Bankers Assn
22	ACLI	American Counc of Life Insurance
23	AEA	American Electronics Assn

Code	Symbol	Name
24	AFBF	American Farm Bureau Fedn
25	AIA	American Insurance Assn
26	AMC	American Mining Congress
27	ATA	American Trucking Assns
28	ABC	Asscd Builders & Contractors
29	AGC	Asscd Genl Contractors of America
30	APPW	Assn of Private Pension & Welfare Plan
31	BCBS	Blue Cross & Blue Shield Assn
32	BRT	Business Roundtable
33	CHAM	Chamber of Commerce of the United States
34	CMA	Chemical Manufacturers Assn
35	CED	Comm for Economic Development
36	DUP	E.I. Du Pont de Nemours & Co
37	Ford	Ford Motor Company
38	GM	General Motors Company
39	HIAA	Health Insurance Assn of America
40	MAN	Manville Corporation
41	NAB	Natl Alliance of Business
42	NAHB	Natl Assn of Home Builders
43	NAII	Natl Assn of Independent Insurers
44	NAM	Natl Assn of Manufacturers
45	NARF	Natl Assn of Rehabilitation Facilities
46	NFIB	Natl Fedn of Independent Business
47	NSBU	Natl Small Business United
48	NTMA	Natl Tooling & Machining Assn
49	PIA	Printing Industries of American
Professional societies		
50	AAA	American Academy of Actuaries
51	AACJ	American Assn of Community & Junior Colleges
52	AHA	American Hospital Assn
53	ALA	American Lung Assn
54	AMA	American Medical Assn
55	ANA	American Nurses Assn
56	ASTD	American Society for Training & Development
57	ASPA	American Society of Pension Actuaries
58	AVA	American Vocational Assn
59	NAS	Natl Academy of Sciences
Labor union		
60	NEA	Natl Education Assn

Code	Symbol	Name
Public Interest Groups		
61	AARP	American Assn of Retired Persons
62	ACLU	American Civil Liberties Union
63	AJC	American Jewish Comm
64	AL	American Legion
65	CCCR	Citizens Comm on Civil Rights
66	CBC	Congressional Black Caucus
67	EEAC	Equal Employment Advisory Counc
68	LCCR	Lawyers Comm for Civil Rights
69	LWV	League of Women Voters
70	LULC	League of United Latin American Citizens
71	MDRC	Manpower Demonstration Research Corp
72	MALD	Mexican American Legal Defense & Ed Fund
73	NAACP	Natl Assn Advancement of Colored People
74	NACO	Natl Assn of Counties
75	NCSL	Natl Conf of State Legislatures
76	NCBM	Natl Conf of Black Mayors
77	NCSC	Natl Counc of Senior Citizens
78	NFB	Natl Fedn of the Blind
79	NGA	Natl Governors Assn
80	NLC	Natl League of Cities
81	NOW	Natl Organization for Women
82	NRWC	Natl Right to Work Comm
83	NUL	Natl Urban League
84	NWLC	Natl Womens Law Center
85	NWPC	Natl Womens Political Caucus
86	NYEC	Natl Youth Employment Coalition
87	PLF	Pacific Legal Fund
88	PRC	Pension Rights Center
89	SER	SER/Jobs for Progress
90	USCM	United States Conf of Mayors
91	URB	Urban Institute
92	WOW	Wider Opportunities for Women
93	WE	Women Employed
94	WEAL	Womens Equity Action League
95	WLDF	Womens Legal & Defense Fund
Federal agencies		
96	CCR	Comm on Civil Rights
97	CEA	Council of Economic Advisors

Code	Symbol	Name
98	DOE	Dept of Education
99	NIOS	Natl Institute of Occ Safety & Health
100	DOJ	Dept of Justice
101	OSL	Office of the Secretary of Labor
102	ASP	Assistant Secretary for Policy
103	ETA	Employment & Training Administration
104	MINS	Mine Safety & Health Administration
105	OSHA	Occupational Safety & Health
106	EEOC	Equal Employment Opportunity Comm
107	GAO	General Accounting Office
108	INS	Immigration & Naturalization Service
109	NCEP	Natl Comm for Employment Policy
110	NLRB	Natl Labor Relations Bd
111	PBGC	Pension Benefit Guaranty Corp
112	SBA	Small Business Admin
113	WHO	The White House Office

Congressional committees

114	HREP	Republican members of House Labor & Education Comm
115	HDEM	Democratic members of House Labor & Education Comm
116	SREP	Republican members of Senate Labor and Human Resources Comm
117	SDEM	Democratic members of Senate Labor and Human Resources Comm

GERMANY

Labor unions

1	CGB	Christian Labor League
2	DAG	German Employees Union
3	DBB	German Civil Service League
4	DGB	German Trade Union Federation
5	GEW	Education & Science Union
6	GGLF	Agriculture & Forestry Union
7	HBV	Trade, Banking & Insurance Union
8	NGG	Restaurant Workers Union
9	ÖTV	Public Service & Transport Union
10	GTB	Textile Workers Union
11	IGBSE	Mining, Stone, & Earth Union

Code	Symbol	Name
12	IGCh	Chemical, Paper & Ceramic Union
13	IGM	Metal Workers Union
14	ULA	Union of Top Employees
15	BrDB	Daimler-Benz Workers Council
16	BrMAN	MAN-Salzgitter Workers Council
17	BrHÖSH	Hoesch Steel Workers Council
18	BrVW	Volkswagen Workers Council

Business associations

19	ASU	Self-Employed Entrepreneurs Assn
20	BAG	Middle & Large Retailers Assn
21	BgsLBS	Savings & Loan Assn
22	BvDB	German Bankers Fedn
23	BVI	German Investment Society Assn
24	BvD	Publishers Assn
25	BvZ	Timework Assn
26	BDI	Federation of German Industry
27	BDA	Confederation German Employers Assns
28	DBäV	German Spa Assn
29	DHG	German Hotel & Guesthouse Assn
30	DIHT	German Industry & Trade Congress
31	DSG	German Savings & Checking Assn
32	Gesmet	Union of Metal Industry Employers
33	HDE	Peak Assn of German Retailers
34	HDB	Peak Assn of German Construction Industry
35	VPBsp	Assn of Private Savings & Loans
36	PKV	Assn of Private Health Insurance
37	ZDB	Central Assn of German Builders
38	ZDH	Central Assn of German Crafts
39	DB	German Railways
40	DBenz	Daimler Benz Co
41	DBV	German Farmers Assn

Public interest groups

42	BvKS	Community Peak Fedn
43	DL	German District Council
44	DS	German City Council
45	DStGB	German City & Community League
46	TGdL	Wage Assn of German Laender
47	VKA	Fedn of Communal Employer Assns

Code	Symbol	Name
Professional societies		
48	BÄK	Federal Physicians Chamber
49	DKG	German Hospital Assn
50	FdV	Administrators of German Hospital Employees
51	HB	Hartmann League
52	KBV	Panel Doctors Union
53	MB	Marburger League
54	VDBW	Union of German Industrial Physicians
55	BFB	Federal League of Free Professions
56	DAB	German Women Academic League
57	HLB	High School Teachers League
58	DHV	German High School Assn
59	RAgb	Judges Assn of the Labor Court

Public interest groups and mandatory insurance assns

60	AGfbA	Labor Assn for Industrial Elder Care
61	BA	Federal Agency for Labor
62	BK	Federal Miners
63	BvBK	Federal Assn Industrial Health Insurance
64	BvIK	Federal Assn Crafts Health Insurance
65	BvLK	Federal Assn Agricultural Health Insur
66	AOK-BV	Federal Assn Local Health Insurance
67	BfA	Federal Insurance Institute for Employees
68	GdLA	Assn of Agrarian Elder Funds
69	HdGB	Peak Assn of Commercial Profess
70	VDR	Union of German Retiree Insurers
71	VdAK	Union of Employee Insurance
72	AVE	Union of Worker-Indemnity Insurance
73	BAGFW	Federal Labor Assn Private Social Work
74	AW	Federal Assn of Worker Welfare
75	DCV	German Charity Union
76	DW	Deacons Enterprise Evang Church
77	EvFAM	Evangelical Action Group for Family Questions
78	FDK	Family Fedn of German Catholics
79	KDB	Commission of German Bishops
80	EKD	Council of German Evangelical Churches
81	BAGWfB	Federal Handicapped Workplaces
82	DBJR	German Youth Fedn
83	DF	German Women's Council
84	RKBSH	Reichs Fedn of Veterans, Handicapped
85	Vdk	Union of War Victims & Veterans

Code	Symbol	Name
Political parties		
86	CDU-BT	CDU-CSU Parliament Fraction
87	CDU-AT	CDU Labor & Social Cmte members
88	CDU-BV	CDU Govt Leader
89	CSU-LL	CSU State Leader
90	CDA	CD Social Cmte German Worker
91	CDU-WR	CDU Economic Advisors
92	MIT	Self-Employed Union of CDU-CSU
93	SPD-BT	SPD Parliament Fraction
94	SPD-AS	SPD Labor & Social Cmte members
95	SPD-PV	SPD Party Leadership
96	AfA	Work Assn for Workers Questions
97	FDP-BT	FDP Parliament Fraction
98	FDP-AS	FDP Labor & Social Cmte members
99	FDP-BV	FDP Govt Leader
100	GRÜ-BT	Green Parliament Fraction
101	GRÜ-AS	Green Labor & Social Cmte members
102	GRÜ-BV	Green Party Leader
Federal agencies		
103	BMI	Ministry of the Interior
104	BMJ	Ministry of Justice
105	BMF	Ministry of Finance
106	BMWI	Ministry of Economic Affairs
107	BMJFFG	Ministry of Youth, Women, Family
108	BMA	Ministry of Labor (general)
109	BMAI	Labor Min: Principle & Planning Dept
110	BMAII	Labor Min: Labor Mkt, Unemploy, Foreign Dept
111	BMAIII	Labor Min: Labor Law, Protection Dept
112	BMAIV	Labor Min: Social Insurance, Social Law Dept
113	BMAV	Labor Min: Health & Illness Insurance Dept
114	BMAVI	Labor Min: War Victims, Rehabilitation Dept
115	BMBW	Labor Min: Education & Science Dept
State representatives (Länder)		
116	LVBW	Baden-Württemberg Land Rep
117	LVBay	Bavaria Land Rep
118	LVBerl	Berlin Land Rep
119	LVBre	Bremen Land Rep
120	LVHH	Hamburg Land Rep

Code	Symbol	Name
121	LVHe	Hessen Land Rep
122	LVNS	Lower Saxony Land Rep
123	LVNRW	North Rhineland-Westfalen Land Rep
124	LVRP	Rhineland-Pfalz Land Rep
125	LVS	Saarland Land Rep
126	LVSH	Schleswig-Holstein Land Rep

JAPAN

Labor unions

1	PTU	Japan Private Sector Trade Union Confedn
2	GCU	General Council of Trade Unions of Japan
3	IMF	Intl Metalworkers of Fedn-Japan Council
4	ISU	Japan Fedn of Iron & Steel Workers Unions
5	NMU	Natl Metalworkers Union
6	MTU	Natl Fedn of Metal Trade Unions
7	EMU	All Japan Fedn of Electrical Machine Workers' Unions
8	SHMU	Natl Fedn of Shipbuilding & Heavy Machinery Workers' Unions
9	AWU	General Fedn of Japan Automobile Workers' Unions
10	CEWU	Intl Chemical & Energy Workers Unions-Japanese Affiliates Fedn
11	PPPU	General Fedn of Paper & Pulp Processing Workers' Unions
12	PIWU	Fedn of Petroleum Industry Workers Unions
13	NGWU	Fedn of Natl Gas Workers Unions
14	EPWU	Fedn of Natl Electric Power Workers Unions
15	FWU	All Japan Fedn of Food Workers Unions
16	MCWU	Conf of Mass Communication, Information & Culture Workers Unions
17	PWU	Japan Postal Workers Union
18	TWU	Telecommunication Workers Union of Japan
19	NCWU	General Fedn of Natl Construction Workers Union
20	CEU	Japan Conference of Construction Employees Unions
21	CBEU	Fedn of City Banks Employees Unions
22	LIWU	Natl Fedn of Life Insurance Workers Unions
23	IIWU	Fedn of Indemnity Insurance Workers Unions
24	RWU	Fedn of All Japan Railway Workers Unions
25	PRWU	General Fedn of Private Railway Workers Unions of Japan
26	MTWU	Fedn of Japan Metropolitan Transport Workers Unions
27	TWU	Fedn of Japan Transport Workers Unions
28	ATU	All Japan Transport Union

Code	Symbol	Name
29	ASU	All Japan Seamens Union
30	JTU	Japan Teachers Union
31	CWU	Fedn of Japan Commerce Workers Unions
32	JTWU	Japan Fedn of Textile Workers Unions
33	PSU	Japan Fedn of Natl Public Servants Unions
34	PMWU	All Japan Prefectural & Municipal Workers Unions
35	GPCW	Conf of Government-related Public Corp Workers Unions
36	MWU	Japan Medical Workers Unions Fedn

Business associations

37	CCI	Fedn of Chambers of Commerce & Industry
38	FEO	Japan Fedn of Economic Organizations
39	FEA	Japan Fedn of Employers Assns
40	CED	Japanese Comm for Economic Development
41	MSEO	Natl Center for Medium & Small-sized Enterprises Orgs in Japan
42	CAC	Natl Center for Agricultural Cooperatives in Japan
43	PPI	Japan Paper Processing Industry Fedn
44	PIO	Fedn of Japan Pharmaceutical Industry Organizations
45	MBE	Maritime Business Employers Assn
46	AIE	Automobile Industry Employers Assn
47	FTA	Japan Fedn of Taxicab Assns
48	CIA	National Construction Industry Assn
49	EIF	Electrical Industry Fedn
50	CIA	Japan Chemical Industry Assn
51	CTI	Japan Chemical Textile Industry Assoc
52	MIA	Japan Machine Industry Assn
53	CIO	Fedn of Japan Construction Industry Organizations
54	JMA	Japan Mining Assn
55	RIA	Japan Rubber Industry Assn
56	IMI	Japan Industrial Machine Industry Assn
57	JSA	Japan Shipowners Assn
58	SBA	Japan Securities Business Assn
59	SIA	Japan Shipbuilding Industry Assn
60	SIF	Japan Steel Industry Fedn
61	PIF	Petroleum Industry Fedn
62	EMI	Japan Electric Machine Industry Assn
63	JSI	Japan Spinning Industry
64	PRA	Japan Private Railway Assn
65	CSA	Japan Chain Store Assn
66	DSA	Japan Department Store Assn
67	JTA	Japan Trade Assn
68	NBA	Natl Fedn of Bank Assns

Code	Symbol	Name
69	LIC	Life Insurance Company Assns
70	IIC	Indemnity Insurance Company Assns
71	RA	Realtor Assn
72	GIA	Japan Gas Industry Assn

Public interest groups

73	HIA	Fedn of Health Insurance Assns
74	WAIF	Fedn of Welfare Annuity Insurance Funds
75	ILOT	Intl Labor Organization Tokyo Office
76	HIA	Fedn of Natl Health Insurance Assns
77	CSBS	Fedn of Natl Civil Servants Benefit Societies
78	SWF	Natl Social Welfare Conference

Professional society

79	JMA	Japan Medical Assn

Public interest groups

80	NGA	Natl Governors Assn
81	NAMM	Natl Assn of Municipal Mayors
82	BLL	Buraku Liberation League
83	FMC	Five Member Comm for Promotion of Administrative Reform
84	SECC	Social Economic Council of Citizens
85	JPC	Japan Productivity Center
86	PECC	Peace Economy Council of Citizens
87	CPSG	Contemporary Policy Studies Group

Federal agencies

88	CS	Cabinet Secretariat
89	AMC	Administrative Management & Coordination Agency
90	EPA	Economic Planning Agency
91	MOLLPB	Ministry of Labor Labor Policy Bureau
92	MLSB	Labor Min: Labor Standards Bureau
93	MESB	Labor Min: Human Resources Bureau
94	MWAB	Labor Min: Womens Affairs Bureau
95	MVDB	Labor Min: Vocational Ability Development Bureau
96	MHWS	Ministry of Health & Welfare Social Affairs Bureau
97	MHWI	Health Min: Social Insurance Bureau
98	MHWP	Health Min: Pension Bureau
99	MITI	Ministry of International Trade & Industry

Code	Symbol	Name
100	MOT	Ministry of Transport
101	MOC	Ministry of Construction
102	MOP	Ministry of Posts & Telecommunications
Advisory boards		
103	EAC	Economic Advisory Council
104	ISAC	Industrial Structure Advisory Council
105	SSAC	Social Security System Advisory Council
106	SPAR	Special Council for Promotion of Administrative Reform
107	MWAC	Central Minimum Wage Advisory Council
108	HIAP	Advisory Council for Health Insurance for Aged Persons
109	SIAC	Social Insurance Advisory Council
110	EAC	Employment Advisory Council
111	CLSC	Central Labor Standards Advisory Council
Federal agencies		
112	EPC	Employment Promotion Corporation
113	JIL	Japan Institute of Labor
Political parties		
114	LDP	Liberal Democratic Party Policy Research Council Labor Comm
115	JSP	Japan Socialist Party Policy Council
116	DSP	Democratic Socialist Party Policy Council
117	CGP	Clean Government Party Policy Council
118	JCP	Japan Communist Party Policy Council
119	SDP	Social Democratic Fedn Policy Council
Federal agencies		
120	MOF	Ministry of Finance
Advisory groups		
121	ESC	Natl Employment Security Council
Federal agencies		
122	APEH	Assn for Promoting Employment of the Handicapped in Japan

Appendix 3

Cluster analyses of labor policy domain issues

Clusters and issues	Mean 0–5	Pct. High
UNITED STATES		
1. Health and safety working conditions	2.33	40.0
16. Enforcement of occupational safety and health standards	3.14	55.5
15. Exposure to radiation, chemicals, & occupational diseases	3.08	55.4
14. Company rights in employer associations	0.86	9.0
2. Collective bargaining and governance	1.70	22.7
17. Employee assistance programs for drug and alcohol abuse	2.64	42.9
24. Use of polygraphs, drug testing of employees	2.47	40.2
2. Collective bargaining procedures & regulation	2.06	32.1
3. Right to work	1.92	26.8
6. Corporate restructuring, mergers & acquisitions affecting employee contracts	1.78	25.0
1. Grievance procedures, arbitration & mediation	1.75	24.1
10. Increasing employee responsibilities for job performance	1.71	16.9
5. Givebacks, contract concessions: wage, benefit, work rules	1.66	23.2
7. Use of temporary, part-time employees hired through subcontracts to avoid union contracts	1.57	20.6
4. Use of bankruptcy to void union contracts	1.49	21.4
11. Anti-racketeering statutes for unions and businesses	1.38	18.7
26. Computer monitoring of employees' work	1.33	11.7

Clusters and issues	Mean 0–5	Pct. High
13. Anti-trust violations by employer associations & unions	1.30	13.4
12. Union election procedures	1.25	15.1
9. Employee representation on company boards of directors	1.06	8.1
3. Social policies		
33. Maternal and parental leave rights	3.29	57.1
28. Pension plan benefits and funding levels	3.13	58.1
29. Employee Retirement Income Security Act (ERISA)	2.93	57.1
32. Health care programs for unemployed workers	2.93	50.0
30. Reform of Social Security retirement	2.77	46.5
31. Pension equity for women	2.65	42.0
22. Mandatory retirement age	2.53	33.9
8. Employee stock ownership programs (ESOP)	1.33	13.4
4. Labor market policies	2.69	43.8
35. Vocational education & job training	3.26	59.8
46. Federal job creation and employment stimulation	3.01	53.5
37. Youth unemployment and training programs	3.01	52.7
20. Changes in minimum wage law	3.01	50.0
23. Child care services at the workplace	2.96	50.0
49. Plant closings and notifications	2.91	48.2
47. Immigration reform	2.86	50.1
27. Unemployment compensation	2.69	39.3
19. Wage and hour standards	2.67	44.7
21. Teenage subminimum wages	2.67	42.8
52. Environmental regulations affects production & employment	2.58	43.8
48. Import tariffs, voluntary quotas & restrictions	2.14	31.2
51. Federal aid to troubled industries, companies, regions	2.13	34.0
34. Trade adjustment assistance	2.11	31.2
50. Underground economy, sweatshops	2.05	25.0
5. Disadvantaged populations and discrimination	2.97	48.1
36. Minorities: blacks, Hispanics, Native Americans	3.57	65.1
42. Equal Employment Opportunity (EEO) policies & enforcement	3.52	58.0
40. Women	3.48	60.7
43. Affirmative Action programs in the workplace	3.29	56.2
45. Comparable pay for jobs of comparable worth	3.12	51.8

Clusters and issues	Mean 0–5	Pct. High
39. Handicapped and disabled workers	2.88	41.1
38. Employment and retirement of older Americans	2.72	45.6
44. Sexual harassment	2.70	42.8
25. Promotion and seniority procedures	2.38	34.8
41. Migrant and seasonal agricultural workers	2.03	25.0
6. *Health and safety working conditions*	1.77	23.7
18. Smoking bans in the workplace	1.83	18.8
53. AIDS: employment discrimination & health insurance aspects	1.70	28.6

GERMANY

1. *Collective bargaining and employment conditions*	2.46	41.8
18. Renewal of retirement law until 1991	3.17	55.6
1. Neutrality of the Federal Labor Institute in labor conflicts	3.07	56.4
2. Authorization of token strikes during on-going negotiations	2.84	52.4
16. Labor law regulations for temporary employment	2.80	44.8
6. Social plan regulations in bankruptcies	2.62	40.8
3. Legal prohibitions on lockouts	2.54	42.1
5. Full parity for enterprise codetermination by amending the codetermination law	2.46	45.2
8. Minority rights for small unions in plant and staff council elections	2.41	40.5
17. Standardization of dismissal intervals for workers and employees	2.40	35.8
40. Regulations for employee quitting	2.29	34.1
4. Coal and steel industry codetermination	2.21	35.2
7. Insertion of spokescommittees for managerial employees into plant constitutions	2.19	35.7
45. Assignment of the Labor Courts to the Justice Ministry's jurisdiction	1.98	24.6
2. *Work time protection*	2.81	46.6
24. Distribution of existing work through shortening of hours	3.58	66.7
10. Cooperation by employee representatives in new technology introduction	3.37	63.5

Clusters and issues	Mean 0–5	Pct. High
26. Rules for Sunday and holiday work	3.18	56.3
27. Maximum allowable hours and establishment of minimal rest breaks	2.97	50.0
42. Filling of job vacancies created by retirement regulations	2.91	50.8
9. Works council codetermination of work time on part-time employees	2.86	46.0
35. Gender-neutral advertising of jobs	2.84	38.8
25. Prohibition of irregular employment hours	2.77	46.0
32. Dismissal protection after professional training for youth and trainers	2.75	41.3
36. Women's promotion plans	2.72	42.8
41. Retrenchment of unemployment in the Labor and Environment Special Fund	2.52	38.9
43. Professional training bill	2.45	36.5
37. Burden of proof in discrimination cases	2.31	28.0
3. Store-closing hours	2.55	39.4
23. Introduction of a store service evening	2.95	46.9
22. Change on rules governing store-closing times	2.55	41.3
11. Association governance law	2.48	37.3
14. Excessive participation of employees in productive capacity	2.38	32.0
4. Employment conditions and social policies	3.11	50.8
13. Limited-work contracts	3.79	69.8
12. Legal relations for part-time workers	3.68	62.7
29. Training funds and training leaves	3.61	65.1
30. Rules for unemployment compensation	3.31	55.6
39. Strengthened support for ABM-measures	3.18	53.2
19. Health risks of new technologies	3.27	55.6
20. Prohibition of dangerous substances in the workplace	3.14	54.8
33. Compensation bill for unfilled openings for care of the severely handicapped	3.09	48.4
28. Deduction of industrial old age pension schemes from survivor pensions	2.86	43.7
38. Support for return preparation of foreign workers	2.75	38.0
34. Assimilation of severely handicapped rules to general regulations on dismissal	2.67	37.3
21. Smoking bans in the workplace	2.31	25.4

Clusters and issues	Mean 0–5	Pct. High
5. Social insurance	2.97	50.0
31. Premium changes in social insurance	3.60	65.9
44. Introduction of a social insurance identity card	3.23	57.2
15. Subsidiary activities of civil servants	2.18	27.0

JAPAN

1. Labor markets and disadvantaged populations	2.62	39.0
25. Employment of elderly, postpone retirement age, retraining	3.78	78.2
30. Job creation, government employment stiumlation	3.38	61.3
31. Opening of labor market to foreign workers	3.17	53.8
34. Federal aid to troubled industries, companies, regions	3.17	49.5
23. Response to foreign workers	3.08	50.4
35. Environmental regulations affecting production and employment	2.68	38.7
44. Increasing employee responsibility for increased productivity	2.30	29.4
32. Import tariffs, self-imposed quotas, allocating production quotas	2.25	28.6
24. Youth unemployment, training programs	2.13	18.5
42. Employee stock ownership programs	2.10	23.5
33. Plant closings, notifications	2.00	24.6
43. Employee representatives on company boards of directors	1.40	11.0
2. Social policies	3.05	45.6
5. Mandatory retirement age	3.84	71.7
14. Pension plan benefits, fund levels	3.82	72.3
15. Retirees income guarantee, lump sum payments	3.50	63.0
28. Implementation of male-female equal employment opportunity law	3.25	47.1
21. Vocational education and job training	3.19	52.1
27. Women workers	3.13	49.6
20. Assist change or adjustment of jobs, redevelop worker ability	3.03	37.1
22. Preparation and adjustment of company welfare plans	2.94	47.9
13. Unemployment compensation	2.89	39.9
18. Health care programs–unemployed workers	2.89	38.7

Clusters and issues	Mean 0–5	Pct. High
17. Pension equity for women	2.89	36.1
26. Handicapped, disabled workers	2.81	34.5
19. Maternal, paternal leave rights	2.77	38.7
29. Sexual harassment	1.55	10.1
3. Collective bargaining and governance	1.62	14.2
37. Collective bargaining, procedures and regulation	2.25	21.8
36. Grievance, arbitration, mediation	2.24	17.6
41. Temporary employees to avoid union contracts	2.03	28.5
40. Corporate restructuring, amalgamation, or takeovers affecting employee contracts	1.87	20.4
39. Givebacks, contract concessions	1.86	15.9
38. Bankrupting company to break labor contract	1.33	7.5
46. Union election procedures	1.28	7.6
47. Anti-trust violations: employer associations and unions	1.26	10.1
48. Company rights in employer associations	1.21	8.4
45. Prohibit use of racketeers threat	0.92	4.2
4. Employment and working conditions	2.75	40.2
2. Hour standards	4.03	76.7
1. Wage standards	3.75	70.8
16. Policies of social security, medical insurance for retirees	3.54	63.1
10. Enforcement of safety, health standards	3.28	54.2
9. Exposure to radiation, chemicals, disease	2.87	47.5
7. Promotion, seniority procedures	2.73	35.9
3. Changes in minimum wage law	2.54	35.8
8. Computer monitoring of employees' work	2.37	21.8
6. Child care at workplace	2.24	23.5
4. Workers beneath minimum wage	2.14	35.8
12. Smoking bans in workplace	1.78	8.4
11. Employee assistance programs for drug & alcohol abuse	1.41	9.2
5. Discrimination	[2.06]	[25.6]
49. Discrimination against workers: Burakumin, Korean-Japanese	[2.35]	[27.6]
50. Placement and advancement of discriminated workers	[2.14]	[24.1]
51. Employment of day laborers	[2.21]	[25.0]

Appendix 4

Labor policy domain legislative bills

UNITED STATES

2.	Dec. 1981	House of Labor Comm reports amendments to Black Lung Benefits and Revenue Act of 1977, revising eligibility and terminating new federal claim processing in 1983 (Public Law 97-119)
3.	Apr. 1982	House Labor Comm reports bill to repeal CETA public service jobs program, creates Job Training Partnership Act (Public Law 97-300)
5.	July 1982	Senate Labor Comm reports bill to amend 1959 Landrum Griffin Act and 1974 ERISA to increase penalties for fraud and abuse by labor union and employee benefit plan officials
6.	Aug. 1982	House Labor Comm reports bill to amend 1974 ERISA to establish reporting standards for public employee pension plans
7.	Sept. 1982	House Energy Comm reports a domestic content bill to require Japanese auto makers to buy up to 75% of parts and labor from U.S. sources
8.	Dec. 1982	House Labor Comm hold hearings to amend 1974 ERISA to provide for recovery by civil action of wrongfully denied employee benefits
9.	Feb. 1983	House Labor Comm reports bill to create an American Conservation Corps providing jobs for unemployed and disadvantaged young people on public and Indian lands (Passed by Congress, vetoed by President Reagan)
10.	July 1983	Senate Labor Comm holds hearings on amendments to 1977 Mine Safety and Health Act to encourage closer cooperation between industry and government in solving mine safety and health problems
11.	Sept. 1983	House Labor Comm holds hearings on bill to provide pension benefits to workers who lost vested pensions from companies failing before 1974 ERISA

12.	Sept. 1983	Senate Labor Comm reports Employment Opportunities Act to authorize labor-intensive public works programs for dislocated workers, and unemployment compensation during retraining
13.	Feb. 1984	Senate Labor Comm holds hearings on amendments to 1938 Fair Labor Standards Act to remove restrictions on garment industry work done in the home
16.	Mar. 1984	House Labor Comm reports a bill to amend 1963 Vocational Education Act, revising and extending federal aid to vocational education programs (Public Law 98-524)
18.	Sept. 1984	House Ways and Means Comm reports bill to revise 1974 ERISA and 1954 Internal Revenue Code to provide greater equity under private pension plans for workers, spouses, and dependents (Public Law 98–397)
19.	May 1985	House Labor Comm holds hearings on bill to amend Job Training Partnership Act to require remedial education in JTPA summer youth employment and training programs
20.	May 1985	Senate Labor Comm holds hearings on bill to create a three-year demonstration program offering a subminimum wage for teenagers
23.	June 1986	House Judiciary Comm reports bill to amend Immigration and Nationality Act to penalize employers who hire aliens without checking their employment eligibility (Public Law 99–603)
24.	Sept. 1986	House Labor Comm reports bill to create an American Boxing Corporation to develop model state boxing health and safety standards
28.	Apr. 1987	Senate Labor Comm reports bill to create Occupational Risk Assessment Board to monitor and notify workers of disease and chemical hazards
29.	May 1987	Senate Labor Subcommittee reports bill to provide unpaid parental or disability leaves with continued employer health insurance benefits and right to reclaim old job or comparable one with full seniority and benefits [Bill not enacted until Bill Clinton became president]
30.	June 1987	House Labor Comm holds hearing to raise minimum wage in steps from \$3.35 to \$4.65 by 1990 [Bill not enacted until George Bush became president]
31.	June 1987	Senate Labor Comm reports bill requiring 60-day advance notice of plant closings and major layoffs [Bill enacted in 1988 after Congress overrode President Reagan's veto]
32.	June 1987	Senate Judiciary Comm reports bill amending 1986 bankruptcy law to prohibit companies from suspending life and

		health insurance benefits by filing for Chapter 11 bankruptcy protection [Public Law 100–334]
33.	June 1987	House Labor Comm reports bill to overrule NLRB and stop "double-breasting" by companies setting up non-union subsidiaries to side-step collective bargaining agreements
35.	July 1987	House Labor Comm reports a bill to ban use of polygraph tests by employers for prospective employees [Public Law 100–347]
36.	July 1987	House Labor Comm reports bill to amend 1974 ERISA to put Pension Benefit Guaranty Corporation on sounder fiscal basis by raising premiums [Bill not enacted until George Bush became president]

GERMANY

1.	June 1983	Submission to *Bundesrat* of bill by Berlin and Schleswig-Holstein on new regulations of jurisdictions in the Labor Court
2.	July 1983	Comment by *Bundesrat* on bill by Hessen on Economic Crime Control: also punishment for unauthorized abandonment of temporary workers
3.	July 1983	Submission to *Bundesrat* of government bill "Household Companion Act 1984": Retrenchment and also unemployment compensation, handicapped subvention, motherhood vacation money, entrance fees in public service (Bill became law)
4.	Oct. 1983	Public hearing by *Bundestag* Labor and Social Committee on government bill "Assistance for Return Preparation of Foreigners" (Bill became law)
5.	Feb. 1984	Public hearing by *Bundestag* Labor and Social Committee on government bill for alleviation of conversion from work to retirement: Pre-Retirement Stipend (Bill became law)
6.	Mar. 1984	Second reading in *Bundestag* of legal intent by SPD "Work Time Act": inclusion of Sunday work in the 40-hour week under adherence to the 8-hour day
7.	May 1984	Public hearing by *Bundestag* Labor and Social Committee on legal intent of SPD to change bankruptcy regulations: Rights from the social plan as privileged bankruptcy assistance
8.	June 1984	Public hearing by *Bundestag* Labor and Social Committee on bill of Rheinland-Palatinate and Schleswig-Holstein "Change in Youth Worker Protection": and also flexible arrangements for daily work time (Bill became law)

9.	Aug. 1984	Submission to the *Bundesrat* of government bill Employment Assistance Act: and also possibility of limiting labor relations (Bill became law)
11.	Oct. 1984	Conference on legal intent of CDU/CSU and FDP about changes of legal specifications in the *Bundestag* Labor and Social Committee: Paraprofessional Occupation Limits Act (Bill became law)
12.	Nov. 1984	Public hearing by the *Bundestag* Labor and Social Committee on legal intent by CDU/CSU and FDP "Labor Assistance–and Annuity Insurance–Change Act": Increase in right to unemployment compensation from 12 to 18 months for older unemployed (Bill became law)
13.	Dec. 1984	Public hearing by *Bundestag* Labor and Social Committee on legal intent of SPD "Guarantees of Equal Treatment of Men and Women in the Workplace": and also burden of proof distribution on employers for the observation of discrimination prohibition in disputes
14.	June 1985	Reading in *Bundestag* of government bill to improve social provisions in rural areas (Rural social supplement) (Bill became law)
15.	Oct. 1985	First reading in *Bundestag* of legal intent of Greens on overtime retrenchment: Overtime only to second hour weekly
16.	Oct. 1985	Public hearing of *Bundestag* Labor and Social Committee on legal intent of CDU/CSU and FDP "Seventh Act on Change of Labor Assistance Law": and also Improvement of instruments for professional education, easier access to ABM for elderly (Bill became law)
18.	Feb. 1986	Public hearing by *Bundestag* Labor and Social Committee on government bill "Change in Severely Handicapped Act": Adjustment of termination protections in general regulations (Bill became law)
20.	Mar. 1986	Public hearing by *Bundestag* Labor and Social Committee on government proposal "Assurance of Neutrality of Federal Labor Institute in Labor Conflict" (Bill became law)
21.	Apr. 1986	Public hearing by *Bundestag* Labor and Social Committee on legal intent of SPD to strengthen industrial codetermination, for example, with the introduction and application of new technologies
22.	May 1986	Reading of government bill on change in occupational assistance law: Renewal of Industrial Training Place Assistance until Dec. 31, 1991 (Bill became law)
23.	May 1986	Submission to *Bundesrat* of government bill to change relief of rural entrepreneurs from premiums for rural social security (Bill became law)

25.	June 1986	First reading in *Bundestag* of SPD legal intent to repeal the deadline rules on deduction of child-education time from annuity insurance (Rubble Women-Baby-Year law)
26.	Sept. 1986	Conference of *Bundestag* Labor and Social Committee on legal intent of SPD "Security of coal-steel codetermination by change of entrepreneurial structure"
27.	Oct. 1986	Public hearing by *Bundestag* Labor and Social Committee on government bill "2. Asset Disclosure Act": indirect nonindustrial participation of workers in intermediate ventures (Bill became law)
28.	Dec. 1986	Public hearing by *Bundestag* Labor and Social Committee on legal intent of Greens "Legal prohibition of lockouts"
29.	Dec. 1986	Second reading in *Bundestag* of legal intent of SPD "Protection of Part-Time Workers"
30.	Feb. 1987	Opinion of *Bundesrat* on bill by North Rheinland-Westphalia and Hessen on the employment impact of Temporary Work Restrictions
31.	May 1987	First reading of government bill in *Bundestag* on extending the expiration date of coal-steel codetermination with combined board until Dec. 31, 1988 (Bill became law)
32.	Oct. 1987	Public hearing by *Bundestag* Labor and Social Committee on legal intent of CDU/CSU and FDP to change the labor assistance law: and also adoption of specific target groups for the disadvantaged program and in furtherance of the educational subsidy law (Bill became law)
33.	Mar. 1988	Public hearing by *Bundestag* Labor and Social Committee on legal intent of CDU/CSU and FDP on training of youth and trained representatives in industry (Bill became law)
34.	Mar. 1988	Submission to *Bundesrat* of government bill to standardize employers' obligation to report about the entrance of general social insurance premiums (Bill became law)
35.	May 1988	Submission to *Bundesrat* of bill by Bremen, North Rhineland-Westphalia, and Saarland to introduce an age limit on admission as a panel doctor
36.	June 1988	First reading of legal intent of CDU/CSU and FDP on change in industrial constitution: spokescommittee of leading employees, report of works council of new techniques, security of coal-steel codetermination (Bill became law)

JAPAN

0.	Aug. 1982	The Diet passed the Elderly Insurance Law as a step toward integrating plural social health insurance systems as well as a fiscal austerity measure. Although medical care

		for the elderly had been free since 1973, this elderly law required the elderly to pay a part of their own medical fees.
3.	May 1983	The Diet passed the Law for the Stabilization of Employment in Depressed Industries and Regions, integrating two related laws. The Ministry of Labor designated 35 industries and 40 regions as serviceable under it.
5.	July 1984	As a fiscal austerity measure, the Diet revised the Employment Insurance Law, the first reform employment insurance in ten years. This revision took the bonus out of the wage base when calculating benefits and changed the number of days for which benefits were given.
6.	Aug. 1984	The Diet passed a revision of the Health Insurance Law. It required the insured to cover 10 percent of their medical costs and set up health insurance for retirees not old enough for elderly insurance.
7.	Aug. 1984	The Diet approved five laws concerning the privatization of the Japan Tobacco and Salt Public Monopoly Corporation.
10.	Dec. 1984	The Diet approved three laws regarding the privatization of the Japan Telegraph and Telephone Public Corporation, to eliminate governmental inefficiencies, to reduce expenses, and to allow other companies to compete in the long distance telephone and the radio-telephone business.
11.	Apr. 1985	The Diet approved a reform of the National Pension Law, making it mandatory for all citizens to contribute to the Basic Pension Fund, which provides common pension payment to all citizens. This reform was the first step toward integrating seven pension systems.
12.	Apr. 1985	The Diet revised the Medium and Small Industries Retirement Funds Law. It expanded the definition of medium and small industries, increased insurance premiums, and increased government subsidies.
13.	May 1985	The Diet revised the occupational training law, changing its title to Occupational Abilities Development Promotion Law. It supported educational training by industry, requiring companies to hire a responsible official and every major city to establish a service center.
14.	May 1985	Following proposals of the Labor Ministry, the Diet passed the Male-Female Equal Employment Opportunity Law which required employers to provide men and women with equal opportunities for recruitment, employment, job assignment, and promotion, but provided no legal sanctions for violators.
15.	June 1985	The Diet passed the Manpower Dispatching Business Law, which acknowledged the legality of manpower dis-

patching businesses, while restricting and guiding their business practices.

16. Dec. 1985 The Diet approved the National Holiday Law, adding May 4 as a national holiday, as a concession to foreign criticism of Japan's long working hours/weeks. It was initiated as a committee bill.

17. Apr. 1986 The Diet approved the Law for the Promotion of Stable Employment for the Elderly, requiring companies to raise the retirement age to 60 years or older, contrary to the common mandatory retirement age of 55. The law included financial incentives for companies with many elderly workers, but no legal sanctions for noncompliance.

19. May 1986 The Diet revised the Workers Accident Compensation & Insurance Law as proposed by the Labor Ministry. The revision corrected compensation inequalities, designating minimum and maximum payments for five-year age intervals.

24. Nov. 1986 The Diet approved eight laws to reform and privatize the Japan National Railways. These laws divided the JNR into six different private companies, resulting in a reduced railroad workforce.

26. Dec. 1986 The Diet passed a revision of the Elderly Insurance Law as a fiscal austerity measure. It raised the contribution from the social health insurance account, reduced the national treasury's contribution, and raised the partial medical fees which the insured had to pay.

27. Apr. 1987 The Diet rejected the Sales Tax Bill introduced by the Government (Cabinet). This rejection damaged the ruling Liberal Democratic Party, especially Prime Minister Nakasone. The tax would have been levied on retailers, who then would pass the tax on to consumers in the form of higher prices.

28. May 1987 The Diet revised the Law to Promote Asset-Building Savings by Salaried Employees, reducing from three to one year the period of a special time deposit necessary to be eligible for a low-interest loan, and increasing the total amount of money loaned per person.

29. May 1987 The Diet passed a revision of the Law for the Promotion of Employment of the Handicapped, introduced by the Labor Ministry. The revision expanded the definition of handicapped to include people with mental disorders and deficiencies.

30. July 1987 The Diet passed the Law for the Promotion of Regional Employment Development, designed to provide

		subsidies to roughly 110 regions with low employment opportunities.
32.	Sept. 1987	The Diet revised the Labor Standards Law. It specified a staged reduction in the workweek from 48 to 40 hours. It also increased the number of paid holidays from 6 to 10 days. On the other hand, it permitted a flexible working hours system by the agreement of labor and management.
33.	Dec. 1988	The Diet passed six laws related to the introduction of the Consumption Tax, which allowed for a 3 percent tax to be imposed on most consumer items. The tax was to be paid at the cash register by the consumer, thus avoiding the retailers objections which scuttled the previous attempt.

References

Abbott, Andrew. 1984. "Event Sequences and Event Duration." *Historical Methods* 17:192–204.

Abbott, Andrew, and Alexandra Hrycak. 1990. "Measuring Resemblance in Sequence Data: An Optimal Matching Analysis of Musicians' Careers." *American Journal of Sociology* 96:144–185.

Abe, Hitoshi, Muneyuki Shindo, and Sadafumi Kawato. 1990. *Gendai Nihon no Seiji.* (The Government and Politics of Japan. Translated by James W. White.) Tokyo: University of Tokyo Press.

Adamy, Wilhelm. 1988. "Deregulierung des Arbeitsmarkts – Zwischenbilanz des Beschäftigungsförderungsgesetzes." *WSI – Mitteilungen* 8:475–482.

Alba, Richard, and Charles Kadushin. 1976. "The Intersection of Social Circles: A New Measure of Social Proximity in Networks." *Sociological Methods and Research* 5:77–102.

Aldenderfer, Mark S., and Roger K. Blashfield. 1984. *Cluster Analysis.* Beverly Hills: Sage.

Alford, Robert R. 1975. "Paradigms of Relations between State and Society." Pp. 145–60 in *Stress and Contradiction in Modern Capitalism,* edited by Leon Lindberg, Robert Alford, Colin Crouch, and Clause Offe. Lexington, MA: Lexington Books.

Alford, Robert R., and Roger Friedland. 1975. "Political Participation and Public Policy." *Annual Review of Sociology* 1:429–479.

———. 1985. *Powers of Theory: Capitalism, the State, and Democracy.* Cambridge, England: University of Cambridge Press.

Allison, Gary D., and Yasunori Sone (eds.). 1992. *Political Dynamics in Contemporary Japan.* Ithaca, NY: Cornell University Press.

Allison, Graham. 1971. *The Essence of Decision: Explaining the Cuban Missile Crisis.* Boston: Little, Brown.

Amenta, Edwin, and Theda Skocpol. 1989. "Taking Exception: Explaining the Distinctiveness of American Public Policies in the Last Century." Pp. 292–333 in *The Comparative History of Public Policy,* edited by Francis G. Castles. Cambridge, England: Polity Press.

Anderson, Stephen. 1992. "The Policy Process and Social Policy in Japan." *Political Science and Politics* 25:36–43.

Aoki, Masahiko. 1984. *Gendai no Kigyo* (The Cooperative Theory of the Firm). Tokyo: Iwanami Shoten.

Arabie, Phipps, Scott A. Boorman, and Paul R. Levitt, 1978. "Constructing Blockmodels: How and Why." *Journal of Mathematical Psychology* 17:21–63.

Armingeon, Klaus. 1988. "Trade Unions Under Changing Conditions: The West German Experience, 1950–1985." *European Sociological Review* 5:1–23.

Baerwald, Hans. 1973. "The Purge of Japanese Leaders under the Occupation." Pp. 36–42 in *Postwar Japan, 1945 to the Present,* edited by Jon Livingston, Joe Moore, and Felicia Oldfather. New York: Pantheon Press.

Balbus, Isaac D. 1971. "The Concept of Interest in Pluralist and Marxian Analysis." *Politics and Society* 1:151–177.

Barker, Anthony (ed.). 1982. *Quangos in Britain.* London: Macmillan.

Barry, Brian. 1965. *Political Argument.* London: Routledge, Kegan Paul.

Bell, Terrel H. 1988. *The Thirteenth Man: A Reagan Cabinet Memoir.* New York: Free Press.

Bellah, Robert, Richard, Madsen, William Sullivan, Ann Swidler, and Steven Tipton. 1985. *Habits of the Heart.* New York: Harper and Row.

Bendix, Reinhard. 1978. *Kings or People: Power and the Mandate to Rule.* Berkeley: University of California Press.

Berger, Suzanne D. (ed.). 1981. *Organizing Interests in Western Europe.* Cambridge, England: Cambridge University Press.

Berry, Jeffrey M. 1977. *Lobbying for the People: The Political Behavior of Public Interest Groups.* Princeton, NJ: Princeton University Press.

———. 1984. *The Interest Group Society.* Boston: Little, Brown.

Block, Fred. 1987. *Revising State Theory: Essays in Politics and Postindustrialism.* Philadelphia: Temple University Press.

Bluestone, Barry, and Bennett Harrison. 1982. *The Deindustrialization of America.* New York: Basic Books.

Boje, David M., and David A. Whetten. 1981. "Effects of Organizational Strategies and Constraints on Centrality and Attributions of Influence in Interorganizational Networks." *Administrative Science Quarterly* 26:378–395.

Boli, John. 1987. "World Polity Sources of Expanding State Authority and Organization, 1870–1970," Pp. 71–91 in *Institutional Structures: Constituting State, Society, and the Individual,* edited by George M. Thomas, John W. Meyer, Francisco O. Ramirez, and John Boli. Newbury Park, CA: Sage.

Bonacich, Phillip. 1987. "Power and Centrality: A Family of Measures." *American Journal of Sociology* 92:1170–82.

Borgatti, Steven, Martin Everett, and Linton Freeman. 1992. *UCINET IV Version 1.0.* Columbia, SC: Analytic Technologies.

Brams, Steven J. 1975. *Game Theory and Politics.* New York: Free Press.

———. 1990. *Negotiation Games: Applying Game Theory to Bargaining and Arbitration.* London: Routledge.

Breiger, Ronald L., Scott A. Boorman, and Phipps Arabie. 1975. "An Algorithm for Clustering Relational Data with Applications to Social Network Analysis and Comparison with Multidimensional Scaling." *Journal of Mathematical Psychology* 12:328–383.

Broadbent, Jeffrey. 1986. "The Ties that Bind: Social Fabric and the Mobilization of Environmental Movements in Japan." *International Journal of Mass Emergencies and Disasters* 4:227–253.

———. 1989a. "Environmental Politics in Japan: An Integrated Structural Analysis." *Sociological Forum* 4:179–202.

———. 1989b. "Strategies and Structural Contradictions: Growth Coalition Politics in Japan." *American Sociological Review* 54:707–721.

Bunn, Ronald F. 1984. "Employers Associations in the Federal Republic of Germany." Pp. 169–201 in *Employers Associations and Industrial Relations: A Comparative Study,* edited by J. P. Windmuller and A. Gladstone. Oxford: Clarendon.

Burawoy, Michael. 1979. *Manufacturing Consent: Changes in the Labor Process Under Monopoly Capitalism.* Chicago: University of Chicago Press.

Burstein, Paul. 1985. *Discrimination, Jobs, and Politics: The Struggle for Equal Employment Opportunity in the United States Since the New Deal.* Chicago: University of Chicago Press.

———. 1991. "Policy Domains: Organization, Culture, and Policy Outcomes." *Annual Review of Sociology* 17:327–350.

Burt, Ronald S. 1976. "Positions in Networks," *Social Forces* 55:93–122.

———. 1980. "Models of Network Structure." *Annual Review of Sociology* 6:79–141.

———. 1987. "Social Contagion and Innovation: Cohesion Versus Structural Equivalence." *American Journal of Sociology* 92:1287–1335.

———. 1989. *STRUCTURE Version 4.1: Reference Manual.* New York: Columbia University Center for the Social Sciences.

Calder, Kent. 1988. *Crisis and Compensation.* Princeton: Princeton University Press.

Campbell, John C. 1977. *Contemporary Japanese Budget Politics.* Berkeley, CA: University of California Press.

———. 1984. "Policy Conflict and Its Resolution within the Governmental System." Pp. 294–334 in *Conflict in Japan,* edited by Ellis Krauss, Thomas Rohlen, and Patricia Steinhoff. Honolulu: University of Hawaii Press.

———. 1992. *How Policies Change: The Japanese Government and the Aging Society.* Princeton, NJ: Princeton University Press.

Cappelli, Peter, and Robert B. McKersie. 1985. "Labor and the Crisis in Collective Bargaining." Pp. 227–246 in *Challenges and Choices Facing American Labor,* edited by Thomas A. Kochan. Cambridge, MA: MIT Press.

Cardoso, Fernando, and Enzo Faletto. 1979. *Dependency and Development in Latin America.* Berkeley: University of California Press.

Carrington, Peter, Greg H. Heil, and Stephen D. Berkowitz. 1980. "A Goodness of Fit Index for Blockmodels." *Social Networks* 2:219–234.

Cawson, Alan. 1986. *Corporatism and Political Theory.* Oxford: Blackwell.

Chamber of Commerce of the United States. 1988. *Issue Strategy Groups.* Washington, DC: mimeo.

Clark, Terry N. 1968. *Community Structure, Decision-making: Comparative Analyses.* San Francisco: Chandler.

Clawson, Dan, Alan Neustadtl, and Denise Scott. 1992. *Money Talks: Corporate PACs and Political Influence.* New York: Basic Books.

Cobb, Roger W., and Charles D. Elder. 1983. *Participation in American Politics: The Dynamics of Agenda-Building.* 2nd ed. Baltimore: Johns Hopkins University Press.

Coleman, James S. 1971. "Foundations for a Theory of Collective Decision." *American Journal of Sociology* 76:615–627.

———. 1973a. *The Mathematics of Collective Action.* Chicago: Aldine.

———. 1973b. "Loss of Power." *American Sociological Review* 38:1–17.

———. 1977. "Social Action Systems." Pp. 11–50 in *Problems of Formalization in the Social Sciences,* edited by K. Szaniawski. Warclaw: Polskiej Akademij Nauk.

———. *1986. Individual Interests and Collective Action: Selected Essays.* New York: Cambridge University Press.

———. 1990. *Foundations of Social Theory.* Cambridge, MA: Harvard University Press.

Collins, Robert M. 1981. *The Big Business Response to Keynes, 1929–1964.* New York: Columbia University Press.

Connolly, William E. 1972. "On 'Interests' in Politics." *Politics and Society* 2:459–477.

Cook, Karen S. 1990. "Exchange Networks and Generalized Exchange: Linking Structure and Action." Pp. 215–229. in *Generalized Political Exchange: Antagonistic Cooperation and Integrated Policy Circuits,* edited by Bernd Marin. Boulder, CO: Westview.

Cook, Karen S., and Richard M. Emerson. 1978. "Power, Equity, and Commitment in Exchange Networks." *American Sociological Review* 43:721–739.

CQ Almanac. 1989. "Minimum Wage Impass Finally Ended." *CQ Almanac* 1989 333–340.

Cyert, Richard M., and James G. March. 1963. *A Behavioral Theory of the Firm.* Englewood Cliffs, NJ: Prentice-Hall.

Davidson, Roger H. (ed.). 1992. *The Postreform Congress.* New York: St. Martin's Press.

Dore, Ronald. 1973. *British Factory-Japanese Factory.* Berkeley: University of California Press.

Downs, Anthony, 1972. "Up and Down with Ecology – The 'Issue Retenion Cycle.'" *The Public Interest* 28:38–50.

Dunleavy, Patrick. 1982. "Quasi-governmental Sector Professionalism: Some Implications for Public Policy-Making in Britain." Pp. 181–205 in *Quangos in Britain,* edited by Anthony Barker. London: Macmillan.

Dyson, Kenneth. 1980. *The State Tradition in Western Europe.* Oxford: Martin Robertson.

Edinger, Lewis J. 1986. *West German Politics.* New York: Columbia University Press.

Eisenstadt, Schmuel N. 1973. *Tradition, Change and Modernity.* New York: Wiley.

Eismeier, Theodore J., and Philip H. Pollock III. 1988. *Business, Money, and the Rise of Corporate PACs in American Elections.* New York: Quorum Books.

Enelow, James M., and Melvin J. Hinich. 1984. *The Spatial Theory of Voting: An Introduction.* Cambridge, England: Cambridge University Press.

Erd, Rainer. 1989. "Amerikanische Gwerkschaften. Strukturprobleme am Beispiel der Teamsters und der Automobilarbeiter." Frankfurt/New York.

Esping-Anderson, Gosta. 1990. *The Three Worlds of Welfare Capitalism.* Cambridge, England: Polity Press.

Esty, Daniel C., and Richard E. Caves. 1983. "Market Structure and Political Influence: New Data on Political Expenditures, Activity, and Success." *Economic Inquiry* 21:24–38.

Etzioni, Amitai. 1975. *A Comparative Analysis of Complex Organizations.* New York: Free Press.

Evans, Peter B., Dietrich Rueschemeyer, and Theda Skocpol (eds.). 1985. *Bringing the State Back In.* Cambridge: Cambridge University Press.

Feldmann, Gerald D. 1981. "German Interest Groups Alliances in War and Inflation, 1914–1923." Pp. 159–184 in *Organizing Interest in Western Europe,* edited by Suzanne Berger. Cambridge: Cambridge University Press.

Fernandez, Roberto, and Roger Gould. 1994. "A Dilemma of State Power: Brokerage and Influence in the National Health Policy Domain." *American Journal of Sociology* 99:1455–1499.

Filippelli, Ronald L. 1990. "The Historical Context of Postwar Industrial Relations." Pp. 137–171 in *U.S. Labor Relations, 1945–1989: Accommodation and Conflict,* edited by Bruce Nissen. New York: Garland.

Fine, Sidney. 1966. "The History of the American Labor Movement with Social Reference to the Developments of the 1930's." Pp. 105–120 in *Labor in a Changing America,* edited by William Haber. New York: Basic Books.

Fireman, Bruce, and William A. Gamson. 1979. "Utilitarian Logic in the Resource Mobilization Perspective." Pp. 8–44 in *The Dynamics of Social Movements: Resource Mobilization, Social Control and Tactics,* edited by Mayer N. Zald and John D. McCarthy. Cambridge, MA: Winthrop.

Fombrum, Charles and Mark Shanley. 1990. "What's in a Name? Reputation Building and Corporate Strategy." *Academy of Management Journal* 33:233–258.

Foster, James C. 1975. *The Union Politic: The CIO Political Action Committee.* Columbia, MO: University of Missouri Press.

Freeman, Linton C. 1977. "A Set of Measures of Centrality Based on Betweenness." *Sociometry* 40:35–41.

———. 1979. "Centrality in Social Networks: Conceptual Clarification." *Social Networks* 1:215–239.

———. 1988. "Computer Programs and Network Analysis." *Connections* 11:26–31.

Freeman, Richard B., and James L. Medoff. 1984. *What Do Unions Do?* New York: Basic Books.

French, John R. P., Jr., and Bertram Raven. 1959. "The Bases of Social Power." Pp. 150–167 in *Studies in Social Power,* edited by Dorwin Cartwright. Ann Arbor, MI: Institute for Social Research.

Friedkin, Noah E. 1993. "Structural Bases of Interpersonal Influence in Groups: A Longitudinal Case Study." *American Sociological Review* 58:861–872.

Fujita, Yoshitaka. 1983. *Gikai ni okeru Rippou Katei no Hikakuhou teki Kenkyu* (The Lifelong Comprehensive Welfare Plan). Tokyo: Sangyo Rodo Chosasho.

———. 1988. "Roshi Kyogisei: Nihon Seisansei Honbu" (Labor-Management Joint Consultation System: Japan Productivity Center). *Jurist* 900:88–89.

Gais, Thomas L., Mark A. Peterson, and Jack L. Walker. 1984. "Interest Groups, Iron Triangles, and Representative Institutions in American National Government." *British Journal of Political Science* 14:161–185.

Galaskiewicz, Joseph. 1979. *Exchange Networks and Community Politics.* Beverly Hills, CA: Sage.

Galtung, Johan. 1990. "Theory Formation in Social Research: A Plea for Pluralism." Pp. 96–112 in *Comparative Methodology: Theory and Practice in International Social Research,* edited by Else Øyen. London: Sage.

Garon, Sheldon. 1987. *The State and Labor in Modern Japan.* Berkeley, CA: University of California Press.

Giddens, Anthony. 1985. *The Nation-State and Violence: Volume Two of a Contemporary Critique of Historical Materialism.* Berkeley: University of California Press.

Glazer, Nathan. 1986. "The 'Social Agenda.'" Pp. 5–30 in *Perspectives on the Reagan Years,* edited by John L. Palmer. Washington: Urban Institute Press.

Godwin, R. Kenneth, and Robert C. Mitchell. 1984. "The Implications of Direct Mail for Political Organizations." *Social Science Quarterly* 65:829–839.

Goldfield, Michael. 1987. *The Decline of Organized Labor in the United States.* Chicago: University of Chicago Press.

Gordon, Andrew. 1988. *The Evolution of Labor Relations in Japan.* Cambridge, MA: Harvard University Press.

Gould, Roger V., and Roberto M. Fernandez. 1989. "Structures of Mediation: A Formal Approach to Brokerage in Transaction Networks." Pp. 89–126 in *Sociological Methodology 1989.* San Francisco: Jossey-Bass.

Granovetter, Mark. 1985. "Economic Action and Social Structure: The Problem of Embededness." *American Journal of Sociology* 91:481–510.

Greenstone, J. David. 1969. *Labor in American Politics.* New York, Knopf.

Griffin, Larry J., Michael E. Wallace, and Beth A. Rubin. 1986. "Capitalist Resistance to the Organization of Labor before the New Deal: Why? How? Success?" *American Sociological Review* 51:147–166.

Halbach, Guenter, Alfred Mertens, Rolf Schwedes, and Otfried Wlotzke. 1987. *Recht der Arbeit,* 2nd ed. Bonn, Germany: Bundesministerium für Arbeit und Sozialordnung.

Hall, Stuart. 1984. "The State in Question." Pp. 1–28 in *The Idea of the Modern State,* edited by Gregor McLennan, David Held, and Stuart Hall. Milton Keynes, England: Open University Press.

Hancock, M. Donald. 1989. *West Germany: The Politics of Democratic Corporatism.* Chatham, NJ: Chatham House.

Hannan, Michael T., and John Freeman. 1977. "The Population Ecology of Organizations." *American Journal of Sociology* 82:929–964.

Hazama, Hiroshi. 1981. *Nihon no Shiyosha Dantai to Roshikankei* (Employers' Association and Industrial Relations in Japan). Tokyo: Nihon Rodo Kyodai.

Heclo, Hugh. 1978. "Issue Networks and the Executive Establishment." Pp. 87–124 in *The New American Political System,* edited by Anthony King. Washington: American Enterprise Institute.

———. 1986. "Reaganism and the Search for a Public Philosophy." Pp. 31–63 in *Perspectives on the Reagan Years,* edited by John L. Palmer. Washington: Urban Institute Press.

Heinz, John P., Edward O. Laumann, Robert L. Nelson, and Robert H. Salisbury. 1993. *The Hollow Core: Private Interests in National Policy Making.* Cambridge, MA: Harvard University Press.

Heinz, John P., Edward O. Laumann, Robert H. Salisbury, and Robert L. Nelson. 1990. "Inner Circles or Hollow Cores? Elite Networks Policy Systems." *Journal of Politics* 52:356–390.

Helm, Jutta. 1986. "Codetermination in West Germany: What Difference Has It Made?" *West European Politics* 9:32–53.

Hentschel, Volker. 1983. *Geschichte der deutschen Sozialpolitik (1880–1980): Soziale Sicherung und kollektives Arbeitsrecht.* Frankfurt: Suhrkamp.

Hikaku Rippo Katei Kenkyukai. 1980. *Gikai niokeru Rippokatei no Hikakuhoteki Kenkyo* (A Comparative Jurisprudent Study on Legislative Process in the Parliament). Tokyo: Keiso Shobo.

Hirsh-Weber, Wolfgang. 1959. *Gewerkschaften in der Politik: Von der Massenstreikdebatte zum Kampf um das Mitbestimmungsrecht.* Köln, Opladen: Westdeutscher Verlag.

Hirschman, Albert O. 1977. *The Passions and the Interests: Political Arguments for Capitalism before Its Triumph.* Princeton, NJ: Princeton University Press.

Holler, Manfred J., and Gerhard Illing. 1991. *Einführung in die Spieltheorie.* Berlin: Springer.

Hollingsworth, J. Rogers, Phillippe Schmitter, and Wolfgang Streeck. 1994. *Governing Capitalist Economies.* New York: Oxford University Press.

Homans, George C. 1974. *Social Behavior: Its Elementary Forms.* Rev. Ed. New York: Harcourt, Brace, Jovanovitch.

Horowitz, Louis Irving. 1982. "Socialization without Politicization: Emile Durkheim's Theory of the Modern State." *Political Theory* 10:353–377.

Hosei Daigaku Ohara Shakai Mondai Kenkyusho. 1982–92. *Nihon Rodo Nenkan* (The Labor Yearbook of Japan). Tokyo: Rodo Shunpou Sha.

———. (ed.). 1992. *'Rengo Jidai' no Rodo Undo: Saihen no Dotei to Shintenkai* (Labor Movement Under the Initiative by Rengo: The Process of Reunification and New Prospectives). Tokyo: Sogo Rodo Kenkyujo.

Huber, Joan, and William Form. 1973. *Income and Ideology.* New York: Free Press.

Iio, Jun. 1993. *Mineika no Seiji Katei: Rincho-gata Kaikaku no Seika to Genkai* (The Politics of Privatization in Japan). Tokyo: Daigaku Shuppan-kai.

Inagami, Takeshi. 1989. "Seifu to Roshi Kankei" (The Government and Industrial Relations). Pp. 93–109 in *Nihon Romu Kankei shi.* Vol 3, edited by Takahashi, Komatsu, and Hutagami. Tokyo: Chuokeizai-sha.

Inagami, Takeshi, et al. 1994. *Neo-Koporatizmu no Kokusai Hikaku: Atarashi Seiji-Keizai Moderu no Tansaku* (Cross-National Comparison of Neo-Corporatism: In Search for New Models of Political Economy). Tokyo: Nihon Rodo Kenkyu Kiko.

Isaak, Robert. 1980. *European Politics.* New York: St. Martin's Press.

Ishida, Takeshi. 1961. *Mineika no Seiji Katei: Rincho-gata Kaikaku no Seika to Genkai* (Contemporary Organizational Politics in Japan). Tokyo: Iwanami Shoten.

———. 1984. "Conflict and its Accommodation: Omote-Ura and Uchi-soto Relations." Pp. 16–38 in *Conflict in Japan,* edited by Ellis Krauss, Thomas Rohlen, and Patricia Steinhoff. Honolulu: University of Hawaii Press.

Ishihata, Nobuo. 1990. *Nihon no Rodo Kumiai: Rekishi to Soshiki* (Labor Union in Japan: Its History and Organization). Tokyo: Nihon Rodo Kenkyu Kiko.

Ito, Mitsutoshi. 1987. "Kokkai no Mekanizumu to Kino." (The Mechanisms and Functions of the Diet). Pp. 129–148 in *Nihon Seiji Gakkai* (The Annuals of The Japanese Political Science Association). Tokyo: Iwanami Shoten.

Ito, Mitsutoshi, and Takashi Momose. 1980. *Jiten Showa Senzenkino Nihon: Seido to Jittai* (A Dictionary of Showa Era Japan before World War II: Its Institutions and Dynamism). Tokyo: Yoshikawa Kobunkan.

Iwai, Tomoaki. 1988. *Rippo Katei* (Legislative Process in Japan). Tokyo: Tokyo Daigaku Shuppan-kai.

Jepperson, Ronald L., and John W. Meyer. 1991. "The Public Order and the Construction of Formal Organizations." Pp. 204–231 in *The New Institutionalism in Organizational Analysis,* edited by Paul J. DiMaggio and Walter W. Powell. Chicago: University of Chicago Press.

Johnson, Chalmers. 1982. *MITI and the Japanese Miracle: The Growth of Industrial Policy, 1925–1975.* Stanford, CA: Stanford University Press.

Johnson, Chalmers, Laura D'Andrea Tyson, and John Zysman. 1989. *Politics and Productivity: How Japan's Development Strategy Works.* New York: Harper Business.

Jordan, A. Grant. 1981. "Iron Triangles, Woolly Corporatism and Elastic Nets: Images of the Policy Process." *Journal of Public Policy* 1:95–123.

Jöreskog, Karl G., and Dag Sörbom. 1989. *LISREL 7: A Guide to the Program and Applications,* 2nd ed., Chicago: SPSS Inc.

Jürgens, Ulrich. 1987. "Arbeitspolitik – Einleitende Bemerkungen." Pp. 208–212 in *Arbeitsmarkt, Arbeitsbeziehungen und Politik in den 80er Jahren (Sonderheft 8: Leviathan),* edited by Heidrun Abromeit and Bernhard Blanke. Opladen: Westdeutscher Verlag.

Jürgens, Ulrich, and Frieder Naschold. 1982. "Arbeitspolitik; – Entwicklungstendenzen und Politikformen." Pp. 327–343 in *Politische Vierteljahresschrift (Sonderheft 13),* edited by Joachim Jens Hesse. Opladen, Germany: Westdeutscher Verlag.

Kabashima, Ikuo, and Jeffrey Broadbent. 1986. "Referent Pluralism: Mass Media and Politics in Japan." *Journal of Japanese Studies* 12:329–361.

Kadushin, Charles. 1968. "Power, Influence, and Social Circles: A New Methodology for Studying Opinion Makers." *American Sociological Review* 33:685–698.

Kakizawa, Koji. 1982. "Kanryo Yui no Sisutemu" (Bureaucratic Dominant System in Japan). Pp. 204–234 in *Amerika no Ginkai vs. Nihon no Kokkai* (American Congress vs. Japanese Diet), edited by Kokusai Koryu Senta. Tokyo: Simul Shuppakai.

Kamens, David H., and Tormod K. Lunde. 1987. "Institutionalizing Theory and the Expansion of Central State Organizations, 1960–80." Pp. 169–197 in *Institutional Patterns and Organizations: Culture and Environment,* edited by Lynne G. Zucker. Cambridge, MA: Ballinger.

Kanbara, Masaru. 1986. *Tenkanki no Seiji Katei: Rincho no Kiseki to sono Kino* (Political Process in the Crossroads: The Process and the Function of the Rincho [Special Advisory Council on Public Administrative Reform]). Tokyo: Sogo Rodo Kenkyujo.

Kappelhoff, Peter. 1989. "Power in Exchange Networks: An Extension and Application of the Coleman Model of Collective Action." Paper presented at first European Conference on Social Network Analysis, Groningen, The Netherlands.

———. 1993. *Soziale Tauschsysteme.* München: Oldenbourg.

Karson, Marc. 1958. *American Labor Unions and Politics, 1900–1918.* Carbondale: Southern Illinois University Press.

Kastendiek, Hans, and Hella Kastendiek. 1987. "Konservative Wende und Industrielle Beziehungen in Groβbritannien und in der Bundesrepublik." Pp. 179–193 in *Arbeitsmarkt, Arbeitsbeziehungen und Politik in den 80er Jahren (Sonderheft 8 des Leviathan),* edited by Heidrun Abromeit and Bernhard Blanke. Opladen: Westdeustcher Verlag.

Katzenstein, Peter (ed.). 1978. *Between Power and Plenty: Foreign Economic Policies of Advanced Industrial States.* Cambridge, MA: Harvard University Press.

Katzenstein, Peter. 1987. *Policy and Politics in West Germany: The Growth of a Semisovereign State.* Philadelphia: Temple University Press.

King, Roger. 1986. *The State in Modern Society: New Directions in Political Sociology.* Chatham, NJ: Chatham House.

Kingdon, John W. 1984. *Agendas, Alternatives, and Public Policies.* Boston: Little, Brown.

Kishimoto, Koichi. 1982. "Niinsei Kokkai to Giin Naikakusei" (A Bicameral Diet and the Parliamentary Cabinet System). Pp. 48–79 in *Amerika no Gikai vs. Nihon no Kokkai* (American Congress vs. Japanese Diet), edited by Kokusai Koryu Senta. Tokyo: Simul Shuppakai.

Knoke, David. 1981. "Power Structures." Pp. 275–332 in *Handbook of Political Behavior* Vol. 3, edited by Samuel L. Long. New York: Plenum.

———. 1983. "Organization Sponsorship and Influence Reputation of Social Influence Associations." *Social Forces* 61:1065–1087.

———. 1986. "Associations and Interests Groups." *Annual Review of Sociology* 12:1–21.

———. 1990a. *Organizing for Collective Action: The Political Economies of Associations.* Hawthorn, NY: Aldine de Gruyter.

———. 1990b. *Political Networks: The Structural Perspective.* New York: Cambridge University Press.

———. 1992a. "Networks as Political Glue: Explaining Public Policy Making." Pp. 164–184 in *Sociology and the Public Agenda,* edited by William Julius Wilson. Newbury Park, CA: Sage.

———. 1992b. "Networks of Elite Structure and Decision Making." *Sociological Methods & Research* 22:23–45.

Knoke, David, and Frank Burleigh. 1989. "Collective Action in National Policy Domains: Constraints, Cleavages, and Policy Outcomes." *Research in Political Sociology* 4:187–208.

Knoke, David, and Ronald S. Burt. 1983. "Prominence." Pp. 195–222 in *Applied Network Analysis: A Methodological Introduction,* edited by Ronald S. Burt and Michael J. Minor. Beverly Hills: Sage.

Knoke, David, and James H. Kuklinski. 1982. *Network Analysis.* Beverly Hills: Sage.

Knoke, David, and Edward O. Laumann. 1982. "The Social Organization of National Policy Domains: An Exploration of Some Structural Hypotheses." Pp. 255–270 in *Social Structure and Network Analysis,* edited by Peter V. Marsden and Nan Lin. Beverly Hills, CA: Sage.

Knoke, David, and Franz Urban Pappi. 1991. "Organizational Action Sets in the U.S. and German Labor Policy Domains." *American Sociological Review* 56:509–523.

Kobayashi, Naoki. 1972. *Kenpo Kogi* (An Annotated Book of The Japanese Constitution). Tokyo: Tokyo University Press.

Kochan, Thomas A., Harry C. Katz, and Robert B. McKersie. 1986. *The Transformation of American Industrial Relations.* New York: Basic Books.

Kohn, Melvin L. 1987. "Cross-National Research as an Analytic Strategy." *American Sociological Review* 52:713–731.

——— (ed.). 1989. *Cross-National Research in Sociology.* Newbury Park: Sage.

Kojima, Kazuo, 1979. *Horitu ga Dekirumade* (The Legislative Procedure in Japan). Tokyo: Gyosei.

Komatsu, Ryuji (ed.). 1988. *Nihon Romu Kanri shi* (The History of Labor Management in Japan, Vol. 3). Tokyo: Chuo Keizai sha.

König, Thomas. 1992. *Entscheidungen im Politiknetzwerk.* Wiesbaden: Deutsche Universitäts Verlag.

———. 1993. "Kollektive Enscheidungsfindung in deutschen Politikfeld 'Arbeit': Ein modellorienterter Politikfeld-Ansatz." *Politisiche Vierteljahrsschrift* 4:597–621.

König, Thomas, Franz Urban Pappi, David Knoke, Jeffrey Broadbent, and Yutaka Tsujinaka. 1993. "Institutional Patterns of Political Exchange: Competitive Versus Cooperative Decision-making in the American, Japanese, and German Labor Policy Domains." Munich, Germany: Paper presented to Third European Social Networks Conference.

Krauss, Ellis S. 1984. "Conflict in the Diet: Toward Conflict Management in Parliamentary Politics." Pp. 242–293 in *Conflict in Japan.* Honolulu: University of Hawaii Press.

Krauss, Ellis S., and Takeshi Ishida. 1989. *Democracy in Japan.* Pittsburgh, University of Pittsburgh.

Kruskal, Joseph B., and Myron Wish. 1978. *Multidimensional Scaling.* Beverly Hills: Sage.

Kumon, Shumpei. 1992. "Japan as a Network Society." Pp. 109–143 in *The Political Economy of Japan.* Vol. 3: *Cultural and Social Dynamics,* edited by Shumpei Kumon and Henry Rosovsky. Stanford, CA: Stanford University Press.

Kuster, George. 1980. "Germany." Cited in Robert Isaak, 1980, *European Politics,* New York: St. Martin's Press.

Laumann, Edward O., and David Knoke. 1986. "Social Network Theory." Pp. 83–104 in *Approaches to Social Theory,* edited by Siegwart Lindenberg, James S. Coleman, and Stefan Nowak. New York: Russell Sage Foundation.

Laumann, Edward O., and David Knoke. 1987. *The Organizational State: A Perspective on National Energy and Health Domains.* Madison, WI: University of Wisconsin Press.

———. 1989. "Policy Networks of the Organizational State: Collective Action in the National Energy and Health Domains." Pp. 17–55 in *Networks of Power: Organizational Actors at the National, Corporate and Community Levels,* edited by Robert Perrucci and Harry R. Potter. New York: Aldine de Gruyter.

Laumann, Edward O., David Knoke, and Yong-Hak Kim. 1985. "An Organizational Approach to State Policymaking: A Comparative Study of Energy and Health Domains." *American Sociological Review* 50:1–19.

Laumann, Edward O., and David Knoke with Yong-Hak Kim. 1987. "Event Outcomes." Pp. 343–373 in *The Organizational State,* edited by Edward O. Laumann and David Knoke. Madison: University of Wisconsin Press.

Laumann, Edward O., and Peter V. Marsden. 1979. "The Analysis of Oppositional Structures in Political Elites: Identifying Collective Actors." *American Sociological Review* 44:713–732.

Laumann, Edward O., Peter V. Marsden, and David Prensky. 1983. "The Boundary Specification Problem in Network Analysis." Pp. 18–34 in *Applied Network Analysis: A Methodological Introduction,* edited by Ronald S. Burt and Michael J. Minor. Beverly Hills, CA: Sage.

Laumann, Edward O., and Franz Urban Pappi. 1976. *Networks of Collective Action: A Perspective on Community Influence Systems.* New York: Academic Press.

Lehman, Edward W. 1988. "The Theory of the State Versus the State of Theory." *American Sociological Review* 53:865–878.

Lehmbruch, Gerhard. 1979. "Liberal Corporatism and Party Government." Pp. 147–183 in *Trends Toward Corporatist Intermediation,* edited by Philippe C. Schmitter and Gerhard Lehmbruch. Beverly Hills: Sage.

———. 1984. "Concertation and the Structure of Corporatist Networks." Pp. 60–80 in *Order and Conflict in Contemporary Capitalism: Studies in the Political Economy of Western European Nations,* edited by John H. Goldthorpe. Oxford: Clarendon Press.

Levitan, Sar A., and Martha R. Cooper. 1984. *Business Lobbies: The Public Good and the Bottom Line.* Baltimore: Johns Hopkins University Press.

Lieberson, Stanley. 1991. "Small N's and Big Conclusions: An Examination of the Reasoning in Comparative Studies Based on a Small Number of Cases." *Social Forces* 70:307–320.

Lijphart, Arend, and Markus M. L. Crepaz. 1991. "Corporatism and Consensus Democracy in Eighteen Countries: Conceptual and Empirical Linkages." *British Journal of Political Science* 21:235–256.

Lindblom, Charles E. 1977. *Politics and Markets.* New York: Basic Books.

Loomis, Burdett A. 1983. "A New Era: Groups and the Grass Roots." Pp. 169–190 in *Interest Group Politics,* edited by Allan J. Cigler and Burdett A. Loomis. Washington: CQ Press.

Lorrain, Francois, and Harrison White. 1971. "Structural Equivalence of Individuals in Social Networks." *Journal of Mathematical Sociology* 1:49–80.

Lowi, Theodore J. 1964. "American Business, Public Policy, Case-Studies, and Political Theory." *World Politics* 16:667–715.

McCarthy, John D. 1983. "Social Infrastructure Deficits and New Technologies: Mobilizing Unstructured Sentiment Pools." Washington, DC: Catholic University.

McFarland, Andrew S. 1984. *Common Cause.* Chatham, NJ: Chatham House.

McQuaid, Kim. 1982. *Big Business and Presidential Power.* New York: William Morrow.

Mann, Michael. 1986. *The Sources of Social Power: Vol. 1: A History of Power from the Beginning to A.D. 1760.* Cambridge: Cambridge University Press.

March, James G., and Johan P. Olsen. 1976. *Ambiguity and Choice in Organizations.* Bergen, Norway: Universitetsforlaget.

March, James, and Johan Olsen. 1984. "The New Institutionalism: Organizational Factors in Political Life." *American Political Science Review* 78:734–749.

———. 1989. *Rediscovering Institutions: The Organizational Basis of Politics.* New York: Free Press.

Marin, Berndt. 1991. "Generalized Political Exchange: Preliminary Considerations." Pp. 37–65 in *Generalized Political Exchange: Antagonistic Cooperation and Integrated Policy Circuits,* edited by Berndt Marin. Boulder, CO: Westview Press.

Marks, Gary. 1989. *Unions in Politics: Britain, Germany, and the United States in the Nineteenth and Early Twentieth Centuries.* Princeton, NJ: Princeton University Press.

Marsden, Peter V. 1981. "Introducing Influence Processes into a System of Collective Decisions." *American Journal of Sociology,* 86:1203–1235.

———. 1982. "Brokerage Behavior in Restricted Exchange Networks." Pp. 201–218 in *Social Structure and Network Analysis,* edited by Peter V. Marsden and Nan Lin. Beverly Hills, CA: Sage.

———. 1983. "Restricted Access in Networks and Models of Power." *American Journal of Sociology* 88:686–717.

Marsden, Peter, and Edward O. Laumann. 1977. "Collective Action in a Community Elite: Exchange, Influence Resources and Issue Resolution." Pp. 199–250 in *Power, Paradigms, and Community Research,* edited by Roland J. Liebert and Allan W. Imersheim. London: Sage.

Marx, Karl. 1978. "Preface to A Contribution to the Critique of Political Economy." Pp. 3–6 in *The Marx-Engles Reader,* 2nd ed., edited by Robert C. Tucker. New York: Norton.

Masumi, Junnosuke. 1988. *Nihon Seiji si 4: Senryo Kaikaku, Jimin-to shihai* (Political History, Vol. 4: Occupational Reform and Dominance by the Liberal Democratic Party). Tokyo: Tokyo Daigaku Shuppankai.

Meyer, John W., John Boli, and George M. Thomas. 1987. "Ontology and Rationalization in the Western Cultural Account." Pp. 12–37 in *Institutional Structures: Constituting State, Society, and the Individual,* edited by George M. Thomas, John W. Meyer, Francisco O. Ramirez, and John Boli. Newbury Park, CA: Sage.

Meyer, John W., and Bryan Rowan. 1977. "Institutional Organizations: Formal Structure as Myth and Ceremony." *American Journal of Sociology* 83:340–363.

Mill, John Stuart. 1974. *Philosophy of Scientific Method.* New York: Hafner Press.

Millis, Henry A., and Emily C. Brown. 1950. *From the Wagner Act to Taft-Hartley: A Study of National Labor Policy and Labor Relations.* Chicago: University of Chicago Press.

Ministry of Labor. 1961. *Rodo Gyosei-shi* (The History of Labor Administration in Japan). 3 volumes. Tokyo: Rodo Horei Kyokai.

———. 1978. *Rodokumiai Kihonchosa 30-nenshi* (30 Year's History of Survey on Labor Unions). Tokyo: Rodo Kijun Kyokai.

Mitchell, J. Clyde. 1983. *Users' Guide to ABBW (Arabie/Boorman/Breiger/White) Block Modelling Program.* Oxford, England: Nuffield College.

Mochizuki, Mike Masato. 1982. "Managing and Influencing the Japanese Legislative Process: The Role of Parties and the National Diet." Ph.D. diss. Harvard University.

———. 1992. "Public Sector Labor and the Privatization Challenge: The Railway and Telecommunications Unions." Pp. 181–199 in *Political Dynamics in Contemporary Japan,* edited by Gary D. Allison and Yasunori Sone. Ithaca, NY: Cornell University Press.

Momose, Takashi. 1990. *Showa Senzennki no Nihon: Seido to Jittai* (Japan in the Pre-war Showa Era: Institutions and Dynamics). Tokyo: Yoshikawa Koubunn Kan.

Moore, Gwen, 1979. "The Structure of a National Elite Network." *American Sociological Review* 44:673–692.

Moretz, Sandy. 1987. "House to Vote on Worker Notification Bill." *Occupational Hazards* (September):112–116.

Mori, Goro (ed.). 1981. *Nihon no Roshi Kankei Sisutemu* (Japanese System of Industrial Relations). Tokyo: Nihon Rodo Kyokai.

Mückenberger, Ulrich. 1986. "Paragraph 116 AGF: Stadien eines Gesetzgebungsprozesses." *Kritische Justiz* 19:166–186.

Mueller, Dennis C. 1989. *Public Choice II: A Revised Edition of Public Choice.* New York: Cambridge University Press.

Muramatsu, Michio, Mitsutoshi Ito, and Yutaka Tsujinaka. 1992. *Nihon no Seiji* (Politics in Japan). Tokyo: Yuhikaku.

Nakamura, Tadashi (ed.). 1988. *Labor in Japan.* Tokyo: Nihon Romu Kenkyu-kai.

Nakane, Chie. 1970. *Japanese Society.* Berkeley: University of California Press.

Nihon Kokusai Koryu Senta (ed.). 1982. *Amerika no Ginkai vs. Nihon no Kokkai* (American Congress vs. Japanese Diet: How They Work). Tokyo: Simul Shuppakai.

Nihon Seisansei Honbu. *Katsuyo Rodo Tokei.* Tokyo: Nihon Seisansei Honbu.

Nixon, Richard Milhous. 1978. *The Memoirs of Richard Nixon.* New York: Grosset and Dunlap.

Ohara Shakai Mondai Kenkyusho. 1982–90. *Nihon Rodo Nenkan* (The Labor Year Book in Japan). Tokyo: Rodo Junpo Sha.

———. 1987. *Nihon Rodo Nenkan* (The Labor Year Book in Japàn). Tokyo: Rodo Junpo Sha.

Okimoto, Daniel I., and Thomas P. Rohlen (eds.). 1988. *Inside the Japanese System: Readings on Contemporary Society.* Stanford, CA: Stanford University Press.

Oleszek, Walter J. 1979. *Congressional Procedures and the Policy Process.* 1st ed. Washington: Congressional Quarterly Press.

———. 1989. *Congressional Procedures and the Policy Process.* 3rd ed. Washington: Congressional Quarterly Press.

Omi, Naoto. 1994. "Gendai Nihon no Macro Corporatism: Chingin Kettei to Seisaku Sanka" (Macro Corporatism in Contemporary Japan: Wage Determination Process and Participation in the Policy Process). Pp. 278–339 in *Neo-Koporatizmu no Kokusai Hikaku: Atarashi Seiji-Keizai Moderu no Tansaku* (Cross-National Comparison of Neo-Corporatism: In Search for New Models of Political Economy), edited by Takeshi Inagami, et al. Tokyo: Nihon Rodo Kenkyu Kiko.

Ooyama, Reiko, 1993. "Gikai: Toron Seiji no Kakuritsu" (The Diet Reform: Toward Establishment of Politics by Discussion). Pp. 115–139 in *Seiji Kaikaku Sengen* (Political Reform Declaration), edited by Nyu Gurando Dezain Kenkyukai, Aki Shobo.

Ordeshook, Peter C. 1990. "The Emerging Discipline of Political Economy." Pp. 9–30 in *Perspectives on Positive Political Economy,* edited by James E. Alt and Kenneth A. Shepsle. Cambridge, England: Cambridge University Press.

Ornstein, Norman J., and Shirley Elder. 1978. *Interest Groups, Lobbying and Policymaking.* Washington: Congressional Quarterly Press.

Otake, Hideo. 1994. *Jiyushugi teki Kaikaku no Jidai* (The Era of Neo-Liberal Reforms). Tokyo: Chuo Koron sha.

Øyen, Else (ed.). 1990. *Comparative Methodology: Theory and Practice in International Social Research.* London: Sage.

Paige, Jeffrey M. 1975. *Agrarian Revolution: Social Movements and Export Agriculture in the Underdeveloped World.* New York: Free Press.

Pappi, Franz Urban. 1984. "Boundary Specifications and Structural Models of Elite Systems: Social Circles Revisited." *Social Networks* 6:79–95.

——— (ed.). 1987. *Methoden der Netzwerkanalyse.* Munich: Oldenbourg.

———. 1988. "Entscheidungsprozesse im Politikfeld 'Arbeit' im internationalen Vergleich." Kiel: Institut für Soziologie.

———. 1990. "Klassenstruktur und Wahlverhalten im sozialen Wandel." Pp. 15–30 in *Wahlen und Wähler, Analyzen aus Anlaβ de Bundestagswahl 1987,* edited by Max Kaase and Hans Dieter Klingemann. Opladen: Westdeutscher Verlag.

———. 1993. "Policy-Netze: Erscheinungsform moderner Politiksteuerung oder methodischer Ansatz?" *Sonderheft 24 der Politischen Vierteljahresschrift* 1993: 84–94.

Pappi, Franz Urban, and Peter Kappelhoff. 1984. "Abhängigkeit, Tausch und kollektive Entscheidung in einer Gemeindeelite." *Zeitschrift für Soziologie* 13:87–117.

Pappi, Franz Urban, and David Knoke. 1992. "Political Exchange in the German and American Labor Policy Domain." Pp. 179–208 in *Policy Networks: Structural Analysis of Public Policy,* edited by Renate Mayntz and Bernd Marin. Frankfurt am Main: Campus Verlag.

Pappi, Franz Urban, and Christian Melbeck. 1984. "Das Macht-potential von Organisationen in der Gemeindepolitik." *Koelner Zeitschrift fuer Soziologie und Sozialpsychologie* 36:557–584.

Parsons, Talcott. 1967. "On the Concept of Political Power." Pp. 297–354 in *Sociological Theory and Modern Society,* edited by Talcott Parsons. New York: Free Press.

Pempel, T. J. 1982. *Policy and Politics in Japan: Creative Conservatism.* Philadelphia: Temple University Press.

———. 1992. "Political Parties and Representation: The Case of Japan." *Political Science and Politics* 25:13–18.

Pempel, T. J., and Keiichi Tsunekawa. 1979. "Corporatism without Labor?" Pp. 231–270 in *Trends Toward Corporatist Intermediation,* edited by Philippe C. Schmitter and Gerhard Lehmbruch, Beverly Hills: Sage.

Pennings, Johannes M., and Paul S. Goodman. 1977. "Toward a Workable Framework." In *New Perspectives on Organizational Effectiveness,* edited by Paul S. Goodman and Johannes M. Pennings. San Francisco: Jossey-Bass.

Peterson, Mark A. 1990. *Legislating Together: The White House and Capitol Hill from Eisenhower to Reagan.* Cambridge, MA: Harvard University Press.

Poggi, Gianfranco. 1978. *The Development of the Modern State: A Sociological Introduction.* Stanford, CA: Stanford University Press.

Prensky, David. 1985. *Interorganizational Structure and Organizational Participation in a National Policy Domain.* Ph.D. diss. University of Chicago.

Pressman, Jeffrey L., and Aaron Wildavsky. 1973. *Implementation.* Berkeley: University of California.

Ragin, Charles. 1987. *The Comparative Method.* Berkeley, CA: University of California Press.

Rainsberger, Paul. 1990. "The Constraints of Public Policy: Legal Perspectives on the Decline of the Labor Movement Since World War II." Pp. 91–136 in *U.S. Labor Rela-*

tions, 1945–1989: Accommodation and Conflict, edited by Bruce Nissen. New York: Garland.

Reeve, Andrew, and Alan Ware. 1983. "Interests in Political Theory." *British Journal of Political Science* 13:379–400.

Rehmus, Charles M. 1966. "Labor in American Politics." Pp. 252–267 in *Labor in a Changing America,* edited by William Haber. New York: Basic Books.

Reindt, Manfred, and Heinz Saffert. 1968. *Das Bundesministerium für Arbeit und Sozialordnung: Geschichte-Gestalt-Aufgaben.* Berlin: Erich Schmidt Verlag.

Ricci, David. 1971. *Community Power and Democratic Theory.* New York: Random House.

Richardson, Bradley M., and Scott C. Flanagan. 1984. *Politics in Japan.* Boston: Little, Brown.

Riker, William H., and Peter C. Ordeshook. 1973. *An Introduction to Positive Political Theory.* Englewood Cliffs, NJ: Prentice-Hall.

Rincho, Gyokakushin OB kai. 1991. *Nihon wo Kaeta 10 nen: Rincho to Gyokakushin* (A Decade of Structural Change). Tokyo: Gyosei Kanri Kenkyu Centre.

Ripley, Randall B., and Grace A. Franklin. 1978. *Congress, the Bureaucracy, and Public Policy.* Homewood, IL: Dorsey Press.

Rockman, Bert A. 1989. "Minding the State – Or a State of Mind? Issues in the Comparative Conceptualization of the State." Pp. 173–203 in *The Eulsive State: International and Comparative Perspectives,* edited by James A. Caporaso. Newbury Park, CA: Sage.

Rosei Kenkyukai (ed.). 1978. *Ishida Rosei: sono Sokuseki to Tenbou* (Ishida Labor Administration: Its History and Perspective). Tokyo: Romu Gyosei Kenkyujo.

Sabatier, Paul A. 1988. "An Advocacy Coalition Framework of Policy Change and the Role of Policy-Oriented Learning Therein." *Policy Sciences* 21:129–168.

Sakurabayashi, Makoto. 1985. *Sangyohokoku-kai no Soshiki to Kino* (The Patriotic Industrial Association: Its Organization and Functions). Tokyo: Ochanomizu Shobo.

Salisbury, Robert H. 1979. "Why No Corporatism in America?" Pp. 213–230 in *Trends Toward Corporatist Intermediation,* edited by Philippe C. Schmitter and Gerhard Lehmbruch. Beverly Hills: Sage.

———. 1984. "Interest Representation: The Dominance of Institutions." *American Political Science Review* 78:64–76.

Scheuch, Erwin. 1967. "Society as Context in Cross-Cultural Comparison." *Social Science Information* 6:7–23.

Schiffman, Susan, M. Lance Reynolds, and Forest Young. 1981. *Introduction to Multidimensional Scaling: Theory, Methods and Applications.* New York: Academic Press.

Schlozman, Kay L., and John T. Tierney. 1983. "More of the Same: Washington Pressure Group Activity in a Decade of Change." *Journal of Politics* 46:1006–1032.

———. 1986. *Organized Interests and American Democracy.* New York: Harper and Row.

Schmid, Günther. 1990. "Beschäftigungs- und Arbeitsmarktpolitik." Pp. 228–254 in *Politik in der Bundersrepublik Deutschland,* edited by Klaus von Beyme and Manfred G. Schmidt. Opladen: Westdeutscher Verlag.

Schmidt, Manfred G. 1989. "Learning from Catastrophes: West Germany's Public Policy." Pp. 56–99 in *The Comparative History of Public Policy,* edited by Francis G. Castles. Cambridge, England: Polity Press.

Schmitter, Phillippe C. 1977. "Modes of Interest Intermediation and Models of Societal Change in Western Europe." *Comparative Political Studies* 10:7–38.

———. 1981. "Interest Intermediation and Regime Governability in Contemporary Western Europe and North America." Pp. 287–330 in *Organizing Interests in Western Europe,* edited by Suzanne D. Berger. Cambridge, England: Cambridge University Press.

Schmitter, Philippe C., and Gerhard Lehmbruch (eds.). 1979. *Trends Toward Corporatist Intermediation.* Beverly Hills: Sage.

Schneier, Edward V., and Bertram Gross. 1993. *Legislative Strategy: Shaping Public Policy.* New York: St. Martin's Press.

Scholten, Ilja (ed.). 1987. *Political Stability and Neo-Corporatism: Corporatist Integration and Societal Cleavages in Western Europe.* Newbury Park, CA: Sage.

Schönhoven, Klaus. 1987. *Die deutschen Gewerkschaften.* Frankfurt: Suhrkamp.

Schumpeter, Joseph A. 1942. *Capitalism, Socialism, and Democracy.* London: Allen & Unwin.

Schwartz, Joseph E. 1977. "An Examination of CONCOR and Related Methods for Blocking Sociometric Data." Pp. 255–282 in *Sociological Methodology 1977,* edited by David R. Heise. San Francisco: Jossey-Bass.

Selznick, Philip. 1949. *TVA and the Grassroots.* Berkeley: University of California Press.

Shaiko, Ronald G. 1991. "More Bang for the Buck: The New Era of Full-Service Public Interest Groups." Pp. 109–129 in *Interest Group Politics, 3rd Ed.,* edited by Allan J. Cigler and Burdett A. Loomis. Washington: CQ Press.

Shakai, Keizai Kokumin Kaigi. 1977. *Henbo suru Ro-shi Kankei* (Japanese Industrial Relations in Transition). Tokyo: Shakai Keizai Kokumin Kaigi.

Shimada, Haruo. 1983. "Wage Determination and Information Sharing: An Alternative Approach to Income's Policy?" *International Industrial Relations Association: Sixth World Congress Reports* 2a:139–164.

Shimizu, Shinzo. 1982. *Sengo Rodo Kumiai Undo shi ron* (The Postwar Labor History in Japan). Tokyo: Nihon Hyoron Sha.

Shinkawa, Toshimitu. 1993. *Nihon-gata Hukushi Kokka no Seiji Keizai gaku* (The Political Economy of the Japanese Welfare State). Tokyo: Sanichi Shobo.

Shinoda, Toru. 1989. *Seiki-matsu no Rodo Undo* (Labor Movement in the End of the 20th Century). Tokyo: Iwanami Shoten.

Shirai, Taishiro, Tadashi Hanami, and Kazuyoshi Koshiro. 1986. *Rodo Kumiai Tokuhon* (An Introduction to Labor Union). Tokyo: Tokyo Keizai Shinpou Sha.

Shrum, Wesley, and Robert Wuthnow. 1988. "Reputational Status of Organizations in Technical Systems." *American Journal of Sociology* 93:882–912.

Skocpol, Theda. 1992. *Protecting Soldiers and Mothers: The Political Origins of Social Policy in the United States.* Cambridge, MA: Harvard University Press.

Slomp, Hans. 1990. *Labor Relations in Europe: A History of Issues and Developments.* New York: Greenwood Press.

Smith, Hedrick. 1988. *The Power Game: How Washington Works.* New York: Random House.

Soltwedel, Rüdiger, and Adrian Bothe. 1990. "Regulierungen auf dem Arbeitsmarkt der Bundesrepublik." *Kieler Studien 223.* Tübingen: Mohr (Siebeck).

Stokman, Frans N., and Jan M. M. Van den Bos. 1992. "A Two-Stage Model of Policymaking with an Empirical Test in the U.S. Energy-Policy Domain." *Research in Politics and Society* 4:219–253.

Streeck, Wolfgang. 1983. "Between Pluralism and Corporatism: German Business Associations and the State." *Journal of Public Policy* 3:265–284.

Streeck, Wolfgang, and Phillippe C. Schmitter (eds.). 1985. *Private Interest Government: Beyond Market and State.* Beverly Hills, CA: Sage.

Taft, Philip. 1957. *The A.F. of L. in the Time of Gompers.* New York: Harper.

Takagi, Ikuo. 1976. *Shunto-ron* (The Spring Wage Bargaining Round). Tokyo: Rodo Junpo-sha.

Takemae, Eiji. 1982. *Sengo Rodo Kaikaku* (Post-War Labor Reform). Tokyo: Tokyo Daigaku Shuppan Kai.

Taylor, D. Garth, and James S. Coleman. 1979. "Equilibrating Processes in Social Networks: A Model for Conceptualization and Analysis." Pp. 257–300 in *Perspectives on Social Network Analysis,* edited by Paul W. Holland and Samuel Leinhardt. New York: Academic Press.

Thaysen, Uwe, Roger H. Davidson, and Robert G. Livingston (eds.). 1990. *The U.S. Congress and the German Bundestag: Comparisons of Democratic Processes.* Boulder, CO: Westview Press.

Tiepelmann, Klaus, and Gregor van der Beek (eds.). 1992. *Theorie der Parafiski.* Berlin: Walter de Gruyter.

Tilly, Charles. 1984. *Big Structures, Large Processes, Huge Comparisons.* New York: Russell Sage.

Tocqueville, Alexis de. 1945. *Democracy in America.* New York: Knopf.

Tominaga, Kenichi. 1981. *Nihon Sangyo Shakai no Tenki* (The Crossroad of Japanese Industrial Society). Tokyo: Tokyo Daigaku Syuppan-kai.

Tomlins, Christopher L. 1985. *The State and the Unions: Labor Relations, Law, and the Organized Labor Movement in America, 1880–1960.* Cambridge: Cambridge University Press.

Troy, Leo, and Neil Sheflin. 1985. *Union Source Book.* West Orange, NJ: Industrial Relations Data Information Services.

Tsujinaka, Yutaka. 1986. "Gendai Nihon Seiji no Koporatizumu-ka" (A Shift Toward Corporatism in Contemporary Japanese Politics). Pp. 223–260 in *Seiji Katei,* edited by Mitsuru Uchida. Tokyo: Sanrei Shobo.

———. 1987. "Rodo-kai no Saihen to 86-nen Taisei no Imi" (Reorganization of Labor Movement and the Significance of Nakasone's 1986 Regime). *Leviathan* 1:47–72.

———. 1988. *Rikei Shudan* (Interest Groups in Japan). Tokyo: Tokyo Daigaku Shuppan-kai.

———. 1993. "Rengo and Its Osmotic Networks." Pp. 200–213 in *Political Dynamics in Contemporary Japan,* edited by Gary Allison and Yasunori Sone. NY: Cornell University Press.

Uchida, Kenzo, Masao Kanazashi, and Masayuki Hukuoka (eds.). 1988. *Zeisei Kaikaku wo Meguru Seiji Rikigaku* (Political Dynamics Over the Tax Reform). Tokyo: Chuou Koron sha.

Useem, Michael. 1983. *The Inner Circle: Large Corporations and Business Politics in the United States and the United Kingdom.* New York: Oxford University Press.

Verba, Sidney, and Steven Kelman. 1987. *Elites and the Idea of Equality: A Comparison of Japan, Sweden, and the United States.* Cambridge: Harvard University Press.

Vogel, David. 1989. *Fluctuating Fortunes: The Political Power of Business in America.* New York: Basic Books.

Wall, Grenville, 1975. "The Concept of Interest in Politics." *Politics and Society* 5:487–510.

Ware, Norman. 1935. *Labor in Modern Industrial Society.* Boston: Heath.

Warren, Roland L., Stephen Rose, and Ann Bergunder. 1974. *The Structure of Urban Reform.* Lexington, MA: Heath.

Wasserman, Stanley, and Katherine Faust. 1992. "Blockmodels: Interpretation and Evaluation." *Social Networks* 14:5–61.

Webber, Douglas. 1987. "Eine Wende in der Deutschn Arbeitsmarktpolitik? Sozialliberale under Christlich-liberale Antworten auf die Beschäftingungskrise." Pp. 74–85 in *Arbeitsmarkt, Arbeitsbeziehungen und Politik in den 80er Jahren (Sonderheft 8 des Leviathan),* edited by Heidrun Abromeit and Bernhard Blanke. Opladen: Westdeutscher Verlag.

Weber, Max. 1930. *The Protestant Ethic and the Spirit of Capitalism* translated by Talcott Parsons. New York: Scribner's.

———. 1946. *From Max Weber: Essays in Sociology,* translated and edited by H. H. Gerth and C. Wright Mills. New York: Oxford.

———. 1947. *The Theory of Social and Economic Organization.* New York: Free Press.

———. 1968. *Economy and Society.* Totowa, NJ: Bedminster Press.

Weitbrecht, Hansjoerg, and Gerhard Berger. 1985. "Zur Geschichte der Arbeitsbeziehungen: Deutschland, Oesterreich, Schweiz." Pp. 483–520 in *Handbuch der Arbeitsbeziehungen,* edited by G. Endruweit et al. Berlin: de Gruyter.

Wiarda, Howard J. 1991. "Comparative Politics Past and Present." Pp. 3–30 in *New Directions in Comparative Politics,* edited by Howard J. Wiarda. Boulder, CO: Westview Press.

Wilensky, Harold L., and Lowell Turner. 1987. *Democratic Corporatism and Policy Linkages: The Interdependence of Industrial, Labor-Market, Incomes, and Social Policies in Eight Countries.* Berkeley, CA: Institute of International Studies, University of California.

Wilks, Stephen, and Maurice Wright. 1987. "Comparing Government-Industry Relations: States, Sectors, and Networks." Pp. 274–313 in *Comparative Government-Industry Relations. Western Europe, the United States, and Japan.* Oxford: Clarendon Press.

Wilson, Frank, 1983. "French Interest Group Politics: Pluralist or Neocorporatist?" *American Political Science Review* 77:895–910.

Wilson, Graham K. 1979. *Unions in American National Politics.* New York: St. Martin's Press.

Wlotzke, Ottfried. 1985. "Das gesetzliche Arbeitsrecht in einer sich wandelden Arbeitswelt." *Der Betrieb* 1985:754–768.

Wolferen, Karl Van. 1989. *The Enigma of Japanese Power: People and Politics in a Stateless Nation.* New York: Knopf.

Wolman, Harold, and Fred Teitelbaum. 1984. "Interest Groups and the Reagan Presidency." Pp. 297–329 in *The Reagan Presidency and the Governing of America,* edited by Lester M. Salamon and Michael S. Lund. Washington: Urban Institute Press.

World Bank. 1990. *World Development Report 1990.* New York: Oxford University Press.

Wrong, Dennis. 1979. *Power: Its Forms, Bases and Uses.* Oxford: Basil Blackwell.

Zachert, Ulrich. 1984. "Hintergrund und Perspektiven der 'Gegenreform im Arbeitsrecht.'" *Kritische Justiz* 17:186–201.

Index